Jon E. Lewis's many previous books include *The Mammoth Book of Life Before the Mast*, *The Mammoth Book of True War Stories*, *The Mammoth Book of Trafalgar* and *The Mammoth Book of Battles*.

Also available

THE MAMMOTH BOOK OF

PIRATES

In which is related many true and eyewitness accounts
of the most notorious plunderers to rove the seas

Edited by Jon E. Lewis

ROBINSON
London

ROBINSON

First published in Great Britain in 2006 by Robinson,
an imprint of Constable & Robinson Ltd

Reprinted by Robinson in 2017

10

A CIP catalogue record for this book
is available from the British Library.

UK ISBN: 978-1-84529-115-0

Printed and bound in Great Britain by
CPI Group (UK) Ltd., Croydon CR0 4YY

Papers used by Robinson are from well-managed forests
and other responsible sources

MIX
Paper from
responsible sources
FSC® C104740

Robinson
An imprint of
Little, Brown Book Group
Carmelite House
50 Victoria Embankment
London EC4Y 0DZ

An Hachette UK Company
www.hachette.co.uk

www.littlebrown.co.uk

CONTENTS

A PIRATE CHRONOLOGY

150 BC	Cicilia flourishes as pirate haven, Mediterranean
AD 67	Pompey crushes Cicilian pirates
1200s	Introduction of Letters of marque
1492	Columbus discovers the New World
1494	Treaty of Tordesillas divides New World between Spain and Portugal
1518	Aruj Barbarossa, creator of the Barbary States, killed by Spaniards
1519	Cortes lands in Mexico
1525	Algiers begins its 300-year history as Barbary pirate haven
1531–3	Pizarro overthrows Incas
1562	John Hawkins; first voyage to the "Spanish Main"
1572	Drake attacks Nombre de Dios
c.1603	Female Irish pirate Granuaile dies in Rockfleet castle
1606	Corsair John Ward seizes the *Reniera e Soderina*, carrying £100,00 cargo, Mediterranean
1616	Simon Danziger (aka Danser) executed in Tunis
c.1630	Buccaneers settle on Tortuga, off Hispaniola
1668	Henry Morgan sacks Portobello; buccaneer Francois L'Olonais (aka l'Olonoise) captured and eaten by cannibals, Gulf of Darien
1671	Morgan raids Panama
1678	A.O. Exquemelin publishes *De Amerikaensche Zee-Rovers*
1688	Morgan dies from "drinking and sitting up late"
1690–1720	Madagascar flourishes as pirate base in Indian Ocean

1692	Earthquake destroys Port Royal
1695	Henry Avery captures Moghul of India's ship *Gang-i-Sawai*, netting a haul of £325,000
1697	Dampier publishes memoir *A New Voyage round the World*
1701	Pirate-chaser turned pirate Captain Kidd hanged at Execution Dock
1704	Execution of pirate John Quelch, among the first to fly the "Jolly Roger"
1718	Blackbeard (aka Edward Teach) dies in hand-to-hand fight with Lieutenant Maynard of the Royal Navy; Edward England active in the Atlantic and Indian oceans
1719	Defoe publishes *Robinson Crusoe*; Robert Bartholomew active in the Atlantic and Caribbean (until 1722); Howell Davis ambushed and killed, Principe Island
1720	"Calico Jack" Rackam hanged
1721	Mary Read dies of fever in prison on Jamaica; Edward Low active in the Caribbean and Atlantic (until 1724)
c.1725	"Golden Age" of piracy at an end in the Atlantic
c.1750–1830	Joasimi pirates active in Persian Gulf, Red Sea and Indian Occean
1807	Master pirate Ching Yih dies, China; succeeded by wife Cheng I Sao
c.1810–1820	Jean Lafitte flourishes in Gulf of Mexico and Caribbean
1811	Scott publishes *The Pirate*
1812–15	War of 1812
1814	Byron publishes *The Corsair*
1816	Anglo-Dutch squadron bombards Algiers and releases over 3,000 Christian prisoners
1883	R.L. Stevenson publishes *Treasure Island*
1904	First performance of J.M. Barrie's *Peter Pan*
1935	Errol Flynn stars in movie *Captain Blood*
2003	Johnny Depp stars in movie *Pirates of the Caribbean*

INTRODUCTION

Piracy might not be the world's oldest profession, but it has a long and dishonourable history. There were pirates in Ancient Greece; Cicero was eloquent in his diatribes against the pirates who infested the Roman seas. The Vikings were snatch-and-row rovers on a nightmarish scale (indeed, 'Viking' is the Old English for 'pirate'), yet it is the sea-robbers of the sixteenth and seventeenth centuries who come foremost into the mind's eye when the word 'pirate' is hoisted. It is the exploits of these pirates – Captain Avery, Blackbeard, Kidd, Morgan and the notorious like – on which this book concentrates.

The 'Golden Age' of sea-robbery was inaugurated by the discovery of the New World, specifically the Spanish conquest of the Aztec and Inca empires. The plundered treasures of these nations, laden on ships destined for Madrid, caused every sailor with a criminal eye to flock to the Spanish Main. The first freeloaders tended to sail with licenses – 'letters of marque' – from the governments of Spain's rivals, because the high seas robbery of the Spanish *flotas*, which were carrying up to 2 million ducats per annum to Iberia, was a means both of enriching their own treasury and of weakening Spanish might. Licensed robbers or 'privateers', of whom England's Sir Francis Drake is the most famous, were succeeded by the buccaneers, who operating with only the semi-official approval of the governments of Spain's enemies. Increasingly, though, sea-robbers operating for purely personal gain came to dominate the Caribbean and beyond, hard-bitten 'pirates' for whom a dangerous life outside the law was better than a monotonous law-abiding life without prospects.

Yet the pirates of the Golden Age were not a disorganized criminal rabble, despite the psychopathic leanings of some of their commanders, like the homicidal Blackbeard. There was honour among sea thieves, with many pirates obliged to sign a code of conduct which regulated how loot was to be divided. The rules of the *Revenge*, under John Phillips, for example ordered that: '. . . the Captain shall have one full share and a half in all prizes: the master, carpenter, boatswain and gunner shall have one share and a quarter'. Other ships had regulations which detailed almost every aspect of life at sea. The ship of Captain Bartholomew Roberts even ruled that lights and candles were 'to be put out at eight o'clock at night' and 'No person [was] to game at cards or dice for money'. The same ship also accorded every 'man . . . a vote in affairs of moment'.

The apparent equality of those under the Jolly Roger has encouraged some modern historians to view the Golden Age pirate ship as a floating utopia. And not just historians looking for evidence of proto-socialism; valiant historical attempts have been made to find evidence that the pirate ship was a haven for women, black people and homosexuals (in the case of the last, prompting the witticism that 'Jolly Roger' now be given a whole new twist.) Black people – refugees from slavery – were certainly a standard component of the pirate crew, but Mary Read and Anne Bonny aside, women rovers were a distinct rarity, and whether the 'matelot' system in the Caribbean, in which two pirates voluntarily fought and lived alongside each other, extended to sex is debatable.

The tendency of modern historians to project onto the Golden Age pirate ship contemporary mores, fears and desires is not quite risible. It is, after all, what people have done to pirates for hundreds of years.

Except for a few minor brigands, pirates had vanished from the Caribbean and the Indian Ocean by the mid-1700s, and by the early 1820s the corsairs of the Mediterranean were on the wane. With real pirates sailing off into the oceanic sunset, it became easy to treat the pirate as a blank page onto which any design could be etched. Byron's epic poem 'The Corsair' (see appendix I), which sold 10,000 copies on the day of its publication in 1814, set the pirate as a figure of romance – a clear response to the reaction and conformity of industrializing Georgian England – with Scott's *The Pirate*, 1821, a sort of novelistic confirmation. A rash of pirate tales, plays and operas followed, culminating in 1883 with

R.L. Stevenson's Treasure Island, featuring Long John Silver, with his 'dreadful stories . . . about hanging and walking the plank'. But real pirates never walked the plank; neither, with the exception of Avery, did they bury their treasure. The fictional pirate had taken over from the real one. Douglas Fairbanks and Erroll Flynn swinging through the rigging in the cinematic swashbucklers of the Thirties and Forties came to completely overshadow l'Olonais and Blackbeard and the other rovers who once went on 'the account'.

True-life pirates and privateers might not have been as glamorous as Flynn or as politically correct as we would like, but they fascinate because their real exploits, like Drake's raid on *Nombre de Dios* in 1572 and Henry 'Long Ben' Avery's seizure of the Moghul of India's treasure ship, *Gang-i-sawai*, in 1695 are as dramatic as anything a Hollywood scriptwriter can conjure up, including those employed on the *Pirates of the Caribbean* cycle. And even Johnny Depp might be pushed to play the cruel, flamboyant Blackbeard, with lighted matches under his hat and 17 wives in port, or the white-suited 'Calico Jack' Rackham who fell hopelessly in love with Ann Bonny. Or, indeed, that masterly sea-warrior, Henry Morgan, who was as fearless and astute as the hero of any pirate tale. All these historical figures, and many more from piracy's Golden Age, rove the pages beyond.

"By the means of this light we saw a huge heap of silver"

THE RAID ON NOMBRE DE DIOS

Sir Francis Drake and Philip Nichols

Francis Drake (c. 1543–1596) began his legendary career at sea serving in the slave-trading ships of his cousin, John Hawkins, before branching out on his own as a pirate in the Spanish Caribbean in 1570. Inspired by the treasure to be plundered there, Drake was equally motivated by a burning Protestantism: he loathed the Roman Catholic Spanish. In 1572 Drake led an attack on the Spanish treasure port of Nombre de Dios in Panama; if not his most lucrative robbery it caught the Western world's imagination for its sheer audacity. Five years later, Drake began his successful voyage around the world (making him the second captain to navigate the globe, after Magellan); with the connivance of Queen Elizabeth he undertook some plundering of the Spanish New World en route and returned a rich man; his personal take of the global piratical proceedings approached £10,000. Elizabeth knighted him in 1581. Thereafter, she retained him as her personal pirate – occasionally licensing him as a privateer – and he led raids on the West Indies in 1585 and 1595. On the latter expedition he was struck down by dysentery and died on 7 February 1596. He was buried at sea near Porto Bello.

Here "the scourge of Spain" describes his night attack on Nombre de Dios of 19 July 1572. He writes in the third person.

On Whitsunday Eve, being the 24 of May in the year 1572, Captain Drake in the *Pascha* of Plymouth, of 70 tons, his admiral; with the *Swan* of the same port, of 25 tons, his vice-admiral, in which his brother John Drake was Captain; (having in both of them of men and boys seventy-three, all voluntarily assembled, of which the eldest was fifty, all the rest under thirty: so divided that there were forty-seven in the one ship and twenty-six in the other, both richly furnished with victuals and apparel for a whole year, and no less heedfully provided of all manner of munition, artillery, artificers, stuff and tools that were requisite for such a man-of-war in such an attempt; but especially having three dainty pinnaces made in Plymouth, taken asunder all in pieces and stowed aboard, to be set up as occasion served), set sail, from out of the Sound of Plymouth, with intent to land at Nombre de Dios.

The wind continued prosperous and favourable at north-east, and gave us a very good passage without any alteration or change, so that albeit we had sight (June 3) of Porto Santo, one of the Madeiras, and of the Canaries also within twelve days of our setting forth: yet we never struck sail nor came to anchor, nor made any stay for any cause, neither there nor elsewhere, until twenty-five days after; when (June 28) we had sight of the Island of Guadeloupe, one of the islands of the West Indies, goodly high land.

The next morning (June 29) we entered between Dominica and Guadeloupe, where we descried two canoes coming from a rocky island, three leagues off Dominica; which usually repair thither to fish, by reason of the great plenty thereof which is there continually to be found. We landed on the south side of it, remaining there three days to refresh our men and water our ships out of one of those goodly rivers, which fall down off the mountain. There we saw certain poor cottages built with palmito boughs and branches, but no inhabitants at that time, civil nor savage: the cottages (it may be, for we could know no certain cause of the solitariness we found there) serving not for continual inhabitation, but only for their uses that came to that place at certain seasons to fish.

The third day after (July 1), about three in the afternoon, we set sail from thence toward the continent of terra firma. And the fifth day (July 6) after we had sight of the high land of Santa Marta, but came not near the shore by ten leagues; but thence directed our course for a place called by us Port Pheasant; for that our Captain had so named it in his former voyage, by reason of the great store of those goodly fowls which he and his company did then kill and feed on in that place. In this course, notwithstanding we had two days calm, yet within six days we arrived (July 12) at our Port Pheasant, which is a fine round bay of very safe harbour for all winds, lying between two high points not past half a cable's length over at the mouth, but within eight or ten cables' length every way, having ten or twelve fathoms water, more or less, full of good fish; the soil also very fruitful, which may appear by this, that our Captain having been in this place within a year and few days before, and having rid the place, with many alleys and paths made, yet now all was so overgrown again as that we doubted, at first, whether this was the same place or no.

At our entrance into this bay, our Captain having given order to his brother what to do if any occasion should happen in his absence, was on his way with intent to have gone aland with some few only in his company, because he knew there dwelt no Spaniards within thirty-five leagues of that place: Tolu being the nearest to the eastwards, and Nombre de Dios to the westwards, where any of that nation dwelt. But as we were rowing ashore we saw a smoke in the woods, even near the place which our Captain had aforetime frequented; therefore thinking it fit to take more strength with us, he caused his other boat also to be manned, with certain muskets and other weapons, suspecting some enemy had been ashore.

When we landed, we found by evident marks that there had been lately there a certain Englishman of Plymouth, called John Garret, who had been conducted thither by certain English mariners which had been there with our Captain in some of his former voyages. He had now left a plate of lead nailed fast to a mighty great tree (greater than any four men joining hands could fathom about) on which were engraven these words, directed to our Captain:

Captain Drake, if you fortune to come to this port, make haste away: For the Spaniards which you had with you here the last year have bewrayed this place, and taken away all that you left here.
I depart from thence this present 7 of July, 1572.
Your very loving friend,
John Garret

The smoke which we saw was occasioned by a fire, which the said Garret and his company had made before their departure in a very great tree (not far from this which had the lead nailed on it) which had continued burning at least five days before our arrival.

This advertisement notwithstanding, our Captain meant not to depart before he had built his pinnaces, which were yet aboard in pieces, for which purpose he knew this port a most convenient place. And therefore, as soon as we had moored our ships, our Captain commanded his pinnaces to be brought ashore for the carpenters to set up, himself employing all his other company in fortifying a place, which he had chosen out as a most fit plot, of three-quarters of an acre of ground, to make some strength or safety for the present, as sufficiently as the means he had would afford; which was performed by felling of great trees and bowsing and haling them together with great pulleys and hawsers, until they were enclosed to the water, and then letting others fall upon them until they had raised with trees and boughs thirty foot in height round about, leaving only one gate to issue at, near the water's side, which every night (that we might sleep in more safety and security) was shut up, with a great tree drawn athwart it.

The whole plot was built in a pentagonal form, to wit, of five equal sides and angles, of which angles two were toward the sea, and that side between them was left open, for the easy launching of our pinnaces: the other four equal sides were wholly (excepting the gate before mentioned) firmly closed up. Without, instead of a trench, the ground was rid for fifty foot space round about.

The rest was very thick with trees, of which many were of those kind which are never without green leaves till they are dead at the root (excepting only one kind of tree amongst them, much like to our ash, which when the sun cometh right over them, causing great rains, suddenly casteth all their leaves, viz., within three days, and yet within six days after becomes all green again. The leaves of the other trees do also in part fall away, but so as the trees continue still green notwithstanding) being of a marvellous height and supported as it were with five or six natural buttresses growing out of their bodies, so far that three men may so be hidden in each of them that they which shall stand in the very next buttress shall not be able to see them. One of them specially was marked to have had seven of those stays or buttresses, for the supporting of his greatness and height, which being measured with a line close by the bark and near to the ground, as it was indented or extant, was found to be above thirty-nine yards about. The wood of those trees is as heavy or heavier than brazil or lignum vitæ, and is in colour white.

The next day after we had arrived (July 13) there came also into that bay, an English bark of the Isle of Wight, of Sir Edward Horsey's, wherein James Rance was Captain and John Overy Master, with thirty men, of which some had been with our Captain in the same place the year before. They brought in with them a Spanish caravel of Seville, which he had taken the day before, athwart of that place, being a caravel of adviso bound for Nombre de Dios, and also one shallop with oars, which he had taken at Cape Blanco. This Captain Rance, understanding our Captain's purpose, was desirous to join in consort with him, and was received upon conditions agreed on between them.

Within seven days after his coming, having set up our pinnaces and despatched all our business, in providing all things necessary out of our ships into our pinnaces: we departed (July 20) from that harbour, setting sail in the morning towards Nombre de Dios, continuing our course till we came to the Isle of Pinos, where, being within three days arrived, we found two frigates of Nombre de Dios lading plank and timber from thence.

The negroes which were in those frigates gave us (July 22) some particular understanding of the present state of the town, and besides told us that they had heard a report that certain soldiers should come thither shortly, and were daily looked for, from the Governor of Panama and the country thereabout, to defend the town against the Cimaroons (a black people which about eighty years past fled from the Spaniards their masters, by reason of their cruelty, and are since grown to a nation, under two kings of their own. The one inhabiteth to the west, the other to the east of the way from Nombre de Dios to Panama) which had near surprised it [Nombre de Dios] about six weeks before.

Our Captain, willing to use those negroes well (not hurting himself) set them ashore upon the Main, that they might perhaps join themselves to their countrymen the Cimaroons and gain their liberty if they would, or if they would not, yet by reason of the length and troublesomeness of the way by land to Nombre de Dios, he might prevent any notice of his coming, which they should be able to give. For he was loth to put the town to too much charge (which he knew they would willingly bestow) in providing beforehand for his entertainment; and therefore he hastened his going thither, with as much speed and secrecy as possibly he could.

To this end, disposing of all his companies according as they inclined most, he left the three ships and the caravel with Captain Rance, and chose into his four pinnaces (Captain Rance's shallop made the fourth) beside fifty-three of our men, twenty more of Captain Rance's company, with which he seemed competently furnished to achieve what he intended; especially having proportioned, according to his own purpose and our men's disposition, their several arms, viz., six targets, six firepikes, twelve pikes, twenty-four muskets and calivers, sixteen bows and six partisans, two drums and two trumpets.

Thus having parted (July 28) from our company, we arrived at the Island of Cativas, being twenty-five leagues distant, about five days afterward. There we landed all in the morning betimes and our Captain trained his men, delivering them their several weapons and arms, which hitherto he had kept very fair and safe in good cask. And exhorting them after his manner, he declared the greatness of the hope of good things that was there, the weakness of the town, being unwalled, and the hope he had of prevailing to recompense his wrongs, especially now that he should come with such a crew, who were like-minded with himself, and at such a time as he should be utterly undiscovered.

Therefore, even that afternoon, he causeth us to set sail for Nombre de Dios, so that before sunset we were as far as Rio Francisco. Thence he led us hard aboard the shore, that we might not be descried of the Watch House, until that being come within two leagues of the point of the bay, he caused us to strike a hull, and cast our grappers, riding so until it was dark night.

Then we weighed again and set sail, rowing hard aboard the shore with as much silence as we could, till we recovered the point of the harbour under the high land. There we stayed, all silent, purposing to attempt the town in the dawning of the day, after that we had reposed ourselves for a while.

But our Captain, with some others of his best men, finding that our people were talking of the greatness of the town and what their strength might be, especially by the report of the negroes that we took at the Isle of Pinos, thought it best to put these conceits out of their heads and therefore to take the opportunity of the rising of the moon that night, persuading them that it was the day dawning. By this occasion we were at the town a large hour sooner than first was purposed, for we arrived there by three of the clock after midnight: At what time it fortuned that a ship of Spain, of sixty tons, laden with Canary wines and other commodities, which had but lately come into the bay and had not yet furled her sprit-sail, espying our four pinnaces, being an extraordinary number and those rowing with many oars, sent away her gundeloe towards the town, to give warning. But our Captain, perceiving it, cut betwixt her and the town, forcing her to go to the other side of the bay; whereby we landed without impeachment, although we found one gunner upon the [gun] platform in the very place where we landed, being a sandy bay and no quay at all, not past twenty yards from the houses.

There we found six pieces of brass ordnance, mounted upon their carriages, some demy, some whole culverins. We presently dismounted them. The gunner fled. The town took alarm (being very ready thereto, by reason of their often disquieting by their near neighbours the Cimaroons) as we perceived, not only by the noise and cries of the people, but by the bell ringing out and drums running up and down the town.

Our Captain, according to the directions which he had given over night to such as he had made choice of for the purpose, left twelve to keep the pinnaces, that we might be sure of a safe retreat if the worst befell. And having made sure work of the platform before he would enter the town, he thought best first to view the mount on the east side of the town, where he was informed by sundry intelligences, the year before, they had an intent to plant ordnance which might scour round about the town.

Therefore, leaving one half of his company to make a stand at the foot of the mount, he marched up presently unto the top of it, with all speed, to try the truth of the report, for the more safety. There we found no piece of ordnance, but only a very fit place prepared for such use, and therefore we left it without any of our men and with all celerity returned down the Mount.

Then our Captain appointed his brother, with John Oxenham[1] and sixteen other of his men, to go about behind the King's Treasure House and enter near the eastern end of the Market Place. Himself with the rest would pass up the broad street into the Market Place, with sound of drum and trumpet.

[1] Spelt "Oxnam" in the original.

The firepikes, divided half to the one and half to the other company, served no less for fright to the enemy than light of our men, who by this means might discern every place very well, as if it were near day; whereas the inhabitants stood amazed at so strange a sight, marvelling what the matter might be and imagining, by reason of our drums and trumpets sounding in so sundry places, that we had been a far greater number than we were.

Yet by means of the soldiers which were in the town, and by reason of the time which we spent in marching up and down the Mount, the soldiers and the inhabitants had put themselves in arms and brought their companies in some order, at the southeast end of the Market Place, near the Governor's house and not far from the gate of the town, which is only one, leading towards Panama; having (as it seems) gathered themselves thither, either that in the Governor's sight they might shew their valour, if it might prevail, or else that by the gate they might best take their *vale* and escape readiest.

And to make a shew of far greater numbers of shot, or else of a custom they had by the like device to terrify the Cimaroons, they had hung lines with matches lighted, overthwart the western end of the Market Place, between the church and the cross, as though there had been in a readiness some company of shot; whereas indeed there was not past two or three that taught these lines to dance, till they themselves ran away as soon as they perceived they were discovered.

But the soldiers, and such as were joined with them, presented us with a jolly hot volley of shot, beating full upon the egress of that street in which we marched, and levelling very low, so as their bullets ofttimes grazed on the sand. We stood not to answer them in like terms, but having discharged our first volley of shot, and feathered them with our arrows (which our Captain had caused to be made of purpose in England; not great sheaf arrows, but fine roving shafts, very carefully reserved for the service) we came to the push of pike, so that our firepikes being well armed and made of purpose, did us very great service. For our men, with their pikes and short weapons, in short time took such order among these gallants (some using the butt-end of their pieces instead of other weapons), that partly by reason of our arrows, which did us there notable service, partly by occasion of this strange and sudden closing with them in this manner unlooked for, and the rather for that at the very instant, our Captain's brother, with the other company with their firepikes, entered the Market Place by the easter street; they, casting down their weapons, fled all out of the town by the gate aforesaid, which had been built for a bar to keep out of the town the Cimaroons, who had often assailed it, but now served for a gap for the Spaniards to fly at.

In the following and returning, divers of our men were hurt with the weapons which the enemy had let fly as he fled, somewhat for that we marched with such speed, but more for that they lay so thick and cross one on the other.

Being returned, we made our stand near the midst of the Market Place, where a tree groweth hard by the cross; whence our Captain sent some of our men to stay the ringing of the alarm bell, which had continued all this while. But the church being very strongly built and fast shut, they could not without firing (which our Captain forbade) get into the steeple where the bell hung.

In the meantime, our Captain having taken two or three Spaniards in their flight, commanded them to shew them the Governor's House, where he understood was the ordinary place of unlading the moyles of all the treasure which came from Panama by the King's appointment, although the silver only was kept there; the gold, pearl, and jewels (being there once entered by the King's officer) was carried from thence to the King's Treasure House not far off, being a house very strongly built of lime and stone, for the safe keeping thereof.

At our coming to the Governor's House we found the great door, where the moyles do usually unlade, even then opened, a candle lighted upon the top of the stairs; and a fair jennet ready saddled, either for the Governor himself, or some other of his household to carry it after him. By means of this light we saw a huge heap of silver in that nether room; being a pile of bars of silver of, as near as we could guess, seventy foot in length, of ten foot in breadth, and twelve foot in height, piled up against the wall. Each bar was between thirty-five and forty pound in weight.

At sight hereof our Captain commanded straightly that none of us should touch a bar of silver, but stand upon our weapons, because the town was full of people, and there was in the King's Treasure House, near the water side, more gold and jewels than all our four pinnaces could carry; which we would presently set some in hand to break open, notwithstanding the Spaniards' reports of the strength of it.

We were no sooner returned to our strength, but there was a report brought by some of our men that our pinnaces were in danger to be taken and that if we ourselves got not aboard before day we should be oppressed with multitude both of soldiers and towns-people. This report had his ground from one Diego, a negro, who in the time of the first conflict came and called to our pinnaces to know whether they were Captain Drake's? And upon answer received continued entreating to be taken aboard, though he had first three or four shot made at him, until at length they fetched him and learned by him that, not past eight days before our arrival, the King had sent thither some 150 soldiers to guard the town against the Cimaroons, and the town at this time was full of people besides; which all the rather believed because it agreed with the report of the negroes which we took before at the Isle of Pinos. And therefore our Captain sent his brother and John Oxenham to understand the truth thereof.

They found our men which we left in our pinnaces much frightened, by reason that they saw great troops and companies running up and down, with matches light, some with other weapons, crying *Que gente? Que gente?* which having not been at the first conflict, but coming from the utter ends of the town (being at least as big as Plymouth), came many times near us and, understanding that we were English, discharged their pieces and ran away.

Presently after this a mighty shower of rain, with a terrible storm of thunder and lightning, fell, which poured down so vehemently (as it usually doth in those countries) that before we could recover the shelter of a certain shade or penthouse at the wester end of the King's Treasure House (which seemeth to have been built there of purpose to avoid sun and rain), some of our bow-strings were wet and some of our match and powder hurt, which while we were careful of, to refurnish and supply, divers of our men harping on the reports lately brought us, were muttering of the forces of the town, which our Captain perceiving, told them that he had brought them to the mouth of the treasure of the world. If they would want it they might henceforth blame nobody but themselves.

And therefore as soon as the storm began to assuage of his fury (which was a long half hour), willing to give his men no longer leisure to demur of those doubts, nor yet allow the enemy farther respite to gather themselves together, he stepped forward, commanding his brother, with John Oxenham and the company appointed them, to break the King's Treasure House; the rest to follow him, to keep the strength of the Market Place till they had despatched the business for which they came.

But as he stepped forward, his strength and sight and speech failed him and he began to faint for want of blood, which, as then we perceived, had in great quantity issued upon the sand, out of a wound received in his leg in the first encounter, whereby, though he felt some pain, yet (for that he perceived divers of the company, having already gotten many good things, to be very ready to take all occasions of winding themselves out of that conceited danger) would he not have it known to any, till this his fainting against his will bewrayed it; the blood having first filled the very prints which our footsteps made, to the great dismay of all our company, who thought it not credible that one man should be able to spare so much blood and live.

And therefore even they which were willingest to have adventured most for so fair a booty would in no case hazard their Captain's life; but (having given him somewhat to drink, wherewith he recovered himself, and having bound his scarf about his leg, for the stopping of the blood) entreated him to be content to go with them aboard, there to have his wound searched and dressed, and then to return ashore again if he thought good.

This when they could not persuade him unto, as who knew it utterly impossible, at least very unlikely, that ever they should (for that time) return again, to recover the state in which they now were, and was of opinion that it were more honourable for himself to jeopard his life for so great a benefit, than to leave off so high an enterprise unperformed, they joined altogether and with force mingled with fair entreaty, they bare him aboard his pinnace and so abandoned a most rich spoil for the present, only to preserve their Captain's life; and being resolved of him, that while they enjoyed his presence and had him to command them, they might recover wealth sufficient; but if once they lost him they should hardly be able to recover home, no, not with that which they had gotten already.

Thus we embarked by break of the day (July 29), having besides our Captain many of our men wounded, though none slain but one trumpeter, whereupon, though our chirurgeons were busily employed in providing remedies and salves for their wounds, yet the main care of our Captain was respected by all the rest; so that before we departed out of the harbour, for the more comfort of our company, we took the aforesaid ship of wines without great resistance.

But before we had her free of the haven they of the town had made means to bring one of their culverins, which we had dismounted, so as they made a shot at us, but hindered us not from carrying forth the prize to the isle of Bastimentos, or the Isle of Victuals; which is an island that lieth without the bay to the westwards, about a league off the town, where we stayed the two next days, to cure our wounded men and to refresh ourselves in the goodly gardens.

THE LAST FIGHT
OF THE *REVENGE*

Sir Walter Raleigh

A sleight of Tudor inky hands – not least those of his kinsman Walter Raleigh – remade Sir Richard Grenville into a selfless naval defender of Elizabethan England. In truth, Grenville both financed and participated in pirate-cum-privateering raids for nearly thirty years. Tellingly, his end came trying to intercept the Spanish treasure fleet from the West Indies. His motives may not have been altruistic, yet his bravery was unsurpassed: for twelve hours on 13 September 1591 Grenville's Revenge *fought a solo-ship battle against the Spanish fleet off the Azores.*

All the powder of the *Revenge* to the last barrel was now spent, all her pikes broken, forty of her best men slain, and the most part of the rest hurt. In the beginning of the fight she had but one hundred free from sickness, and fourscore and ten sick, laid in hold upon the ballast. A small troop to man such a ship, and a weak garrison to resist so mighty an army. By those hundred all was sustained, the volleys, boardings, and enterings of fifteen ships of war, besides those which beat her at large. On the contrary, the Spanish were always supplied with soldiers brought from every squadron: all manner of arms and powder at will. Unto ours there remained no comfort at all, no hope, no supply of either ships, men, or weapons; the masts all beaten overboard, all her tackle cut asunder, her upper work altogether rased, and in effect evened she was with the water, but the very foundation or bottom of a ship, nothing being left overhead either for fight or defence. Sir Richard [Grenville] finding himself in this distress, and unable any longer to make resistance, commanded the Master-gunner, whom he knew to be a most resolute man, to split and sink the ship; that thereby nothing might remain of glory or victory to the Spaniards, seeing in so many hours' fight, and with so great a navy they were not able to take her, and persuaded the company, or as many as he could induce, to yield themselves unto God, and to the mercy of none else; but as they had like valiant resolute men repulsed so many enemies, they should not now shorten the honour of their nation, by prolonging their own lives for a few hours, or a few days. The Master-gunner readily condescended, and divers others; but the Captain and the Master were of another opinion, and besought Sir Richard to have care of them.

And as the matter was thus in dispute, and Sir Richard refusing to hearken to any of those reasons, the Master of the *Revenge* (while the Captain was unto him the greater party) was convoyed aboard the *General Don Alonso Bassan*. Who finding none over hasty to enter the *Revenge* again, doubting lest Sir Richard would have blown them up and himself, and perceiving by the report of the Master of the *Revenge* his dangerous disposition: yielded that all their lives should be saved, the company sent for England, and the better sort to pay such reasonable ransom as their estate would bear, and in the mean season to be free from galley or imprisonment. To this he so much the rather condescended as well, as I have said, for fear of further loss and mischief to themselves, as also for the desire he had to recover Sir Richard Grenville; whom for his notable valour he seemed greatly to honour and admire.

When this answer was returned, and that safety of life was promised, the common sort being now at the end of their peril, the most drew back from Sir Richard and the Master-gunner, being no hard matter to dissuade men from death to life. The Master-gunner finding himself and Sir Richard thus prevented and mastered by the greater number, would have slain himself with the sword, had he not been by force withheld and locked into his cabin. Then the *General* sent many boats aboard the *Revenge*, and divers of our men fearing Sir Richard's disposition, stole away aboard the *General* and other ships. Sir Richard, thus overmatched, was sent unto by Alonso Bassan to remove out of the *Revenge*, the ship being marvellous unsavoury, filled with blood and bodies of dead and wounded men like a slaughter house. Sir Richard answered that he might do with his body what he list, for he esteemed it not, and as he was carried out of the ship he swooned, and reviving again desired the company to pray for him. The *General* used Sir Richard with all humanity, and left nothing unattempted that tended to his recovery, highly commending his valour and worthiness, and greatly bewailed the danger wherein he was, being unto them a rare spectacle, and a resolution seldom approved, to see one ship turn towards so many enemies, to endure the charge and boarding of so many huge Armadoes, and to resist and repel the assaults and entries of so many soldiers.

Sir Richard died, as it is said, the second or third day aboard the *General*, and was by them greatly bewailed. What became of his body, whether it were buried in the sea or on the land we know not: the comfort that remaineth to his friends is, that he hath ended his life honourably in respect of the reputation won to his nation and country, and of the same to his posterity, and that being dead, he hath not outlived his own honour.

CORSAIRS OF THE BARBARY COAST

Christopher Lloyd

The long infamy of John Ward and Simon Danser stemmed as much from their apostasy as their plunderings; they were Christians who served as privateers for the Muslim states of the North African coast.

> All the world about has heard
> Of Danseker and Captain Ward
> And of their proud adventures every day.

No pirate enjoyed greater notoriety in his own day than Captain Ward. The hero – or anti-hero – of three ballads, two blackletter pamphlets and a play by Robert Osborne, *A Christian turn'd Turke*, he is seldom heard of today. A good deal of his career is obscured by legend, but its outlines may be pieced together from the numerous complaints about him in the Venetian State Papers and the citations in the records of the High Court of Admiralty. Since he only operated in the Mediterranean, he escaped the censure of the formidable judge of that court, Sir Julius Caesar, and since he made a success of his career, the last we hear of him is living in a palace at Tunis and enjoying his hobby of rearing chicks from incubators.

According to the earliest pamphlet about him, printed by Andrew Barker, "Master of a ship, who was taken by the confederates of Ward and by them detained prisoner", Ward was born at Faversham in Kent and began life as a fisherman. In the last years of Elizabeth's reign he drifted to Plymouth, hoping, no doubt, to join a privateering expedition to the West Indies. When these hopes failed, he joined the navy and was posted to a pinnace of the Channel Guard called the *Lion's Whelp*, on which he spent his time lamenting the good old times of the privateers "when we might sing, drab, swear and kill men as freely as your cakemakers do flies; when the whole sea was our empire where we robbed at will, and the world was our garden where we walked for sport".

Since he was not the sort of man to accept naval discipline for long, he was soon plotting to seize a bark belonging to a Catholic recusant who was said to have shipped a large treasure on board before embarking for Spain. When Ward and his friends seized the vessel they found "the goldfinches flowen out of their nest", so they sailed her to southern Ireland where, by pretending to be a friendly merchantman, they captured a large French ship which Ward later called the *Little John*.

He now saw himself as the Robin Hood of the high seas. He made his way to Algiers, but found that Englishmen were not popular there at the moment because another Englishman in the service of the Duke of Tuscany, Captain Giffard, had recently burned a prize in the middle of the harbour by way of protest against the price offered, thereby endangering the whole of the Algerine fleet.

He proceeded to Tunis, where he enjoyed the protection of Cara Osman, Black Osman, Captain of the Janissaries. A French report of 1606 credits him with commanding ships with combined crews amounting to 500 men; and in that year John Keye of Limehouse, captain of the *John Baptist* of 90 tons, found himself pursued by Ward off Greece "in a flemish flyboate of 200 tons called the *Gift*, having 30 cast pieces and 67 Christian English, Dutch and Spanish and 28 Turks serving him". Keye was on board as a prisoner when Ward went on to capture a Venetian "argosy" called *Rubin* of 300 tons, which he took back to Tunis. There Keye and 140 other Englishmen were freed.

Ward made his fortune by the capture of the Venetian *Reinera e Soderina*, a galeasse of 1500 tons, on her way back from Cyprus, valued at "one hundred times a thousand pounds" or two million ducats. A bill of indictment was filed in the High Court of Admiralty and some of those named therein ended their days at Execution Dock, but Ward himself went from strength to strength. It was deposed that one member of his crew received five and a half shares, each worth £15, and another £80 after the capture of the *Soderina*.

The three hours fight resulting in her surrender caused a sensation at Venice, where it was described in these words:

> The captain after deciding on the advice of everybody to fight, divided up all the crew and stationed some on the quarter deck, others on the main deck and the poop, and thus they all seemed to be very gallant soldiers with weapons in their hands. The two ships that came to attack, even though two or three shots were fired at them, strove without further ado to lay themselves alongside, and on coming within range fired off twelve shots, six each, always aiming at the crew and the sails, without once firing into the water. Their plans, designed to terrify, succeeded excellently, because two of those who were defending the quarter deck were hit by one of their shots, and when they were wounded and indeed torn to pieces, all the rest fled, leaving their weapons lying on the quarter deck and all of them running to their own property, even while the two vessels were coming alongside.

As a result of such successes, Ward gathered round him a formidable group of pirates: Captain Sampson was appointed to the command of prizes, Richard Bishop of Yarmouth became Ward's first lieutenant and James Procter of Southampton and John Smith of Plymouth his gunners. Though Danser still rivalled him in the western Mediterranean, Ward ruled the central seas. When asked if he would like to join the French as Danser had done, he replied, "I favour the French? I tell you if I should meet my own father at sea I would rob him and sell him when I had done." When a seaman called Richard Bromfield upbraided him for turning Turk and living in such a heathenish country, Ward merely called him "a Puritan knave and a Puritan rogue".

Yet at this moment he opened negotiations for a royal pardon. One of his acquaintances deposed that he was offered £200 "in Barbary gold" to take to friends in England in order to impress the Lord Admiral. The Venetian ambassador said that he was offered 30,000 crowns. But even James I jibbed at accepting

bribes from such a notorious pirate and went so far as to name
Ward specifically in a proclamation of January, 1609, for the
apprehension of pirates. Ward seems to have been much annoyed
at the rejection of his suit: "Tell those flat caps who have been the
reason I was banished that before I have done with them I will
make them sue for *my* pardon."

One of the ballads about Ward – "The Famous Sea Fight
between Captain Ward and the Rainbow" – refers to this plea for
a pardon, but as the author confuses the *Rainbow* with the ships of
Captain Rainsborough or Rainsborrow, whom we have seen
stoutly defending the *Sampson*, no great reliance can be put upon
it. Three verses are, however, worth quoting:

> Strike up, ye lusty gallants, with musick and sound of drum
> For we have descry'd a rover upon the sea is come;
> For his name is Captain Ward, right well it doth appear
> There has not such a rover found out this thousand year.
>
> For he hath sent unto our king, the sixth of January,
> Desiring that he might come in, with all his company;
> "And if your King will let me come, till I my tale have told
> I will bestow for my ransome full thirty ton of gold."
>
> "Go tell the King of England, go tell him this from me,
> If he reign king of all the land, I will reign king at sea."

Barker's pamphlet concludes with the names of 23 captains of
English ships taken by Ward. Two of them belonged to the
Fursman brothers of Dartmouth, who were turned adrift in a
rough sea, but were rescued by a Venetian vessel. We need not
expend too much sympathy on them because their names appear
on another list of pirates compiled a few years earlier.

Ward's attacks on Venetian shipping are constantly referred to
in the Venetian State Papers. He is reported as having captured
the galleons *Balbi* and *Spelgata* and special escorts were ordered
to convoy the galley fleets. The commander of a galleon specified
for this purpose sensibly complained that she stood too high out
of the water to be efficient as a pirate chaser and that a great galley
was much better for the purpose.

A striking portrait of Ward at the height of his fame is provided by an English seaman interviewed by our ambassador at Venice, Sir Henry Wotton. He describes Ward as a man of about fifty-five years of age, nearly bald, with a fringe of white hair round his swarthy face – "speaks little, always swearing. Drunk from morn till night. Most prodigal and plucky. Sleeps a great deal. A fool and an idiot out of his trade."

By this time he had given up all hopes of returning to England. As the principal renegade at Tunis, life there was very comfortable. Osman Bey's patronage was continued by his successor Yussuf, who valued the prizes Ward brought in. He put an old castle at his disposal which Ward converted into "a palace more fit for a prince than a pirate". Such favour stood him in good stead when he once condemned his flagship as unseaworthy and abandoned her together with her Turkish crew. When he returned to Tunis he was nearly lynched by the mob, but saved by his protector. After that he carried few Turks on board, his reputation being sufficient to attract plenty of European volunteers.

When the Scottish traveller, William Lithgow, visited him in 1616, Ward was living in great style, retired from the sea and enjoying the fruits thereof.

Here in Tunneis I met an English Captain, general Waird [such was Lithgow's Scottish pronunciation: Father Dan called him Edouart], once a great pirate and commander at sea; who in despite of his denied acceptance in England, had turned Turk and built there a fair palace, beautified with rich marble and alabaster stones. With whom I found domestics, some fifteen circumcised English renegades, whose lives and countenances were both alike, even as desperate as disdainful. Yet old Waird their master was placable and joined me safely with a passing land conduct to Algier; yea, and diverse times in my ten days staying there I dined and supped with him, but lay aboard in the French ship.

His legendary fame lived on because Edward Coxere, a captive at Tunis a few years later, says that Ward always "had a Turkish habit on, he was to drink water and no wine, and wore little irons under his Turk's shoes like horseshoes".

John Ward died of the plague at Tunis in 1622. He had long outlived his rival, Simon Danser. Lithgow misleadingly describes the manner of Danser's death after his return from Algiers and Fez in 1616, though a more probable date for the event is 1611.

Simon Danser is a more shadowy figure than Ward. His name is spelled in a variety of ways – Danser, Dansker, Tantzer, the Dancer – though it was actually Simon Simonsen of Dordrecht. Like so many of his countrymen, he was a common seaman who took to piracy as soon as he reached the Mediterranean. According to Father Dan, "after some years as a pirate, he arrived at Algiers in a northern type of ship in 1606 and stayed three years. He was the first who taught the corsairs of Algiers the use of round ships . . . Another English pirate called Edouart (Ward) did the same for those of Tunis." He is credited with 40 prizes during the three years he sailed under Turkish colours from Algiers, where he was known as Dali Capitan or Captain Devil.

In 1608, an English supercargo being examined by Venetian authorities attested that he had seen Spanish ships chasing Danser's four ships, which were then sailing in company with Ward off Malaga. He added that Danser had taken 23 sail in a month although he had only been "on the account" a year. Next year the English consul reported Danser's arrival at Algiers in a ship built at Lubeck "of great force", manned by Turks and Dutch seamen. He was now forcing English and Dutch seamen into his service and "was like to overthrow all the merchants here and bring the name of Englishmen into great disrepute". That year he caused an international diplomatic scandal by capturing a Spanish ship with ten Jesuits on board. The King of Spain complained to the King of France who complained to the Sultan. Danser saw the opportunity of getting a pardon and returning to his home at Marseilles if he ransomed the prisoners himself for 27,000 livres, but he could not resist stealing two bronze cannon from the Moors as he sailed for France in 1609. These he presented to his patron, the Duke of Guise, and for many years these guns prevented any settlement between France and Algiers.

He married and settled down at Marseilles, having sold his prizes for 60,000 crowns, retaining 500,000 crowns worth of property for himself. He was evidently in high favour because he accompanied the Duke of Guise to Paris, making the King of England feel very virtuous when he pointed out to the Venetian ambassador that he himself had just refused a pardon to Danser's rival.

Apparently Ward and Danser were still on good terms, though they quarrelled soon afterwards over the division of prizes.

Danser had five ships at Marseilles while "that scoundrel Ward" had nine at Tunis. Both were attacking Venetian shipping, but life at Marseilles was not altogether comfortable. There were many merchants residing there whose ships Danser had plundered, so that "when crossing the street he was accompanied by some of his bravos, who carried loaded pistols in their hands and formed his bodyguard."

The events which led to his death began when the king ordered him out of his retirement to go to Tunis to negotiate the release of some French ships there. According to Lithgow's circumstantial account, Danser opened negotiations by inviting the Bey to dinner "and mainly feasted him with good cheer, great quaffing, sounding trumpets and roaring shots, and none more familiar than the dissembling Bashaw".

In return, the Bey invited Danser on shore to dinner the next night. Danser arrived at the castle with a bodyguard, but, as he crossed the drawbridge, the gate was suddenly shut on his followers. The Bey then taxed him with past crimes, for the prizes he had seized and "the merciless murders of Moorish lives, for he never spared any. Whereupon he was straight beheaded and his body thrown over the walls in a ditch; which done, off went the ordnance of the fort to have sunk two of Danser's ships, but they cutting their cables, with much ado escaped . . . Lo, there was a Turkish policy more sublime and crafty than the best European alive could have performed," concludes Lithgow with Machiavellian glee, evidently echoing the pleasure his host, Captain Ward, expressed at the story.

The evil which Danser had done in his lifetime lived after him. The Algerines were still complaining about his theft of the two bronze cannon and they were still intercepting French merchantmen coming from the Levant. The French consul warned of a large corsair fleet "armed with Flemish and English guns which, being heavier than their own, gives them the advantage in the chase". He lists 21 ships already taken that year and adds that ships from Alexandretta were in particular danger. Then in 1620 a noted Barbary corsair called Regeb Reis seized a French ship off Marseilles. Two young men escaped to tell their story with such effect that the mob rose and massacred 48 Turkish prisoners. Some sort of accommodation with Algiers was now essential, so the story ends in 1623 when Marseilles merchants raised 30,000 livres to ransom Algerian prisoners held by the Duke of Guise, Danser's old patron, and the Duke at long last sent back the two bronze guns.

Ward and Danser were not only a pair of colourful rogues. It was their example and above all their ships and crews which transformed corsair warfare in the Mediterranean. The skills which they taught the Algerines and Tunisians introduced a far more dangerous form of commerce raiding than in the days of galleys with a limited range. Corsairs were now sailing into the Atlantic, to Ireland and even on one occasion to Iceland. As Sir Francis Cottington, our ambassador at Madrid, informed the Duke of Buckingham, now Lord High Admiral, "the strength and boldness of the Barbary pirates is now grown to that height both in the ocean and the Mediterranean seas as I have never known anything to have wrought greater sadness and distraction at this court than the daily advice thereof. Their whole fleet consists of 40 sail of tall ships of between 200 and 400 tons apiece; their admiral (flagship) of 500. They are divided into two squadrons, the one of 18 remaining before Malaga in sight of the city, the other about the Cape of S. Maria which is between Lisbon and Seville . . . To this day they remain before Malaga intercepting all ships that pass that way, and also prohibiting all trade into these parts of Spain."

No wonder that Andrew Barker, the author of the pamphlet about Ward which now only exists in one copy, warned that the corsairs "have been so readied by the instruction of our apostate countrymen (I mean Ward and others) to tackle their ships, to man and manage a fight that unless they are suppressed Christendom must expect no traffic at sea".

PIRACY IN ANCIENT ROME

Piracy plagued Ancient Rome. Eventually, in 67 BC, Pompey was given special powers – and millions of sesterces – to rid the Med-

iterranean of sea robbers – and did so in three months. Cicero's account of piracy in Mare Nostrum *is from his prosecution speech against Verres, the governor of Sicily, for extortion.*

Cleomenes left harbour on board the quadrireme from Centuripa, followed by ships from Segesta, Tyndaris, Herbita, Heraclea, Apollonia and Haluntium. It had all the appearance of a fine fleet, but was actually feeble and weak because of the leave of absence given to the marines and sailors. Our wonderful, industrious governor only had his eyes on this fleet of his command for as long as it sailed past his notorious debauch. He had not been seen for several days, but he allowed the sailors a brief look at him then, as he, a governor of the Roman people, stood in sandals, a purple cloak and a tunic that reached the ankles, leaning on a woman on the beach. This was the dress in which very many Sicilians and Roman citizens had seen him.

The fleet moved on and finally reached Pachynus after four days' sailing, where the sailors in their agony of hunger collected the roots of the wild palms, which are very plentiful there as in most of Sicily, and on these the poor desperate men fed. Cleomenes, on the other hand, who considered himself a second Verres in point of luxury, wickedness and leadership, drank himself silly all day long in his tent erected on the shore. While he was incapable and the rest starving, news suddenly came of a pirate vessel in the port of Odyssea (our fleet still being at Pachynus). Cleomenes was relying on the theoretical but far from actual existence of some land forces to bring his complement of sailors and oarsmen up to strength. But the same greedy method of Verres was found to have been applied to these as well as to the fleets and there were only a few left, for most had been dismissed. First Cleomenes gave orders for the mast to be raised in his own ship, sails to be set, anchors to be weighed, and instructed the signal to be given for the rest to follow him. This vessel from Centuripa had a remarkable turn of speed under canvas, though no one knew a ship's potential under oars during Verres's governorship, in spite of the fact that Cleomenes was short of fewer oarsmen and marines as a mark of special honour and favour.

The quadrireme quickly disappeared as if in flight, while the remaining ships were struggling in one spot. But they had more courage. Although they were few and their situation critical, they shouted out that they were prepared to fight, and were willing to offer in battle the part of their lives and strength still left to them by hunger. If Cleomenes had not fled so far in front, there could have been some plan for resistance, for his was the only decked ship; it was of such a size that it could have protected the rest, and in a pirate battle would have seemed like a city among those pirate sloops. But hungry, in want, and deserted by their leader and admiral, they could do nothing except begin to follow him on the same course. Like Cleomenes, they made for Helorus, not so much in flight from the pirates' attack as in pursuit of their commander. As each dropped back last of the column, so it came first into danger, as the pirates attacked the rear ship . . . While all this was happening, Cleomenes had reached the shore at Helorus, where he jumped out, leaving the quadrireme wallowing in the sea. The remaining commanders, once their admiral had gone ashore, could not fight back or make their escape by sea, and so they followed Cleomenes to Helorus. Then Heracleo, the pirate chief, suddenly finding himself the victor quite beyond his expectation, not by any valour of his own but because of the greed and wickedness of Verres, gave orders for the glorious fleet of the Roman people to be set on fire and burnt as it lay drawn up on the beach. The time was early evening . . .

News of this dreadful tragedy was brought to Syracuse late at night. Everyone converged on the governor's residence . . . Cleomenes, in spite of the dark, did not dare to show his face in public, but shut himself up at home, without even the company of his wife, who could perhaps have consoled her husband in his misfortune [she was with Verres]. The domestic discipline of our singular governor was so strict that in such a crisis and at the receipt of such momentous news, no one was allowed in, and no one dared to wake Verres from his sleep or interrupt him if awake. When the news was known throughout the city, a great crowd gathered . . . The governor was asked for, and when it was agreed that no one had told him the news, there was a sudden rush on the house . . . While he was still half-asleep in a drunken stupor, the crowd gained control of themselves, took their arms and manned the Forum and the Island, which comprises a great part of the city.

The pirates waited for just one night at Helorus, then left our ships still smouldering and proceeded on their way to Syracuse. The first part they approached was the summer quarters of the governor, that part of the beach where throughout those days he had placed his tents and camp of luxury. They found the spot deserted and, realizing that the governor had moved, they at once began to penetrate quite fearlessly into the harbour itself. When I say the harbour, I mean that the pirates entered the city and the inmost part of the city. For at Syracuse the buildings do not come to an end at the harbour, but the harbour is surrounded by and contained in the town, which means that the edges of the walls are washed by the sea, and the water, as it were, ebbs into a bay formed by the town. Here, under your governorship, Verres, the pirate Heracleo sailed at his fancy with his four little pirate sloops . . . And as he passed the Island, the roots of the wild palms found in our ships were thrown out to let everyone know of the crimes of Verres and the disaster that had come upon Sicily.

From *They Saw It Happen in Classical Times*, ed. B.K. Workman, Basil Blackwell & Mott Ltd. Copyright © 1964 Basil Blackwell & Mott Ltd.

"Pistol in one hand and cutlass in the other"

ENTER THE BUCCANEERS

Howard Pyle

The Golden Age of piracy began in the mid sixteenth century with the birth of the "buccaneers" in the Caribbean. The pirate historian Howard Pyle charts their early progress.

Just above the northwestern shore of the old island of Hispaniola – the Santo Domingo of our day – and separated from it only by a narrow channel of some five or six miles in width, lies a queer little hunch of an island, known, because of a distant resemblance to that animal, as the Tortuga de Mar, or sea turtle. It is not more than twenty miles in length by perhaps seven or eight in breadth; it is only a little spot of land, and as you look at it upon the map a pin's head would almost cover it; yet from that spot, as from a center of inflammation, a burning fire of human wickedness and ruthlessness and lust overran the world, and spread terror and death throughout the Spanish West Indies, from St Augustine to the island of Trinidad, and from Panama to the coasts of Peru.

About the middle of the seventeenth century certain French adventurers set out from the fortified island of St Christopher in longboats and hoys, directing their course to the westward, there to discover new islands. Sighting Hispaniola "with abundance of joy", they landed, and went into the country, where they found great quantities of wild cattle, horses, and swine.

Now vessels on the return voyage to Europe from the West Indies needed revictualing, and food, especially flesh, was at a premium in the islands of the Spanish Main; wherefore a great profit was to be turned in preserving beef and pork, and selling the flesh to homeward-bound vessels.

The north-western shore of Hispaniola, lying as it does at the eastern outlet of the old Bahama Channel, running between the island of Cuba and the great Bahama Banks, lay almost in the very main stream of travel. The pioneer Frenchmen were not slow to discover the double advantage to be reaped from the wild cattle that cost them nothing to procure, and a market for the flesh ready found for them. So down upon Hispaniola they came by boatloads and shiploads, gathering like a swarm of mosquitoes, and overrunning the whole western end of the island. There they established themselves, spending the time alternately in hunting the wild cattle and buccanning[1] the meat, and squandering their hardly earned gains in wild debauchery, the opportunities for which were never lacking in the Spanish West Indies.

At first the Spaniards thought nothing of the few travel-worn Frenchmen who dragged their longboats and hoys up on the beach, and shot a wild bullock or two to keep body and soul together; but when the few grew to dozens, and the dozens to scores, and the scores to hundreds, it was a very different matter, and wrathful grumblings and mutterings began to be heard among the original settlers.

But of this the careless buccaneers thought never a whit, the only thing that troubled them being the lack of a more convenient shipping point than the main island afforded them.

This lack was at last filled by a party of hunters who ventured across the narrow channel that separated the main island from Tortuga. Here they found exactly what they needed – a good harbor, just at the junction of the Windward Channel with the old Bahama Channel – a spot where four-fifths of the Spanish-Indian trade would pass by their very wharves.

There were a few Spaniards upon the island, but they were a quiet folk, and well disposed to make friends with the strangers; but when more Frenchmen and still more Frenchmen crossed the narrow channel, until they overran the Tortuga and turned it into one great curing house for the beef which they shot upon the neighboring island, the Spaniards grew restive over the matter, just as they had done upon the larger island.

Accordingly, one fine day there came half a dozen great boatloads of armed Spaniards, who landed upon the Turtle's Back

[1] Buccanning, by which the "buccaneers" gained their name, was of process of curing thin strips of meat by salting, smoking, and drying in the sun.

and sent the Frenchmen flying to the woods and fastnesses of
rocks as the chaff flies before the thunder gust. That night the
Spaniards drank themselves mad and shouted themselves hoarse
over their victory, while the beaten Frenchmen sullenly paddled
their canoes back to the main island again, and the Sea Turtle was
Spanish once more.

But the Spaniards were not contented with such a petty
triumph as that of sweeping the island of Tortuga free from
the obnoxious strangers, down upon Hispaniola they came,
flushed with their easy victory, and determined to root out every
Frenchman, until not one single buccaneer remained. For a time
they had an easy thing of it, for each French hunter roamed the
woods by himself, with no better company than his half-wild
dogs, so that when two or three Spaniards would meet such a one,
he seldom if ever came out of the woods again, for even his resting
place was lost.

But the very success of the Spaniards brought their ruin along
with it, for the buccaneers began to combine together for self-
protection, and out of that combination arose a strange union of
lawless man with lawless man, so near, so close, that it can scarce
be compared to any other than that of husband and wife. When
two entered upon this comradeship, articles were drawn up and
signed by both parties, a common stock was made of all their
possessions, and out into the woods they went to seek their
fortunes; thenceforth they were as one man; they lived together
by day, they slept together by night; what one suffered, the other
suffered; what one gained, the other gained. The only separation
that came betwixt them was death, and then the survivor in-
herited all that the other left. And now it was another thing with
Spanish buccaneer hunting, for two buccaneers, reckless of life,
quick of eye, and true of aim, were worth any half dozen of
Spanish islanders.

By and by, as the French became more strongly organized for
mutual self-protection, they assumed the offensive. Then down
they came upon Tortuga, and now it was the turn of the Spanish
to be hunted off the island like vermin, and the turn of the French
to shout their victory.

Having firmly established themselves, a governor was sent to
the French of Tortuga, one M. le Passeur, from the island of St
Christopher; the Sea Turtle was fortified, and colonists, consist-

ing of men of doubtful character and women of whose character there could be no doubt whatever, began pouring in upon the island, for it was said that the buccaneers thought no more of a doubloon than of a Lima bean, so that this was the place for the brothel and the brandy shop to reap their golden harvest, and the island remained French.

Hitherto the Tortugans had been content to gain as much as possible from the homeward-bound vessels through the orderly channels of legitimate trade. It was reserved for Pierre le Grand to introduce piracy as a quicker and more easy road to wealth than the semi-honest exchange they had been used to practice.

Gathering together eight-and-twenty other spirits as hardy and reckless as himself, he put boldly out to sea in a boat hardly large enough to hold his crew, and running down the Windward Channel and out into the Caribbean Sea, he lay in wait for such a prize as might be worth the risks of winning.

For a while their luck was steadily against them; their provisions and water began to fail, and they saw nothing before them but starvation or a humiliating return. In this extremity they sighted a Spanish ship belonging to a "flota" which had become separated from her consorts.

The boat in which the buccaneers sailed might, perhaps, have served for the great ship's longboat; the Spaniards out-numbered them three to one, and Pierre and his men were armed only with pistols and cutlasses; nevertheless this was their one and only chance, and they determined to take the Spanish ship or to die in the attempt. Down upon the Spaniard they bore through the dusk of the night, and giving orders to the "chirurgeon" to scuttle their craft under them as they were leaving it, they swarmed up the side of the unsuspecting ship and upon its decks in a torrent – pistol in one hand and cutlass in the other. A part of them ran to the gun room and secured the arms and ammunition, pistoling or cutting down all such as stood in their way or offered opposition; the other party burst into the great cabin at the heels of Pierre le Grand, found the captain and a party of his friends at cards, set a pistol to his breast, and demanded him to deliver up the ship. Nothing remained for the Spaniard but to yield, for there was no alternative between surrender and death. And so the great prize was won.

It was not long before the news of this great exploit and of the

vast treasure gained reached the ears of the buccaneers of Tortuga and Hispaniola. Then what a hubbub and an uproar and a
tumult there was! Hunting wild cattle and buccanning the meat
was at a discount, and the one and only thing to do was to go a-
pirating; for where one such prize had been won, others were to
be had.

In a short time freebooting assumed all of the routine of a
regular business. Articles were drawn up betwixt captain and
crew, compacts were sealed, and agreements entered into by the
one party and the other.

In all professions there are those who make their mark, those
who succeed only moderately well, and those who fail more or
less entirely. Nor did pirating differ from this general rule, for in
it were men who rose to distinction, men whose names, something tarnished and rusted by the lapse of years, have come down
even to us of the present day.

Pierre Francois, who, with his boatload of six-and-twenty
desperadoes, ran boldly into the midst of the pearl fleet off the
coast of South America, attacked the vice admiral under the very
guns of two men-of-war, captured his ship, though she was
armed with eight guns and manned with threescore men, and
would have got her safely away, only that having to put on sail,
their mainmast went by the board, whereupon the men-of-war
came up with them, and the prize was lost.

But even though there were two men-of-war against all that
remained of six-and-twenty buccaneers, the Spaniards were glad
enough to make terms with them for the surrender of the vessel,
whereby Pierre Francois and his men came off scot-free.

Bartholomew Portuguese was a worthy of even more note. In a
boat manned with thirty fellow adventurers he fell upon a great
ship off Cape Corrientes, manned with threescore and ten men,
all told.

Her he assaulted again and again, beaten off with the very
pressure of numbers only to renew the assault, until the Spaniards who survived, some fifty in all, surrendered to twenty
living pirates, who poured upon their decks like a score of bloodstained, powder-grimed devils.

They lost their vessel by recapture, and Bartholomew Portuguese barely escaped with his life through a series of almost
unbelievable adventures. But no sooner had he fairly escaped

from the clutches of the Spaniards than, gathering together another band of adventurers, he fell upon the very same vessel in the gloom of the night, recaptured her when she rode at anchor in the harbor of Campeche under the guns of the fort, slipped the cable, and was away without the loss of a single man. He lost her in a hurricane soon afterward, just off the Isle of Pines; but the deed was none the less daring for all that.

Another notable no less famous than these two worthies was Roch Braziliano, the truculent Dutchman who came up from the coast of Brazil to the Spanish Main with a name ready-made for him. Upon the very first adventure which he undertook he captured a plate ship of fabulous value, and brought her safely into Jamaica; and when at last captured by the Spaniards, he fairly frightened them into letting him go by truculent threats of vengeance from his followers.

Such were three of the pirate buccaneers who infested the Spanish Main. There were hundreds no less desperate, no less reckless, no less insatiate in their lust for plunder, than they.

The effects of this freebooting soon became apparent. The risks to be assumed by the owners of vessels and the shippers of merchandise became so enormous that Spanish commerce was practically swept away from these waters. No vessel dared to venture out of port excepting under escort of powerful men-of-war, and even then they were not always secure from molestation. Exports from Central and South America were sent to Europe by way of the Strait of Magellan, and little or none went through the passes between the Bahamas and the Caribbees.

So at last "buccaneering", as it had come to be generically called, ceased to pay the vast dividends that it had done at first. The cream was skimmed off, and only very thin milk was left in the dish. Fabulous fortunes were no longer earned in a ten days' cruise, but what money was won hardly paid for the risks of the winning. There must be a new departure, or buccaneering would cease to exist.

Then arose one who showed the buccaneers a new way to squeeze money out of the Spaniards. This man was an Englishman – Lewis Scot.

The stoppage of commerce on the Spanish Main had naturally tended to accumulate all the wealth gathered and produced into the chief fortified cities and towns of the West Indies. As there no longer existed prizes upon the sea, they must be gained upon the land, if they were to be gained at all. Lewis Scot was the first to appreciate this fact.

Gathering together a large and powerful body of men as hungry for plunder and as desperate as himself, he descended upon the town of Campeche, which he captured and sacked, stripping it of everything that could possibly be carried away.

When the town was cleared to the bare walls Scot threatened to set the torch to every house in the place if it was not ransomed by a large sum of money which he demanded. With this booty he set sail for Tortuga, where he arrived safely – and the problem was solved.

After him came one Mansvelt, a buccaneer of lesser note, who first made a descent upon the isle of Saint Catherine, now Old Providence, which he took, and, with this as a base, made an unsuccessful descent upon Neuva Granada and Cartagena. His name might not have been handed down to us along with others of greater fame had he not been the master of that most apt of pupils, the great Captain Henry Morgan, most famous of all the buccaneers, one time governor of Jamaica, and knighted by King Charles II.

After Mansvelt followed the bold John Davis, native of Jamaica, where he sucked in the lust of piracy with his mother's milk. With only fourscore men, he swooped down upon the great city of Nicaragua in the darkness of the night, silenced the sentry with the thrust of a knife, and then fell to pillaging the churches and houses "without any respect or veneration".

Of course it was but a short time until the whole town was in an uproar of alarm, and there was nothing left for the little handful of men to do but to make the best of their way to their boats. They were in the town but a short time, but in that time they were able to gather together and to carry away money and jewels to the value of fifty thousand pieces of eight, besides dragging off with them a dozen or more notable prisoners, whom they held for ransom.

And now one appeared upon the scene who reached a far greater height than any had arisen to before. This was Francois l'Olonoise, who sacked the great city of Maracaibo and the town of Gibraltar. Cold, unimpassioned, pitiless, his sluggish blood was never moved by one single pulse of human warmth, his icy heart was never touched by one ray of mercy or one spark of pity for the hapless wretches who chanced to fall into his bloody hands.

Against him the governor of Havana sent out a great war vessel, and with it a negro executioner, so that there might be no inconvenient delays of law after the pirates had been captured. But l'Olonoise did not wait for the coming of the war vessel; he went out to meet it, and he found it where it lay riding at anchor in the mouth of the River Estra. At the dawn of the morning he made his attack sharp, unexpected, decisive. In a little while the Spaniards were forced below the hatches, and the vessel was taken. Then came the end. One by one the poor shrieking wretches were dragged up from below, and one by one they were butchered in cold blood, while l'Olonoise stood upon the poop deck and looked coldly down upon what was being done. Among the rest the negro was dragged upon the deck. He begged and implored that his life might be spared, promising to tell all that might be asked of him. L'Olonoise questioned him, and when he had squeezed him dry, waved his hand coldly, and the poor black went with the rest. Only one man was spared; him he sent to the governor of Havana with a message that henceforth he would give no quarter to any Spaniard whom he might meet in arms – a message which was not an empty threat.

The rise of l'Olonoise was by no means rapid. He worked his way up by dint of hard labor and through much ill fortune. But by and by, after many reverses, the tide turned, and carried him with it from one success to another, without let or stay, to the bitter end.

Cruising off Maracaibo, he captured a rich prize laden with a vast amount of plate and ready money, and there conceived the design of descending upon the powerful town of Maracaibo itself. Without loss of time he gathered together five hundred picked scoundrels from Tortuga, and taking with him one Michael de Basco as land captain, and two hundred more buccaneers whom he commanded, down he came into the Gulf of Venezuela and upon the doomed city like a blast of the plague. Leaving their vessels, the buccaneers made a land attack upon the fort that stood at the mouth of the inlet that led into Lake Maracaibo and guarded the city.

The Spaniards held out well, and fought with all the might that

Spaniards possess; but after a fight of three hours all was given up
and the garrison fled, spreading terror and confusion before
them. As many of the inhabitants of the city as could do so
escaped in boats to Gibraltar, which lies to the southward, on the
shores of Lake Maracaibo, at the distance of some forty leagues or
more.

Then the pirates marched into the town, and what followed
may be conceived. It was a holocaust of lust, of passion, and of
blood such as even the Spanish West Indies had never seen
before. Houses and churches were sacked until nothing was left
but the bare walls; men and women were tortured to compel them
to disclose where more treasure lay hidden.

Then, having wrenched all that they could from Maracaibo,
they entered the lake and descended upon Gibraltar, where the
rest of the panic-stricken inhabitants were huddled together in a
blind terror.

The governor of Merida, a brave soldier who had served his
king in Flanders, had gathered together a troop of eight hundred
men, had fortified the town, and now lay in wait for the coming of
the pirates. The pirates came all in good time, and then, in spite of
the brave defense, Gibraltar also fell. Then followed a repetition
of the scenes that had been enacted in Maracaibo for the past
fifteen days, only here they remained for four horrible weeks,
extorting money – money! ever money! – from the poor poverty-
stricken, pest-ridden souls crowded into that fever hole of a town.

Then they left, but before they went they demanded still more
money – ten thousand pieces of eight – as a ransom for the town,
which otherwise should be given to the flames. There was some
hesitation on the part of the Spaniards, some disposition to haggle,
but there was no hesitation on the part of l'Olonoise. The torch
WAS set to the town as he had promised, whereupon the money
was promptly paid, and the pirates were piteously begged to help
quench the spreading flames. This they were pleased to do, but in
spite of all their efforts nearly half of the town was consumed.

After that they returned to Maracaibo again, where they
demanded a ransom of thirty thousand pieces of eight for the
city. There was no haggling here, thanks to the fate of Gibraltar;
only it was utterly impossible to raise that much money in all of
the poverty-stricken region. But at last the matter was compro-
mised, and the town was redeemed for twenty thousand pieces of

eight and five hundred head of cattle, and tortured Maracaibo was quit of them.

In the Ile de la Vache the buccaneers shared among themselves two hundred and sixty thousand pieces of eight, besides jewels and bales of silk and linen and miscellaneous plunder to a vast amount.

Such was the one great deed of l'Olonoise; from that time his star steadily declined – for even nature seemed fighting against such a monster – until at last he died a miserable, nameless death at the hands of an unknown tribe of Indians upon the Isthmus of Darien.

BUCCANEER WEAPONS

The rovers' rise to world-wide predominance during the second half of the seventeenth century can be attributed primarily to one factor: firepower. No matter how few in numbers, most pirate bands felt they could carry any objective through guile, mobility and superior musketry. This was not only true on land, but in ship-to-ship encounters as well, where a dozen well-aimed muskets were held to be the equivalent of a heavy gun. (Rather than attacking with a broadside of roundshot, French *flibustiers* favoured a volley of musketry followed by a boarding-party, their prizes being less likely to sustain grievous damage.)

Given the absence of armament factories and powder-mills in the Americas during this period, most weaponry had to be imported from Holland, France or England. This gave the West Indian privateers a distinct advantage over their Spanish-American foes, for whom firearms remained an expensive luxury because of Madrid's more antiquated trade policies – thus hampering their colonies' defensive capabilities, while at the same time contributing to the buccaneers' increasing arrogance, as the latter came to believe all Spaniards were easy prey.

The buccaneers equipped themselves with the best firearms they could obtain, and in considerable profusion. For example, the members of the expedition which Laurens de Graaf and the Sieur de Grammont led against Veracruz in May 1683 were instructed to bring as many firearms with them as possible, in order to offset the defenders' heavier numbers. During the attack itself, more than one inhabitant noticed how the raiders brushed aside its garrison because each "carried three or four firearms", while later, when thousands of Spanish captives were being herded on to Sacrificios Island, they were guarded by a few score pirates, "each one with three firearms and a short sword or cutlass".

With the exception of Saint-Domingue's *boucaniers* and other such sharpshooting hunters, most privateersmen waited until they could unleash volleys from close range during battle. For this reason they were often armed with either a musket or blunderbuss, plus two or more pistols for point-blank work (the effects of this latter fire being so murderous that the term "pistol-proof" became a byword among buccaneers, to denote anything invincible or outstanding). For the rest, rovers would carry additional charges – nick-named "apostles", perhaps because these usually numbered a dozen – in their bandoliers or cartridge belts, plus the usual vicious assortment of swords, dirks and axes for hand-to-hand combat.

In lieu of artillery, their land forays often involved the use of grenades, a particularly favoured assault weapon. Not wishing to be encumbered, the pirates substituted hand-grenades for siege-guns in order to sow confusion and panic within enemy fortifications, or redoubts. For example, during this same attack on Veracruz, a contingent of forty buccaneers rushed the northern Caleta bastion at dawn, tossing grenades through its apertures before swarming on to the rooftop. The resultant detonations were so loud that they could be heard three-quarters of a mile away on San Juan de Ulua island, and caused the bastion to surrender immediately, without a struggle.

Grenades could be made of either iron or glass. The French chronicler and priest Jean-Baptiste Labat recorded an instance of this latter usage, when the *flibustiers* of Capitaine Pinel swarmed over the bows of a British 18-gun ship off Barbados in early 1694 (during the War of the League of Augsburg, known in America as King William's War). The English crew barricaded itself inside the forecastle, but Pinel's boarders found a small hatch:

through which they flung a glass jar filled with gunpowder and surrounded by four or five lit fuses, which ignited the powder when the jar burst and burned seven or eight Englishmen so horribly, they called for quarter.

"Quicker even than gunpowder,
I next drew my sword and thrust to right and left"

HOW HALF-ARSE
BECAME CAPTAIN

Louis Le Golif

According to his autobiography, Louis Le Golif – nicknamed "Half-Arse" after one buttock was shot away by cannon – was a French buccaneer who fought with Roche Brasiliano and Laurens de Graeff. It is possible that Golif's Memoirs of a Buccaneer, *which were discovered in France at the end of the Second World War, are a forgery; even so they accurately depict many aspects of buccaneer life.*

It was between Cape Saint Thomas and the reefs known as Les Grenouilles that we saw one morning a ship which to Bigourdin could not be other than a merchantman. She was sailing before the wind as if to hug the southern shore of the great island of Jamaica. We took to the open sea, on the port tack, headed south by south-east, so as to lead them to think that we were another merchantman making sail for Cartagena, which would result in our cutting in on them and placing ourselves ahead. But they made such good pace that we soon saw that this would not be easy. We had hoisted the Galician merchant flag astern, for we had no doubt that this vessel was Spanish.

In order to be able to sail across her bows, we had to bear away, and it was in this perhaps that we were mistaken. Thereby we came to expose our beam, and that at quite close range, and we were preparing to hail them noisily in Spanish in order to mislead them, when, quite suddenly, they dropped the sails which hid their batteries and enveloped themselves in smoke. We were treated at once to the finest volley of two-headed angels[1] it was possible to receive. It was the first time I had seen this diabolical trick used, and I certainly believe that not one of their shots missed.

With a crash that is still in my ears, our mainmast and all its sails fell over the starboard side, and our fore topmast, being no longer supported, ended by falling on the head, crushing that of the storm-jib; during which the ship, which now bore nothing but the mizzen-sail, veered helplessly, despite the efforts of the helmsman, thereby showing her bows to the enemy. This certainly was for us the most deadly position imaginable. It was exactly where Bigourdin had hoped to place his enemy, and we were wholly prevented from making even the slightest retort, since our cannon faced nothing but the sea.

We had just broken our teeth on one of the first vessels, disguised as merchantmen but armed for war, that the Spaniards were then beginning to put to sea to deceive the filibusters and to crush them by means of this pretence.

Bigourdin was stretched out in his own blood, without any legs, his belly burst open and his guts exposed, while all around me the deck was strewn with my friends, some without arms, others without heads, not counting those who had been crushed by yards, blocks, the debris of tops and other heavy objects which had fallen from above in great disorder.

When I sought to move, the planks had become so sticky with the blood that was spurting from every direction that I fell. I was not long in pulling myself together and, as the command fell to me, I cried above the uproar:

"Brethren of the Coast! To your posts! I will give orders! No gun to be fired!"

This I did because disorder was beginning to raise its ugly head aboard.

I was obeyed. I could only escape from the position we were in by a ruse. I saw that the enemy had hove-to, and I did not wish to wait for him to pepper us with a second broadside. I did not

---

[1]Two-headed angels, or chain-shot, were the names given to two cannon-balls linked by a strong chain and fired by the same charge. The chain became taut in the air, cut or smashed everything it encountered and did great damage among the masts and rigging.

hesitate for long over the decision I had to take. We had to surrender, or at least to appear to do so.

I told one man, who was near me and still on his feet, to go at once and find our stern flag, which was for the time being, as I have already said, that of the Galician merchantmen, and to wave it at the bow with the sole purpose of leading the enemy to think that they had been mistaken and had blasted their own country-men. After which I sent another to collect twenty of the most determined of our men he might find unwounded and send them to me. I had the hope that, seeing my signal and our distress, the Spaniards would put a boat to sea in order either to assist us if we were friends or to receive my sword if things should work out otherwise.

When the twenty adventurers I had sent for had joined me, I told them that they would have to take side-arms in order, without a sound and at a signal from me, to massacre all those who would presently climb aboard, after which we would take their clothes and would go aboard their vessel, which we would have to carry by great surprise and sharp attack.

It was not one boat but two that they put in the water by means of the blocks of their lower yards, which took a long time and gave us the opportunity to prepare our ambush well.

In each boat there were about ten soldiers, with six sailors at the oars and another forward with the boathook. I had reason to fear that their distrust would uncover my ruse when I saw them make a great circle around us. At first they called out vocifer-ously, enquiring who we were, where we had come from and where we were going. Having foreseen this, I had placed near me a Brother of the Coast who was a native of Vianna do Castello in Portugal and who spoke Spanish to perfection. I made him reply that we were merchants from Vigo, going to the town of Carta-gena, and that they themselves were criminal and scurvy butchers to have massacred their own countrymen, and that they would all be damned for a crime that had never been seen since there were ships on the sea and poor mariners to sail the waves. This speech dismayed them. They asked for the master of the ship, and my Portuguese told them he was dead, in which he did not lie, that the only surviving officer, to his knowledge, was unconscious, having his belly crushed by tackle fallen from the mainmast, and that he did not know where the third could be, perhaps squashed and cut to death under some pile of debris, and while saying all this, good actor that he was, he had tears in his voice and a very whinning and querulous tone, and he said further that they would have done well to have brought the priest with them so that he might confess and fortify in God all those good Christians and Roman Catholics who, by their error, were now about to depart this life, and to say a prayer for those who had already done so.

All of this, to which was doubtless added the fact that they were under the poop and could not fail to recognise that this was a Spanish ship, as the *Salagrun* certainly was, ended by convincing them. Luckily our starboard side being all encumbered with the debris of our rigging, they had to come alongside our port, that is to say on the side where the men of their own ship could not see them. They began to climb up one behind the other, as was natural. My Portuguese awaited them at the top of the ladder, fooling them all the time with his jeremiads.

The first to reach our deck was the officer who led them and who had hailed us. Scarcely was he there than I saw him struck in the right place by a knife thrown from a distance, without his being able to breathe a word nor open his mouth. And he did not even fall, being seized at once by four hands and thrown aside with a gag in his mouth in case he was not quite dead. The first soldier to follow him was served likewise and also the third. I counted eleven who met the same fate.

It will perhaps be surprising that these men should thus be massacred so quietly, one after the other in single file. It will be understandable when I say that these Greek soldiers are ordinarily individuals more limited in mind than sheep or donkeys, and when they have been deprived of their officers, they are quite stupid enough to fall into any trap.

Only the last was kept alive, quickly gagged and securely bound, to serve as a decoy to make the men of the second boat climb up. They brought him to me and I gave him to hope that he would save his life if he obeyed my orders without trickery or deception. I directed him to go to the ladder, and tell his companions that their officer had sent word for them to give succour quickly to all their unfortunate countrymen who were dying and suffering so much as a result of their fatal mistake. This *jean-foutre* was so fearful of dying that he promised to do all we wanted. Having untied him, he was led to the side by my

Portuguese and, while he made the fine speech I had dictated to him, this Portuguese, pretending to be with him as a friend, was pricking his back with his knife, ready to dispatch him at once if he showed the slightest inclination to betray us. But this did not happen. The others took to the tale like larks to a mirror; they came alongside and climbed up, and were butchered one by one, just as I have told of the first.

After that there still remained seven sailors in each boat, to guard them and hold them alongside. We had to rid ourselves also of them, and it did not take us long. Seven adventurers dropped suddenly into each boat, each one upon his man. Having only their oars in their hands, they could not put up much of a defence.

When everything had ended well, it only remained for us to disguise ourselves. I exchanged my clothes for those of the Spanish officer. They were certainly just a little tight, but at that time I had not half the corpulence that I have since acquired, and I was nevertheless able to get into the breeches and jacket of this little runt, though rather badly. As for the rest of my men, everything went well with them since they had some choice and each managed as best he could. When we saw ourselves so well bedecked, we had a great desire to laugh, although the scene gave not the least grounds for it and the moans which rose unceasingly everywhere did not invite gaiety. But we had to put off until later the succouring of these poor men, the hardest task remaining to be done, to wit: to capture the vessel quickly by surprise and daring, which might well seem a mad undertaking. I took the time to give a large bowl of rum to each of the forty-eight men who were coming with me. I was not in any great hurry, since evening was falling and that could only assist me. It was my wish that they should only recognise our faces when it was too late, and I waited until after sunset before descending into the boats and pushing off.

We were more in number than those who had come in them, but I desired that we should be as many as possible, and I made it appear that we were bringing with us those who were in the worst state. These sham casualties had swathed their heads or limbs in bloodstained linen and bandages, and lying at the bottom of the boats they gave further help by concealing beneath them the weapons and boxes of grenades that I had to carry.

Seeing us approach, the Spaniards, who crowded at the top of the ladder, cried out:

"*Quien?*"

On this day my Portuguese revealed himself so fine an actor that I think he might have been able to cut a good figure at the Theatre de Bourgogne, reputed at that time to be the best in Paris. He answered with a fine gesture of calamity and in a pitiable voice that there had certainly been a terrible mistake, that they had shattered and massacred some poor Galician mariners, that we were bringing the most moribund to the surgeon, and that we were also going to send for the priest, of whom we were in great need. In response there came a loud murmur of regret and lamentation. We drew alongside the ladder and I ascended first, taking care to keep my head lowered and well hidden by my hat, like someone overwhelmed by the deepest consternation. But you may well imagine that I went up the last rungs like lightning and, leaving no one the time to recognise me nor to take it all in, I fired my two pistols almost at point-blank into the faces of the two officers whom I thought to be of the highest rank. Quicker even than my powder, I next drew my sword and thrust to right and left as much as I could before they had unsheathed their own, and I thereby stretched out a half-dozen in less than no time.

My men were now joining me in great clusters, helping themselves up by the wales and chains. The enemy was fleeing on all sides, having allowed themselves to be caught without weapons, which they were now running to fetch. Those who had them, having found time to draw, began to face up with some obstinacy and courage. One of them hurled himself upon me with a great sabre, but I parried his blow and ran him through cleanly, after which I picked up his weapon and held it in my left hand, and was soon well pleased with it, as we shall see.

Having rallied in imposing numbers, they charged us and broke up our company, which I had wanted to hold together. A fine melee followed, each man for himself without being able to attend to his neighbour. At one moment I was alone against three of them, two with swords and the last with a sabre. It was then that I saw the fruits of the fine lessons which my good fencing-master of Dieppe had once given me. I parried all their blows and thrust all three of them in the belly. I had only just extricated myself when I saw that I had seven on my hands, who assailed me from all sides, armed with pikes, axes and sabres. As soon as I had floored one, two others would run up, so that there were soon more than a dozen pressing in on me. Ridding myself of one of them who had come too close by a great kick to the genitals, and another, who had fallen and sought to stab me from below with his knife, whom I quietened by crushing his face with my heel, it might well be said that I fought with all four limbs, and without any presumption I assert that, so doing. I am, properly speaking, invulnerable and invincible. On that day I even knew how to ward off pistol and musket balls with a twirl of my sabre.

Seeing with whom they were engaged, all these *bougres* began to take care and to keep their distance. I charged them at once, which made them flee like a flock of sparrows. There remained only a great devil who raised a huge axe and thought to split my head in two, but before he could do so I nailed him to a rack of belaying-pins. I had some difficulty in withdrawing my sword, and was only able to do so by giving him a good push in the belly with my foot. It was then, without a doubt, that I received a slight sword-thrust in my left shoulder, but I did not become aware of the pain until after the fight. It was given me, I think, by an officer who gave me the greatest trouble in all this merry-making. I fenced with him in a fine fashion, and I was grateful to have only two like him before me, since this bully was joined by one of his companions who, by way of greeting, began by firing his two pistols into my face. They only just missed me, for the balls carried away my hat. I was not long in seeing that the man was more expert with a sword than with a firearm, nor in finding myself uncomfortable with these two fellows. But for my courage and steadiness of mind, I would not have come out of it at all. It was then that Pulverin, my good brother and *matelot*,[1] who later became my second-in-command, saved the situation by coming up behind them with a sabre in his right hand and an axe in his left. He opened the shoulders of one and all the back of the head of the other, and thereby rid me of these heroes who had been two to one.

While we took time to breathe, we saw that our men had rallied together and had already almost mastered the deck between the

[1]For explanation of the term *matelot*, see Glossary

mainmast and foremast, but that behind the balusters of the forecastle a large number of soldiers, who were lying in wait there under a petty officer full of malice, were preparing to send us a murderous discharge from their muskets. This was no time to hesitate, and it was necessary for us to sweep them all away. I was about to spring forward when they fired. But they were too hasty and their bullets were badly aimed, so that they passed above our ears. We leapt to the attack. At the starboard ladder I was forced to run through several pikemen who aspired to stop me with their weapons, which gave me little to fear; it was enough for me to parry the blow with my sabre and with it to hold the lance low, after which I had plenty of time to pierce the lancer with my sword wherever I liked, and to send him quite nicely to God or the Devil, which I did not fail to do five or six times in succession. Then the others, fearful of such a fate, gave me passage, and I was able to reach the upper deck, where I did great carnage beneath the mizzen.

We were fighting one against ten. Darkness was falling and each had difficulty in recognising his fellows, more especially as our Spanish clothes added to the confusion. Several, thinking that I was an officer of their king, summoned me to their aid, which was a most desirable convenience to me since, under the guise of helping them, I could slay them without respite. Seeing which, they began to challenge one another and to strike at one another with sabre, axe or pike, in the belly and elsewhere, which is by no means usual or courteous between friends. They shouted like demons in order to make themselves known, calling out their names, so that I knew if the *bougre* I was piercing was called Pedro, Pepe or Juanito. There was less risk for us in this respect, since we had known one another for a long time, while many wore large golden ear-rings, which proved for us a very distinctive and recognisable mark. I really think that I made a mistake only once. They, the Spaniards, hesitated before striking, allowing us time to do so first, which, as is known, is a great advantage in war. One small youth, doubtless misled by my clothing, cried out on seeing me approach:

"*Querido padre! No me mata!*" ("Don't kill me, father!")

I had not the least difficulty in showing him, with my sword, that he was mistaken in thinking that I was his father.

It was soon no more than a massacre, and for one whose heart was not too hardened it was somewhat distasteful. In the end, those who remained let themselves drop into the lower battery. I have said that we brought grenades with us. We exploded a few of them between their legs. They cried out for mercy, but we sent them a few more with the sole object of bringing them completely to wisdom.

However, it was certainly necessary to halt. I had all the hatchways battened down promptly so as to shut the monkeys up, and all of us rejoiced very much at having won an engagement that had begun so badly. It was only then that Pulverin saw that my left hand was all sticky with the blood that was running down my sleeve and I felt that I had a painful shoulder, but as the arm and all the fingers of the hand were working normally, I did not worry about it very much. At the same time, Pulverin was filled with mirth on seeing that my clothes, which, as I have said, were a little tight, had burst on all sides in the violence of the fighting, and that since the breeches had suffered like the rest I was an offence to decency, which was, after all, of no importance, there being no ladies with us.

We were very thirsty and very hungry, but I did not consider going to fetch victuals and drink from the stores, for the *bougres* were still too numerous below and further fighting might result, however little they might have recovered themselves. I contented myself, nevertheless, with opening the doors which led to the crew's quarters and to the main cabin, where we first of all searched for a lantern. Having found one and having lit it with a flint, we visited those places that were deserted, and found there only a few biscuits and sweetmeats, and four flagons of brandy, with which we regaled ourselves at once.

We could not go to the *Salagrun* because, when we had climbed up to the attack, having by no means too many men, I had ordered that none should remain in the boats and that time should not be wasted in making them fast. In doing so, I knew well that they would drift away, having wished thereby to put my men to the necessity of conquering or perishing.

I ordered that the vessel should lie-to while awaiting daybreak. When that had come, I saw that the still disabled *Salagrun*, as well as the two boats, had moved off a long way. We filled our sails and first went to fetch the two long-boats, after which, having fixed to the mainmast the filibuster's flag that I had taken care to bring with me, rolled under my belt, we approached the *Salagrun*. The joy of all those who had remained behind, when they recognised our ensign, can be imagined. When we had come near, I saw them dancing and throwing their bonnets and hats into the air. I had myself taken alone to the *Salagrun*, with only four men at the oars, leaving the others on the vessel as a prize crew, with Pulverin as chief. First of all they had to busy themselves with throwing the dead into the sea, and were strictly forbidden to descend into the battery except in case of fire. My plan was to let all those monkeys wallow there and to allow them out only when we had dropped anchor at Tortuga, where I wanted to go, not being sorry that they would see me return there all covered with glory, after having left the place so meanly, as already related.

I decided to make all my men move over to the Spanish vessel, which was named the *Santa Clara*, and to scuttle the *Salagrun*, which was in no condition for sailing the seas; then I made sail for Tortuga, where we dropped anchor after three days' voyage without incident.

Our sails were not yet furled when we saw ourselves surrounded by a host of boats filled with all sorts of people, very impatient to know what this fine vessel was that had arrived for the first time in their harbour and that many thought was a king's ship.

Having learned that a vessel captured from Spain had just dropped anchor below the fort of La Roche, Monsieur d'Ogeron, who was then Governor on behalf of the King and the gentlemen of the West Indian Company of Tortuga and the coast of Santo Domingo, did not hesitate to come on board. I received him as pleasantly as I could, making the cannon thunder while he was mounting the ladder. Having named me as captain, he gave me, as well as the persons of quality who accompanied him, a thousand embraces and civilities. After I had conducted them to the main cabin and had filled for them large pots of punch or good Spanish wine, I had to tell them the details of my very glorious feat of arms, at which their friendliness towards me redoubled and they embraced me yet again. Seeing that I was so much in favour with Monsieur the Governor, I ventured to ask him what had happened to M. Piedouille. In truth, I had some fear that this skinflint would make difficulties for me with the gentlemen of the Company, and would demand compensation from me for having fled from his estate well before I had finished the three years of my contract. But in America, he who is in the good graces of Monsieur the Governor fears nothing and I was there already. I was reassured when he informed me that the said M. Piedouille had passed away, having been quite neatly dispatched by one of his men.

I left the care of the prisoners who were lying in the battery to the governor of the fort, who was at that time M. de Curbezac. They emerged only a little fatigued, since they had been able to use their victuals and wine as they pleased. They numbered forty-eight. I learned later that the majority were afterwards exchanged for some of our own. The priest was allowed to reach the Spanish town of San Domingo as best he could. As to the booty, nothing much came out of this ship, except a lot of powder and cannon-balls. We had only one hundred and fifty pieces of eight, which were in the chest, to share, and a few effects, some of which, however, were quite fine. I at once appointed my good brother and *matelot* Pulverin as second captain and, leaving to him the task of seeing to everything on the ship, I went ashore in the same boat as Monsieur the Governor and together with him.

You can imagine that I was received there in the most flattering and glorious fashion. All the inhabitants of Tortuga, adventurers, Brethren of the Coast and gentlemen of fortune, were on the shore when I landed to a great chorus of cheering, and there were even some who fired their guns into the air to honour me. Although my left arm was still in a sling because my scratch had not completely closed, I had donned the finest doublet I had found in the Spanish captain's cabin. It was of gold-embroidered satin, and doubtless destined for some governor of New Spain.

Setting foot on shore in this attire, I could not refrain from thinking of that night, a few years earlier, when I had at that very spot made off with a wretched skiff in order to flee with Bournizot. It will be admitted that I had come a long way since then.

THE PIRATE'S CODE OF HONOUR

Contrary to the stereotypical view of pirates as an anarchic rabble, many lived in a well-ordered self-government. Usually each crew member swore – on the Bible – allegiance to the ship's rules (articles) before departure. Articles varied from pirate ship to pirate ship, but the main provisions were similar and dealt with the division of booty. Below is the code of piratical conduct from Captain Bartholomew Robert's squadron, circa 1722.

i. Every man has a vote in affairs of moment: has equal title to the fresh provisions or strong liquors at any time seized, and [may] use them at pleasure unless a scarcity make it necessary for the good of all to vote a retrenchment.

ii. If they defrauded the Company to the value of a dollar, in plate, jewels or money, marooning was the punishment. If robbery was only between one another they contented themselves with slitting the ears and nose of him that was guilty, and set him on shore, not in an inhabited place but somewhere where he was sure to encounter hardships.

iii. No person to game at cards or dice for money.

iv. The lights and candles to be put out at eight o'clock at night. If any of the crew after that hour still remained inclined to drinking, they were to do it on open deck.

v. To keep their piece, pistols and cutlass clean and fit for service.

vi. No boy or woman to be allowed among them. If any man were found seducing any of the latter sex, and carried her to sea disguised, he was to suffer Death.

vii. To desert the ship or their quarters in battle was punished by Death or Marooning.

viii. No striking another on board, but every man's quarrels to be ended on shore, at sword and pistol.

ix. No man to talk of breaking up their way of living till each had a share of £1,000. If, in order to do this, any man should lose a limb or become a cripple in their service, he was to have 800 dollars out of the public stock, and for lesser hurts proportionately.

xi. The musicians to have rest on the sabbath day, but the other six days and nights none, without special favour.

Reprinted from *Captain Johnson's A General History of the Robberies and Murders of the Most Notorious Pirates*, 1724

"Morgan called on the defenders to surrender,
or else they would receive no quarter"

MORGAN'S WAY

A.O. Exquemelin

The Welsh-born Henry Morgan was the greatest of the Caribbean
buccaneers or "Brethren of the Coast". Licensed by the Council of
Jamaica as a privateer to attack Spanish ships, he routinely over-
stepped his jurisdiction and launched raids on Spanish ports. His
methods were vile – even to contemporaries: he applied torture to men
and women captives as a matter of course – but brought such rich
successes that few protested.

Alexander Exquemelin knew Morgan better than most; he served
under him in his glory days. Here he recounts Morgan's raids on
Porto Bello and Maracaibo, 1688–9.

So that the reader may better understand this audacious exploit, I
must give a short description of Porto Bello. This city is in Costa
Rica [in Panama, in fact] latitude 10° north, some forty leagues
from the Gulf of Darien and eight leagues west of Nombre de Dios.
With the exception of Havana and Cartagena, it is the strongest city
which the King of Spain possesses in all the West Indies. Two
strong forts stand at the entrance of the bay, protecting the town
and harbour. These forts are always manned by a garrison of 300
soldiers, and not a single vessel can enter the bay without consent.
Four hundred families have their permanent residence in the city,
but the merchants only stay there when there are galleons in port, as
the place is very unhealthy on account of the mountain vapours.
The merchants reside in Panama, but have their warehouses in
Porto Bello, kept up by their servants. Silver is brought from
Panama on pack-mules, ready for the arrival of the galleons, or the
ships of the slave trade, delivering Negroes.

Morgan, who was very familiar with this coast, arrived with his fleet about dusk off Puerto de Naos, some ten leagues west of Porto Bello, and crept along the coast by night until they reached Puerto del Pontin, four leagues from the city. There they cast anchor, and the buccaneers all jumped into canoes and small rowing-boats, leaving just enough men on board to manage the ships and bring them into port next day.

About midnight they landed at a place called Estero Longa Lemo, and marched overland until they reached the first outpost of the city. Their guide was an Englishman who had formerly been a prisoner there and so knew the roads well. This Englishman and three or four others went ahead and captured the sentry, without firing a shot or making any noise. They bound him fast and brought him to Morgan, who immediately questioned him as to the arrangements of the town's defences and the strength of the garrison, and the prisoner told what he knew. Still with his hands tied, they made him march in the vanguard, threatening that if he had not told them the truth it would cost him his life.

After marching about a quarter of an hour they came to a redoubt, which they surrounded. Morgan called on the defenders to surrender, or else they would receive no quarter. Despite this threat the defenders proved stubborn and bravely fired on their attackers, so that at least they could give warning to the people in the city. In fact, the alarm was immediately sounded there. But the redoubt could not hold out long, and as soon as the buccaneers entered they blew up the inner fortification with all the Spaniards inside.

Then the buccaneers rushed on to the city, where most of the people were still in bed – for no one had thought the corsairs would have been so bold as to attack a place like Porto Bello. As the rovers entered, those citizens who were up grabbed what they had and flung it down cisterns and wells, hoping to foil the invaders. One band of buccaneers went to assault the forts and another went to the cloisters, where they took all the monks and nuns prisoner.

The governor had retired to one of the forts, from which he directed a fierce fire against the buccaneers, who were not slow to answer him. They kept up such a steady aim on the gun-platforms that the Spaniards lost seven or eight men before they could load and fire. The battle lasted all morning till noon, and still the invaders could not conquer the fort. Their ships lay in the harbour-mouth, and no one could enter for the withering fire from the forts on both sides. Finally, as they had lost many men and were gaining no advantage, the buccaneers began throwing in hand grenades and endeavoured to burn down the gate of the fort. But when they came in close for this attack the Spaniards soon made them turn back, for they hurled down at least fifty pots full of gunpowder as well as huge stones, which did much damage among the raiders.

Morgan and his men were beginning to despair, when they saw the English flag flying from the smaller fort and a troop of their fellows approaching, shouting "Victory!" This sight made Morgan pluck up courage, despite the drubbing he'd had. He entered the town to think of some means of capturing the fort, which was a matter of great importance to the buccaneers as the principal citizens were inside, with their gold and silver and jewels, and the silver ornaments from the churches.

Morgan had a dozen huge ladders made, broad enough for four men to climb at the same time. He fetched out all the monks and nuns, and the governor was informed that unless he surrendered the fort these people would be made to set the scaling ladders against its walls. All the answer Morgan received was that he should never have the fort so long as the governor lived.

The ladders were brought out, carried by the monks, priests and women, urged on by the buccaneers, who never thought the governor would fire on his own people – but he spared them as little as he had the raiders. The monks began to implore the governor by all the saints in heaven to give up the fort and save their lives, but their cries went unheeded. Willing or not, they had no choice but to carry out the ladders. As soon as these were set against the walls the buccaneers immediately swarmed up, furiously attacking the Spaniards with hand grenades and stink-pots – but they were forced to turn back by the ferocious resistance of the defenders.

The buccaneers refused to be daunted. One troop managed to set the fort gate on fire, while the rest clambered up the ladders with the same violence as before. When the Spaniards saw they were attacking with such vehemence, they gave up the defence – all except the governor, who like a desperate madman slew his own folk as well as the enemy. The buccaneers demanded if he would accept quarter, and he answered no. He used these very words: "*Más vale morir como soldado honrado que ser ahorcado como un cobardo.*" ("Better to die as an honourable soldier than be hanged as a coward.") They attempted to take him prisoner but could not, and were forced to shoot him dead. His own wife and daughter, who were in the fort with him, had begged him to save his life, but to no avail.

After the surrender of the fort, which was in the evening, all the prisoners were brought inside the town, the men and women being housed separately, and a guard set to look after them. The rovers brought their own wounded into a house near by. Having put everything in order, they began making merry, lording it with wine and women. If fifty stout-hearted men had been at hand that night they could have wiped out all the buccaneers.

Next day the rovers began collecting the loot, searching all the houses. Some of the prisoners were made to point out who were the richest among them, and then these citizens were asked where their wealth was. If they refused to tell they were immediately put to the rack and tortured there until they gave up the ghost or confessed the hiding-place. Many innocent souls, who in fact had nothing to hide, died like martyrs under the torments their captors subjected them to. No one was spared, except those who revealed where their goods were hidden.

Meanwhile, the president of Panama, having received news of the conquest of Porto Bello, was busy gathering together a force sufficient to drive the corsairs out of that city. The buccaneers were warned of this activity by some prisoners they had taken, but they paid little attention to the news. Their ships lay in the harbour, and if they could no longer hold the town they would set it on fire and put to sea.

When they had been there a fortnight diseases began to rage among them, caused by air foul with the stench of so many corpses, and by their furious debaucheries with drink and women. Most of their wounded died. As for the Spanish, very few survived – but these did not die from excesses, but through want and discomfort. Instead of sipping their customary morning cup of chocolate, they were glad to get a bit of bread or a lump of mule's flesh.

Meantime, Morgan was getting everything ready for their departure. The booty was stowed on board, together with as much foodstuff as they could obtain. Morgan informed the prisoners he must have a ransom for the city, otherwise he would set it on fire and demolish the forts. So that they could attend to this matter, he gave them permission to send out two men to collect the levy, which amounted to 100,000 pieces of eight. The two men sent to fetch this contribution went to the president of Panama and told him what was happening in Porto Bello.

The president had already raised a considerable army, and now led these troops to Porto Bello. The buccaneers, who were on the alert, were warned of his advance and lay in wait for him with 100 well-armed men at a narrow passage. They succeeded in destroying many of the president's troops and then retired to the fort. The president then sent word to Morgan that unless the buccaneers moved out he would attack with a huge army and grant no quarter whatsoever. Morgan was not afraid, knowing he could get away whenever he chose, and answered that he would not abandon the forts until the demanded ransom was produced. And, in the extreme event of his having to leave, he would at least demolish the forts beforehand and put all his prisoners to death.

Seeing no means of coercing the buccaneers, the president left the citizens of Porto Bello to manage as best they could and withdrew with his troops from the city. In the end, the citizens contrived to collect the 100,000 pieces of eight to secure their liberty.

The president of Panama was astounded that 400 men could have conquered such strong fortresses, whose defenders had not lacked courage, with nothing but small-arms. He sent a messenger to Morgan, asking that he might be allowed to see the weapon which had given him such power. Morgan received the president's envoy with great civility and gave him a French musket with a barrel four and a half feet long, firing a one ounce bullet; he also sent a cartouche which he'd had expressly made in France, containing thirty cartridges full of powder. He charged the messenger to tell his master that Morgan presented him with this musket, and that within a year or two he would come to Panama to fetch it back again.

The president sent the messenger back with a present for Morgan – a gold ring set with a rosette of emeralds – and thanked him cordially for the musket. He begged Morgan not to call on

him in the manner he had visited Porto Bello, for in that case he
might not get such a good reception.

Morgan, having stocked his ships with all kinds of provisions
and marine stores, of which there were plenty in Porto Bello,
finally took his departure. He could not resist taking some of the
brass cannon from the forts as a keepsake, and the rest of the guns
were spiked.

Shortly after abandoning Porto Bello, the fleet arrived at the
South Cays of Cuba, where, according to custom, the booty was
shared out. The buccaneers found they had 215,000 pieces of
eight in ready money, jewels and silver, besides other spoils of
linen, silk and other goods. Having shared out the plunder,
Morgan entered Jamaica with great honour and magnificence,
as he brought so much wealth with him.

After Morgan had been some time in Jamaica and his men had
squandered their money, he decided to renew his attacks on the
Spaniards. He gave as rendezvous the Isla de la Vaca, off the
south coast of Hispaniola. This was a good place for careening the
ships and also for obtaining provisions, as there are many wild
boar to hunt on the big island. Many English and French
buccaneers arrived to join forces with Morgan, for he had made
a great name for himself on account of the immense success of his
previous raids.

At this time a naval vessel mounting thirty-six guns arrived in
Jamaica from New England. The governor sent this warship to
join Morgan's fleet, to encourage him still further to attack some
place of consequence, where there would be good plunder.
Morgan was delighted at the arrival of such a ship, for he had
not a single vessel in his fleet fit to prevail against a fort if the need
arose. There was also a French ship, mounting twenty-four
cannon and twelve brass swivel-guns, which Morgan would
gladly have had in his company. But the men on board dared
not trust themselves among the English, fearing reprisals. At a
time when they had run short of food they had encountered an
English ship at sea and had helped themselves to victuals with no
payment except a bill of exchange payable in Jamaica and Tortuga.

Seeing the French would not accompany him willingly, Morgan invited the captain and crew on board the great ship, without

rousing their suspicions, then took them all prisoner, laying claim to the French ship on account of the victuals they had taken.

Morgan then held a council of war with the captains of the buccaneer fleet to decide which place on the Spanish coast to attack. They resolved to sail first for the island of Savona, off the eastern point of Hispaniola, and having come together at this rendezvous take a further decision as to where they would go.

They drank the health of the King of England and toasted their good success and fired off salvoes. The gentlemen made merry in the poop and the men did the same in the fo'c'sle – but when they were at the height of their joy, events swiftly changed to a sorrowful conclusion. For, as the festive guns were being fired, some sparks landed in the gunpowder – and the ship blew up with 300 Englishmen on board, as well as the French prisoners. There were only about thirty survivors. All those who had been in the great cabin saved their lives, with little harm done, Morgan being slightly injured in the leg. The survivors had all been in the stern of the ship, for in English ships the powder-room is generally forward. More might have escaped, but most of the men had been drunk.

The English, having no excuse for the disaster which had overtaken the warship, justified matters by taking the French vessel. They said the French had blown up the king's ship, and that they had been sailing with a Spanish privateering commission to attack the English wherever they could. As proof, they showed a pass from the governor of Baracao on the island of Cuba which they had found on the French ship, permitting the French to cruise against the English pirates, as the Jamaican buccaneers were daily committing hostilities against the Spaniards although there was no war between England and Spain.

In fact, the French had obtained this commission not to give them excuse for attacking the English buccaneers, but in order to trade with the Spaniards. The captain of the French ship was also among the survivors, and tried vainly to explain how matters stood. The ship was taken to Jamaica, where again the French captain tried to plead his cause – but instead of giving him a hearing, they threw him into prison and threatened to hang him.

Meanwhile, Morgan refused to lose heart, and decided to pursue his plans with the men who remained. A week after the ship had blown up, they had fished out all the corpses floating in the water. This was not in order to give them a decent burial, but for the sake of their clothes and the gold rings on their fingers. As soon as they had fished out a body they pulled off the garments and hacked off the fingers which were beringed, then threw back the corpse to be a floating prey for the sharks. Their bones are still to be found on the beaches, washed up by the sea.

Morgan kept to his original plan of meeting on Savona and there holding a council to decide where to attack. He set sail for this rendezvous with his companion ships, which numbered fifteen. Morgan sailed in the largest, which mounted only fourteen guns. Altogether, he had a force of about 960 men. A few days later they came to Cabo de Lobos, situated midway along the south coast of Hispaniola between Cabo Tiburon and Punta del Espada, where Morgan was held up for three weeks by the strong east wind. Every day they attempted to round the cape, but failed. Finally they succeeded, and seven or eight leagues farther on sighted a ship come from England. A few of the ships went off to see what they could get from this vessel, but Morgan continued his course, saying he would wait for them at the Bay of Ocoa.

Two days later Morgan reached this bay, where he put in to fetch aboard fresh water and to wait for the rest of his fleet. Every day five or six men from each ship were sent ashore to look for food to save their own supplies. They shot everything they found – horses, donkeys, cattle and sheep. The Spaniards of course did not suffer this gladly. Noticing that on each trip only a few men came ashore, they laid a trap for the rovers. They sent for three or four hundred soldiers from the nearby garrison at San Domingo, and meanwhile drove all the cattle inland.

The buccaneers, about fifty strong, had wandered three leagues or so through the woods when the Spaniards let them see a fine herd of cattle, driven along by a few cowherds for the look of the thing. The buccaneers fell on their prey and the Spaniards let them get on with it – but when they were in the act of carrying off the beasts they had shot, the soldiers attacked in full force, crying, "*Mata! Mata!*" ("Kill, kill!")

The buccaneers abandoned the slaughtered animals and put themselves in a posture of defence. They resisted the Spaniards furiously: while half were firing, the rest were loading. Keeping up a continuous fire, they retired in good order until they reached the shelter of the forest once more. The Spaniards would have liked to have pursued them, but, as the rovers seldom missed their mark and had already killed and wounded a large number, they turned back again.

The buccaneers were still in the woods, binding up their comrades' wounds as best they could, and they could see the Spaniards carrying off their dead and wounded. Among the casualties was a dead buccaneer, and a group of Spaniards were moving round this man, plunging their naked swords into the corpse and shouting, "*El cornudo ladron!*"

The buccaneers in the woods, seeing that the main Spanish force had withdrawn, rushed out on this troop, killing many of them. They took the corpse of their comrade, which had received more than a hundred stabs after death, and buried it in the forest. After this, they killed a few horses so as not to return without meat, and brought their wounded back on board.

Next day Morgan himself landed with 200 men, but by that time the Spaniards had already gone, and had driven away all their cattle. So they set fire to a few houses and returned to the ships.

As the rest of his fleet did not arrive, Morgan proceeded with those ships he had with him to the final rendezvous on Savona. There were no signs of the other vessels there, either, so he decided to wait a few days for them. In the meantime, he sent out a party of 150 men to land on Hispaniola and plunder the villages in the neighbourhood of San Domingo for supplies, as they were beginning to run short of food. But the marauding party returned without success, for the Spaniards, warned that the corsairs were on the coast, had all been up in arms. The buccaneers, who only cared to fight for booty, had not fancied doing battle.

As his companions still did not arrive, Morgan mustered the men who were with him. He found he had about 500 men, and eight vessels, his own ship being the biggest. His original plan had been to plunder all the towns and villages along the coast of Caracas, but his present forces were too weak for this, so he had to make another decision. Among his men was a French captain, who had been with l'Olonnais at the capture of Maracaibo. He had observed the features of the lake so accurately he was convinced he could bring in Morgan's fleet. After he had discussed with Morgan the way they must set about taking the place, the men were informed, and they agreed unanimously to go on this enterprise.

The resolve having been taken, Morgan and his fleet steered towards Curacao and, on sighting this island, put in at another called Ruba, which lies about twelve leagues off the western tip of Curacao. It belongs to the Dutch West India Company, who have installed a sergeant there as governor, with fifteen soldiers. Otherwise, the island is inhabited by Indians, who speak Spanish and are under Spanish religious influence. Every year a priest comes from a village called Coro on the opposite coast, who preaches to them and gives them the sacrament after the Roman Catholic manner.

These Indians trade with the buccaneers when they call in, exchanging sheep and goats for linen, thread and anything else they need. The island is infertile – very barren, and mostly overgrown with scrub. There are sheep and goats in great numbers and a little maize is planted. There are also many horses, and whatever the Indians do, they do on horseback – even if it's only to go five hundred paces from their home to fetch water. There are many rattlesnakes and some extremely venomous spiders. Anyone who has been bitten by one of these creatures is tied in a hammock and left there twenty-four hours without food or drink. The inhabitants believe the victim must be prevented from drinking, otherwise he will die.

Morgan, having come to anchor at this island, traded with the Indians for as many sheep and goats as were required for the whole fleet, and two days later left by night, so that they should not see in which direction he sailed – but they did notice it, nevertheless.

Next day the fleet entered the Bay of Maracaibo. They anchored in eight fathoms of water in the middle of the bay, out of view of Look-out Island, and sailed on when darkness fell. At daybreak they were at the bar of the lake. The Spaniards had built a new fort, from which they welcomed Morgan with the heavy artillery they had installed.

All the smaller boats were employed to land the buccaneers with the utmost speed. The Spaniards too were busy with their preparations at the fort. They burned down several near-by houses to give them a clear field of fire, and kept up a heavy cannonade all day long.

It was dusk when Morgan and his men reached the fort. They found nobody inside, for when they saw the buccaneers close by the walls the Spaniards had let off some gunpowder and made for the woods under cover of the smoke. Morgan was amazed to find no defenders, for the fort was very well equipped to hold out. They found a cellar full of gunpowder, much of it scattered about – and a length of burning match about an inch away from the powder, so that the buccaneers narrowly missed being blown up with the fort and all.

The match was snatched away, and Morgan had all the gunpowder instantly carried outside. The walls were pulled down where necessary, and the guns dismantled. There were sixteen cannon, firing balls of eight, twelve and twenty-four pounds, eighty muskets and other weapons besides. The cannon were thrown down from the fortress walls and the gun-carriages were burnt.

Early next morning the buccaneer fleet entered the lake, and the powder was shared out among those vessels which carried artillery. The cannon thrown down from the fort were spiked, and buried in the sand. The men immediately embarked again, to sail for Maracaibo as quickly as possible, but the water was so shallow above the bar in the mouth of the lagoon the ships could barely pass over, and some went aground. Yet, in order to lose no time in proceeding to the city, the crews were immediately transferred to other vessels.

About noon next day they arrived before Maracaibo and brought the vessels close inshore, so that the men could land under the protection of the light artillery they carried. But all went as easily as at the Fuerte de la Barra, for all the Spaniards had fled to the woods, leaving the city empty apart from a few poor cripples – who could neither flee nor had anything to lose.

The buccaneers entered the city, and searched everywhere to make sure there were no soldiers concealed in any of the houses or in the woods round about the city. Finding no danger, each ship's company took up its quarters in the houses around the market-place. The great church was made into a guardhouse, where a watch was kept continuously. On the same day as they occupied the city, a party of a hundred men was at once sent out to bring back prisoners and plunder. They returned next evening with about fifty mules laden with various goods, and thirty prisoners –

men and women, children and slaves. The prisoners were
promptly tortured in the usual manner to make them say where
the fugitive citizens were hiding. One was strappado'd and
beaten, another was spread-eagled with burning fuses between
his fingers and toes, another had a cord twisted so tight round his
head his eyes protruded like eggs. If they still would not tell they
were put to death, when there were no further torments that
could be inflicted on them.

This went on for three weeks, and every day the buccaneers
sent out a marauding party, who always brought back plenty of
loot, never returning empty-handed. After they had taken about
100 prisoners from the most important families of Maracaibo and
had robbed them of their wealth, Morgan decided to proceed to
Gibraltar.

The buccaneers instantly made all the ships ready, stowed the
booty and the prisoners on board and weighed anchor. They
steered for Gibraltar, making preparations for battle: every man
knew what he had to do. Some of the prisoners were sent on shore
in advance to command the people of Gibraltar, in Morgan's
name, to surrender. Should they prove intransigent, he would
give them no quarter: they would receive no better treatment
from these buccaneers than they did from the French two years
ago.

After a few days Morgan and his fleet sailed within sight of
Gibraltar, where the Spaniards put up a bold fire with their heavy
guns. Instead of making any changes on this account, the rovers
plucked up their courage, saying if there was going to be a tussle,
there'd be plenty of booty – and that was sugar enough to sweeten
any sour sauce.

The crews landed at dawn next day. Instead of taking the main
road, the Frenchman – who had been there before and knew the
lie of the land – remembered another way through the woods,
from which they could descend on the town from the rear. They
left a few men in the road, to make the Spaniards think this would
be the route they would take.

But in fact the buccaneers had no need of such precautions, for
the Spaniards still vividly recalled the events of two years ago
when the French were there, and would rather give up the place
than lose as many lives as they had done then. They had set a few
ambuscades outside the village along the way they were fleeing so

that if they were overtaken they could defend their retreat. They had also spiked the guns at the fort, and carried away the gunpowder.

The buccaneers found nobody in the village but a poor ignorant simpleton. They asked him where the folks had fled. He said he did not know – he had not inquired. They asked whether he knew of any plantations; he said he must have been on twenty in his lifetime. Then they demanded whether he knew where to find the gold and silver of the churches. Yes, he replied, and brought them to the church sacristy, saying he had seen all the gold and silver there, but he did not know where it was now. When they could get no more answers out of him, they tied him up and beat him. Then the simple fellow began to shout, "Let me go! I will show you my house and my goods and my money!"

This made the rovers think they were dealing with a rich man, who had been pretending to be a fool. They unbound him, and he brought them to a hovel, where he had buried a few earthenware dishes, plates and other trash, together with three pieces of eight. They asked him his name. "I am Don Sebastian Sanchez," he said, "brother of the governor of Maracaibo." Then they began to torture him anew, tying him up and beating him till the blood ran down his body. He cried out that if they would let him go, he would take them to his sugar-mill, where they would find all his wealth and his slaves, but when they untied him he was unable to walk. They flung him on a horse, but in the forest he told them he had no sugar-mill, nor anything in the world, and that he lived on the charity of the hospital. This was true, as they afterwards discovered.

Again they took him and bound him, hanging stones from his neck and his feet. They burned palm leaves under his face, making it so sooty with smoke he did not look like a man, and they beat him violently. He died after half an hour of these torments. They cut the rope and dragged his body into the woods, where they left him lying. So ended this simple wretch's life, as a martyr.

The same day a gang of buccaneers brought back a poor cottager with his two daughters. Early next morning they went out with this man, who had promised to bring them where the villagers were hiding. He took them to various plantations where the people certainly had been, but the Spaniards, knowing the rovers were on the prowl, kept out of sight in the forest, making little huts of branches to protect their goods from the rain. When the poor man could find nobody, the buccaneers thought he was purposely misleading them. In their rage, they killed him, hanging him from a tree, although the poor soul earnestly begged and prayed for his life. The buccaneers then spread out to lie in wait for the villagers here and there around the plantations, where they would be obliged to come to gather food to live on.

At last they captured a slave, whom they promised to take back to Jamaica, and give him as much money as a man could carry, and Spanish clothes to wear. This prospect suited the Negro very well, and he promptly led them to the hiding-places. They let the slave kill some of the prisoners they captured so that he would not run away, and he did great havoc among the Spaniards. The rovers were out on this expedition eight days, making the prisoners march along with them, and loading the captured goods on mules. Finally they had so many prisoners it was impracticable to go farther, so they decided to return to Gibraltar, bringing with them over 250 captives.

On arrival, every prisoner was interrogated as to whether he had money hidden away, or whether he knew where other people's wealth was concealed. Those who would not confess were subjected to the cruellest tortures imaginable. Among those who suffered most heavily was an old Portuguese in his sixties, because a Negro had denounced him as being very rich. This old man was seized and asked where his money was. He swore by every oath that all the money he'd had in the world was a hundred pieces of eight, and that a young man who lived near him had taken this money and run off with it.

The rovers did not believe him, but strappado'd him so violently that his arms were pulled right out of joint. He still would not confess, so they tied long cords to his thumbs and his big toes and spreadeagled him to four stakes. Then four of them came and beat on the cords with their sticks, making his body jerk and shudder and stretching his sinews. Still not satisfied, they put a stone weighing at least two hundredweight on his loins and lit a fire of palm leaves under him, burning his face and setting his hair alight – yet despite all these torments he would not confess to having money.

Then they took him and bound him to one of the pillars of the church, which they were using as a guardhouse, and gave him one little bit of meat a day, just enough to keep him alive. After four or five days of this suffering, he begged that some friends of his from among the prisoners might be sent to him, so that he might contrive to get money to give the rovers. After talking with his friends, he offered 500 pieces of eight. The rovers would not listen to him, but instead gave him a beating and said he must talk of thousands, not hundreds, or it would cost him his life. In the end, after he had produced all the evidence he could that he really was a poor man, who earned his bread keeping a tavern, they settled for 1,000 pieces of eight.

Yet even this man had not suffered all the torments which the buccaneers inflicted on the Spaniards to make them divulge their hidden wealth. Some they hung up by their genitals, till the weight of their bodies tore them loose. Then they would give the wretches three or four stabs through the body with a cutlass, and leave them lying in that condition until God released them from their miserable plight by death. Some poor creatures lingered on for four or five days. Others they crucified, with burning fuses between their fingers and toes. Others they bound, smeared their feet with grease and stuck them in the fire.

When they had finished with the white men, the buccaneers started on the slaves. Eventually they found a slave who promised to bring them to a river which flowed into the lake, where there was a ship and four barques, laden with rich cargo, belonging to Maracaibo. Another slave was denounced as knowing the whereabouts of the governor of Gibraltar and most of the women. This man was instantly seized, but he denied it. When the rovers threatened to hang him, however, he admitted he knew and promised to lead them to the governor.

The buccaneers decided that a hundred of them should go in two small vessels to the river where the ships lay, and the rest should go and capture the governor. They set out next day, leaving the prisoners on board their ships. Morgan marched with 350 men to seek out the governor, who had retired to an island in the middle of a river, which he had fortified.

Here they arrived after marching two days. The governor's spies had warned him of their approach, so he and his people had retreated to a mountain-top, which could only be reached in single file by a narrow passage. He had also prepared some fireballs, to check the invaders should they try to climb up.

But heavy rains and the great damage the buccaneers suffered crossing a river prevented them from pressing the attack. They had lost several mules, laden with money and goods, and several women and children were drowned. Some of their weapons were unfit for use, and their powder was wet. In fact, if fifty well-armed lancers had tackled them, they could easily have killed all the buccaneers – but the Spaniards were in such a state of terror they thought the very trees in the forest as they rustled in the wind were the *ladrones*, as they called the rovers.

Finally, after many hardships, the buccaneers struggled through the water. They were able to save their own skins, but the poor women and little children fared so badly it was pitiful to see. They had to travel half a league through the forest, wading through water up to their middles. The land is very low-lying, and the rivers, swollen by the rains and the water from the mountains, had overflowed their banks.

Twelve days after their departure the rovers were back in Gibraltar bringing back a large number of prisoners, but their main attempt had miscarried. Two days later the ships returned from the river bringing the captured ship and the four barques, together with goods and prisoners. They had been unable to capture these vessels complete with their original cargo, because Spaniards in canoes had given warning of their coming. They had hurriedly unloaded most of the merchandise, intending to set fire to the vessels once they were empty. But before they could manage this, the buccaneers attacked and took the ships while there were still some goods on board, such as linen and silks.

The buccaneers had been in occupation five weeks, and had sent out various other expeditions, when they decided to leave Gibraltar. They dispatched some of their prisoners to collect a ransom for the town, threatening as usual to burn the place down if it were not forthcoming. The Spaniards returned saying they had been unable to find anybody, and that the governor had forbidden the payment of any ransom. But if Morgan would have patience, they promised to gather together 5,000 pieces of eight among themselves, and he should take hostages with him to Maracaibo until all was paid.

Morgan was anxious to leave: he had been away from Maracaibo so long and did not know how things stood there. The Spaniards had had time to assemble a big enough force to prevent his getting out of the lake. So he accepted the proposal and took four hostages. He let the prisoners go (after they had paid a ransom) but kept the slaves. They wanted to pay a ransom for the Negro who had been the rovers' guide, but Morgan would not surrender him, for without doubt the Spaniards would have burnt him alive if they could have laid hands on him.

The buccaneers weighed anchor and set sail, and four days later arrived at Maracaibo, where they found everything as they had left it. But they received news they had not expected. A poor man, who had been living at the hospital, told Morgan there were three Spanish men-of-war in the mouth of the lake, lying in wait for him, and the fort had again been well equipped with artillery and soldiers.

Morgan instantly sent out a sloop to report on these ships. The boat returned next evening, and confirmed all the old man had said. They had seen the warships and been under fire from their cannon. The warships were full of troops, and the biggest carried at least forty guns, the next thirty, and the smallest twenty-four. The fort also was well defended.

These forces were disproportionately greater than Morgan's, for his heaviest ship only carried fourteen guns. No one dared betray the fear and anxiety he felt, least of all Morgan. What were they to do? There was no exit except through the mouth of the lake where the warships lay – there was no chance of escape overland. Morgan would have preferred the warships to have sailed up to the city, rather than wait for him in the straits where their heavy guns could do him great injury. Nevertheless, it appears that God (for the punishment of the Spaniards) provided means for these raiders to save themselves from the clutches of their righteous enemies.

Morgan, to show he was not afraid, sent a Spaniard to demand ransom for the city of Maracaibo. Two days later the man came back with a letter from the Spanish admiral, which read as follows:

*Letter from the Spanish general, Don Alonzo del Campo y Espinosa
to Morgan, admiral of the buccaneers.*

Having, through our friends and neighbours, received news that
you have had the audacity to commit hostilities in the territories
and cities owing obedience to His Catholic Majesty, the King of
Spain my master, I have come to this place, according to my
bounden duty, and have built up again that fortress which you
took from a set of faint-hearts and from which you flung down the
guns, that I may prevent your escape from this lake and do you all
the injury my duty requires.

Nevertheless, if you will surrender with humility all which you
have taken, including all the slaves and other prisoners, I will
have the clemency to let you pass, that you may return to your
own country. Should you obdurately resist these honourable
conditions which I propose, I shall send for sloops from Caracas,
in which I shall embark my troops to sail for Maracaibo, with
orders to destroy you utterly and put every man to the sword.
This is my final resolution: take heed, and be not ungrateful for
my kindness. I have with me valiant soldiers, yearning to be
allowed to revenge the unrighteous acts you have committed
against the Spanish nation in America.

Signed on board His Majesty's ship, *Magdalena*, at anchor in
the entry of the Lake of Maracaibo, 24 April 1669.

                          Don Alonzo del Campo y Espinosa.

Morgan had all the buccaneers assemble in the market-place
and read out the letter, first in English and then in French. Then
he asked them how they felt – would they rather surrender their
booty in order to gain a free passage, or would they fight for it?
The buccaneers answered with one accord that they would rather
fight till the death than hand over their spoils. They'd risked their
lives for it once, and were ready to do so a second time.

One of the crowd came up to Morgan and said he would undertake to destroy the great ship, with only twelve men, in the following
manner. They would make a fire-ship out of the ship they had
captured in the lake, fitting her out like a man-of-war, with the flag
flying. On the deck would stand logs of wood with caps on top, to
look like the crew, and big hollow logs (the kind called Negroes'
drums) would stick out of the ports to look like guns.

This suggestion was approved, considering their dire need, yet first Morgan wanted to see if he could not get some other concession from the Spanish general. He sent back a messenger with the following proposals: that the buccaneers would leave Maracaibo without doing any harm to the city by burning or other means, and without claiming any ransom; that they would give up half of the slaves, and set free all the prisoners without ransom; and that they would refrain from exacting the contribution for Gibraltar, which had still not been paid, and would let the hostages go free.

The Spanish general replied that he refused to consider such proposals, and that if they did not surrender upon the conditions imposed by him within two days, he would destroy them by fire and sword. Upon receiving this answer, Morgan and his men instantly resolved to do everything they could to get out of the lake without surrendering their booty.

All the prisoners were shut up and closely guarded. The slaves, who had been employed fetching water and doing other jobs, were also locked up, and the buccaneers themselves did the work. They collected all the tar, pitch, brimstone and other combustibles that could be found in the city, ready to prepare the fire-ship. They filled the hold with palm leaves dipped in a mixture of pitch, tar and brimstone, covered the counterfeit cannon on deck with the same stuff and laid six pots of gunpowder under each, and sawed up half the woodwork inside the ship so that it could blow up and burn with greater force. They also made new portholes through which they stuck the long hollow logs known as Negroes' drums in place of artillery. Along the deck they set wooden props, each fitted with a cap or hat to look like a man, and then hoisted the admiral's flag.

Now the fire-ship was ready they decided to set sail for the mouth of the lake. All the prisoners were put aboard one large barque, and in another all the plunder, together with the most important women prisoners, each vessel being manned by twelve well-armed buccaneers. The barques were ordered to keep to the rear of the convoy, and at a given signal to come into the midst of the fleet as they slipped out of the trap.

The fire-ship had orders to sail on ahead, in front of the admiral's flagship, and grapple the Spanish man-of-war. If the fire-ship failed to fall foul of the Spaniard on account of the current, the admiral himself would assault the man-of-war. To mislead the enemy still further, another vessel, got up to look like a fire-ship, with kindled rope smoking on deck, was to sail behind the flagship.

After Morgan had given all these orders a general oath was taken that the buccaneers would all stand by one another to the last drop of blood. Whatever happened, they would never cry for quarter but fight to the last man. Those who behaved courageously and performed any deed of extraordinary valour, or captured a ship, should be rewarded out of the common plunder.

Upon this resolution, Morgan set sail, and on 30 April 1669, came in sight of the Spanish men-of-war, riding at anchor directly in the middle of the fairway. It was too late in the evening to go into battle, so Morgan dropped anchor about a cannon-shot from the enemy, taking the men off the fire-ship in the evening in accordance with the custom of war. All night both sides kept up a vigilant watch, and the buccaneers prepared themselves for the day to come. As soon as day began to dawn, the buccaneers were under sail with the ebb tide. The Spaniards thought the rovers had resolved to slip out with the tide; they cut their cables and got under way.

The fire-ship bore down on the Spanish man-of-war and grappled to her side. Realizing the danger, the Spanish general instantly ordered men to leap across to the fire-ship, cut down her masts and push her clear so she would drift free with the tide. Scarcely had the men jumped aboard when the deck blew up. All the combustible debris caught in the sails, setting them on fire and giving out huge flames and smoke. The general was forced to abandon ship.

The second Spanish ship, seeing their flagship on fire, was making for the shelter of the fort with all speed when she ran aground. The third ship also attempted to escape, but was too quickly pursued by one of the buccaneer fleet and soon was captured. Those of the second ship, which lay aground below the fort, knowing the buccaneers would soon assail them, took what they could out of her and set the ship on fire themselves.

The great ship drifted burning along the shore, and very few men had escaped from her. The buccaneers sailed between the shore and the ship to rescue the crew, but the Spaniards drowned rather than fall into the rovers' hands, for reasons that I shall explain later.

The buccaneers were in high spirits, having fought such a victorious battle within the space of two or three hours, and they intended to follow up their success. They all came ashore to take the fort, from which came the fierce fire of heavy artillery. The buccaneers had no other weapons but their muskets and a few hand grenades; their ships' guns were too light to breach such strong walls. All the rest of the day they engaged the fort with brisk musket-fire, and when they caught sight of any of the defenders they seldom missed their mark. But when they attempted to come in close to the wall to throw their hand grenades – then it was their turn to suffer. The Spaniards began hurling down fireballs and pots of gunpowder tied to lighted fuses with such effect the buccaneers were forced to retire, with the loss of more than thirty dead and about the same number wounded.

At dusk the buccaneers went on board again, without having achieved their objective. The Spaniards, fearing they would bring their artillery on shore, worked the whole night levelling certain mounds which might have given the enemy some advantage, and still felt confident of preventing the corsairs' escape from the lake.

The great ship had broken up about evening time and some Spaniards attempted to swim to the wreck, but were prevented by the rovers. Several prisoners had been taken, and Morgan interrogated a steersman from the small ship they had captured to find out what forces the Spaniards had had, whether reinforcements were expected, and where they would come from.

"Sir," answered the man, in Spanish, "I am a foreigner. Please do not harm me: I will tell you the truth of all that has occurred. We were sent out to the West Indies from Spain with six ships to cruise against the corsairs and destroy them, for the Court had received strong protests on the capture of Porto Bello. The Spanish court complained to the court of England, and the King replied that he had never given commissions for any hostility to be employed against the subjects of His Catholic Majesty. Consequently these six ships were fitted out, and sent here from Spain under the command of Don Augustin de Gusto. [Bustos?]

"His flagship was the *Nuestra Señora de la Soledad*, carrying forty-eight cannon and eighteen swivel-guns. The vice-admiral was Don Alonzo del Campo y Espinosa, commanding *La Concepcion*, mounting forty-four cannon and eighteen swivel-guns. Besides these were four other ships: *La Magdalena*, with thirty-six cannon, twelve swivels and two hundred and fifty men; the *San Luis*, with twenty-six cannon, twelve swivels and two hundred men; *La Marquesa*, with sixteen cannon, eight swivels and one hundred and fifty men; and the *Nuestra Señora del Carmen*, similarly armed and manned.

"We first arrived in Cartagena, where the two great ships were sent back to Spain, as they were too large for cruising in these waters. The four remaining vessels were sent to Campeche, under the command of Don Alonzo, to sail against the corsairs. Here we lost the *Carmen* in a storm which blew up from the north, and the three other ships sailed into harbour at San Domingo in Hispaniola. We were informed that a fleet from Jamaica had passed that way, landing a few men at a place called Alta Gracia. One of these had been taken prisoner and had stated that the rovers intended to take Caracas. Don Alonzo instantly weighed anchor and we steered for the mainland. We met a barque, which we hailed, and they told us the fleet from Jamaica – seven small ships and a boat – was in the Lake of Maracaibo.

"Upon this news we sailed here, and coming to rest before the bar fired a shot to signal for a pilot. Those on land saw we were Spanish ships and came on board. They told us the English had taken Maracaibo, and were at present in Gibraltar. Don Alonzo put heart into us for battle, and promised us all the plunder we should take from the English. He had the cannon we had salvaged from the wrecked ship carried to the fort, with two brass eighteen-pounders from his own ship.

"The pilot brought us over the bar, and Don Alonzo came ashore and rallied all the people to him, and reinforced the garrison with a hundred more men. Shortly after we received news that your people were at Maracaibo, whereupon Don Alonzo wrote you a letter. When he understood you did not intend to hand over your captures, he again roused and encouraged us, promising us the plunder. All the men then took Mass in the manner of the Roman Catholic church, and swore an oath to give no quarter nor accept quarter from the English. This is why so many drowned, for they dare not cry for mercy.

"Two days before you came upon us, a Negro informed Don Alonzo that you had made a fire-ship, but he would not believe this. He said such men did not understand how to fit up a fire-ship, and had no materials for such a purpose."

Morgan treated this steersman well, offering him a share with the rest of the crews if he would stay with them. The man accepted, since he could do no better than stay with the rovers, and told them furthermore that there had been a good 30,000 pieces of eight on board the great ship, which was why some of the Spaniards had tried to get to the wreck. Leaving one of his ships to keep the Spaniards at bay and fish up the silver, Morgan retired with the rest of his fleet to Maracaibo. Here they repaired the captured Spanish ship, which Morgan took for his own. He sent a messenger to the general, again demanding a ransom for Maracaibo or he would burn it down.

The Spaniards, in view of the defeat they had suffered at sea, decided to pay the ransom as they could think of no other way to be rid of the rovers (although Don Alonzo would never agree to this course). They asked how much Morgan demanded and he stipulated 30,000 pieces of eight and 500 cattle to provision his ships, promising to do no damage to the city and to set the prisoners free. Finally, they settled for 20,000 pieces of eight and 500 cattle.

Next day, the Spaniards brought all the cattle and part of the money. The buccaneers slaughtered the beasts and salted the flesh, and by the time this was finished the Spaniards had brought the rest of the promised ransom. They then expected the prisoners to be released, but Morgan did not see it this way: he said he would give up the prisoners when he was out of cannon-range from the fort – hoping to get an undisputed passage for the sake of the captives.

The buccaneers weighed anchor and sailed towards the entry of the lake. The ship they had left there was awaiting them, and the crew had salvaged about 15,000 pieces of eight from the wreck of the burnt ship, together with some wrought silver and various sword-hilts and daggers, all of silver. Some of the coins had melted in the great heat and had flowed together into big lumps, weighing as much as thirty pounds.

Morgan made all the prisoners understand they must persuade the general to agree to let the buccaneers pass the fort unmolested; if he would not consent they should all be hanged from the yard-arm. The prisoners discussed what to do, and sent a messenger to Don Alonzo in the fort, beseeching him to let the rovers pass in peace, for otherwise it would cost them their lives. They sought to move him by every argument, pointing out that there were many women and little children among them, and begging him to be pleased to spare their lives.

Far from conceding, the governor returned a brusque answer, upbraiding them for cowards. If they had maintained their fort against the entrance of the corsairs as strongly as he intended to dispute their exit, the raiders would not have got in so easily. On no account was he minded either to surrender the fort or to give the pirates any loophole of escape. On the contrary, he would send the lot of them to the bottom. The fort was his, he himself had wrested it from the enemy, and therefore he could do with it whatever he thought good for the advantage of his King and the maintenance of his own honour.

The Spanish messengers returned very fearfully on board and told Morgan all Don Alonzo had said. Morgan replied that he would find a means of getting out, notwithstanding. In the meantime, he thought it best to share out the booty, for there was no convenient rendezvous near at hand. The next place was Hispaniola, and before they were able to reach that island they might be separated by a storm – in which case the ship with the plunder might perhaps not care to seek out the others to give them their share.

The money, together with the jewels and wrought silver, came to the value of 250,000 pieces of eight, apart from the other goods and the slaves. This treasure was first divided among the ships according to the number of men on board, and shared out among each crew. So that all should be uprightly done, they took an oath that no man had held back so much as six pennyworth, be it in gold, silver, jewels, pearls or precious stones such as diamonds, emeralds and bezoar-stones. Morgan himself first took the oath on the Bible, and all the rest followed suit, down to the last man.

Having shared out all the booty, the buccaneers had to seek a way of getting out of the lake, and they decided to put the following stratagem into effect. Many of the men embarked in canoes, as if intending to land, and came ashore under the shelter of the trees. But most of them in fact lay flat on their bellies at the bottom of the canoes and so returned to the ships, without more than three or four men being visible on the return journey. Various trips like this were made from all the ships, so that the Spaniards became convinced the rovers intended a night attack on the fort with scaling-ladders. In consequence, they made great preparations for defending the fort from the landward side, bringing all the artillery to bear in that direction.

Night came, and the moon shone bright. The buccaneers were all ready: they slipped anchor and let the ships drift with the tide until they came level with the fort – then they clapped on all sail and sped with the land wind behind them beyond the bar. Instantly the Spaniards shifted part of their artillery round to the seaward side, but the rovers were almost out of reach by then, so little damage was done. Moreover, the Spaniards dared not bring all their big guns to face the sea, fearing that, while they were concentrating their fire in this direction, another band of rovers might be approaching overland to attack them.

Next day Morgan sent a canoe to the fort, bringing back some of the prisoners, whom the Spaniards had given up for dead. He also gave a barque to the rest of the prisoners and let them sail off in it – all except the hostages from Gibraltar, who had not been liberated. Morgan did not choose to let these men go, that they might be an example to the Spaniards for another occasion. He also fired off seven salvoes in farewell to the fort – but his salute was not answered.

The following day the buccaneers were caught in a storm which blew up from the north-east. The fleet dropped anchor in five fathoms of water, but the sea was so rough the anchors could not hold, so they were forced to sail on. Some of the vessels had sprung leaks and they were in great peril. They dared not put in to the shore, for they could expect mercy neither from the Spaniards nor the Indians if they fell into their hands. At last the gale began to die out, after they had passed many days in extreme danger.

While Morgan had acquired good booty and won a great victory over the Spaniards, his fellow buccaneers, who had left him near Cabo de Lobos to go and plunder the English ship, had suffered a terrible beating at Comanago on the coast of Caracas. They had come to the rendezvous on the island of Savona, but failed to find the letter Morgan had left for them inside a jar. As they did not know where Morgan had gone to, they decided to attack some place on their own. They were about 500 strong, and had five ships and a barque. They chose for their leader a certain Captain Ansel, who had conducted himself valiantly in the capture of Porto Bello, and decided that the town of Comanago should be their objective. This town lies on the mainland coast of the province of Caracas, about sixty leagues west of Trinidad.

On arrival, the rovers came on shore in their usual manner, and killed some Indians who were on the beach. But when they reached the town, they were surrounded on every side by Spaniards and Indians. They had no thoughts of booty, but only of how to get back to the shore. Nevertheless, the rovers put up a determined fight, and won back to the ships again – but not as whole as they had set out, for they left more than 100 dead, and had fifty wounded men among them.

When they reached Jamaica once more, the buccaneers who had been with Morgan mocked and jeered at them, asking what sort of coins were struck in Comanago.

PIRATE SONGS

Sailors sang chanties or work songs during their labors. Half-sung, half-chanted in a call-response pattern, chanties included ample profanity. The leader improvised, commenting on recent events and insulting the officers. After working hours, sailors entertained themselves with ballads. Many were sad songs of separation from home and family, known generically as "the sailor's lament". Also popular were ballads of danger and adventure, sea battles, storms and shipwrecks.

At least some seamen continued to enjoy music after they turned pirate. In the early 1600s, Captain STEPHENSON kidnapped a man because he was expert on some kind of pipe. On Bartholomew ROBERTS' warship – much larger than most pirate vessels – "musicians" entertained or accompanied the men. Roberts' ARTICLES allow "The Musicians to have Rest on the Sabbath Day, but the other six Days and Nights, none without special favour." Whether they sang or played instruments is unknown.

Some sailors' songs were written down from the late seventeenth century. Some individual mariners probably remained faithful to their favorite ballads after turning pirate. But others may have preferred foreign ditties learned during their travels or from captives.

Pirates may have celebrated each other's exploits. However, the only surviving songs about pirates are ballads, composed by professional (although usually anonymous) authors. From the early 1600s, these ballads were sold to the London public, often in connection with hangings. Since their authors knew little about individual brigands, each ballad tells the same story. Pirates are bad men, who slaughter their victims and spend their money "in drunkenness and letchery", to quote "*The* SEAMAN'S SONG" (1609). "CAPTAIN KID'S FAREWEL TO THE SEAS" (1701), the most successful ballad, remained popular in America for two centuries.

Bill Bones sings "FIFTEEN MEN ON A DEAD MAN'S CHEST" at the Admiral Benbow Inn in TREASURE ISLAND. In *The* PIRATES OF PENZANCE (1879), the Pirate King soars in "OH, BETTER FAR TO LIVE AND DIE", while the pirates in PETER PAN (1904) chant "AVAST BELAY". The lyrics and music were invented for these works and are not based on sailors' ballads.

From *The Wordsworth Dictionary of Pirates*, Jan Rogozinski, Wordsworth Editions Ltd, 1997. Copyright © 1995 Jan Rogozinski.

THE TAKING OF PANAMA

Howard Pyle

Henry Morgan's greatest exploit:

And now Captain Morgan determined to undertake another venture, the like of which had never been equaled in all of the annals of buccaneering. This was nothing less than the descent upon and the capture of Panama, which was, next to Cartagena, perhaps, the most powerful and the most strongly fortified city in the West Indies.

In preparation for this venture he obtained letters of marque from the governor of Jamaica, by virtue of which elastic commission he began immediately to gather around him all material necessary for the undertaking.

When it became known abroad that the great Captain Morgan was about undertaking an adventure that was to eclipse all that was ever done before, great numbers came flocking to his standard, until he had gathered together an army of two thousand or more desperadoes and pirates wherewith to prosecute his adventure, albeit the venture itself was kept a total secret from everyone. Port Couillon, in the island of Hispaniola, over against the Ile de la Vache, was the place of muster, and thither the motley band gathered from all quarters. Provisions had been plundered from the mainland wherever they could be obtained, and by the 24th of October, 1670 (O.S.), everything was in readiness.

The island of Saint Catharine, as it may be remembered, was at one time captured by Mansvelt, Morgan's master in his trade of piracy. It had been retaken by the Spaniards, and was now thoroughly fortified by them. Almost the first attempt that Morgan had made as a master pirate was the retaking of Saint Catharine's Isle. In that undertaking he had failed; but now, as there was an absolute need of some such place as a base of operations, he determined that the place must be taken. And it was taken.

The Spaniards, during the time of their possession, had fortified it most thoroughly and completely, and had the governor thereof been as brave as he who met his death in the castle of Porto Bello, there might have been a different tale to tell. As it was, he surrendered it in a most cowardly fashion, merely stipulating that there should be a sham attack by the buccaneers, whereby his credit might be saved. And so Saint Catharine was won.

The next step to be taken was the capture of the castle of Chagres, which guarded the mouth of the river of that name, up which river the buccaneers would be compelled to transport their troops and provisions for the attack upon the city of Panama. This adventure was undertaken by four hundred picked men under command of Captain Morgan himself.

The castle of Chagres, known as San Lorenzo by the Spaniards, stood upon the top of an abrupt rock at the mouth of the river, and was one of the strongest fortresses for its size in all of the West Indies. This stronghold Morgan must have if he ever hoped to win Panama.

The attack of the castle and the defense of it were equally fierce, bloody, and desperate. Again and again the buccaneers assaulted, and again and again they were beaten back. So the morning came, and it seemed as though the pirates had been baffled this time. But just at this juncture the thatch of palm leaves on the roofs of some of the buildings inside the fortifications took fire, a conflagration followed, which caused the explosion of one of the magazines, and in the paralysis of terror that followed, the pirates forced their way into the fortifications, and the castle was won. Most of the Spaniards flung themselves from the castle walls into the river or upon the rocks beneath, preferring death to capture and possible torture; many who were left were put to the sword, and some few were spared and held as prisoners.

So fell the castle of Chagres, and nothing now lay between the buccaneers and the city of Panama but the intervening and trackless forests.

And now the name of the town whose doom was sealed was no secret.

Up the river of Chagres went Capt. Henry Morgan and twelve hundred men, packed closely in their canoes; they never stopped, saving now and then to rest their stiffened legs, until they had come to a place known as Cruz de San Juan Gallego, where they were compelled to leave their boats on account of the shallowness of the water.

Leaving a guard of one hundred and sixty men to protect their boats as a place of refuge in case they should be worsted before Panama, they turned and plunged into the wilderness before them.

There a more powerful foe awaited them than a host of Spaniards with match, powder, and lead – starvation. They met but little or no opposition in their progress; but wherever they turned they found every fiber of meat, every grain of maize, every ounce of bread or meal, swept away or destroyed utterly before them. Even when the buccaneers had successfully overcome an ambuscade or an attack, and had sent the Spaniards flying, the fugitives took the time to strip their dead comrades of every grain of food in their leathern sacks, leaving nothing but the empty bags.

Says the narrator of these events, himself one of the expedition, "They afterward fell to eating those leathern bags, as affording something to the ferment of their stomachs."

Ten days they struggled through this bitter privation, doggedly forcing their way onward, faint with hunger and haggard with weakness and fever. Then, from the high hill and over the tops of the forest trees, they saw the steeples of Panama, and nothing remained between them and their goal but the fighting of four Spaniards to every one of them – a simple thing which they had done over and over again.

Down they poured upon Panama, and out came the Spaniards to meet them; four hundred horse, two thousand five hundred foot, and two thousand wild bulls which had been herded together to be driven over the buccaneers so that their ranks might be disordered and broken. The buccaneers were only eight hundred strong; the others had either fallen in battle or had dropped along the dreary pathway through the wilderness; but in the space of two hours the Spaniards were flying madly over the plain, minus six hundred who lay dead or dying behind them.

As for the bulls, as many of them as were shot served as food there and then for the half-famished pirates, for the buccaneers were never more at home than in the slaughter of cattle.

Then they marched toward the city. Three hours' more fighting and they were in the streets, howling, yelling, plundering, gorging, dram-drinking, and giving full vent to all the vile and nameless lusts that burned in their hearts like a hell of fire. And now followed the usual sequence of events – rapine, cruelty, and extortion; only this time there was no town to ransom, for Morgan had given orders that it should be destroyed. The torch was set to it, and Panama, one of the greatest cities in the New World, was swept from the face of the earth. Why the deed was done, no man but Morgan could tell. Perhaps it was that all the secret hiding places for treasure might be brought to light; but whatever the reason was, it lay hidden in the breast of the great buccaneer himself. For three weeks Morgan and his men abode in this dreadful place; and they marched away with one hundred and seventy-five beasts of burden loaded with treasures of gold and silver and jewels, besides great quantities of merchandise, and six hundred prisoners held for ransom.

Whatever became of all that vast wealth, and what it amounted to, no man but Morgan ever knew, for when a division was made it was found that there was only *two hundred pieces of eight to each* man.

When this dividend was declared a howl of execration went up, under which even Capt. Henry Morgan quailed. At night he and four other commanders slipped their cables and ran out to sea, and it was said that these divided the greater part of the booty among themselves. But the wealth plundered at Panama could hardly have fallen short of a million and a half of dollars. Computing it at this reasonable figure, the various prizes won by Henry Morgan in the West Indies would stand as follows: Panama, $1,500,000; Porto Bello, $800,000; Puerto del Principe, $700,000; Maracaibo and Gibraltar, $400,000; various piracies, $250,000 – making a grand total of $3,650,000 as the vast harvest of plunder. With this fabulous wealth, wrenched from the Spaniards by means of the rack and the cord, and pilfered from his companions by the meanest of thieving, Capt. Henry Morgan retired from business, honored of all, rendered famous by his deeds, knighted by the good King Charles II, and finally appointed governor of the rich island of Jamaica.

Morgan continued in this office for almost a decade until a political change of climate in 1682 made it expedient to sack the Spanish-loathing sea dog. He died in 1688, aged 45, of dropsy from "drinking and sitting up late".

*"The buccaneers' main exercises are target-shooting
and keeping their guns clean"*

"ON THE ACCOUNT": THE LIVES OF THE BUCCANEERS OF THE CARIBBEAN, BY ONE OF THEIR NUMBER

A.O. Exquemelin

*Born in France circa 1645 Alexander Oliver Exquemelin trained as a
barber-surgeon before determining "to enter into the wicked order of
pirates, or robbers of the sea". He served in the Caribbean with both
L'Olonnais and Henry Morgan (see pages 51–77); after breaking
with Morgan, whose sadism he deplored. Exquemelin returned to
Europe, settling in Holland, where he drew upon his piratical experi-
ences to pen* De Amerikaensche Zee-Rovers, 1678. *The book was an
overnight success and translation from the Dutch into other European
languages followed quickly; the first English edition of the memoir
appeared in 1684 as* The Buccaneers of America.

*Below, Exquemelin recounts buccaneer life in the Golden Age of
the mid seventeenth century.*

The rovers can fit out an expedition cheaply, and easily come by
new vessels, in the way I have described. When a buccaneer is
going to sea he sends word to all who wish to sail with him. When
all are ready, they go on board, each bringing what he needs in the
way of weapons, powder and shot.

On the ship, they first discuss where to go and get food
supplies. This means meat – for they eat nothing else on their
voyages, unless they capture other foodstuffs from the Spaniards.

The meat is either pork or turtle, which is also salted. Sometimes they go and plunder the Spaniards' *corrales*, which are pens where they keep perhaps a thousand head of tame hogs. The rovers go at night and find the house of the farmer who looks after the pigs and fetch him out of his bed. Unless he gives them as many hogs as they demand, they hang him without mercy.

When the rovers have to do their own hunting, they employ a hunter of their own nationality who has a pack of hounds, letting him have whatever share of the catch they think fit. Some of them go with the hunter to help salt and smoke the flesh, while others stay on board to get the vessel shipshape – careening and greasing and doing all that is necessary. When the hunting party have salted as much meat as they think will suffice for the voyage, they bring it to the ship, where it is piled in the hold on the ballast.

They cook two meals a day of this meat, without rationing. When it is boiled, the fat is skimmed off the cauldron and put into little calabashes, for dipping the meat in. The meal consists of only one course, and often it tastes better than the food to be found on a gentleman's table. The captain is allowed no better fare than the meanest on board. If they notice he has better food, the men bring the dish from their own mess and exchange it for the captain's.

When the provisions are on board and the ship is ready to sail, the buccaneers resolve by common vote where they shall cruise. They also draw up an agreement or *chasse partie*, in which is specified what the captain shall have for himself and for the use of his vessel. Usually they agree on the following terms. Providing they capture a prize, first of all these amounts would be deducted from the whole capital. The hunter's pay would generally be 200 pieces of eight. The carpenter, for his work in repairing and fitting out the ship, would be paid 100 or 150 pieces of eight. The surgeon would receive 200 or 250 for his medical supplies, according to the size of the ship.

Then came the agreed awards for the wounded, who might have lost a limb or suffered other injuries. They would be compensated as follows: for the loss of a right arm, 600 pieces of eight or six slaves; for a left arm, 500 pieces of eight or five slaves. The loss of a right leg also brought 500 pieces of eight or five slaves in compensation; a left leg, 400 or four slaves; an eye, 100 or one slave, and the same award was made for the loss of a finger. If a man lost the use of an arm, he would get as much as if it had been cut off, and a severe internal injury which meant the victim had to have a pipe inserted in his body would earn 500 pieces of eight or five slaves in recompense.

These amounts having first been withdrawn from the capital, the rest of the prize would be divided into as many portions as men on the ship. The captain draws four or five men's portions for the use of his ship, perhaps even more, and two portions for himself. The rest of the men share uniformly, and the boys get half a man's share.

When a ship has been captured, the men decide whether the captain should keep it or not: if the prize is better than their own vessel, they take it and set fire to the other. When a ship is robbed, nobody must plunder and keep his loot to himself. Everything taken – money, jewels, precious stones and goods – must be shared among them all, without any man enjoying a penny more than his fair share. To prevent deceit, before the booty is distributed everyone has to swear an oath on the Bible that he has not kept for himself so much as the value of a sixpence, whether in silk, linen, wool, gold, silver, jewels, clothes or shot, from all the capture. And should any man be found to have made a false oath, he would be banished from the rovers, and never more be allowed in their company.

The buccaneers are extremely loyal and ready to help one another. If a man has nothing, the others let him have what he needs on credit until such time as he can pay them back. They also see justice done among themselves. If anyone has a quarrel and kills his opponent treacherously, he is set against a tree and shot dead by the one whom he chooses. But if he has killed his opponent like an honourable man – that is, giving him time to load his musket, and not shooting him in the back – his comrades let him go free. The duel is their way of settling disputes.

When they have captured a ship, the buccaneers set the prisoners on shore as soon as possible, apart from two or three whom they keep to do the cooking and other work they themselves do not care for, releasing these men after two or three years.

The rovers frequently put in for fresh supplies at some island or other, often one of those islets lying off the south coast of Cuba. Here they drag the ship up the beach to careen her. Everyone goes ashore and sets up his tent, and they take turns to go on marauding expeditions in their canoes. They take prisoner the turtle-fishers of Bayamo – poor men who catch and sell turtles for a living, to provide for their wives and children. Once captured, these men have to catch turtle for the rovers as long as they remain on the island. Should the rovers intend to cruise along a coast where turtles abound, they take the fishermen along with them. The poor fellows may be compelled to stay away from their wives and families four or five years, with no news whether they are alive or dead.

Having mentioned turtles, which may be quite unfamiliar to many readers, I shall briefly describe them. In America there are four kinds of marine turtle. One species is immensely big, weighing up to three or four thousand pounds. These reptiles have no hard shell, so their flesh may easily be pierced with a knife, but they are full of oil and not fit to eat. The second sort are the green turtles; they are of middling size, being a good four feet in breadth. Their shell is thicker, covered with small scales about as thick as the horn used in lanterns. These turtles are extremely good to eat – the flesh very sweet and the fat green and delicious. This fat is so penetrating that when you have eaten nothing but turtle flesh for three or four weeks, your shirt becomes so greasy from sweat you can squeeze the oil out and your limbs are weighed down with it. The third kind is of similar size but with a bigger head, and is not fit to eat, for it reeks of oil. The fourth variety, known as caret, is smaller and longer in the body, and has a shell like those we know in Europe.

These turtles live among rocks under the water, feeding on the moss and sea-apples found there. The other varieties live on grass which grows under water: there are some banks as green and lush as the meadows in Holland. Here the turtles come at night to feed. They cannot stay long on the bottom without coming up to take breath; as soon as they have blown, they descend once more.

They lay eggs like the crocodiles, but without a shell, being covered only with a thin membrane like the skin inside a hen's egg. They produce such prodigious quantities of eggs that, if many were not destroyed by the birds, people could scarcely sail a boat in these parts without running into turtles. They lay three times a year, in May, June and July – and every time each turtle lays 150 or even 190 eggs. They come ashore, scratch out a hole in the sand to lay their eggs in, then cover them over again. The heat of the sun hatches the eggs in three weeks, and out come the young turtles and make for the sea. No sooner are they in the water than the gulls swoop down and snap them up, for they cannot submerge until nine days after their birth. It is lucky if two or three survive out of a hundred.

The turtles have particular places where they come every year to lay their eggs, their main haunt being the Cayman Islands. These are three in number, one big and two small, lying at 20° 15′ north, some forty-five leagues south of Cuba. The turtles come to these islands in such immense numbers that every year a good twenty ships, English as well as French, take on a cargo of turtle flesh, which they salt. The males come to these places to mate with the females, and when two turtles copulate, they remain one or two whole days upon one another.

It is incomprehensible how these creatures manage to find the islands, having quitted other regions to get there; they come from the Gulf of Honduras, some 150 leagues away. Sometimes, ships which have missed their landfall through adverse currents and have been unable to find their latitude have finally set course by the noise of turtles blowing, and so reached the islands.

No special implements are carried for catching the green turtles (the only kind good to eat) but when these creatures come on shore every night to lay their eggs, they can be levered over by two men with a hand-spike. Once laid on their backs, the turtles cannot budge. When many ships lie waiting to load, the beach is divided so that the men from each ship have a certain stretch of sand to clear. In the length of 500 paces as many as a hundred turtles may be turned upside down.

When their season is over on the Cayman Islands, the turtles make for Cuba, where the sea-bed is clean, and here they eat – for all the time they are on the Caymans they eat nothing. Similarly, when a turtle has been caught it can stay about a month lying on its back and remain alive, but by then its fat will have changed to slime, and its flesh be tasteless.

When the turtles have been in Cuban waters a month or so and grown fat again, along come the Spanish fishers, such as those poor men the rovers capture and keep in slavery, to catch them and so provide food for their towns and villages. They fix a four-sided nail, about two inches long and barbed like a harpoon, to a long pole. When the turtle comes up to blow, they hurl this spear so that the dart sticks in its body. Then they pay out some fifteen or sixteen fathoms of line, and when the turtle comes up again to take breath, they throw another harpoon into its side, and so are able to haul the creature into the canoe. Sometimes they are shot on the seabed in four fathoms of water, the darker the better, for in the dark of night as the turtle swims its four feet give off a flickering light and its shield looks quite white, so it can easily be seen. These creatures have very keen sight but cannot hear, so far as one can tell.

The buccaneers' main exercises are target-shooting and keeping their guns clean. They use good weapons, such as muskets and pistols. Their muskets are about four and a half feet long, and fire a bullet of sixteen to a pound of lead. They use cartridges, and have a cartouche containing thirty, which they carry with them always, so they are never unprepared.

When they have stayed long enough in one place, they deliberate where they shall go to try their luck. If any man happens to be familiar with particular coasts where the merchantmen trade, he offers his services. The trading-ships cruise to different places according to the season of the year, for these regions cannot be reached at all times on account of settled winds and currents. The people of New Spain and Campeche do most of their commerce in ships sailing in winter from Campeche to the coasts of Caracas, Trinidad and Margarita, as the north-east trade winds do not permit this voyage in summer. When summer comes, they turn their vessels homewards again. The privateers, knowing the passage through which they must sail, lie in wait for them.

If the rovers have been at sea a considerable time without accomplishing anything, they may take on desperate odds – and sometimes with success. For example, there was a buccaneer called Pierre Francois, of Dunkirk, who had been long at sea in a barque with a crew of twenty-six. He had been cruising in wait for ships coming from Maracaibo and bound for Campeche, but having missed his prey, he and his men resolved to go to Rancherias. This is a place lying off the mouth of the Rio de Hacha, at a latitude of 12½° north, where there are oyster-beds. Every year a fleet of ten to twelve barques, protected by a convoy-ship of twenty-four guns, comes from Cartagena to fish there for pearls. Every boat has two Negro divers, who go down four to six fathoms. Francois resolved to attack the pearl-fishers, and this is how he did it.

The boats lay at anchor on the pearl-bank, with the man-of-war about half a league away, towards the coast. The weather was calm so the buccaneers were able to approach without sails, like a Spanish coaster coming from Maracaibo. But when they drew near the oysterbeds, they rowed towards the flagship of the fleet, which was mounted with eight guns and had sixty well-armed men aboard. As they came alongside, Francois ordered the flagship to surrender, but instead, she opened fire at once. After the broadside, the buccaneers opened fire so accurately that a number of the Spaniards fell, and before the flagship's gun-crews could reload, the rovers had clambered on board and compelled the Spaniards to cry for quarter.

They hoped the man-of-war would come to their aid, but Francois, to mislead the enemy, sank his own vessel and left the Spanish flag flying on the ship he had captured until he was ready to set sail. The Spaniards were sent below and the buccaneers put to sea. The man-of-war fired a victory salute, thinking the rovers had been defeated, but on seeing the ship move seawards, at once cut its cable and set off in pursuit. Dusk fell, and the warship was beginning to gain on the rover. The wind rose, but still the rover crammed on all sail, in order to escape. But misfortune overtook the fugitives, for the mainmast came crashing down to the deck, on account of the canvas the ship carried.

Nevertheless, the buccaneers' courage did not forsake them. They reloaded their muskets, tied the Spanish prisoners together two by two, and prepared to fight the man-of-war with only twenty-two men – for the rest of the crew had been wounded and were unfit for combat. They dropped the mainmast overboard and rigged as many sails as they could on the foremast and the bowsprit.

But at last the man-of-war overtook them and attacked so fiercely that Francois was forced to surrender, but on the terms that neither he nor his crew should be made to labour carrying lime or stone and that they should all be sent to Spain at the first opportunity. (When the Spaniards capture any buccaneers, they usually keep them three or four years at such labour, like slaves, only sending them back to Spain in the galleons when they have no more use for them.) These terms were granted, and Francois gave up the booty with infinite regret, as it included pearls to the value of 100,000 pieces of eight, for the entire catch of all the fleet had been on board. This would have been an immense prize for the rover had he been able to keep it – which doubtless would have been the case if the mainmast had not split.

Here is another example, which began no less boldly and ended no less unluckily. A man known as Bartolomeo el Portugues sailed from Jamaica in a barque mounting four guns and thirty men. Rounding Cabo de Corrientes on the island of Cuba, he saw a ship approaching, come from Maracaibo and Cartagena and bound for Havana and thence for Hispaniola. This ship carried twenty guns and other armament, and had seventy people on board, passengers as well as seamen. The buccaneers resolved to board her and carried out the attempt with great courage, but were bravely beaten back by the Spaniards. On the second attempt they took the ship, with a loss of ten dead and four wounded, although the Spaniards still had forty men alive, counting those fit for service and the wounded.

The buccaneers could not return to Jamaica as the wind was against them, so decided to make for Cabo San Antonio (in the western corner of Cuba) as they were short of water. Near the cape they encountered three ships, come from New Spain and bound for Havana. These ships came alongside, forced the rovers to give up their plunder and moreover took them all prisoner. It grieved them no little, having to hand over such precious booty – for the ship had been laden with 120,000 pounds of cacao, and had 70,000 pieces of eight on board.

Two days after their capture, the ships were separated in a huge gale which blew up, and the trading-ship where the buccaneers were held prisoner touched in at Campeche. Various traders came on board the merchantman to welcome the captain. These men knew Bartolomeo, the rovers' chief, for he had inflicted terrible havoc along this coast, murdering people and burning houses.

Next day, the town's officers of justice came on board asking the captain to hand over the buccaneers, a demand which he dared not refuse. But as the townspeople feared the pirate chief might give them the slip – as he had frequently done before – they made Bartolomeo remain on board ship while they erected a gallows on which to hang him next morning. Bartolomeo spoke good Spanish, and overheard the sailors discussing the hanging. He at once looked for some means of saving his life. He took two empty wine-jars and stoppered them tightly with cork. That night, when everyone was asleep except the sentry who stood guarding him, Bartolomeo did all he could to persuade the man to go to his hammock. But as he showed no intention of doing so, Bartolomeo decided to cut his throat. This he did, without giving the sentry a chance to cry out. Immediately Bartolomeo lowered himself gently into the water with his two jars, and with their help swam to the shore. He made for the forest, where he hid himself for three days before deciding on any course of action.

Early next morning soldiers were sent to patrol the shore, where they guessed he might be. But Bartolomeo was too cunning for them. He watched their movements from the shelter of the woods, and only when they returned to the city began making his way along the coast towards El Golfo Triste (about thirty leagues from Campeche). He reached this place at last, after a journey of fourteen days – not without much hardship from hunger and thirst and the discomforts of travel. He dared not take the main road for fear of falling into the hands of the Spaniards. For four days he was laboriously clambering through the thickets of trees which grow along the shore, with as many roots in the water as branches up above, without setting a foot on the ground. During those four days he had nothing but a small calabash of water, and ate nothing except periwinkles which he pulled off the rocks.

To make matters worse, he had to cross several rivers, though he could hardly swim – yet a man desperately trying to save his life will undertake hazards another would not dream of. He found an old plank washed up on the beach, with some big nails sticking out of it. These he hammered flat with stones, and ground their edges until they were sharp enough to cut with. Then he hacked down creepers and bound together pieces of driftwood he had gathered, and so made a raft on which to cross the rivers.

Finally he came to Triste, where he found a buccaneers' ship from Jamaica. When he had told them his adventures, he urged them to give him a canoe and twenty men, to make a surprise attack by night on the ship where he had been a prisoner, at anchor in Campeche. The buccaneers agreed. Eight days later, Bartolomeo and his twenty men arrived at dead of night at

Campeche harbour, and instantly, without speaking a word, boarded the ship. The men on the ship had thought it was one of the canoes from the city carrying contraband – but they soon found their mistake when the buccaneers all leapt on board and captured the vessel. The rovers immediately cut the anchor cable and set sail. There was still plenty of merchandise on board, but the gold had been taken out.

Bartolomeo el Portugues now forgot all the hardships he had suffered, for he had a good ship once more, with high hopes of making his fortune. But just when he thought he was on top of all his difficulties, the ill-luck which constantly dogged him brought him down again in a short time. He had set his course for Jamaica and was sailing in the region of the Isle of Pines, to the south of Cuba, when his ship ran aground on the reefs of Los Jardines, in a southerly gale. With bitter heartache, he and his men had to abandon ship and flee in their canoe to Jamaica. They did not linger there, but soon made ready to go off in quest of booty once again – yet fortune always went against el Portugues. He made many violent attacks on the Spaniards without gaining much profit from marauding, for I saw him dying in the greatest wretchedness in the world.

There is a buccaneer still living in Jamaica whose exploits have been no less bold. He was born in Groningen, and lived for a long time in Brazil, but when the Portuguese retook that country from the Dutch, various settlers there had to leave. Some went to Holland, others to the French or English islands, and some to the Virgin Isles. This man went to Jamaica, and not knowing what else to do, joined the buccaneers, who called him Rock the Brazilian. First he shipped as a common seaman, and became very popular with the crew. A party of malcontents rallied to his side and parted company with their captain, taking a barque, of which they made Rock the captain.

Soon they captured a ship from New Spain, with much money on board, and brought it to Jamaica. Rock acquired great renown from this exploit, and in the end became so audacious he made all Jamaica tremble. He had no self-control at all, but behaved as if possessed by a sullen fury. When he was drunk, he would roam the town like a madman. The first person he came across, he would chop off his arm or leg, without anyone daring to intervene, for he was like a maniac. He perpetrated the greatest atrocities possible against the Spaniards. Some of them he tied or spitted on wooden stakes and roasted them alive between two fires, like killing a pig – and all because they refused to show him the road to the hog-yards he wanted to plunder.

Once he was cruising after prey along the coast of Campeche when his ship ran aground in a storm. He and his crew had to abandon ship and make for the shore, without being able to rescue anything but their muskets and some powder and shot. This occurred between Campeche and Triste. Straight away they hurried towards El Golfo Triste, where the rovers always put in to repair their ships. After three or four days they were worn out with hunger and thirst and the rough road, so that they could hardly go another step – but worst of all, they were observed by a party of a hundred Spanish cavalry who chanced to come that way.

Captain Rock urged his comrades on, saying he had no intention of giving himself up, but would rather die than be taken prisoner by the Spaniards. The rovers were thirty in number, all well armed, and as their captain had put good heart into them, resolved to die with him rather than surrender. Meantime, the Spaniards were riding violently down on them. The rovers let them approach until they could not miss their aim, and every bullet found its mark. The battle went on for an hour, when the surviving Spaniards took flight. The buccaneers killed the wounded Spaniards instantly, and took their horses and the food they had been carrying. They could now proceed on their way with ease, without having lost more than two of their mates killed, and two wounded.

They rode on horseback along the coast road, and before they arrived at the Gulf, they noticed a Spanish barque off shore, come to cut logwood. The rovers turned back, sending out six of their men in advance to spy on the enemy's movements. In the morning, when the Spaniards came on shore, these men took their canoe and all six jumped on board, rowed out to the barque and captured it as well. As there were few provisions on the vessel, they slaughtered some of their horses and salted the flesh with salt they found on board, to live on till they came across better fare.

Not long after this, the buccaneers captured a ship come from New Spain, laden with meal and many pieces of eight, which had been bound for Maracaibo to purchase cacao. Captain Rock sailed for Jamaica with this prize, and lorded it there with his mates until all was gone. For that is the way with these buccaneers – whenever they have got hold of something, they don't keep it for long. They are busy dicing, whoring and drinking so long as they have anything to spend. Some of them will get through a good two or three thousand pieces of eight in a day – and next day not have a shirt to their back. I have seen a man in Jamaica give 500 pieces of eight to a whore, just to see her naked. Yes, and many other impieties.

My own master often used to buy a butt of wine and set it in the middle of the street with the barrel-head knocked in, and stand barring the way. Every passer-by had to drink with him, or he'd have shot them dead with a gun he kept handy. Once he bought a cask of butter and threw the stuff at everyone who came by, bedaubing their clothes or their head, wherever he best could reach.

The buccaneers are generous to their comrades: if a man has nothing, the others will come to his help. The tavern-keepers let them have a good deal of credit, but in Jamaica one ought not to put much trust in these people, for often they will sell you for debt, a thing I have seen happen many a time. Even the man I have just been speaking about, the one who gave the whore so much money to see her naked, and at that time had a good 3,000 pieces of eight – three months later he was sold for his debts, by a man in whose house he had spent most of his money.

But to return to our tale. Captain Rock soon squandered all his money, and was obliged to put to sea again with his mates. He went back to the coast of Campeche, which was his usual place for marauding. After barely fourteen days there, he went off in a canoe to reconnoitre the shipping in the roadstead of Campeche to see if he could take a vessel. But his ill-luck decreed that he himself should be captured by the Spaniards, together with his canoe and ten of his comrades besides.

He was instantly brought before the governor, who had him shut up in a dark hole with little to eat. The governor would gladly have had him hanged, but dare not, because the buccaneer had thought of a crafty ruse. He wrote a letter to the governor, as if it had come from his comrades among the other buccaneers, threatening they would show no mercy in future however many Spaniards they took, if the governor did Rock any harm.

The governor, on receiving this letter, feared he himself might share such a fate, for previously Campeche had almost fallen into the hands of the rovers, under the leadership of a certain Mansveldt [*sic*] who had been a celebrated buccaneer of Jamaica. The governor therefore decided to send Captain Rock to Spain with the galleons. He made the buccaneer promise on his oath that he would never more return to piracy, threatening he would hang him without mercy if Rock ever fell into his clutches again.

Captain Rock had not been long in Spain before he was on the lookout for a chance of returning to Jamaica. On the journey from the West Indies he had gained some 500 pieces of eight by fishing, with which he bought clothes and other necessaries, and back he went to the island. Having arrived in Jamaica, he set about the work of marauding with more cunning and boldness than ever, devoting all his energy to every exploit which promised to harm the Spaniards.

The Spaniards, seeing there was no getting rid of the buccaneers, were driven to reduce the number of their voyages – but this did them no good. When the buccaneers were unable to capture their ships at sea, they gathered together and came on land, plundering many villages and towns. The rover who initiated these land attacks was Lewis Scot. He took the town of Campeche, plundered the place and forced the citizens to pay ransom before abandoning it. After him came Mansveldt, who undertook to land in New Granada and ravage as far as the South Sea – which in fact he did, but was forced to turn back eventually from lack of food. First he captured the island of St Catalina, where he took some prisoners who set him on the way to the city of Cartagena.

Another buccaneer – John Davis of Jamaica – led a daring enterprise in this same territory. For a long time he had been lurking in the Gulf of Boca del Toro, on the look-out for ships from Cartagena bound for Nicaragua, but had missed them. He and his men decided to leave their ship in the mouth of the Nicaragua river and make their way upstream in canoes, to arrive at the city by night and plunder the churches and the property of the principal merchants. They were a band of ninety strong, and had three canoes among them. Leaving ten men on the ship, which was concealed among the trees at the river mouth so as not to be seen by Indians coming to fish, all the rest took to the canoes: They travelled upriver by night, hiding by day under the trees along the bank.

At about midnight on the third night they reached the town. The sentry took them for fishers from the lagoon, for several of the rovers spoke good Spanish. Also, they had an Indian with them who used to live there and had fled because the Spaniards wanted to make him a slave. This Indian sprang on shore, approached the sentry and murdered him. Then they all landed and paid a visit to the mansions of three or four of the principal citizens. They took all the money they could lay hands on, and also robbed several churches, but by this time some fugitives who had managed to escape their clutches were setting up an outcry through the town.

The citizens and the garrison began to rouse up, so the rovers were compelled to flee, carrying off as much loot as they could manage. They also took along a few prisoners, to use them to obtain quarter, should they be overtaken.

As soon as they reached the river mouth, the rovers made ready their ship with the utmost speed and put to sea. They had made the prisoners, for their ransom, procure them as much meat as was needed for the return journey to Jamaica. While they were still in the mouth of the river, some 500 armed Spaniards rode up, but the buccaneers' bold cannon-fire repelled them. To their great ignominy, the Spaniards had to watch them sail away with their goods. Ninety rovers had dared to land, reach a town more than forty leagues from the shore and garrisoned by a good 800 men, and in so short a time had carried off such splendid booty. The buccaneers had taken over 40,000 pieces of eight in ready money, as well as silver and jewels.

Soon afterwards they came with their loot back to Jamaica, where they promptly squandered it all, so once more they had to go in quest of prey. John Davis was chosen by a group of rovers as chief of their seven or eight ships, as he was a good leader. They resolved to cruise along the north coast of Cuba to lie in wait for the fleet from New Spain and plunder some of its ships. This plan did not succeed, yet, rather than return home without booty, they decided to sail for the coast of Florida. Here they landed and took a small town called San Augustin. This town had a fort, garrisoned by two companies of soldiers, yet despite this the rovers plundered the place and got away without the Spaniards being able to do them any injury.

"One band of rogues . . . took off their shoes, rolled up
their hose and waded through the ooze to their 'prize'"

PIRATES OF THE THAMES

Clive Senior

For though Pyrates exempted be
From fatall Tyburne's wither'd tree,
They have an Harbour to arrive
Call'd Wapping, where as ill they thrive
As those that ride up Holbourne Hill,
And at the Gallows make their Will
                    – Samuel Rowlands,
                         Knave of Hearts

Proportionately, the Thames was the scene of more acts of piracy
than any other stretch of water in England, owing to the number
of vessels on the river and the existence of a large number of
disaffected seamen who lodged in the shanty settlements east of
London Bridge. Of eight-six indictments drawn up in the High
Court of Admiralty for piracies committed on the English coast
between 1603 and 1640, no less than fifty-one relate to depredations on the Thames. Although the records of the London court
might be expected to exaggerate the relative importance of
Thames-side crime, it is nevertheless clear that London was
an important centre of piracy.

It might seem strange that such crimes should find a place in a
history of piracy, especially when the robbers did not even need a
boat from which to launch their attacks. For example, when one
band of rogues spied the *Green Hat* of Dordrecht lying in the
mud below Gravesend, they took off their shoes, rolled up their
hose and waded through the ooze towards their "prize". When
they clambered aboard they discovered the crew had gone ashore,
and proceeded to ransack the ship. Despite the circumstances,

this crime and many others like it were treated as piracy. The reason for this was the territorial division between the admiralty and the common law courts. Piracy was simply the maritime equivalent of robbery; whether a crime was piracy or robbery depended on where it was committed. The jurisdiction of the lord high admiral extended all round the coasts of England up to high-water mark (whether the tide was in or not), and as far up the rivers as the lowest bridges. If a crime which would have constituted a robbery on land was committed in the admiral's jurisdiction, then the criminals were likely to be treated as pirates.

Apart from the legal definition, there is ample justification for treating such crimes as piracy rather than robbery. Most of the offenders were seafaring men who made their living from the water in some way or other: usually as sailors, ferrymen, or fishermen. The value of prizes may have been small compared with captures made by pirates on the high seas, but then there were fewer men involved, so shares tended to be larger. The type of piracy could vary enormously. Some crimes occurred as the impromptu result of a heavy drinking bout in a waterside tavern; others were planned and executed by organised bands who successfully managed to escape detection for many years. If some of the unfortunates who were caught do not seem to merit the description of "pirate", the same could be said of many of their brethren who were at large on the ocean. The sentence was the same for all and, perhaps because of this, river and coastal pirates could be every bit as desperate and violent as pirates on the high seas.

The two types of piracy were not completely separate, however. Some of the most illustrious pirate careers had the humblest of beginnings. All of John Ward's wealth and magnificence can be directly traced back to the small bark which he and his men boarded in Portsmouth harbour. Many small-time pirates began with similar ambitions of building up their strength and riches. Some, like Ward, given patience, perseverance and luck, actually graduated to the ranks of the deep-sea pirates; most cruised aimlessly about, plundered a few weak vessels and then ran ashore with their loot.

Spoils were committed all round the English coast in the early seventeenth century, but in this chapter it is intended to concentrate on one area only – the River Thames and its estuary.

Because London was the seat of the High Court of Admiralty, crimes on this stretch of water were more likely to come to light than those committed elsewhere. Accounts of piracy in the outports and on the coasts are rare, but the record of piracy in the capital is continuous and detailed. There is probably more evidence relating to piracy on the Thames in this period than almost anywhere else. During the first half of the century nearly a third of all piracy indictments in the High Court of Admiralty were for spoils committed on the Thames itself.

Riverside piracy was not exclusively a seventeenth-century phenomenon. John Stow, in his *Survey of London*, made mention of piracy on the Thames in medieval times. He tells how the Londoners sent out a fleet of ships in 1216 which succeeded in capturing many pirates, "besides innumerable others that they drowned, which had robbed on the river of Thames". Stow's next mention of riverside piracy comes more than two centuries later. One night in the spring of 1440, six foreign vessels lay anchored in the Thames after unloading cargoes of fish which they had brought to London for Lent. As the crews were sleeping, a band of pirates stole alongside in a barge, cut their throats and threw the bodies overboard. After pillaging the ships the pirates sank them in an effort to hide all trace of their crime, apparently unsuccessfully, for two of the offenders were caught and hung in chains on a specially raised hill at East Smithfield in full view of the river.

From these two isolated examples it can be seen that riverside piracy was nothing new in the seventeenth century. Indeed, it was destined to continue well into modern times. Bracebridge Hemyng, the Victorian author, wrote in about 1870 that "for a long time piracy and smuggling had been going on in the river just below the bridge", and furnished his readers with stories of bands of cut-throats who operated from hideouts in Limehouse and Wapping in the latter half of the nineteenth century.

Because Thameside pirates were parasites who lived off the trade of London, their activity was closely linked with the life and vitality of the metropolis. London in the late sixteenth and early seventeenth centuries was undergoing an expansion, the like of which had not been seen in England before. By 1603 its population was probably approaching a quarter of a million. In sheer size it dwarfed every other city in the kingdom. London's wealth was prodigious too. In 1619 the city's share of the naval expedition which was sent against the pirates of Algiers was assessed at £40,000 – more than four times the sum of all the other ports put together! Merchants in the provinces, jealous and fearful of the rapid growth of the capital, voiced fears that the head was becoming too great for the body to support; that the growth of London was sapping the nation's strength. Such fears were not completely unfounded. To feed and clothe so large a population presented problems for which the government was completely unprepared. Yet the city did not starve: it continued to grow. Carts came from further and further afield laden with food and dairy produce and barks navigated the Thames to meet the growing needs of the city, while the Newcastle colliers beat up and down the east coast in an effort to keep the Londoners warm.

Seaborne traffic was the secret of London's spectacular growth and the Thames, as the main highway of traffic, was the artery connecting the heart of the city with the rest of the world. Foreigners who visited London came away impressed not only with its size and wealth, but also with the importance of the river. Paul Hentzner, who was in the city in 1597, observed that:

> The wealth of the world is wafted to it by the Thames, swelled by the tide, and navigable to merchant ships through a safe and deep channel for sixty miles from its mouth to the City.

From docks all along these sixty miles of river vessels sailed on voyages of trade and discovery. Most of the important trading companies of the day were firmly established in London. As trade grew and ships increased in size, so larger docks were constructed downstream further away from the city at places such as Ratcliffe, Wapping, Greenwich, Deptford, Woolwich and Gravesend. The proliferation of shipping on the Thames was picturesquely described by William Camden, when he remarked that "a man would say, that seeth the shipping there, that it is, as it were, a very wood of trees disbranched to make glades and let in light; so shaded is it with masts and sailes."

The importance of the river in London's trade was matched by its importance for transport and communications within the city. The streets of old London were crowded, unhealthy and unsafe for travellers. Many of the roads were still unpaved and the risk from footpads was compounded by the increase in the numbers of carts and coaches. Apart from carts delivering produce, the streets were clogged up by private and public coaches, known to contemporaries as "Hackney hell carriages", which were totally unsuited to negotiating the intricate and overcrowded streets and passages of medieval London. Small wonder that people took to the river. Travelling by water was more soothing, less noxious and far quicker. It was also essential for travellers wishing to cross from one side of the river to the other. Stuart London was only blessed with one bridge over the Thames. Even for those wanting to visit the theatres and pleasure houses on Bankside, the river was by far the most convenient form of travel.

The taxi-drivers of Elizabethan and Jacobean London were the wherrymen – oarsmen and scullers who piled for hire in their small boats or wherries along the numerous water stairs and landing places. It has been said that there were "as many wherries on the Thames in early Stuart times as there were gondolas in Venice". Stow put their number at 2,000 in Westminster, the City and Southwark alone. John Taylor, the "water poet", thought that if all the dependants of these watermen were included, then the number of those who lived "by the oar and skull, betwixt the bridge of Windsor and Gravesend, cannot be fewer than forty thousand".

Thus, in the sixteenth and seventeenth centuries, the Thames played a part in London life which it is difficult to appreciate today. The hustle of trade and the frantic activity on the river was not, however, without its seedy side. It was only natural that as seaborne trade began to utilise docks further down river, new settlements should appear east of the city which were mainly inhabited by seafarers and others who relied in some way on the river for a living. Growth took place on the north bank, on Tower Hill, at St Katherines, Ratcliffe, Shadwell, Limehouse, Poplar and Wapping, and on the south bank, at Redruth and Rother- hithe. The burial registers of these places bear ample witness to the seafaring character of the new settlements, being full of the names of sailors, mariners, shipwrights, anchorsmiths, chandlers, carpenters, ropemakers and others who looked to boats and ships for their livelihood.

Despite government attempts at control, London's eastward

expansion was haphazard. The whole area soon became a maze of wharfs, docks, piers, small creeks and crowded houses. Buildings sprang up almost overnight, often in defiance of government proclamations. Stow bemoaned the deterioration that had taken place close to his own native Ratcliffe, where he had witnessed the construction of "a continuall streete, or filthy straight passage, with Alleyes of small tenements or cottages builded, inhabited by saylors' victualers". The riverside east of London, which even in the late sixteenth century had still been regarded as a rural retreat from the overcrowding and filth of the city, became, in only a short space of time, a place to be shunned even more than the city, especially when the plague was raging. At least one contemporary believed the plagues of the first half of the seventeenth century to have been imported to London aboard foreign ships and to have first gained a foothold in the overcrowded and insanitary conditions prevailing in the East End.

Not only was the East End a fertile breeding ground for the plague, it also provided ideal conditions in which crime could flourish. There was, of course, no proper police force in Stuart England and law and order were little in evidence. This was particularly true of the new developments, which were outside the city's jurisdiction. The attitude of the government was to isolate the crime which existed within these areas and to try to prevent it from spreading to the city. For example, when East Enders caused trouble in the more law-abiding districts of Lambeth and Southwark, the Council's solution was to impose a curfew and to forbid passengers from being ferried over from Ratcliffe, Blackwall and Wapping after nine o'clock at night. Still, London could not hope to exclude completely the population of the new areas, and the eastern settlements soon had the reputation of being "a great source of beggars and other loose persons swarming about the City".

Alehouses, always prime centres of crime and disorder, expanded rapidly along the whole waterfront. In 1630, the justices of Wapping reported that they had closed down as many as twenty-six taverns in Wapping itself, but this still left a total of thirty-seven to serve the needs of the inhabitants. Because of the periodic and seasonal nature of their employment, sailors and fishermen usually had plenty of time to idle away. Alehouses provided ideal meeting-places and information centres where trouble-makers and the criminal elements had ample opportunity to drown their sorrows, hatch their plots and recruit allies and helpers.

Usually the pirates who met in the alehouses to the east of the city went downstream to look for their prey. Some went as far as Gravesend or Tilbury before attempting to capture a vessel, and the more adventurous posed a threat to shipping in the estuary and even attacked vessels further out to sea. In 1613, a band of about ten men commandeered a fishing boat at Leigh and sailed to Shoeburyness, where they succeeded in capturing a better boat. They then sailed up the coast as far as Orford Ness, where they robbed the crew of the *Golden Cock* of Haarlem. Seizing the *Desire* of Barking, they sailed to the south side of the estuary, and off Reculver attacked the *Cock* of St Omer, making off with her cargo of lawns and cambrics worth nearly £200. Getting ashore at Gillingham, the pirates made their way overland to London and were able to dispose of some of their loot at St Bartholomew's Fair. Only two men, Thomas Brooker, a ship's carpenter from Rochester, and Henry Stakes, a gunner from Somerset, were ever brought to trial for this crime.

The lord admiral's jurisdiction on the Thames only extended as far as London Bridge, so only attacks on shipping below the bridge were treated as piracy. The dividing line between piracy and robbery was, however, more than just a purely legal distinction. Old London Bridge, supported by a series of narrow arches, and straining under the weight of houses and shops, provided a serious obstacle to shipping on the river. Vessels of burden could not pass the bridge and had to anchor downstream, where they either unloaded their cargoes or transferred them to smaller craft for the journey upstream. It was because ships of size and consequence were confined to the waters east of the bridge that acts of piracy were likely to be of greater consequence than robberies committed higher up the river.

Still, some piracies were little more than drunken forays which were ill-conceived and ended disastrously. Five days before Christmas 1607, Garret Scottle and some friends boarded a wherry after a heavy drinking bout in a Limehouse tavern. Rowing downstream, they encountered a hoy lying between Greenwich and Deptford. Boarding the ship, they took £50 in coin before fleeing ashore. Scottle was the only one to be caught and he paid for his indiscretion with his life.

Most crimes, however, were more carefully planned and executed and few of the offenders were ever caught. It was not
difficult for pirates to gain intelligence of vessels newly arrived in
the river with details of their cargoes, for such news travelled fast
amongst the seafaring community. Likely ships could be recon-
noitred to see how well they were guarded or, alternatively, bands
of men could simply row downstream in the hope of encountering
some suitable prize.

There was little risk of these pirates being caught. The navy
was responsible for patrolling the river, but usually only one
ketch or pinnace was employed on active service at a time. During
the first half of the century, the navy appears to have had only one
isolated success – in 1629 when a naval ketch challenged the *Angel*
of Halstow at Tilbury and arrested a band of sailors who had
recently captured her. The lords of the admiralty had little
appreciation of the difficulty of preventing piracy on the river.
In 1633 they wrote to Captain Coke, the commander of the king's
ship, upbraiding him for his failure to stop the "dayly pilfrings
and insolencies comitted in the Ryvers of Thamise and Medway
by pyrattes, pickerons and pettie men of warre". With only one
ship the task was impossible. Pirates often knew the whereabouts
of the patrol vessel and were able to choose the time and place for
their attacks carefully.

The only other means of preventing piracy was to arrest any
suspicious persons and to stop wherries which were carrying
abnormally large numbers of men (although members of a band
could easily avoid detection by travelling overland and meeting
their accomplices at a prearranged destination). In 1613, after a
complaint had been received from the Merchant Strangers in
London concerning the increasing number of depredations on
the river, the Council declared that the problem was caused by
"loose and ill disposed marriners and other seafaringmen as are
suffered to passe in wherries and other boates by that towne of
Gravesende, and soe falling further downe joyne themselves in
partnershipp and sease upon such pinckes and boates as they
fined fitt". The Council's remedy was for the searchers of
Gravesend to take into custody any suspicious-looking men
who could not account for their employment.

The searchers were soon able to report that they had indeed
arrested several suspects who "without all doubt were mynded to

have putt som suche lyke matter in practis". Such a course of action was clearly impractical and can only have been prompted by desperation. Men could not be charged with crimes before they had committed them, and keeping suspects in prison was a costly business. It was impossible to hold every suspicious-looking person on the busiest stretch of water in the world.

Because some of the most successful pirates were never caught, references to them appear only briefly in the records of the period. In 1620, a man whose fishing trawler had been taken by a band of pirates at Holehaven, described the leader as a man "called Will, a blacke fellowe with longe haire, who saied hee knewe hee shoulde never bee taken, for hee had used that trade allmoste these twentie yeares". The only other mention of this pirate's activities on the Thames comes earlier in the same year, when a band led by a man dressed in a black cloth suit, who was known as "Black Will", rowed downstream from Limehouse and plundered several vessels before getting ashore with their loot. Perhaps this was the same Black Will who was master's mate on an English pirate ship which captured a Portuguese carvel near Madeira in 1608 and whose share of the prize amounted to £335. The true identity of Black Will may never be known, but whoever he was he deserves to be numbered amongst the most successful pirates of his day.

Another Thameside pirate who enjoyed a career of some notoriety was "Dick of Dover". His real name was Richard Catro and he was a sailor from the Isle of Thanet. He was first questioned in the admiralty in 1613 in connection with several piracies, but at that time he strongly denied being known as Dick of Dover. He next appears in connection with piracy six years later, when he "made a match" at the "Three Tuns" in Ratcliffe to go down river in search of likely prizes. Catro and his men took a hoy as far as Tilbury, plundered the *Gift of God* of Calais of her cargo of cloth worth about £150, and finally returned to Ratcliffe with the booty laden in two wherries. Catro was arrested and arraigned as Dick of Dover. He was sentenced to death, but may have escaped, for the following year Dick of Dover was again at large, this time leading an attack on the *Primrose* at Long Reach and plundering two other vessels near Tilbury. Perhaps some pirates' nick-names were perennial.

Thameside pirates took pains to ensure that they could not be easily identified. They were helped by the long winter nights and by the river mists that formed on the Thames. Crews of ships often had little time to notice their assailants before being stowed unceremoniously below hatches. Lawrence Tatum, the master of the *James* of London, which was taken at Blackwall on a winter's night in 1624, described how a dozen or more men "entred the said shippe in the darcke and presently masked and covered the faces of this examinant's men then aboard the said shippe [so] that they coulde not discerne them to take any notice of them".

Some pirates even went so far as to disguise themselves by wearing false beards or by blacking their faces with powder. Others wore masks or visors and one man actually boarded vessels wearing an iron helmet shaped like a skull. Even when identification was possible it was still difficult, because witnesses who had last seen their attackers wearing rough seamen's clothes might be asked to identify the same men when they were well dressed and groomed. Only the most foolish helped to incriminate themselves – like Arthur Halse, who appeared in court wearing the very stockings which formed part of the cargo he was accused of stealing.

*"Captain Spragge sailed into the harbour of Port Royal
with four buccaneers hanging by the neck from his
yardarms"*

TWILIGHT OF THE BUCCANEERS

Neil Grant

The free-for-all in the West Indies was over. Spain was now just
one of several European countries that held bases and colonies in
the region. She was no longer everyone's enemy. England or
France might be found in alliance with Spain against each other,
or against the Dutch. It no longer suited the European powers to
let loose a band of adventurers against the Spanish empire. But
the buccaneers could not be organized to fight any enemy except
Spain. Their usefulness was at an end.

The writing had been on the wall since the days of Morgan –
and Morgan himself had read the message clearly. For a long time
the English government had been in two minds about the
buccaneers. Sometimes the buccaneers were encouraged, sometimes they were discouraged. Governors in the West Indies
received conflicting orders. They were told to stop buccaneering
at the same time as they were congratulated on the success of a
buccaneer raid.

As time went on, the scales were weighted ever more heavily
against the buccaneers. When the English had captured Jamaica,
it had few colonists, no town of any size, no large farms and little
trade. In forty years, Jamaica had changed rapidly. Large plantations lay where scrub and forest had been, and English merchants
made big profits in trading slaves for Jamaican sugar. Their
business did not benefit from the presence of a thousand unruly
buccaneers in the colony. As long as there was "no peace beyond
the line", trade was upset.

The rich planters and merchants were powerful men. They sat
on the council for Jamaica, and they could bring pressure on the

English government. They demanded an end to lawlessness, an end to piracy.

There was no hope of ending international conflict in the Caribbean. The nations of Europe would go on wrestling for an advantage in the West Indies for most of the 18th century. But England, like France and the Netherlands, was no longer on the outside, banging on the Spanish door and demanding to be let in. These countries were in a position like that of Spain a hundred years before. They had colonies to guard, trade to conduct, and interests to protect. Buccaneering could hurt them as badly as it had hurt Spain in the past. In the future, the international contest would be carried on by regular navies, by royal ships commanded by professional officers, not by the uncontrolled ravages of the buccaneers.

In 1687 an English naval squadron, under the command of Sir Robert Holmes, was sent to the West Indies to clear the pirates from the Caribbean. For a few months, no buccaneer vessel dared show herself in the sea lanes.

In his report, Sir Robert said that he found the buccaneers had already disappeared from the major West Indian colonies. They had been forced to find new havens, in the Bahamas, in the Danish island of St Thomas, or in the colonies on the mainland of North America. The ports of New England and Virginia were popular with pirates of all kinds. The American colonists were usually willing to buy – at cheap prices – the goods stolen from Spanish ships and settlements, and without asking awkward questions.

In this same year, Captain Spragge sailed into the harbour of Port Royal with four buccaneers hanging by the neck from his yardarms. (One of them was a certain Captain Bannister, who had been dodging frigates sent from Jamaica to catch him for more than two years). A few years earlier, this sight would have displeased most of the people of Port Royal, but not now. According to the governor of Jamaica, the gruesome evidence of Captain Spragge's success against the buccaneers was "a spectacle of great satisfaction to all good people".

A dramatic and terrifying event brought down the curtain on the buccaneers of Port Royal in 1692. To the people of the time, it seemed as though God had signified his disapproval of the city.

Port Royal had a reputation (which it deserved) as the wildest –

and perhaps the richest – city in the world. One visitor described it as "hot as hell and wicked as the devil". Wine ran in the streets, money changed hands freely, and hardly a night passed without a knifing somewhere among its taverns and brothels.

The town was built on the end of a narrow spit of land, which enclosed a bay. It made a perfect harbour, one of the best in the West Indies.

The disaster happened just before mid-day on 7 June 1692. It happened very quickly, faster than the time it takes to tell.

Far below the ground, a mighty earthquake erupted. It began with a shattering roar. Suddenly, the quays along the harbour sagged like wet sand, and plunged into the water. Though the weather was clear, the waters of the bay rose in huge waves as if a storm was raging. The cables of vessels moored in the harbour snapped in two, and the ships plunged about help-lessly, like paper boats in a flood. Within seconds, the houses nearest the waterside toppled as the ground sank beneath them, and disappeared into the waves. A man drinking in a tavern saw, with horror, the stones in the floor heave themselves upwards. He raced outside, to see the street rising in waves like the sea.

The earth split in huge cracks. Carts, buildings and people suddenly disappeared into the ground. A few people, with ex-traordinary good fortune, fell into one great rift and were thrown up, unharmed, out of another, a long way from the spot where they had disappeared.

The whole city was collapsing as though made of cardboard. The water came rolling in, and most of the houses were drowned under several fathoms. A frigate that had been moored in the harbour was carried over the roofs of the houses. Some of the people struggling in the water were able to clamber to safety on board.

In just three minutes, the city of Port Royal was destroyed. Nine-tenths of the buildings had disappeared, and about three thousand of the inhabitants had lost their lives. The quays where so many buccaneer ships had tied up, the taverns where their crews had drunk and gambled, the houses where the richer captains had lived – all were gone. It was the end of an era.

★ ★ ★

The French buccaneers of Hispaniola flourished for a little longer than the English of Jamaica. D'Orgeron and De Pouancay had managed to gain some control over them and use them as an effective privateering force. Saint Domingue remained open to the buccaneers for some years after Jamaica had ceased to welcome them.

King Louis XIV sent a firm order to put an end to buccaneering in 1683, soon after the death of De Pouancay. Like earlier orders, this one was not fully carried out. But the great raid on Vera Cruz, which took place in the same year, was the last really large-scale expedition of the French buccaneers against Spain.

The Brethren of the Coast had one final fling four years later. After a twelve-year truce, war had broken out again between France and Spain. The French sent a naval expedition to the Caribbean under an aristocratic commander, De Pointis.

It was agreed that this fleet should join with a force of buccaneers from Saint Domingue to attack the Spaniards.

The buccaneers were led by the governor of Saint Domingue, Ducasse. In the tradition of D'Orgeron, Ducasse had managed to keep control of the buccaneers without losing their loyalty. He was himself a tough and courageous general.

His position was not easy. De Pointis, the commander-in-chief, looked on the buccaneers as a gang of ruffians. He despised them, and insisted that they should obey naval discipline like the rest of the expedition. It is not hard to imagine what the buccaneers thought of De Pointis. Ducasse needed all his skill and power of command to keep the two parts of the expedition together.

The object of the expedition was Cartagena, the largest, the richest, and the most strongly defended city in all of Spanish America. Drake had captured it in 1585, when it was smaller and weaker. The buccaneers had never taken it. Even Morgan had decided that Cartagena was too strong for him.

De Pointis had over four thousand men, mostly soldiers. The buccaneers numbered about six hundred and fifty, in nine or ten ships. De Pointis's fleet included a bomb vessel, a ship specially built to fire shells from enormous mortars. She was able to toss her deadly missiles over the defences and into the city, causing severe damage and some panic.

Cartagena was fiercely defended. In fact, if the outlying forts had been more heavily manned, the siege might have failed. The stone walls of the outer fort that guarded the harbour were so thick that the French artillery could not pierce them. But the buccaneers knew of a path round the fort, which led to the road connecting the fort with the city. The road was cut and the fort surrounded. The commander, seeing his position was hopeless, surrendered. As he handed the keys of the fort to the French, he said, "I put into your hands the keys of all the Spanish Indies."

It was not as easy as that. More forts had to be overcome before the city was reached. But the garrison in these forts seems to have been rather small, and the guns too few. One by one they fell, though not without fierce fighting. The sharp-shooting of the buccaneers, whose pinpoint musket fire picked off the defenders, made the task of the French easier.

When the last fort had fallen, the French were within a musket shot of the suburbs of the city. The buccaneers' muskets kept the streets clear, but heavy gunfire from strongpoints within the suburbs kept the French at bay. For a week, their artillery pounded the walls, and at last a breach was made. It was hardly wide enough for more than one man, and the French lost many killed when they charged the breach. But they got through, killing every Spaniard they found, and drove the rest back into the main part of the city.

Cartagena was doomed. It was surrounded on all sides, suffering heavy fire from the French artillery, which had been brought up close to the walls, and from the shells fired from the ships in the harbour. After a siege that, all together, had lasted more than two weeks, the governor of Cartagena surrendered.

Vast booty was found within, probably three or four million pieces of eight. The French had promised no looting, but it was not easy to prevent a victorious army – still less the buccaneers – from grabbing everything they could. Some of the citizens of Cartagena actually hired groups of the buccaneers to stand guard over their property.

When all the treasure had been gathered, Ducasse went to De Pointis and asked for the share due to the buccaneers. To his surprise, the amount was very small. De Pointis insisted that the buccaneers should have the same prize money as the regular soldiers. This piece of news was not received kindly by the Brethren of the Coast.

Amid much grumbling from the buccaneers, the fleet sailed from Cartagena on 1 June, four weeks after the city had fallen. No sooner were they at sea than the buccaneers left the main fleet and reversed their course, back to Cartagena. That dog De Pointis had cheated them, they swore. They would return to the city and take what was rightfully owed them. Ducasse, who had been wounded during the siege, was unable to stop them. Probably, he did not try very hard.

The horrified citizens of Cartagena watched as the buccaneer ships sailed into the harbour they had left so recently. All the defences of the city had been destroyed by De Pointis before leaving, and there was nothing to stop the buccaneers marching in. They took hostages, tortured some of them, and demanded a huge ransom for the city. Once more, the wretched citizens had to dig deep into their pockets. In four days, enough was collected to give each of the buccaneers a sum of about a thousand pieces of eight.

As they sailed away, making for Cow Island to share out the loot, the buccaneers met a squadron of English and Dutch warships, which had been sent from Europe to intercept the French fleet. De Pointis had avoided them, but the buccaneers were not so fortunate. Two of their ships were captured, and they happened to be the largest ships, carrying the lion's share of the plunder. A third ship was driven ashore near Cartagena, where her crew was put to work by the Spaniards rebuilding the defences. A fourth ship was chased to Hispaniola, forced ashore near Santo Domingo, and burned.

The rest escaped to various havens in Saint Domingue. But they were not safe even there. The English ships swept into Petit Gouave and seized more of the buccaneers' plunder, as well as burning part of the town.

The siege of Cartagena was one of the largest military operations in which the buccaneers were involved. But it showed only too clearly how their power had shrunk. They formed only a small part of the invading force, and were treated with contempt by the commander. They could never have held Cartagena to ransom if the city had not been defenceless. Then they were attacked and defeated by the English and Dutch fleet, losing nearly all their loot. At last – the final insult – their base was raided by the English and their houses burned.

Plenty of work remained in future wars for privateers in the West Indies. And piracy continued for many years on a smaller scale. But the days when the Brethren of the Coast roamed at will from the Gulf of Mexico to Barbados were over.

JOURNAL OF A BUCCANEER

William Dampier

The son of a Somerset farmer, Dampier fled the rural round for adventure at sea at the age of sixteen. When the entire crew of his Jamaican merchantman deserted to the pirate band of Bartholomew Sharp in 1680, Dampier went with them. Later, he joined the band of John Cook, who stole the Batchelor's Delight. *In early 1684 the* Batchelor's Delight *arrived in the Pacific:*

In this Sea we made the best of our way toward the Line, till the Lat, of 24 S., where we fell in with the main Land of South America. All this course of the Land, both of Chili and Peru is vastly high. Therefore we kept 12 or 14 Leagues offshore, being unwilling to be seen by the Spaniards dwelling there. The Land is of a most prodigious Height. It lies generally in Ridges parallel to the Shore and 3 or 4 Ridges one with another, each surpassing the other in height. Those that are farthest within Land, are much higher than others. They always appear blue when seen at Sea. Sometimes they are obscured with Clouds, but not so often as the high Lands in other parts of the World, for here are seldom or never any Rains on these Hills, any more than in the Sea near it. Neither are they subject to Fogs. These are the highest Mountains that I ever saw, far surpassing the Pike of Tenariffe or Santa Marta, and, I believe, any Mountains in the World.

In Sir John Narborough's Voyage to Baldivia (a City on this Coast) mention is also made of very high Land seen near Baldivia, and the Spaniards with whom I have discoursed have told me that there is very high Land all the way between Coquimbo (which lies in about 30d. South lat.) and Baldivia which is in 40 South. So that by all likelihood these Ridges of Mountains run in a continued Chain from one end of Peru and Chili to the other, all along this South Sea Coast; called usually the *Andes* or *Sierra Nuevada des Andes*. The excessive Height of these Mountains may possibly be the reason that there are no Rivers of Note that fall into these Seas. Some small Rivers indeed there are, but very few of them, for in some places there is not one that comes out into the Sea in 150 or 200 Leagues, and where they are thickest they are 30, 40 or 50 Leagues asunder, and too little and shallow to be navigable. Besides, some of these do not constantly run, but are dry at certain Seasons of the Year. The River Ylo runs flush with a quick Current at the latter End of January, and so continues till June, and then it decreases by degrees, growing less and running slow till the latter End of September, when it fails wholly and runs no more till January again. This I have seen at both Seasons in two former Voyages I made here, and have been informed by the Spaniards that other Rivers on this Coast are of a similar Nature, being Torrents or Land-floods caused by the Rains at certain Seasons far within Land, rather than perennial Streams.

We still kept along in sight of this Coast, but at a good distance from it, encountering with nothing of note till, in the Lat. of 9 deg. 40 min. South. on the 3rd of May, we descried a Sail to the Northward of us, plying to Windward. We chased her and, Capt. Eaton being ahead, soon took her. She had come from Guiaquil about a Month before, laden with Timber, and was bound to Lima. Three Days before we took her, she had come from Salta, where she had gone for Water, and where they had had news of our being in these Seas by an express from Baldivia. For, as we afterwards heard. Capt. Swan had been at Baldivia to seek a Trade there; and he having met Capt. Eaton in the Straits of Magellan, the Spaniards of Baldivia had doubtless been informed of us by him, suspecting him also to be one of us, though he was not. Upon this News the Viceroy of Lima sent Expresses to all the Seaports, so that they might provide themselves against our Assaults.

We immediately steered away for the Island Lobos, which lies in Lat. 6d. 24m. South Lat. I took the Elevation of it ashore with an Astrolabe, and it is 5 Leagues from the Main.

Here we scrubbed our Ships, and being in a readiness to sail, the Prisoners were examined to know if any of them could conduct us to some Town where we might make an Attempt. For they had informed us before that we had been described by the Spaniards, and by that we knew that they would send no Riches by Sea so long as we were here. Many Towns were considered on, such as Guiaquil, Zana, Truxillo, and others. At last Truxillo was pitched on as the most important, and therefore the likeliest to make us a Voyage if we could conquer it. We did not much question this, though we knew it to be a very populous City. But the greatest difficulty was in Landing. For Guanchaquo, which is the nearest Seaport to it, but six Miles off, is an ill place to Land, since sometimes the very Fishermen that live there are not able to go out in three or four Days. However the 17th of May in the Afternoon, our Men were mustered from both Ships' Companies, and their Arms proved. We were in all 108 Men fit for Service, besides the sick. And the next Day we intended to sail and take the Wood-Prize with us. But the next day, one of our Men being ashore early on the Island, descried three Sail bound to the Northward; two of them outside the Island to the Westward, the other between it and the Continent.

We soon got our Anchors up and chased, and Captain Eaton, who drew the least draught of Water, put through between the Westernmost Island and the Rocks, and went after those two that were outside the Islands. We in Captain Cook's Ship went after the other, which stood in for the Main Land, but we soon fetched her up, and having taken her, stood in again with her to the Island. For we saw that Captain Eaton wanted no help, having taken both those that he went after. He came in with one of his Prizes, but the other was so far to Leeward, and so deep, that he could not then get her in, but he hoped to get her in the next Day. Being deep laden, however, and designed to go down before the Wind to Panama, she would not bear Sail.

The 19th Day she turned all Day, but got no nearer the Island. Our Moskito-strikers, according to their Custom, went and struck six Turtles, for here are indifferent plenty of them. The Ships that we took the Day before we came from Guanchaquo, were all three laden with Flour and bound for Panama. Two of them were laden as deep as they could swim. The other was not more than half-laden, but was ordered by the Viceroy of Lima to sail with the other two, or else she should not sail till we had gone out of the Seas. For he hoped they might escape us by setting out early. In the biggest Ship was a Letter to the President of Panama from the Viceroy of Lima, assuring him that there were Enemies come into that Sea, for which reason he had dispatched these three Ships with Flour, that they might not be wanting (for Panama is supplied from Peru), and he desired him to be frugal with it, for he did not know when he would send more. In this Ship were likewise 7 or 8 Tons of Quince Marmalade and a stately Mule sent to the President, together with a very large Image of the Virgin Mary in Wood, carved and painted to adorn a new Church at Panama, and sent from Lima by the Viceroy. She brought also from Lima 800,000 Pieces of Eight, to carry with her to Panama. But while she was lying at Guanchaquo taking in her lading of Flour, the Merchants, hearing of Capt. Swan's being in Baldivia, ordered the Money ashore again. These Prisoners likewise informed us that the Gentlemen (Inhabitants of Truxillo) were building a Fort close by the Sea, purposely to hinder the designs of any that should attempt to land there. Upon this News we altered our former Resolutions, and resolved to go with our three Prizes to the Gallapagos, which are a great many large Islands, some lying under the Equator, others on each side of it.

The 19th Day in the Evening we sailed from the Island Lobos, with Captain Eaton in our Company. We carried the three Flour Prizes with us, but our first Prize laden with Timber we left here at an Anchor. When we came within 40 Minutes of the Equator, we steered West, having the Wind at South, a very moderate gentle Gale. It was the 31st Day of May when we first had sight of the Gallapagos Islands. Some of them appeared on our Weather-bow, some on our Lee-bow, others right ahead. We at first sight trimmed our Sails, and steered as near the Wind as we could, striving to get to the Southernmost of them, but our Prizes being deep laden, their Sails but small and thin, and a very small Gale, they could not keep up with us. Therefore we edged away again, a point from the Wind, to keep near them. And in the Evening, the Ship that I was in, and Capt. Eaton's, anchored on the East-side of one of the Easternmost Islands, a Mile from the shore, in sixteen Fathoms Water, clean, white, hard Sand.

The Gallapagos Islands are a great number of uninhabited Islands, lying under and on both sides of the Equator. The Easternmost of them are about 110 Leagues from the Main. They are laid down in the Longitude of 181, reaching to the

Westward as far as 176, therefore their Longitude from England Westward is about 68 degrees. But I believe you Hydrographers do not place them far enough to the Westward. The Spaniards who first discovered them, and in whose draughts alone they are laid down, report them to be a great number stretching North-West from the Line, as far as 5 degrees N., but we saw no more than 14 or 15. Some of them are 7 or 8 Leagues long, and 3 or 4 broad.

They are of a good height, most of them flat and even on the top. Four or five of the Easternmost are rocky, barren and hilly, producing neither Tree, Herb, nor Grass, except a few Dildo-trees by the Seaside. The Dildo-tree is a green prickly shrub, that grows about 10 or 12 feet high, without either Leaf or Fruit. It is as big as a Man's Leg, from the root to the top, and it is full of sharp prickles, growing in thick rows from top to bottom. This shrub is fit for no use, not so much as to burn. Close by the Sea there grows in some Places Bushes of Burton-wood which is very good firing. This sort of Wood grows in many Places in the West Indies, especially in the Bay of Campeachy and the Samballoes. I never saw any in these Seas but here. There is Water on these barren Islands, in ponds and holes among the Rocks. Some of the other Islands are mostly plain and low, and the Land more fertile, producing Trees of diverse sorts, unknown to us. Some of the Westernmost of these Islands are nine or ten Leagues long, and six or seven broad, the Mould deep and black. These produce Trees of great and tall Bodies, especially Mammee-trees, which grow here in great Groves. In these large Islands there are some pretty big Rivers; and in many of the other lesser Islands there are Brooks of good Water.

The Spaniards, when they first discovered these Islands, found Multitudes of Guanoes and Land-turtle, or Tortoise, and named them the Gallapagos Islands. I believe there is no place in the World that is so plentifully stored with those Animals. The Guanoes here are as fat and large as any that I ever saw, and they are so tame that a Man may knock down twenty in an Hour's Time with a Club. The Land-turtle are here so numerous that 5 or 600 Men might subsist on them alone for several Months without any other sort of Provision. They are extraordinarily large and fat, and so sweet that no Pullet eats more pleasantly. One of the largest of these Creatures will weigh 150 or 200 weight, and some of them are 2 feet, or 2 feet 6 inches, over the Calipee, or Belly. I never saw any but at this place that weighed above 30 pounds weight. I have heard that at the Isle of St. Lawrence, or Madagascar; and at the English Forest, an Island near it, also called Don Mascarin and now possessed by the French, there are very large ones, but whether so big, fat and sweet as these, I do not know. There are 3 or 4 sorts of these Creatures in the West Indies. One is called by the Spaniards Hecate. These live mostly in fresh Water-ponds, and seldom come on Land. They weigh about 10 or 15 pounds. They have small Legs and flat Feet, and small long Necks. Another sort is called Tenapen. These are a great deal less than the Hecate: the Shell on their Backs is all carved naturally, finely wrought, and well clouded. The Backs of these are rounder than those before-mentioned. They are otherwise much of the same form. They delight to live in wet swampy places, or on the Land near such places. Both these sorts are very good Meat. They are in great plenty on the Isles of Pines near Cuba. There, the Spanish Hunters, when they meet them in the Woods, bring them home to their Huts, and mark them by notching their Shells, then let them go. This they do to have them at Hand, for they never ramble far from there. When these Hunters return to Cuba after about a Month or six Weeks' stay, they carry with them 3 or 400 or more of these Creatures to sell. For they are very good Meat, and every Man knows his own by their Marks. These Tortoise in the Gallapagos are more like the Hecate, except that, as I said before, they are much bigger and have very long small Necks and little Heads. There are some green Snakes on these Islands, but no other Land Animal that I ever saw. There are great plenty of Turtle-Doves, so tame that a Man may kill 5 or 6 dozen in a Forenoon with a stick. They are somewhat less than a Pigeon, and are very good Meat, and commonly fat.

The Air of these Islands is temperate enough, considering the Clime. There is constantly a fresh Sea-breeze all Day, and cooling, refreshing Winds in the Night. Therefore the Heat is not so violent here as in most Places near the Equator. The time of the Year for the Rains is in November, December and January. Then there is oftentimes excessively hard, tempestuous Weather, mixed with much Thunder and Lightning. Sometimes, before and after these Months, there are moderate refreshing showers, but in May, June, July and August, the Weather is always very fair.

We stayed at one of these Islands which lies under the Equator just one Night, because our Prizes could not get in to Anchor. We refreshed ourselves very well both with Land and Sea-Turtles, and the next Day we sailed from there. The next Island of the Gallapagos that we came to is but two Leagues from this. As soon as we came to an Anchor, we made a Tent ashore for Capt. Cook who was sick. Here we found Sea-Turtle lying ashore on the Sand. This is not customary in the West Indies. We turned them on their Backs so that they might not get away. The next Day more came up, and we found it to be their custom to lie in the Sun. So we never took care to turn them afterwards, but sent ashore the Cook every Morning, who killed as many as served for the Day. This Custom was observed all the time we lay here, feeding sometimes on Land-Turtle, sometimes on Sea-Turtle, there being plenty of either sort. Capt. Davis came here again a second time, and then he went to other Islands on the West-side of these. There he found such plenty of Land-Turtle that he and his Men ate nothing else for the three Months that he stayed there. They were so fat that he saved sixty Jars of Oil out of those that he spent. This Oil served instead of Butter, to eat with Doughboys on his return out of these Seas. He found very convenient Places to career, and good Channels between the Islands and very good anchoring in many Places. He also found plenty of Brooks of good Fresh-water and Fire-wood enough, there being plenty of Trees fit for many uses. Capt. Harris, one that we shall speak of hereafter, came here likewise, and found some Islands that had plenty of Mammee-trees, and pretty large Rivers. We stayed here but 12 Days, in which time we put ashore 5000 Packs of Flour for a Reserve, in case we should have occasion of any before we left these Seas. Here one of our Indian Prisoners informed us that he was born at Ria Lexa, and that he would engage to carry us there. He, being examined of the Strength and Riches of it, satisfied the Company so well that they were resolved to go there.

We had very fair Weather and small Winds on this Voyage from the Gallapagos, and at the Beginning of July we fell in with Cape Blanco, on the Main of Mexico. This is so called from two white Rocks lying off it. When we are off at Sea right against the

Cape, they appear as part of the Cape, but being near the Shore, either to the Eastward or Westward of the Cape, they appear at first view like two Ships under sail. Coming nearer, they are like two high Towers, small, high and steep on all sides, and they are about half a Mile from the Cape. This Cape is in Lat. 9 d. 56 m. It is about the height of Beachy-head in England, on the Coast of Sussex. It is a full Point, with steep Rocks to the Sea. The Top of it is flat and even for about a Mile, and then it gradually falls away on each side with a gentle Descent. It appears very pleasant, being covered with great lofty Trees. From the Cape, on the N.W. side, the Land runs in N.E. for about 4 Leagues, making a small Bay, called by the Spaniards Caldera. From the bottom of this Bay, it is but 14 or 15 Leagues to the Lake of Nicaragua on the North Sea Coast. The way between is somewhat mountainous, but mostly Savannah.

Capt. Cook, who was sick at John Fernando's, continued so till we came within 2 or 3 Leagues of Cape Blanco, and then died of a sudden, though he seemed that Morning to be as likely to live, as he had been some Weeks before. But it is usual with sick Men coming from the Sea, where they have nothing but the Sea-Air, to die off as soon as ever they come within the view of the Land. About four Hours after, we all (namely the Ship that I was in, Captain Eaton, and the great Meal-Prize) came to an Anchor, within a League of the Cape, right against a Brook of fresh Water. Capt. Cook was carried ashore to be buried, and twelve Men carried their Arms to guard those that were ordered to dig the Grave. For although we saw no appearance of Inhabitants, we did not know if the Country might not be thickly inhabited. And before Capt. Cook was interred, three Spanish Indians came to the Place where our Men were digging the Grave, and demanded what they were, and from where they had come. Our Men answered that they had come from Lima and were bound to Ria Lexa, but that, the Captain of one of the Ships dying at Sea, we had been obliged to come to this Place to give him a Christian Burial. The three Spanish Indians, who were very shy at first, began to be very bold, and drawing near, asked many silly Questions. Our Men did not stick at soothing them up with many Falsehoods, purposely to draw them into their clutches. Our Men often laughed at their temerity, and asked them if they had never seen any Spaniards before. They told them that they themselves were Spaniards, and that they lived among Spaniards, and that although they were born there, they had never seen 3 Ships there before. Our Men told them that they might not have seen so many now, if it had not been on an urgent occasion. At length they drilled them by Discourse so near, that our Men laid hold on all three at once. But before Captain Cook was buried, one of them made his escape. The other two were brought off aboard our Ship. Captain Eaton immediately came aboard and examined them. They confessed that they had come purposely to view our Ship, and if possible, to inform themselves what we were. For not long before, the President of Panama had sent a Letter of advice to Nicoya, informing the Magistrates there that some Enemies had come into these Seas and that therefore it behoved them to be careful of themselves.

Nicoya is a small Mulatto Town, about 12 or 14 Leagues East from here, standing on the Banks of a River of that Name. It is a Place very fit for building Ships, therefore most of the Inhabitants are Carpenters, and are commonly employed in building new Ships or repairing old ones. It was here that Capt. Sharp (just after I left him, in the Year 1681) got Carpenters to fix his Ship, before he returned to England. And for that reason it behoved the Spaniards to be careful (according to the Governor of Panama's Advice), lest any Men at other times, wanting such Necessaries as the Place afforded, might again be supplied there. These Spanish Indians likewise told us that they had been sent to this Place in order to view our Ships, fearing these were the ones mentioned by the President of Panama. It being demanded of them to give an account of the Estate and Riches of the Country, they said that the Inhabitants were mostly Husbandmen who were employed either in the Planting and Manuring of Corn, or chiefly about Cattle, they having large Savannahs well stored with Bulls, Cows and Horses; and that by the Seaside in some Places, there grew some Red-wood useful in Dying. Of this they said there was little Profit made, because they were forced to send it to the Lake of Nicaragua, which runs into the North Seas. They also sent there great quantities of Bull and Cow-Hides, and brought from there in Exchange European Commodities, such as Hats, Linen and Woollen, with which they clothed themselves.

After they had given this Relation, they told us that if we wanted Provision there was a Beef-Estantion about three Miles off, where we might kill what we pleased. This was welcome News, for we had had no sort of Flesh since we left the Galla-pagos. Therefore Twenty-four of us immediately entered into two Boats, taking one of these Spanish Indians with us for a Pilot, and went ashore about a League from the Ship. There we hauled our Boats up dry, and all marched away, following our Guide, who soon brought us to some Houses and a large Pen for Cattle. This Pen stood in a large Savannah, about two Miles from our Boats. There were a great many fat Bulls and Cows feeding in the Savannahs. Some of us would have killed three or four to carry on board, but others opposed it, and said it was better to stay all Night, and in the Morning drive the Cattle into the Pen, and then kill 20 or 30, or as many as we pleased. I was minded to return aboard, and endeavoured to persuade them all to go with me, but some would not. Therefore I returned with 11, which was half, and left the other 12 behind. At this place, I saw three or four Tons of the Red-wood, which I take to be the sort of Wood called in Jamaica Blood-wood or Nicaragua-wood. We who returned aboard met no one to oppose us, and the next Day, we expected our Consorts that we had left ashore. But none came: therefore at four o'clock in the Afternoon, ten Men went in our Canoe to see what had become of them. When they came to the Bay where we had landed to go to the Estantion, they found our Men all on a small Rock, half a Mile from the shore, standing in the Water up to their Waists. These Men had slept ashore in a House, and turned out early in the Morning to pen the Cattle. Two or three went one way, and as many another way to get the Cattle to the Pen, and others stood at the Pen to drive them in. When they were thus scattered, about 40 or 50 armed Spaniards came in among them. Our Men immediately called to each other, and drew together in a Body before the Spaniards could attack them, and marched to their Boat, which was hauled up dry on the Sand. But when they came to the sandy Bay, they found their Boat all in Flames. This was a very unpleasing sight, for they did not know how to get aboard, unless they marched by Land to the Place where Capt. Cook was buried, which was near a League. The greatest part of the way was thick Woods where the Spaniards might easily lay an Ambush for them, at which they are very expert. On the other side, the Spaniards now thought them secure, and therefore came to them and asked them if they would be pleased to walk to their Plantations, with many other such flouts. But our Men answered never a Word.

It was about half-ebb when one of our Men took notice of a Rock a good distance from the shore, just appearing above Water. He showed it to his Consorts and told them it would be a good Castle for them if they could get there. They all wished themselves there, for the Spaniards, who lay as yet at a good distance from them behind the Bushes, being secure of their Prey, began now and then to whistle a shot among them. Having therefore well considered the place, together with the danger they were in, they proposed to send one of the tallest Men to try if the Sea between them and the Rock were fordable. This Counsel they presently put in Execution, and found it according to their desire. So they all marched over to the Rock where they remained till the Canoe came to them, which was about seven Hours. It was the latter part of the Ebb when they first went over, and then the Rock was dry. But when the Flood-tide returned again, the Rock was covered, and the Water still flowing, so that if our Canoe had stayed but one Hour longer, they might have been in as great a danger of their Lives from the Sea, as before from the Spaniards, for the Tide rises here about eight feet.

The Spaniards remained on the shore, expecting to see them destroyed, but never came from behind the Bushes, where they had first planted themselves. They had no more than 3 or 4 Hand-guns, the rest of them being armed with Lances. The Spaniards in these parts are very expert in heaving or darting the Lance, with which upon Occasion, they will do great Feats, especially in Ambuscades. And by their good Will, they care not for fighting otherwise, but content themselves with standing aloof, threatening and calling Names, at which they are as expert as the other; so that if their Tongues be quiet, we always take it for granted they have laid some Ambush. Before Night, our Canoe came aboard, and brought our Men all safe.

The Day before we left here, Mr. Edward Davis, the Company's Quarter-Master, was made Captain by consent of all the Company, for it was his Place by Succession. The 20th Day of July we sailed from this Bay of Caldera, with Capt. Eaton, and our Prize which we had brought from the Gallapagos in Company, directing our Course for Ria Lexa.

Dampier continued the pirate life for another four years. He profited nothing, and returned to England destitute. Aside from a half-share in a tattooed South Sea islander his possessions stretched to little save for a hollow-bamboo tube in which was stashed a diary of his life on the waves. Revised and extended, Dampier's journal was published in two volumes, A New Voyage round the World, *1697, and* Voyages and Descriptions, *1699. A major source of information about the buccaneers, they also provided accurate and rich reports of the natural phenomena Dampier had encountered on his travels. Indeed, it was as a naturalist, rather than as a pirate that Dampier found his fame (fortune tended to avoid him), and the government commissioned him to explore Australia. Dampier, however, made a poor captain and little emerged from his Australia voyage – apart from the book,* A Voyage to New Holland *– save for Dampier's own court martial for mistreating his men. A decade of privateering with, among others, Thomas Stradling and Woodes Rogers ensued, before Dampier retired to a modestly comfortable old age.*

"the spoil . . . which they received from that ship
was almost incalculable"

AVERY'S PRIZE

Charles Ellms

Henry Avery's seizure of the Moghul of India's treasure ship, Gang-i-sawai, *ranks as one of the most successful of piratical exploits. Although the 19th century pirate historian Charles Ellms suggests that Avery died in poverty, this may be wishful moral thinking. The end of Avery (who also sailed under the names of Every, Long Ben, Benjamin Bridgeman) is unknown.*

During his own time the adventures of Captain Avery were the subject of general conversation in Europe. It was reported that he had married the Great Mogul's daughter, who was taken in an Indian ship that fell into his hands, and that he was about to be the founder of a new monarchy – that he gave commissions in his own name to the captains of his ships, and the commanders of his forces, and was acknowledged by them as their prince. In consequence of these reports, it was at one time resolved to fit out a strong squadron to go and take him and his men; and at another time it was proposed to invite him home with all his riches, by the offer of his Majesty's pardon. These reports, however, were soon discovered to be groundless, and he was actually starving without a shilling, while he was represented as in the possession of millions. Not to exhaust the patience, or lessen the curiosity of the reader, the facts in Avery's life shall be briefly related.

He was a native of Devonshire (Eng.), and at an early period sent to sea; advanced to the station of a mate in a merchantman, he performed several voyages. It happened previous to the peace of Ryswick, when there existed an alliance between Spain, England, Holland, and other powers, against France, that the

French in Martinque carried on a smuggling trade with the
Spaniards on the continent of Peru. To prevent their intrusion
into the Spanish dominions, a few vessels were commanded to
cruise upon that coast, but the French ships were too strong for
them; the Spaniards, therefore, came to the resolution of hiring
foreigners to act against them. Accordingly, certain merchants of
Bristol fitted out two ships of thirty guns, well manned, and
provided with every necessary munition, and commanded them
to sail for Corunna to receive their orders.

Captain Gibson commanded one of these ships, and Avery
appears to have been his mate, in the year 1715. He was a fellow of
more cunning than courage, and insinuating himself into the
confidence of some of the boldest men in the ship, he represented
the immense riches which were to be acquired upon the Spanish
coast, and proposed to run off with the ship. The proposal was
scarcely made when it was agreed upon, and put in execution at
ten o'clock the following evening. Captain Gibson was one of
those who mightily love their bottle, and spent much of his time
on shore; but he remained on board that night, which did not,
however, frustrate their design, because he had taken his usual
dose, and so went to bed. The men who were not in the confederacy went also to bed, leaving none upon deck but the
conspirators. At the time agreed upon, the long boat of the other
ship came, and Avery hailing her in the usual manner, he was
answered by the men in her, "Is your drunken boatswain on
board?" which was the watchword agreed between them. Avery
replying in the affirmative, the boat came alongside with sixteen
stout fellows, who joined in the adventure. They next secured the
hatches, then softly weighed anchor, and immediately put to sea
without bustle or noise. There were several vessels in the bay,
besides a Dutchman of forty guns, the captain of which was
offered a considerable reward to go in pursuit of Avery, but he
declined. When the captain awoke, he rang his bell, and Avery
and another conspirator going into the cabin, found him yet half
asleep. He inquired, saying, "What is the matter with the ship?
does she drive? what weather is it?" supposing that it had been a
storm, and that the ship was driven from her anchors. "No, no,"
answered Avery, "we're at sea, with a fair wind and a good
weather." "At sea!" said the captain: "how can that be?"
"Come," answered Avery, "don't be in a fright, but put on your

clothes, and I'll let you into a secret. You must know that I am captain of this ship now, and this is my cabin, therefore you must walk out; I am bound to Madagascar, with a design of making my own fortune, and that of all the brave fellows joined with me."

The captain, having a little recovered his senses, began to understand his meaning. However, his fright was as great as before, which Avery perceiving, desired him to fear nothing; "for," said he, "if you have a mind to make one of us, we will receive you; and if you turn sober, and attend to business, perhaps in time I may make you one of my lieutenants; if not, here's a boat, and you shall be set on shore." Gibson accepted of the last proposal; and the whole crew being called up to know who was willing to go on shore with the captain, there were only about five or six who chose to accompany him.

Avery proceeded on his voyage to Madagascar, and it does not appear that he captured any vessels upon his way. When arrived at the northeast part of that island, he found two sloops at anchor, which, upon seeing him, slipped their cables and ran themselves ashore, while the men all landed and concealed themselves in the woods. These were two sloops which the men had run off with from the East Indies, and seeing Avery's ship, supposed that he had been sent out after them. Suspecting who they were, he sent some of his men on shore to inform them that they were friends, and to propose a union for their common safety. The sloops' men being well armed, had posted themselves in a wood, and placed sentinels to observe whether the ship's men were landing to pursue them. The sentinels only observing two or three men coming towards them unarmed, did not oppose them. Upon being informed that they were friends, the sentinels conveyed them to the main body, where they delivered their message. They were at first afraid that it was a stratagem to entrap them, but when the messengers assured them that their captain had also run away with his ship, and that a few of their men along with him would meet them unarmed, to consult matters for their common advantage, confidence was established, and they were mutually well pleased, as it added to their strength.

Having consulted what was most proper to be attempted they endeavoured to get off the sloops, and hastened to prepare all things, in order to sail for the Arabian coast. Near the river Indus, the man at the mast-head espied a sail, upon which they gave

chase; as they came nearer to her, they discovered that she was a
tall vessel, and might turn out to be an East Indiaman. She,
however, proved a better prize; for when they fired at her she
hoisted Mogul colors, and seemed to stand upon her defence.
Avery only cannonaded at a distance, when some of his men
began to suspect that he was not the hero they had supposed. The
sloops, however attacked, the one on the bow, and another upon
the quarter of the ship, and so boarded her. She then struck her
colors. She was one of the Great Mogul's own ships, and there
were in her several of the greatest persons in his court, among
whom, it was said, was one of his daughters going upon a
pilgrimage to Mecca; and they were carrying with them rich
offerings to present at the shrine of Mahomet. It is a well-known
fact, that the people of the east travel with great magnificence, so
that these had along with them all their slaves and attendants,
with a large quantity of vessels of gold and silver, and immense
sums of money to defray their expenses by land; the spoil therefore which they received from that ship was almost incalculable.

Taking the treasure on board their own ships, and plundering
their prize of every thing valuable, they then allowed her to depart.
As soon as the Mogul received this intelligence, he threatened to
send a mighty army to extirpate the English from all their settlements upon the Indian coast. The East India Company were
greatly alarmed, but found means to calm his resentment, by
promising to search for the robbers, and deliver them into his
hands. The noise which this made over all Europe gave birth to the
rumors that were circulated concerning Avery's greatness.

In the mean time, our adventurers made the best of their way
back to Madagascar, intending to make that place the deposit of
all their treasure, to build a small fort, and to keep always a few
men there for its protection. Avery, however, disconcerted this
plan, and rendered it altogether unnecessary.

While steering their course, Avery sent a boat to each of the
sloops, requesting that the chiefs would come on board his ship to
hold a conference. They obeyed, and being assembled, he suggested to them the necessity of securing the property which they
had acquired in some safe place on shore, and observed that the
chief difficulty was to get it safe on shore; adding that, if either of
the sloops should be attacked alone, they would not be able to
make any great resistance, and thus she must either be sunk or

taken with all the property on board. That, for his part, his ship was so strong, so well manned, and such a swift-sailing vessel, that he did not think it was possible for any other ship to take or overcome her. Accordingly, he proposed that all their treasure should be sealed up in three chests; that each of the captains should have keys and that they should not be opened until all were present; that the chests should be then put on board his ship, and afterwards lodged in some safe place upon land.

This proposal seemed so reasonable, and so much for the common good, that it was without hesitation agreed to, and all the treasure deposited in three chests, and carried to Avery's ship. The weather being favorable, they remained all three in company during that and the next day; meanwhile Avery, tampering with his men, suggested that they had now on board what was sufficient to make them all happy; "and what," continued he, "should hinder us from going to some country where we are not known, and living on shore all the rest of our days in plenty?" They soon understood his hint, and all readily consented to deceive the men of the sloops, and fly with all the booty; this they effected during the darkness of the following night. The reader may easily conjecture what were the feelings and indignation of the other two crews in the morning, when they discovered that Avery had made off with all their property.

Avery and his men hastened towards America, and being strangers in that country, agreed to divide the booty, to change their names, and each separately to take up his residence, and live in affluence and honor. The first land they approached was the Island of Providence, then newly settled. It however occurred to them, that the largeness of their vessel, and the report that one had been run off with from the Groine, might create suspicion; they resolved therefore to dispose of their vessel at Providence. Upon this resolution, Avery, pretending that his vessel had been equipped for privateering, and having been unsuccessful, he had orders from the owners to dispose of her to the best advantage, soon found a merchant. Having thus sold his own ship, he immediately purchased a small sloop.

In this he and his companions embarked, and landed at several places in America, where, none suspecting them, they dispersed and settled in the country. Avery, however, had been careful to conceal the greater part of the jewels and other valuable articles, so that his riches were immense. Arriving at Boston, he was almost resolved to settle there, but, as the greater part of his wealth consisted of diamonds, he was apprehensive that he could not dispose of them at that place, without being taken up as a pirate. Upon reflection, therefore, he resolved to sail for Ireland, and in a short time arrived in the northern part of that kingdom, and his men dispersed into several places. Some of them obtained the pardon of King William, and settled in that country.

The wealth of Avery, however, now proved of small service, and occasioned him great uneasiness. He could not offer his diamonds for sale in that country without being suspected. Considering, therefore, what was best to be done, he thought there might be some person at Bristol he could venture to trust. Upon this he resolved, and going into Devonshire, sent to one of his friends to meet him at a town called Bideford. When he had unbosomed himself to him and other pretended friends, they agreed that the safest plan would be to put his effects into the hands of some wealthy merchants, and no inquiry would be made how they came by them. One of these friends told him, he was acquainted with some who were very fit for the purpose, and if he would allow them a handsome commission, they would do the business faithfully. Avery liked the proposal, particularly as he could think of no other way of managing this matter, since he could not appear to act for himself. Accordingly, the merchants paid Avery a visit at Bideford, where, after strong protestations of honor and integrity, he delivered them his effects, consisting of diamonds and some vessels of gold. After giving him a little money for his present subsistence, they departed.

He changed his name, and lived quietly at Bideford, so that no notice was taken of him. In a short time his money was all spent, and he heard nothing from his merchants though he wrote to them repeatedly; at last they sent him a small supply, but it was not sufficient to pay his debts. In short, the remittances they sent him were so trifling, that he could with difficulty exist. He therefore determined to go privately to Bristol, and have an interview with the merchants himself – where, instead of money, he met with a mortifying repulse; for, when he desired them to come to an account with him, they silenced him by threatening to disclose his character; the merchants thus proving themselves as good pirates on land as he was at sea.

Whether he was frightened by these menaces, or had seen some other person who recognised him, is not known; however, he went immediately to Ireland, and from thence solicited his merchants very strongly for a supply, but to no purpose; so that he was reduced to beggary. In this extremity he was determined to return, and cast himself upon the mercy of these honest Bristol merchants, let the consequence be what it would. He went on board a trading-vessel, and worked his passage over to Plymouth, from whence he travelled on foot to Bideford. He had been there but a few days, when he fell sick and died; not being worth so much as would buy him a coffin!

RICHEST PRIZES TAKEN BY PIRATES IN THE INDIAN OCEAN AND RED SEA, 1690–1722

Captain	Probable Value	Prize
John TAYLOR in the *Cassandro*, Olivier LA BOUCHE in the *Victory* (1721)	£500,000 in diamonds and treasure, £375,000 in other cargo. Divided into shares worth at least £3,600 each	*Nostra Senhora de Cabo*, a Portuguese vessel taken at Reunion Island
Henry AVERY in the *Fancy* and five other captains (1695)	£325,000 (estimate, probably low, by East India Company). The *Fancy* took most of the loot, about £1,000 cash per man plus jewels	*Fateh Mohammed* and *Gang-i-sawai (Gunsway)* taken in the Red Sea
Edmund CONDENT in the *Flying Dragon* (1720)	£150,000 (East Indian Company estimate) in money, drugs, spices, and silk. About £2,000 per share	A large (Arab?) ship taken near Bombay

Captain	Probable Value	Prize
Dirk CHIVERS and Robert CULLIFORD commanding the *Soldado* and the *Mocha* (1698)	£130,000 in cash. More than £700 per share	*Great Mohammed*, Indian ship taken in the Red Sea
John BOWEN in the *Speaker* (1700 or 1701)	£100,000	Indian vessel taken near the mouth of the Red Sea
Edward ENGLAND with the *Fancy* and the *Victory* (1720)	£75,000 according to some reports	*Cassandra*, an East India Company vessel taken at Johanna Island in the Comoros
Thomas HOWARD in consort with John Bowen in the *Speedy Return* (1703)	More than £70,000	Two Indian vessels taken in the Red Sea
John HALSEY with the *Charles* (1701)	£50,000 in cash	Two British ships taken at Mocha in the Red Sea
William KIDD in the *Adventure Galley* (1698)	£45,000 (estimate by Indian merchants), £22,500 (East India Company estimate)	*Quedah Merchants*, an Indian vessel taken off Cochin, India

From *The Wordsworth Dictionary of Pirates*, Jan Rogozinski, Wordsworth Editions Ltd., 1997. Copyright © 1995 Jan Rogozinski

VOYAGE TO EXECUTION DOCK: THE UNFORTUNATE CAREER OF CAPTAIN KIDD

Charles Ellms

Little is known of William Kidd's early life, save that he was born in Scotland. He first enters the records in 1689 when the British, needy of men and vessels to fight the Nine Years' War, licensed the pirate William Kidd as privateer in the Caribbean. He was also found to be useful to the Union Jack during King William's War, at the end of which he settled in New York and married a wealthy widow. It was in New York that Kidd became involved in the project that brought him his infamy and his early demise.

The easy access to the harbor of New York, the number of hiding-places about its waters, and the laxity of its newly organized government, about the year 1695, made it a great rendezvous of pirates, where they might dispose of their booty and concert new depredations. As they brought home with them wealthy lading of all kinds, the luxuries of the tropics, and the sumptuous spoils of the Spanish provinces, and disposed of them with the proverbial carelessness of freebooters, they were welcome visitors to the thrifty traders of New York. Crews of these desperadoes, therefore, the runagates of every country and every clime, might be seen swaggering in open day about the streets, elbowing its quiet inhabitants, trafficking their rich outlandish plunder at half or quarter price to the wary merchant; and then squandering their prize-money in taverns, drinking, gambling, singing, carousing and astounding the neighborhood with midnight brawl and revelry. At length these excesses rose to such a height as to become a scandal to the provinces, and to call loudly for the interposition of government. Measures were accordingly taken to put a stop to this widely extended evil, and to drive the pirates out of the colonies.

Among the distinguished individuals who lurked about the colonies, was Captain Robert Kidd,* who in the beginning of King William's war, commanded a privateer in the West Indies, and by his several adventurous actions, acquired the reputation of a brave man, as well as an experienced seaman. But he had now become notorious, as a nondescript animal of the ocean. He was somewhat of a trader, something more of a smuggler, but mostly a pirate. He had traded many years among the pirates, in a little rakish vessel, that could run into all kinds of water. He knew all their haunts and lurking places, and was always hooking about on mysterious voyages.

Upon the good old maxim of "setting a rogue to catch a rogue", Capt. Kidd was recommended by the Lord Bellamont, then governor of Barbadoes, as well as by several other persons, to the government here, as a person very fit to be entrusted to the command of a government ship, and to be employed in cruising upon the pirates, as knowing those seas perfectly well, and being acquainted with all their lurking places; but what reasons governed the politics of those times, I cannot tell, but this proposal met with no encouragement here, though it is certain it would have been of great consequence to the subject, our merchants suffering incredible damages by those robbers.

Upon this neglect, the Lord Bellamont and some others, who knew what great captures had been made by the pirates, and what a prodigious wealth must be in their possession, were tempted to fit out a ship at their own private charge, and to give the command of her to Captain Kidd; and to give the thing a greater reputation, as well as to keep their seamen under better command, they procured the king's commission for the said Capt. Kidd, of which the following is an exact copy:

William Rex,
WILLIAM THE THIRD, by the grace of God, King of England, Scotland, France and Ireland, defender of the faith, &c. To

---

* His real name was William Kidd.

our trusty and well beloved Capt. ROBERT KIDD, commander of the ship the Adventure galley, or to any other, the
commander of the same for the time being, *Greeting:*
Whereas we are informed, that Capt. Thomas Too, John
Ireland, Capt. Thomas Wake, and Capt. William Maze or
Mace, and other subjects, natives or inhabitants of New
York, and elsewhere, in our plantations in America, have
associated themselves with divers others, wicked and ill-
disposed persons, and do, against the law of nations, commit many and great piracies, robberies and depredations on
the seas upon the parts of America, and in other parts, to the
great hindrance and discouragement of trade and navigation, and to the great danger and hurt of our loving subjects,
our allies, and all others, navigating the seas upon their
lawful occasions. Now KNOW YE, that we being desirous to
prevent the aforesaid mischiefs, and as much as in us lies, to
bring the said pirates, free-booters and sea-rovers to justice,
have thought fit, and do hereby give and grant to the said
Robert Kidd, (to whom our commissioners for exercising
the office of Lord High Admiral of England, have granted a
commission as a private man-of-war, bearing date the 11th
day of December, 1695,) and unto the commander of the
said ship for the time being, and unto the officers, mariners,
and others which shall be under your command, full power
and authority to apprehend, seize, and take into your
custody as well the said Capt. Thomas Too, John Ireland,
Capt. Thomas Wake, and Capt. Wm. Maze or Mace, as all
such pirates, free-booters, and sea-rovers, being either our
subjects, or of other nations associated with them, which
you shall meet with upon the seas or coasts of America, or
upon any other seas or coasts, with all their ships and
vessels, and all such merchandizes, money, goods, and
wares as shall be found on board, or with them, in case
they shall willingly yield themselves; but if they will not
yield without fighting, then you are by force to compel them
to yield. And we also require you to bring, or cause to be
brought, such pirates, free-booters, or sea-rovers, as you
shall seize, to a legal trial, to the end they may be proceeded
against according to the law in such cases. And we do
hereby command all our officers, ministers, and other

our loving subjects whatsoever, to be aiding and assisting to you in the premises. And we do hereby enjoin you to keep an exact journal of your proceedings in execution of the premises, and set down the names of such pirates, and of their officers and company, and the names of such ships and vessels as you shall by virtue of these presents take and seize, and the quantities of arms, ammunition, provision, and lading of such ships, and the true value of the same, as near as you judge. And we do hereby strictly charge and command you, as you will answer the contrary at your peril, that you do not, in any manner, offend or molest our friends or allies, their ships or subjects, by colour or pretence of these presents, or the authority thereby granted. *In witness whereof*, we have caused our great seal of England to be affixed to these presents. Given at our court in Kensington, the 26th day of January, 1695, in the 7th year of our reign.

Capt. Kidd had also another commission, which was called a commission of reprisals; for it being then war time, this commission was to justify him in the taking of French merchant ships, in case he should meet with any; but as this commission is nothing to our present purpose, we shall not burthen the reader with it.

Previous to sailing, Capt. Kidd buried his bible on the seashore, in Plymouth Sound; its divine precepts being so at variance with his wicked course of life, that he did not choose to keep a book which condemned him in his lawless career.

With these two commissions he sailed out of Plymouth in May, 1696, in the *Adventure* galley, of 30 guns, and 80 men; the place he first designed for was New York; in his voyage thither, he took a French banker, but this was no act of piracy, he having a commission for that purpose, as we have just observed.

When he arrived at New York, he put up articles for engaging more hands, it being necessary to his ship's crew, since he proposed to deal with a desperate enemy. The terms he offered, were, that every man should have a share of what was taken, reserving for himself and owners forty shares. Upon which encouragement he soon increased his company to 155 men.

With this company he sailed first for Madeira, where he took in wine and some other necessaries; from thence he proceeded to Bonavista, one of the Cape de Verd Islands, to furnish the ship with salt, and from thence went immediately to St. Jago, another of the Cape de Verd Islands, in order to stock himself with provisions. When all this was done, he bent his course to Madagascar, the known rendezvous of pirates. In his way he fell in with Capt. Warren, commodore of three men of war; he acquainted him with his design, kept them company two or three days, and then leaving them, made the best of his way for Madagascar, where he arrived in February, 1696, just nine months from his departure from Plymouth.

It happened that at this time the pirate ships were most of them out in search of prey; so that according to the best intelligence Capt. Kidd could get, there was not one of them at that time about the island; wherefore, having spent some time in watering his ship and taking in more provisions, he thought of trying his fortune on the coast of Malabar, where he arrived in the mouth of June following, four months from his reaching Madagascar. Hereabouts he made an unsuccessful cruise, touching sometimes at the island of Mohila, and sometimes at that of Johanna, between Malabar and Madagascar. His provisions were every day wasting, and his ship began to want repair; wherefore, when he was at Johanna, he found means of borrowing a sum of money from some Frenchmen who had lost their ship, but saved their effects, and with this he purchased materials for putting his ship in good repair.

It does not appear all this while that he had the least design of turning pirate; for near Mohila and Johanna both, he met with several Indian ships richly laden, to which he did not offer the least violence, though he was strong enough to have done what he pleased with them; and the first outrage or depredation I find he committed upon mankind, was after his repairing his ship, and leaving Johanna; he touched at a place called Mabbee, upon the Red Sea, where he took some Guinea corn from the natives, by force. After this, he sailed to Bab's Key, a place upon a little island at the entrance of the Red Sea. Here it was that he first began to open himself to his ship's company, and let them understand that he intended to change his measures; for, happening to talk of the Mocha fleet, which was to sail that way, he said, "*We have been unsuccessful hitherto; but courage, my boys, we'll make our fortunes out of this fleet;*" and finding that none of them appeared averse to it, he ordered a boat out, well manned, to go upon the coast to make discoveries, commanding them to take a prisoner and bring him to him, or get intelligence any way they could. The boat returned in a few days, bringing him word, that they saw fourteen or fifteen ships ready to sail, some with English, some with Dutch, and some with Moorish colors.

We cannot account for this sudden change in his conduct, otherwise than by supposing that he first meant well, while he had hopes of making his fortune by taking of pirates; but now weary of ill success, and fearing lest his owners, out of humor at their great expenses, should dismiss him, and he should want employment, and be marked out for an unlucky man; rather, I say, than run the hazard of poverty, he resolved to do his business one way, since he could not do it another.

He therefore ordered a man continually to watch at the mast head, lest this fleet should go by them; and about four days after, towards evening, it appeared in sight, being convoyed by one English and one Dutch man-of-war. Kidd soon fell in with them, and getting into the midst of them, fired at a Moorish ship which was next him; but the men-of-war taking the alarm, bore down upon Kidd, and firing upon him, obliged him to sheer off, he not being strong enough to contend with them. Now he had begun hostilities, he resolved to go on, and therefore he went and cruised along the coast of Malabar. The first prize he met was a small vessel belonging to Aden; the vessel was Moorish, and the owners were Moorish merchants, but the master was an Englishman; his name was Parker. Kidd forced him and a Portuguese that was called Don Antonio, which were all the Europeans on board, to take on with him; the first he designed as a pilot, and the last as an interpreter. He also used the men very cruelly, causing them to be hoisted up by the arms, and drubbed with a naked cutlass, to force them to discover whether they had money on board, and where it lay; but as they had neither gold nor silver on board, he got nothing by his cruelty; however, he took from them a bale of pepper, and a bale of coffee, and so let them go.

A little time after he touched at Carawar, a place upon the same coast, where, before he arrived, the news of what he had done to the Moorish ship had reached them; for some of the English merchants there had received an account of it from the owners, who corresponded with them; wherefore, as soon as Kidd came in, he was suspected to be the person who committed this piracy;

and one Mr. Harvey and Mr. Mason, two of the English factory, came on board and asked for Parker, and Antonio, the Portuguese; but Kidd denied that he knew any such persons, having secured them both in a private place in the hold, where they were kept for seven or eight days, that is, till Kidd sailed from thence.

However, the coast was alarmed, and a Portuguese man-of-war was sent out to cruise. Kidd met with her, and fought her about six hours, gallantly enough; but finding her too strong to be taken, he quitted her; for he was able to run away from her when he would. Then he went to a place called Porca, where he watered his ship and bought a number of hogs of the natives to victual his company.

Soon after this, he came up with a Moorish ship, the master whereof was a Dutchman, called Schipper Mitchell, and chased her under French colors, which they observing hoisted French colors too; when he came up with her, he hailed her in French, and they having a Frenchman on board, answered him in the same language; upon which he ordered them to send their boat on board; they were obliged to do so, and having examined who they were, and from whence they came, he asked the Frenchman who was a passenger, if he had a French pass for himself; the Frenchman gave him to understand that he had. Then he told the Frenchman that he must pass for captain, and by—, says he, you are the captain; the Frenchman durst not refuse doing as he would have him. The meaning of this was, that he would seize the ship as fair prize, and as if she had belonged to French subjects, according to a commission he had for that purpose; though one would think, after what he had already done, he need not have recourse to a quibble to give his actions a colour.

In short, he took the cargo, and sold it some time after; yet still he seemed to have some fears upon him, lest these proceedings should have a bad end; for, coming up with a Dutch ship some time after, when his men thought of nothing but attacking her, Kidd opposed it; upon which a mutiny arose, and the majority being for taking the said ship, and arming themselves to man the boat to go and seize her, he told them, such as did, never should come on board him again; which put an end to the design, so that he kept company with the said ship some time, without offering her any violence. However, this dispute was the occasion of an accident, upon which an indictment was grounded against Kidd;

for Moor, the gunner, being one day upon deck, and talking with Kidd about the said Dutch ship, some words arose between them, and Moor told Kidd, that he had ruined them all; upon which Kidd, calling him a dog, took up a bucket and struck him with it, which breaking his scull, he died next day.

But Kidd's penitential fit did not last long; for coasting along Malabar, he met with a great number of boats, all of which he plundered. Upon the same coast he also fell in with a Portuguese ship, which he kept possession of a week, and then having taken out of her some chests of India goods, thirty jars of butter, with some wax, iron and a hundred bags of rice, he let her go.

Much about the same time he went to one of the Malabar islands for wood and water, and his cooper being ashore, was murdered by the natives; upon which Kidd himself landed, and burnt and pillaged several of their houses, the people running away; but having taken one, he caused him to be tied to a tree, and commanded one of his men to shoot him; then putting to sea again, he took the greatest prize which fell into his hands while he followed this trade; this was a Moorish ship of 400 tons, richly laden, named the *Queda Merchant*, the master whereof was an Englishman, by the name of Wright; for the Indians often make use of English or Dutchmen to command their ships, their own mariners not being so good artists in navigation. Kidd chased her under French colors, and having come up with her, he ordered her to hoist out her boat and send on board of him, which being done, he told Wright he was his prisoner; and informing himself concerning the said ship, he understood there were no Europeans on board, except two Dutch and one Frenchman, all the rest being Indians or Armenians, and that the Armenians were part owners of the cargo. Kidd gave the Armenians to understand, that if they would offer anything that was worth his taking for their ransom, he would hearken to it. Upon which, they proposed to pay him 20,000 rupees, not quite £3,000 sterling; but Kidd judged this would be making a bad bargain, wherefore he rejected it, and setting the crew on shore, at different places on the coast, he soon sold as much of the cargo as came to ten thousand pounds. With part of it he also trafficked, receiving in exchange provisions, or such other goods as he wanted; by degrees he disposed of the whole cargo, and when the division was made, it came to about £200 a man; and having reserved forty shares to himself, his dividend amounted to about £8,000 sterling.

The Indians along the coast came on board and trafficked with all freedom, and he punctually performed his bargains, till about the time he was ready to sail; and then thinking he should have no further occasion for them, he made no scruple of taking their goods and setting them on shore, without any payment in money or goods, which they little expected; for as they had been used to deal with pirates, they always found them men of honor in the way of trade; a people, enemies to deceit, and that scorned to rob but in their own way.

Kidd put some of his men on board the *Queda Merchant*, and with this ship and his own sailed for Madagascar. As soon as he had arrived and cast anchor, there came on board of him a canoe, in which were several Englishmen, who had formerly been well acquainted with Kidd. As soon as they saw him they saluted him, and told him they were informed he was come to take them, and hang them, which would be a little unkind in such an old acquaintance. Kidd soon dissipated their doubts, by swearing he had no such design, and that he was now in every respect their brother, and just as bad as they; and calling for a cup of bomboo, drank their captain's health.

These men belonged to a pirate ship, called the *Resolution*, formerly the *Mocha Merchant*, whereof one Capt. Culliford was commander, and which lay at anchor not far from them. Kidd went on board with them, promising them his friendship and assistance, and Culliford in his turn came on board of Kidd; and Kidd, to testify his sincerity in iniquity, finding Culliford in want of some necessaries, made him a present of an anchor and some guns, to fit him out for sea again.

The *Adventure* galley was now so old and leaky, that they were forced to keep two pumps continually going; wherefore Kidd shifted all the guns and tackle out of her into the *Queda Merchant*, intending her for his man-of-war; and as he had divided the money before, he now made a division of the remainder of the cargo; soon after which, the greatest part of the company left him, some going on board Capt. Culliford, and others absconding into the country, so that he had not above 40 men left.

He put to sea, and happened to touch at Amboyna, one of the Dutch spice islands, where he was told that the news of his actions had reached England, and that he was there declared a pirate.

The truth of it is, his piracies so alarmed our merchants that some motions were made in parliament, to inquire into the commission that was given him, and the persons who fitted him out. These proceedings seem to lean a little hard upon Lord Bellamont, who thought himself so touched thereby, that he published a justification of himself in a pamphlet, after Kidd's execution. In the meantime it was thought advisable, in order to stop the course of these piracies, to publish a proclamation, offering the king's free pardon to all such pirates as should voluntarily surrender themselves, whatever piracies they had been guilty of, at any time before the last day of April, 1699 – that is to say, for all piracies committed eastward of the Cape of Good Hope, to the longitude and meridian of Socatora, and Cape Cormorin; in which proclamation, Avery and Kidd were excepted by name.

When Kidd left Amboyna he knew nothing of this proclamation, for certainly had he had notice of his being excepted in it, he would not have been so infatuated, as to run himself into the very jaws of danger; but relying upon his interest with the Lord Bellamont, and fancying that a French pass or two he found on board some of the ships he took, would serve to countenance the matter, and that part of the booty he got would gain him new friends – I say, all these things made him flatter himself that all would be hushed, and that justice would but wink at him. Wherefore he sailed directly for Boston laden with booty, with a crew of swaggering companions at his heels. But no sooner did he show himself in Boston, than the alarm was given of his reappearance, and measures were taken to arrest him. The daring character which Kidd had acquired, however, and the desperate fellows who followed like bull-dogs at his heels, caused a little delay in his arrest. He took advantage of this to bury the greater part of his immense treasure, which has never been found, and then carried a high head about the streets of Boston. He even attempted to defend himself when arrested, but was secured and thrown into prison. Such was the formidable character of this pirate and his crew, that a frigate was sent to convey them to England for trial.

Accordingly a sessions of admiralty being held at the Old

Bailey, in May 1701, Capt. Kidd, Nicholas Churchill, James How, Robert Lumly, William Jenkins, Gabriel Loff, Hugh Parrot, Richard Barlicorn, Abel Owens and Darby Mullins, were arraigned for piracy and robbery on the high seas, and all found guilty except three; these were Robert Lumly, William Jenkins and Richard Barlicorn, who proving themselves to be apprentices to some of the officers of the ship, and producing their indentures in court, were acquitted.

The three above mentioned, though they were proved to be concerned in taking and sharing the ship and goods mentioned in the indictment, yet, as the gentlemen of the long robe rightly distinguished, there was a great difference between their circumstances and the rest; for there must go an intention of the mind and a freedom of the will to the committing an act of felony or piracy. A pirate is not to be understood to be under constraint, but a free agent; for in this case, the bare act will not make a man guilty, unless the will make it so.

Now a servant, it is true, if he go voluntarily, and have his proportion, he must be accounted a pirate, for then he acts upon his own account, and not by compulsion; and these persons, according to the evidence, received their part, but whether they accounted to their masters for their shares afterwards, is the matter in question, and what distinguishes them as free agents, or men that did go under the compulsion of their master; which being left to the consideration of the jury, they found them *not guilty*.

Kidd was tried upon an indictment of murder also, viz. for killing Moor, the gunner, and found guilty of the same. Nicholas Churchill, and James How pleaded the king's pardon, as having surrendered themselves within the time limited in the proclamation, and Col. Bass, governor of West Jersey, to whom they surrendered, being in court, and called upon, proved the same. However, this plea was overruled by the court, because there being four commissioners named in the proclamation, viz. Capt. Thomas Warren, Israel Hayes, Peter Delannoye, and Christopher Pollard, Esquires, who were appointed commissioners, and sent over on purpose to receive the submissions of such pirates as should surrender, it was adjudged no other person was qualified to receive their surrender, and that they could not be entitled to the benefit of the said proclamation, because they had not in all circumstances complied with the conditions of it.

Darby Mullins urged in his defence, that he served under the king's commission, and therefore could not disobey his commander without incurring great punishments; that whenever a ship or ships went out upon any expedition under the king's commission, the men were never allowed to call their officers to an account, why they did this, or why they did that, because such a liberty would destroy all discipline; that if any thing was done which was unlawful, the officers were to answer it, for the men did no more than their duty in obeying orders. He was told by the court, that acting under the commission justified in what was lawful, but not in what was unlawful. He answered, he stood in need of nothing to justify him in what was lawful, but the case of seamen must be very hard, if they must be brought into such danger for obeying the commands of their officers, and punished for not obeying them; and if they were allowed to dispute the orders, there could be no such thing as command kept up at sea.

This seemed to be the best defence the thing could bear; but his taking a share of the plunder, the seamen's mutinying on board several times, and taking upon them to control the captain, showed there was no obedience paid to the commission; and that they acted in all things according to the custom of pirates and freebooters, which weighing with the jury, they brought him in guilty with the rest.

As to Capt. Kidd's defence, he insisted much on his own innocence, and the villainy of his men. He said, he went out in a laudable employment and had no occasion, being then in good circumstances, to go a pirating; that the men often mutinied against him, and did as they pleased; that he was threatened to be shot in the cabin, and that ninety-five left him at one time, and set fire to his boat, so that he was disabled from bringing his ship home, or the prizes he took, to have them regularly condemned, which he said were taken by virtue of a commission under the broad seal, they having French passes. The captain called one Col. Hewson to his reputation, who gave him an extraordinary character, and declared to the court, that he had served under his command, and been in two engagements with him against the French, in which he fought as well as any man he ever saw; that there were only Kidd's ship and his own against Monsieur du Cass, who commanded a squadron of six sail, and they got the better of him. But this being several years before the facts mentioned in the indictment were committed, proved of no manner of service to the prisoner on his trial.

As to the friendship shown to Culliford, a notorious pirate, Kidd denied, and said, he intended to have taken him, but his men being a parcel of rogues and villains refused to stand by him, and several of them ran away from his ship to the said pirate. But the evidence being full and particular against him, he was found guilty as before mentioned.

When Kidd was asked what he had to say why sentence should not pass against him, he answered, that *he had nothing to say, but that he had been sworn against by perjured and wicked people.* And when sentence was pronounced, he said, *My Lord, it is a very hard sentence. For my part, I am the most innocent person of them all, only I have been sworn against by perjured persons.*

Wherefore about a week after, Capt. Kidd, Nicholas Churchill, James How, Gabriel Loff, Hugh Parrot, Abel Owen, and Darby Mullins, were executed at Execution Dock, and afterwards hung up in chains, at some distance from each other, down the river, where their bodies hung exposed for many years.

Kidd died hard, for the rope with which he was first tied up broke with his weight and he tumbled to the ground. He was tied up a second time, and more effectually. Hence came the story of Kidd's being twice hung.

Such is Captain Kidd's true history; but it has given birth to an innumerable progeny of traditions. The report of his having buried great treasures of gold and silver which he actually did before his arrest, set the brains of all the good people along the coast in a ferment. There were rumors on rumors of great sums of money found here and there, sometimes in one part of the country sometimes in another; of coins with Moorish inscriptions, doubtless the spoils of his eastern prizes.

Some reported the treasure to have been buried in solitary, unsettled places about Plymouth and Cape Cod; but by degrees, various other parts, not only on the eastern coast but along the shores of the Sound, and even Manhattan and Long Island were gilded by these rumors. In fact the vigorous measures of Lord Bellamont had spread sudden consternation among the pirates in every part of the provinces; they had secreted their money and jewels in lonely out-of-the-way places, about the wild shores of the sea coast, and dispersed themselves over the country. The hand of justice prevented many of them from ever returning to regain their buried treasures, which remain to this day thus secreted, and are irrecoverably lost. This is the cause of those frequent reports of trees and rocks bearing mysterious marks, supposed to indicate the spots where treasure lay hidden; and many have been the ransackings after the pirates' booty. A rocky place on the shores of Long Island, called Kidd's Ledge, has received great attention from the money diggers; but they have not as yet discovered any treasures.

PIRATES OF THE SILVER SCREEN

Ten classic pirate movies:

1) *The Black Pirate*, starring Douglas Fairbanks Snr, 1926
2) *Captain Blood*, starring Errol Flynn, 1935
3) *The Buccaneer*, starring Frederic March, 1938
4) *The Sea Hawk*, starring Errol Flynn, 1940
5) *The Black Swan*, starring Tyrone Power, 1942
6) *The Princess and the Pirate*, starring Bob Hope, 1944
7) *Treasure Island*, starring Robert Newton, 1950
8) *The Crimson Pirate*, starring Burt Lancaster, 1952
9) *Hook*, starring Dustin Hoffman, 1991
10) *Pirates of the Caribbean: The Black Pearl*, starring Johnny Depp, 2003

"The privateers rubbed their hands
in pleasure at the profitable deal"

THE TOWN HELD FOR RANSOM

Alexander Winton

To encourage privateering against Spanish commerce the English
government in 1708 surrendered its 20 per cent share of booty taken.
Those duly encouraged by the government "tax relief" included the
burghers of Bristol, who supplied two 300-ton frigates for the
expedition to South America of the young local captain, Woodes
Rogers. The expedition's navigator was the now-famous William
Dampier (see pp 114–25). In early 1709 Rogers's expedition
rounded Cape Horn into the Pacific.

Snow-capped mountains daubing the eastern horizon announced
that the privateers had come for the first time into waters of the
chase. They heeled and tallowed on the placid sea, and rigged the
pinnaces with pursuit guns. The council appointed reliable hands
to search all boarders returning from a prize. Gambling was
outlawed "to prevent men losing all they had", swearing was
forbidden as well, the officers being armed with "ferulas" to rap
any foul-mouthed fellow, "by which we found the men much
broken of that vice".

Two weeks of tedious patrol without a catch made these
precautions look like a sorry joke. Rogers worried about crew
morale: "Our Men begin to repine, that tho come so far, we have
met with no Prize in these Seas." On March 15 a scrap of a vessel,
a sixteen-tonner, sailed innocently under their guns. She wasn't
much, but she was a beginning and Rogers renamed her that. She
would come in handy as courier, or for river work. He took her
along to the inshore Lobos Islands where next night, by the light
of a full moon, they anchored.

The gaunt clay islands were named for their combative breed of seal – *lobos marinos*, sea wolves – noisy, stinking brutes, so fierce that one of them painfully mauled a Dutchman off the *Duke*, and nearly dragged him to his death in the surf. A large bird that Cooke shot as turkey turned out to be vulture, smelling worse than the seal.* However unpleasant, the Lobos provided moorage to fit out the *Beginning* for action. Rogers stepped in a new mast, decked her over, put a well-armed crew aboard, and sent her out to scour nearby waters with the *Duchess*. "She looks very pretty," he thought. Soon the two were back in with a fifty-ton prize. Rogers aptly named this one the *Increase*, and appointed Selkirk her master.* The few sick were put aboard her, she was taken in two by the *Duke*, and the four-ship flotilla sailed north from Lobos.

On April 1 their bows cut through ominous waters of blood-red spawn, but next day they gave – or seemed to give – this omen the lie by capturing two prizes as bloodlessly as one could wish. The *Ascensión*, owned and commanded by the brothers Morel, showed her sail seaward at dawn and struck colors, at a musket shot, before the sun was halfway up the sky. "I saw not so much as a Pistol in her," reported Cooke. A high-pooped galleon of 450 tons, she carried a load of timber and dry goods, some Spanish passengers, and fifty Negro slaves. That evening the *Beginning* took a thirty-five-ton coaster, equally unarmed, with £95 in coin and plate aboard.

Being themselves caught, the prisoners gabbled eagerly of bigger fish still aswim. A bishop worth 200,000 pieces of eight was coming in easy stages from Panama; the widow of Peru's late viceroy was bound up from Lima with the whole fat treasure of her husband's office. Rogers spread the six ships in a sea net for a week, eyes glued to the horizon, but neither appeared. By April 12 water was in short supply, and their position close in to the coast daily increased the danger of a general alarm. The officers decided that if they must land on the continent they might as well attack it, and resolved to storm the north Peru port of Guayaquil.

The crewmen greeted this decision with sullen murmurs of discontent. They were seamen, they argued, and would fight any ship afloat, but they had not signed on with the intention of

* The marooner Alexander Selkirk. See pp. 157–60

storming towns ashore. Rogers thought it best to encourage them
a bit more; grumblers would make a poor assault party. The
council proceeded to expand its rules on plunder:

> Imprim. All manner of Bedding and Clothes without strip-
> ping, all manner of Necessaries, Gold Rings, Buckles,
> Buttons, Liquors, and Provisions for our own expending
> and use, with all sorts of Arms and Ammunition, except
> great Guns for Ships, is Plunder, and shall be divided
> equally amongst the Men of each Ship, with their Prizes,
> wither aboard or ashore, according to the whole Shares.
> 2.   It is also agreed, that any sort of wrought Silver or Gold
> Crucifixes, Gold and Silver Watches, or any other Mova-
> bles found about the Prisoners, or wearing Apparel of any
> kind, shall likewise be Plunder: Provided always we make
> this Reserve, that Mony and Womens Ear-Rings, with loose
> Diamonds, Pearls, and precious Stones be excepted.

Booty captured by one party, declared the council, would be
shared by all. Every man had free and unhampered right of
appeal before an impartial committee if he thought the division of
spoil unfair. Should anyone be missing in action, hostages of the
enemy would be held until he was accounted for.

These added benefits only strengthened responsibilities, the
council warned. Drunkenness, disobedience to orders, cowardice
in the face of danger, debauchery with prisoners, or concealment
of plunder would, at the very least, deprive a man of his share. "If
all the foregoing Rules be strictly follow'd," concluded the
council, "we hope to exceed all other Attempts of this nature
before us in these Parts; and not only to enrich and oblige our
selves and Friends, but even to gain Reputation from our Enemies." Excellent resolve; if wars could be won on paper, the
Spanish were already driven to their knees. Heartened, the flotilla
moved off on the night of April 14 toward the wide gulf of
Guayaquil.

The wind fell to a breeze, the breeze to a calm, and they drifted
all night under limp, dew-drenched canvas. Dawn showed a ship
miles eastward, as though risen from the glassy sea. Frye and
Cooke took the two pinnaces after her. Men rushed gaily over the
Duke's side, John Rogers among them, and dug oars for the

distant quarry. By nine o'clock the *Duke* pinnace, far in the lead, came within musket range. The Spaniard ran up a fringed white satin banner and fired a warning gun. Frye's crew cheered the white banner – surely the bishop clutching his pieces of eight! – but the gunshot sobered them. They shipped oars to await the other pinnace.

When Frye, Cooke and John Rogers put their heads together to devise a battle plan, they were aghast at their careless departure from the ships. Neither pinnace had bothered to mount its swivel gun or fetch water; both were thinly manned, some of the crew had not even brought muskets, and those who had were short of ammunition. There was nothing to do but board.

A stern-chase swivel gun poked over the Spaniard's taffrail, muskets sprouted from her cabin lights. On the chance that the bow would be more vulnerable, the attackers swung wide around the enemy and dashed for her bow quarter. Frye could see the bobbing heads of the musketeers as they ran through the waist of the ship to the forecastle. Halfway in, he backed oars and steadied to see if a volley from his men would clear the bow deck. Muskets blazed in return; a ball crashing into John Rogers' skull killed him instantly. Frye had another dead and two wounded from the enemy's single burst of fire, Cooke had two wounded in his boat.

The sight of blood running down their floorboards quickly put an end to their foolish attack. While Cooke stood guard out of range, the *Duke*'s boat brought back to Woodes Rogers its sad cargo. "To my unspeakable Sorrow," he wrote in his journal, "but as I began this Voyage with a Resolution to go thro it, and the greatest Misfortune or Obstacle shall not deter me, I'll as much as possible avoid being thoughtful and afflicting my self for what can't be recall'd, but indefatigably pursue the Concerns of the Voyage, which has hitherto allow'd little Respite."

By midafternoon a light wind carried the *Duke* and *Duchess* within gunshot. The *Duchess* lobbed two shots over the Spaniard, who struck down her ensign without reply. Cooke ran his pinnace in at once. She was French-built, Captain Jose de Arizabala told him, still bore the French name *Havre de Grâce*, rated 270 tons, was cargoed with dry goods, plate and pearls, and carried fifty Spanish passengers and a hundred slaves. Although the *Havre* had but six guns aboard, she was ported for twenty-four, and was Lima-bound to fit out as a man-of-war.

Next day Woodes Rogers sat down to make a mournful entry in his journal. "About twelve," he wrote, "we read the Prayers for the Dead, and threw my dear Brother overboard, with one of our Sailors, another lying dangerously ill. We hoisted our Colours but half-mast up: We began first, and the rest follow'd, firing each some Volleys of small Arms. All our Officers express'd a great Concern for the Loss of my Brother, he being a very active hopeful young Man, a little above twenty Years of Age."

Tears would not bring John back; if they would, he could weep an ocean.

To reach Guayaquil they must penetrate an immense gulf, pass the low tangled growth of Puna Island, and make their way 30 miles up the Guayas River. The town was not much to look at – plank and bamboo houses squatting under church spires – and lay on boggy ground, but it boasted 2000 people, and was the foremost shipbuilding center on the Pacific coast. For a small force to take it, secrecy and surprise were essential.

The attack party would have to be reduced in order to secure the fleet, cumbered as it was with captured ships and more than 300 prisoners. Slaves and crewmen inclined to be docile, but the passengers, some of whom Cooke thought "the briskest Spaniards I ever saw", might plot an uprising. Rogers put most of these brisk gentlemen in irons. Don Jose Arizabala and a few others, too dangerous to leave behind, would go in with the assault boats. A hundred and eleven privateers stayed to work ships and stand guard. They would hold off to sea until the attack was well launched, then anchor at Point Arena, on the north side of the gulf, to await the return.

Rogers, Dover and Courtney split the remaining privateers into three commands of sixty-five men each. Every ten men had a leader, "the best and soberest Man we could pick", and every man pocketed a marked ticket to tell him which squad was his. At midnight on April 17 the ships stood to on a quiet sea, sixty miles from the gulf. Small boats lowered away, pinnaces and barques set oars to locks, men swung down the ropes, and from the decks Cooke and Frye bade them good hunting.

Through the dark early hours and all that day they rowed, until the night tide slowed them to anchor. At four o'clock next morning Rogers and Courtney took two small boats ahead to silence Puna. The barque would follow after a single tide. It was still daylight when they reached the flat, leafy lower end of the island and hid among the mangroves. When darkness fell they crept up the shore to the tiny settlement, pounced on it while it slept, secured its lieutenant, and knocked holes in every canoe drawn to the shallow beach.

The barque did not come up. The noon sun beat down like a white-hot hammer, and still the barque failed to appear. Rogers found it at four o'clock, wandering a dozen miles below Puna, unsure of its bearings. He loaded in what men he had room for and rowed away to rejoin Courtney and Dampier above Puna. The small boats pitched woefully as a fresh wind blew the dirty waters of the gulf into rollers. "I had rather be in a Storm at Sea than here," Rogers moaned. Again daylight had to be worn away batting mosquitoes in the steaming mangrove shallows. At six o'clock on April 21 they thanked God and put out oars for Guayaquil. A hundred and ten men with muskets – rarely had a thriving town been stormed by so few, and so feeble.

Rounding the point, they were dismayed to see all Guayaquil awake. Lights filled the streets, a great beacon fire blazed on the hill, church bells clanged, cannon boomed. A saint's-day fete? An alarm? No one knew. For an hour the boats lay on the dark surface of the river while the officers debated their next move. Rogers argued for going in at once, to take advantage of the confusion. He had little backing; most of the others thought that a night landing into crowded streets would be as confusing to the attackers as to the attacked. They turned for final opinion to the experienced Dampier, who told them that buccaneers never attacked an alerted town. The tide was now ebbing, and the barque unable to come up against it, Rogers could only agree to drop downriver, out of sight, for the time being.

Next morning, as the tide turned and the barque came up with reinforcements, Rogers again urged immediate attack. Dover held out for full consultation of all officers in a boat payed out astern of the barque, where they could discuss in private the most reasonable course. Dover was not bred to the iron; by "reasonable" he meant cautious. During the consultation he raised the specter of heavy losses should so small a force assault an alerted town, and argued that they should negotiate for ransom. He remained obdurate when the majority voted with Rogers to go in without delay. Rogers himself, Dover grimly warned, would be responsible for any disastrous results. A minority sided with him, and Rogers saw that a halfhearted landing would be worse than none. He reluctantly agreed to give negotiation a try. Don Jose and the Puna lieutenant went into Guayaquil for this purpose, armed with the threat that if they had not returned in an hour's time, the attack would proceed. The boats followed and stood off the quay.

Within an hour the emissaries came out with their reply: the governor would negotiate. Not that it was in the slightest degree necessary, the governor had informed them. Was he not Don Jeronimo Bosa y Solis y Pacheco, Knight of the Order of Santiago, and an officer in His Most Catholic Majesty's victorious army? Had he not 1000 horse and foot at his muster in Guayaquil? These invaders, he scoffed, were mere boys; he could sweep them into the river with a brush of his hand. Still, if they had the good sense to refrain from hostilities, he would graciously deign to negotiate.

The governor rowed out that afternoon, and a comfortable discussion went on until five o'clock. It was all immensely promising: the town would ransom itself for 50,000 pieces of eight and would buy the perishable goods of the captured ships. The privateers rubbed their hands in pleasure at this profitable deal. They were going to get more without a fight than if they sacked the town. The governor saluted them genially and went ashore with the promise to conclude arrangements at eight o'clock that evening.

Aboard the barque the privateers laid out refreshments, lighted the candles, and sat down to wait like expectant lovers. The governor failed to come. After midnight a gentleman rowed out to them with propitiatory gifts of meat and brandy. He apologized for Don Jeronimo's absence – a very influential merchant was away – momently expected – the governor awaited his return before settling matters finally. True, reinforcements had filled the town with armed men, so it was well able to defend itself, but since the governor had bound himself to negotiate, and was a man of the highest honor, he would continue to do so. Rogers listened to these blandishments in chill silence. In view of the town's danger, he replied, the governor's absence could hardly be explained away. Rogers would allow him until seven next morning; at one minute after seven they would storm the town.

A good negotiator, as Don Jeronimo was, knows in his bones when to retreat and when to rally. He made it a point to have his oars in the river before the church bells chimed seven. Yes, to be sure, he could arrange purchase of the prize cargoes, even the ships, but 50,000 pieces of eight for the town – ah, that was beyond reason! By noon he conceded that 40,000 might, perhaps, be possible; he could make no binding agreement until leading citizens had discussed it fully. He went ashore at one o'clock pledged to a prompt reply.

The reply, by messenger, was neither prompt nor pleasing. It offered 30,000 pieces of eight for the town, and ignored the prizes entirely. Rogers gave them another half-hour of grace. The boats moved closer in as men loaded their muskets for the attack. Three gentlemen, who came to the riverside brandishing white hand-kerchiefs, raised the ransom by 2000 pieces of eight. Rogers waved them off. His linguist shouted in Spanish for everyone in the line of fire to clear out for their lives. The barque hauled down her flag of truce and trained her cannon on the town, men poured off her deck into boats, and the landing party dug oars for the quay.

Militiamen crowded out of back streets to meet them, and a company of horse charged to the riverbank, yanking at their swords. "They made a formidable Show in respect to our little Number that was to attack them," Rogers admitted. His pinnace grated on the stone landing. Men scrambled out shouting, and fired off a ragged volley toward the militia, who fled back into the town faster than they had come. The cavalry wheeled and pressed after the rout. Pausing only to signal cease-fire to the barque's crew, Rogers marched his little band double-quick after the retreating Spaniards. At the plaza four cannon faced them, the gunners with matches at the touchholes, and the defense forces solidly regrouped behind. Rogers and a few men dashed with a whoop straight for the cannon mouths. The guns belched smoke, a blast of shot swept by; then horse, foot and gunners scattered like dust in a gale. While Rogers halted to secure the great church facing the plaza, Dover and Courtney marched their companies unopposed to the far edge of town. A short half-hour had put Guayaquil in their possession. "With a Handful of raw, undis-ciplin'd Men," was Rogers's contemptuous note, not one of them lost to enemy fire.

But Guayaquil was now hardly worth possessing. The tortuous negotiations had bought time for the town's citizens to carry off everything of value. Privateers broke open locked doors, rooted in barren rooms, ransacked cupboards, and were about to tear up the floor of the plaza church. Rogers ruled the church off bounds; too many buried under it had died of a recent plague.

On the hint of an Indian prisoner, Lieutenant Connely and Selkirk took two boats up the river to see if they could lay hands on some fugitives and, literally, did. Houses along the bank were full of Guayaquil women who had not been able to part with all their jewelry, as a few genteel pats by the privateers discovered. 'Some of their largest Gold Chains were conceal'd, and wound about their Middles, legs and Thighs, etc., but the Gentlewomen of those hot Countries being very thin clad with Silk and fine Linnen, and their Hair dressed with Ribbons very neatly, our Men by pressing felt the Chains, etc., with their Hand on the Outside of the Lady's Apparel, and by their Linguist modestly desired the Gentlewomen to take 'em off and surrender 'em." This gallantry so impressed the grateful ladies of one house that they spread food for the searchers and broke out a cask of choice liquor.

Spanish men were less cordial. Without ever mounting a counterattack, they kept the English nervously on edge by sniping, feints in force, and night alarms. Strengthened by reinforcements, they might retake the town. At the right moment, Rogers thought, a ransom agreement should be struck, and on April 26 he dispatched his ultimatum: 30,000 pieces of eight, payable in six days at Puna, with sufficient hostages as surety, or he would burn Guayaquil to the ground at three o'clock that afternoon.

An hour before the deadline Spanish horsemen rode in to accept the demand and to exchange written guarantees of the terms. To save his dignity, the governor requested clear statement that the town had been taken by storm. It was agreed that the Puna lieutenant, and three Guayaquil gentlemen already in Rogers' custody, would stand as hostages.

Getting out of Guayaquil was more trouble than getting in. Most plunder was bulky – bags of flour, beans and rice; some cordage and ironware, bales of cloth, a ton of tar – and men fainted under the load in the deadly heat. Rain turned the dirt streets to quagmires. When they tried to carry the Spanish

cannon to the riverside, the men sank to their knees, and Rogers
had to contrive a huge bamboo frame that sixty men could put
their shoulders under. That night the whole company of privateers slept in the plaza church; next day they loaded the barque
with plunder, and on April 28, with a loud display of trumpets
and drums to announce their departure, dropped down the ebb
tide to Puna.

ROBINSON CRUSOE RESCUED

Woodes Rogers

*The 1708–11 expedition to South America of privateer Woodes
Rogers found more than booty (£150,000-worth of it): it also
discovered, on 2 February 1709, on uninhabited Mas a Trierra
Island in the Juan Fernandez archipelago the marooner Alexander
Selkirk.*

*The son of a Scottish shoemaker Selkirk had run away to sea to join
the buccaneers, but had subsequently fallen out with his superior,
Thomas Stradling, and requested to be put ashore; Selkirk had been
alone when Rogers's expedition landed. Later Rogers transcribed
Selkirk's adventures in his journal, which was eventually published
in 1712 as* A Cruising Voyage around the World. *Among the readers
of* A Cruising Voyage around the World *was Daniel Defoe, who
found in Selkirk's adventures the inspiration for* Robinson Crusoe.

Our pinnace return'd from the shore, and brought abundance of
craw-fish with a man cloth'd in goat-skins, who look'd wilder
than the first owners of them. He had been on the island four
years and four months, being left there by Captain Stradling in
the *Cinque-Ports*. His name was Alexander Selkirk, a Scotchman,
who had been Master of the *Cinque-Ports*, a ship that came here
last with Captain Dampier, who told me that this was the best

man in her; so I immediately agreed with him to be a mate on board our ship.

'Twas he that made the fire last night when he saw our ships, which he judg'd to be English. During his stay here he saw several ships pass by but only two came in to anchor. As he went to view them he found them to be Spanish and retired from 'em, upon which they shot at him. Had they been French, he would have submitted, but chose to risque dying alone on the Iland, rather than fall into the hands of the Spaniards in these parts, because he apprehended they would murder him, or make a slave of him in the mines; for he fear'd they would spare no stranger that might be capable of discovering the South Sea. The Spaniards had landed before he knew what they were, and they came so near him that he had much ado to escape: for they not only shot at him, but pursue'd him into the woods, where he climb'd to the top of a tree at the foot of which they made water, and kill'd several goats just by, but went off again without discovering him. He told us he was born at Largo in the county of Fife, Scotland, and was bred a sailor from his youth. The reason of his being left here was a difference betwixt him and his captain . . . He had with him his clothes and bedding, with a firelock, some powder, bullets, and tobacco, a hatchet, a knife, a kettle, a Bible, some practical pieces, and his mathematical instruments and books.

He diverted and provided for himself as well as he could; but for the first eight months had much ado to bear up against melancholy, and the terror of being left alone in such a desolate place. He built two huts with piemento trees, cover'd them with long grass, and lin'd them with the skins of goats which he killed with his gun as he wanted, so long as his powder lasted, which was but a pound, and that being near spent, he got fire by rubbing two sticks of piemento wood together upon his knee. In the lesser hut, at some distance from the other, he dressed his victuals, and in the larger he slept, and employed himself in reading, singing Psalms, and praying, so that he said he was a better Christian while in this solitude, than ever he was before, or than he was afraid he should ever be again. At first he never eat anything till hunger constrain'd him, partly for grief, and partly for want of bread and salt; nor did he go to bed till he could watch no longer. The piemento wood, which burnt very clear, serv'd him both for firing and candle, and refresh'd him with its fragrant smell. He might have had fish enough, but could not eat 'em for want of salt, because they occasion'd a looseness; except Crawfish, which are there as large as lobsters and very good. These he sometimes boiled, and at other times broiled as he did his goats flesh, of which he made very good broth, for they are not so rank as ours; he kept an account of 500 that he kill'd while there, and caught as many more, which he marked on the ear and let go. When his powder fail'd he took them by speed of foot; for his way of living, and continual exercise of walking and running, clear'd him of all gross humours, so that he ran with wonderful swiftness thro the woods, and up the rocks and hills, as we perceiv'd when we employ'd him to catch goats for us. We had a bull dog which we sent with several of our nimblest runners to help him in catching goats; but he distanc'd and tir'd both the dog and the men, catch'd the goats and brought 'em to us on his back. He told us that his agility in pursuing a goat had once like to have cost him his life; he pursue'd it with so much eagerness that he catch'd hold of it on the brink of a precipice of which he was not aware, the bushes having hid it from him so that he fell with the goat down the said precipice a great height, and was so stun'd and bruised with the fall that he narrowly escap'd with his life, and when he came to his senses found the goat dead under him. He lay there about 24 hours and was scarce able to crawl to his hut which was about a mile distant, or to stir abroad again in ten days. He came at last to relish his meat well enough without salt or bread, and in the season had plenty of good turnips which had been sow'd there by Captain Dampier's men, and have now overspread some acres of ground. He had enough of good cabbage from the cabbage trees and season'd his meat with the fruit of the piemento trees, which is the same as the Jamaica pepper, and smells deliciously. He found there also a black pepper called *Maragita*, which was very good to expel wind, and against griping of the guts. He soon wore out all his shoes and clothes by running thro the woods; and at last, being forced to shift without them, his feet became so hard that he ran everywhere without annoyance, and it was some time before he could wear shoes after we found him. For not being used to any so long, his feet swelled when he came first to wear 'em again. After he had conquer'd his melancholy he diverted himself sometimes by cutting his name on the trees, and the time of his being left and continuance there. He was at first much pester'd with cats and rats, that had bred in great numbers from some of each species which had got ashore from ships that put in there to wood and water. The rats gnaw'd his feet and clothes while asleep, which obliged him to cherish the cats with his goats flesh; by which many of them became so tame that they would lie about him in hundreds, and soon deliver'd him from the rats.

He likewise tam'd some kids, and to divert himself would now and then sing and dance with them and his cats; so that by the care of Providence, and vigour of his youth, being now about 30 years old, he came at last to conquer all the inconveniences of his solitude and to be very easy. When his clothes wore out he made himself a coat and cap of goatskins, which he stitch'd together with little thongs of the same that he cut with his knife. He had no other needle but a nail, and when his knife was wore to the back, he made others as well as he could of some iron hoops that were left ashore, which he beat thin and ground upon stones. Having some linen cloth by him, he sow'd himself shirts with a nail and stitch'd 'em with the worsted of his old stockings, which he pull'd out on purpose. He had his last shirt on when we found him in the island.

At his first coming on board us, he had so much forgot his language for want of use, that we could scarce understand him, for he seemed to speak his words by halves. We offer'd him a dram, but he would not touch it, having drank nothing but water since his being there, and 'twas some time before he could relish our victuals. He could give us an account of no other product of the Island than what we have mentioned except small black plums, which are very good, but hard to come at, the trees which bear 'em growing on high mountains and rocks.

"And the God of infinite Mercy be merciful to your soul"

THE LIFE, ROBBERIES
AND HANGING OF THE
NOTORIOUS MAJOR BONNET

Captain Charles Johnson

The British pirate Stede Bonnet, as Johnson relates below, took an original route to piracy: he bought his own ship.

The major was a gentleman of good reputation in the island of Barbados, was master of a plentiful fortune, and had the advantage of a liberal education. He had the least temptation of any man to follow such a course of life, from the condition of his circumstances. It was very surprizing to every one, to hear of the major's enterprize, in the island where he lived; and as he was generally esteemed and honoured, before he broke out into open acts of piracy, so he was afterwards rather pitied than condemned, by those that were acquainted with him, believing that this humour of going a-pirating, proceeded from a disorder in his mind, which had been but too visible in him, some time before this wicked undertaking; and which is said to have been occasioned by some discomforts he found in a married state; be that as it will, the major was but ill qualified for the business, as not understanding maritime affairs.

However, he fitted out a sloop with 10 guns and 70 men, entirely at his own expense, and in the night-time sailed from Barbados. He called his sloop the *Revenge*; his first cruize was off the Capes of Virginia, where he took several ships, and plundered them of their provisions, clothes, money, ammunition, etc. in particular the *Anne*, Capt. Montgomery, from Glasgow; the

Turbet from Barbados, which for country sake, after they had taken out the principal part of the lading, the pirate crew set her on fire; the *Endeavour*, Captain Scot, from Bristol, and the *Young* from Leith. From hence they went to New York, and off the east end of Long Island, took a sloop bound for the West Indies, after which they stood in and landed some men at Gardener's Island, but in a peaceable manner, and bought provisions for his company's use, which they paid for, and so went off again without molestation.

Some time after, which was in August 1717, Bonnet came off the bar of South Carolina, and took a sloop and a brigantine bound in; the sloop belonged to Barbados, Joseph Palmer master, laden with rum, sugar, and Negroes; and the brigantine came from New England, Thomas Porter master, whom they plundered, and then dismissed; but they sailed away with the sloop, and at an inlet in North Carolina careened her, and then set her on fire.

After the sloop had cleaned, they put to sea, but came to no resolution what course to take; the crew were divided in their opinions, some being for one thing, and some another, so that nothing but confusion seemed to attend all their schemes.

The major was no sailor as was said before, and therefore had been obliged to yield to many things that were imposed on him, during their undertaking, for want of a competent knowledge in maritime affairs; at length happening to fall in company with another pirate, one Edward Teach (who for his remarkable black ugly beard, was more commonly called Blackbeard). This fellow was a good sailor, but a most cruel hardened villain, bold and daring to the last degree, and would not stick at perpetrating the most abominable wickedness imaginable; for which he was made chief of that execrable gang, that it might be said that his post was not unduly filled, Blackbeard being truly the superior in roguery, of all the company, as has been already related.

To him Bonnet's crew joined in consortship, and Bonnet himself was laid aside, notwithstanding the sloop was his own; he went aboard Blackbeard's ship, not concerning himself with any of their affairs, where he continued till she was lost in Topsail Inlet, and one Richards was appointed captain in his room. The major now saw his folly, but could not help himself, which made him melancholy; he reflected upon his past course of life, and was confounded with shame, when he thought upon what he had done: His behaviour was taken notice of by the other pirates, who liked him never the better for it; and he often declared to some of them, that he would gladly leave off that way of living, being fully tired of it; but he should be ashamed to see the face of any English man again; therefore if he could get to Spain or Portugal, where he might be undiscovered, he would spend the remainder of his days in either of those countries, otherwise he must continue with them as long as he lived.

When Blackbeard lost his ship at Topsail Inlet, and surrendered to the King's proclamation, Bonnet reassumed the command of his own sloop, *Revenge*, goes directly away to Bath Town in North Carolina, surrenders likewise to the King's pardon, and receives a certificate. The war was now broke out between the Triple Allies and Spain; so Major Bonnet gets a clearance for his sloop at North Carolina to get to the island of St. Thomas, with a design (at least it was pretended so) to get the emperor's commission, to go a-privateering upon the Spaniards. When Bonnet came back to Topsail Inlet, he found that Teach and his gang were gone, and that they had taken all the money, small arms and effects of value out of the great ship, and set ashore on a small sandy island above a league from the main, seventeen men, no doubt with a design they should perish, there being no inhabitant, or provisions to subsist withal, nor any boat or materials to build or make any kind of launch or vessel, to escape from that desolate place. They remained there two nights and one day, without subsistance, or the least prospect of any, expecting nothing else but a lingering death; when to their inexpressible comfort they saw redemption at hand; for Major Bonnet happening to get intelligence of their being there, by two of the pirates who had escaped Teach's cruelty, and had got to a poor little village at the upper end of the harbour, sent his boat to make discovery of the truth of the matter, which the poor wretches seeing, made a signal to them, and they were all brought on board Bonnet's sloop.

Major Bonnet told all his company that he would take a commission to go against the Spaniards, and to that end was going to St. Thomas, therefore if they would go with him, they should be welcome; whereupon they all consented, but as the sloop was preparing to sail, a bumboat, that brought apples and

cider to sell to the sloop's men, informed them that Captain
Teach lay at Ocracoke Inlet, with only eighteen or twenty hands.
Bonnet who bore him a mortal hatred for some insults offered
him, went immediately in pursuit of Blackbeard, but it happened
too late, for he missed of him there, and after four days cruize,
hearing no farther news of him, they steered their course towards
Virginia.

In the month of July, these adventurers came off the Capes and
meeting with a pink with a stock of provisions on board, which
they happened to be in want of; they took out of her ten or twelve
barrels of pork, and about four hundred weight of bread; but
because they would not have this set down to the account of
piracy, they gave them eight or ten casks of rice, and an old cable,
in lieu thereof.

Two days afterwards they chased a sloop of 60 tons, and took
her two leagues off of Cape Henry; they were so happy here as to
get a supply of liquor to their victuals, for they brought from her
two hogsheads of rum and as many of molasses, which, it seems,
they had need of, though they had not ready money to purchase
them. What security they intended to give, I can't tell, but
Bonnet sent eight men to take care of the prize sloop, who,
perhaps, not caring to make use of those accustomed freedoms,
took the first opportunity to go off with her, and Bonnet (who was
pleased to have himself called Captain Thomas) saw them no
more.

After this, the major threw off all restraint, and though he had
just before received His Majesty's mercy, in the name of Stede
Bonnet, he relapsed in good earnest into his old vocation, by the
name of Captain Thomas, and recommenced a down-right pirate,
by taking and plundering all the vessels the met with. He took off
Cape Henry, two ships from Virginia, bound to Glasgow, out of
which they had very little besides a hundred weight of tobacco.
The next day they took a small sloop bound from Virginia to
Bermuda, which supplied them with twenty barrels of pork, some
bacon, and they gave her in return, two barrels of rice, and a
hogshead of molasses; out of this sloop two men entered voluntarily. The next they took was another Virginiaman, bound to
Glasgow, out of which they had nothing of value, save only a few
combs, pins and needles, and gave her instead thereof, a barrel of
pork, and two barrels of bread.

From Virginia they sailed to Philadelphia, and in the latitude of 38° North, they took a schooner, coming from North Carolina, bound to Boston, they had out of her only two dozen of calfskins, to make covers for guns, and two of their hands, and detained her some days. All this was but small game, and seemed as if they designed only to make provision for their sloop after they arrived at St. Thomas; for they hitherto had dealt favourably with all that were so unhappy as to fall into their hands; but those that came after, fared not so well, for in the latitude of 32°, off of Delaware River, near Philadelphia, they took two snows bound to Bristol out of whom they got some money, besides goods, perhaps to the value of 150 pounds; at the same time they took a sloop of 60 tons bound from Philadelphia to Barbados, which after taking some goods out, they dismissed along with the snows.

The 29th day of July, Captain Thomas took a sloop of 50 tons, six or seven leagues off Delaware Bay bound from Philadelphia to Barbados, Thomas Read master, loaden with provisions, which they kept, and put four or five of their hands on board her. The last day of July, they took another sloop of 60 tons, commanded by Peter Manwaring, bound from Antigua to Philadelphia, which they likewise kept with all the cargo, consisting chiefly of rum, molasses, sugar, cotton, indigo, and about 25 pounds, in money valued in all to 500 pounds.

The last day of July, our rovers with the vessels last taken, left Delaware Bay, and sailed to Cape Fear River, where they stayed too long for their safety, for the pirate sloop which they now new named the *Royal James*, proved very leaky, so that they were obliged to remain here almost two months, to refit and repair their vessel. They took in this river a small shallop, which they ripped up to repair the sloop, and retarded the further prosecution of their voyage, as before mentioned, till the news came to Carolina, of a pirate sloop's being there to careen with her prizes.

Upon this information, the council of South Carolina was alarmed, and apprehended they should receive another visit from them speedily; to prevent which, Colonel William Rhet, of the same province, waited on the governor, and generously offered himself to go with two sloops to attack this pirate; which the governor readily accepted, and accordingly gave the colonel a commission and full power, to fit such vessels as he thought proper for the design.

In a few days two sloops were equipped and manned: the *Henry* with 8 guns and seventy men, commanded by Captain John Masters, and the *Sea Nymph*, with 8 guns and sixty men, commanded by Captain Fayrer Hall, both under the entire direction and command of the aforesaid Colonel Rhet, who, on the 14th of September, went on board the *Henry*, and, with the other sloop, sailed from Charles Town to Suillivants Island, to put themselves in order for the cruize. Just then arrived a small ship from Antigua, one Cock master, with an account, that in sight of the bar he was taken and plundered by one Charles Vane, a pirate, in a brigantine of 12 guns and ninety men; and who had also taken two other vessels bound in there, one a small sloop, Captain Dill master, from Barbados; the other a brigantine, Captain Thompson master, from Guinea, with ninety odd Negroes, which they took out of the vessel, and put on board another sloop then under the command of one Yeats, his consort, with twenty-five men. This proved fortunate to the owners of the Guineaman, for Yeats having often attempted to quit this course of life, took an opportunity in the night, to leave Vane and to run into North Edisto River, to the southward of Charles Town, and surrendered to His Majesty's pardon. The owners got their Negroes, and Yeats and his men had certificates given them from the government.

Vane cruized some time off the bar, in hopes to catch Yeats, and unfortunately for them, took two ships coming out, bound to London, and while the prisoners were aboard, some of the pirates gave out, that they designed to go into one of the rivers to the southward. Colonel Rhet, upon hearing this, sailed over the bar the 15th of September, with the two sloops before mentioned; and having the wind northerly, went after the pirate Vane, and scoured the rivers and inlets to the southward; but not meeting with him, tacked and stood for Cape Fear River, in prosecution of his first design. On the 26th following, in the evening, the colonel with his small squadron, entered the river, and saw, over a point of land, three sloops at an anchor, which were Major Bonnet and his prizes; but it happened that in going up the river, the pilot ran the colonel's sloops aground, and it was dark before they were on float, which hindered their getting up that night. The pirates soon discovered the sloops, but not knowing who they were, or upon what design they came into that river, they manned three canoes, and sent them down to take them, but they quickly found their mistake, and returned to the sloop, with the unwelcome news. Major Bonnet made preparations that night for engaging and took all the men out of the prizes. He showed Captain Manwaring, one of his prisoners, a letter, he had just wrote, which he declared he would send to the Governor of Carolina; the letter was to this effect, viz. that if the sloops, which then appeared, were sent out against him, by the said governor, and he should get clear off, that he would burn and destroy all ships or vessels going in or coming out of South Carolina. The next morning they got under sail, and came down the river, designing only a running fight. Colonel Rhet's sloops got likewise under sail, and stood for him, getting on each quarter of the pirate, with intent to board him; which he perceiving, edged in towards the shore, and being warmly engaged, their sloop ran aground. The Carolina sloops, being in the same shoal water, were in the same circumstances; the *Henry*, in which Colonel Rhet was, grounded within pistol shot of the pirate, and on his bow; the other sloop grounded right ahead of him, and almost out of gun-shot, which made her of little service to the colonel, while they lay aground.

At this time the pirate had a considerable advantage; for their sloop, after she was aground, lifted from Colonel Rhet's, by which means they were all covered and the colonel's sloop lifting the same way, his men were much exposed; notwithstanding which, they kept a brisk fire the whole time they lay thus aground, which was near five hours. The pirates made a wiff in their bloody flag, and beckoned several times with their hats in derision to the colonel's men, to come on board, which they answered with cheerful huzza's, and said that they would speak with them by and by; which accordingly happened, for the colonel's sloop being first afloat, he got into deeper water, and after mending the sloop's rigging, which was much shattered in the engagement, they stood for the pirate, to give the finishing stroke, and designed to go directly on board him; which he prevented, by sending a flag of truce, and after some time capitulating, they surrendered themselves prisoners. The colonel took possession of the sloop, and was extremely pleased to find that Captain Thomas, who commanded her, was the individual person of Major Stede Bonnet, who had done them the honour several times to visit their own coast of Carolina.

There were killed in this action, on board the *Henry*, ten men, and fourteen wounded; on board the *Sea Nymph*, two killed and four wounded. The officers and sailors in both sloops behaved themselves with the greatest bravery; and had not the sloops so unluckily run aground, they had taken the pirate with much less loss of men; but as he designed to get by them, and so make a running fight, the Carolina sloops were obliged to keep near him, to prevent his getting away. Of the pirates there were seven killed and five wounded, two of which died soon after of their wounds. Colonel Rhet weighed the 30th of September, from Cape Fear River, and arrived at Charles Town the 3rd of October, to the great joy of the whole province of Carolina.

Bonnet and his crew, two days afterwards, were put ashore, and there not being a public prison, the pirates were kept at the watch-house, under a guard of militia; but Major Bonnet was committed into the custody of the marshal, at his house; and in a few days after, David Hariot the master, and Ignatius Pell the boatswain, who were designed for evidences against the other pirates, were removed from the rest of the crew, to the said marshal's house, and every night two sentinals set about the said house; but whether through any corruption, or want of care in guarding the prisoners, I can't say; but on the 24th of October, the major and Hariot made their escape, the boatswain refusing to go along with them. This made a great noise in the province, and people were open in their resentments, often reflecting on the governor, and others in the magistracy, as though they had been bribed, for conniving at their escape. These invectives arose from their fears, that Bonnet would be capable of raising another company, and prosecute his revenge against this country, for what he had lately, though justly, suffered: But they were in a short time made easy in those respects; for as soon as the governor had the account of Bonnet's escape he immediately issued out a proclamation, and promised a reward of 700 pounds to any that would take him, and sent several boats with armed men, both to the northward and southward, in pursuit of him.

Bonnet stood to the northward, in a small vessel, but wanting necessaries, and the weather being bad, he was forced back, and so returned with his canoe, to Suillivants Island, near Charles Town, to fetch supplies; but there being some information sent to the governor, he sent for Colonel Rhet, and desired him to go in pursuit of Bonnet; and accordingly gave him a commission for that purpose; wherefore the colonel, with proper craft, and some men, went away that night for Suillivants Island, and, after a very diligent search, discovered Bonnet and Hariot together; the colonel's men fired upon them, and killed Hariot upon the spot, and wounded one Negro and an Indian. Bonnet submitted, and surrendered himself; and the next morning, being November the 6th, was brought by Colonel Rhet to Charles Town, and by the governor's warrant, was committed into safe custody, in order for his being brought to his trial.

On the 28th of October, 1718, a court of vice-admiralty was held at Charles Town in South Carolina, and, by several adjournments, continued to Wednesday, the 12th of November following, for the trial of the pirates taken in a sloop formerly called the *Revenge*, but afterwards the *Royal James*, before Nicholas Trot, Esq, judge of the vice-admiralty, and chief justice of the said province of South Carolina, and other assistant judges.

The King's commission to Judge Trot was read, and a grand jury sworn, for the finding of the several bills, and a learned charge given them by the said judge, wherein he first showed, that the sea was given by God, for the use of men, and is subject to dominion and property, as well as the land.

Secondly, he particularly remarked to them, the Sovereignty of the King of England over the British seas.

Thirdly, he observed, that as commerce and navigation could not be carried on without laws; so there have been always particular laws, for the better ordering and regulating marine affairs; with an historical account of these laws, and origin.

Fourthly, he proceeded to show, that there have been particular courts and judges appointed; to whose jurisdiction maritime causes do belong, and that in matters both civil and criminal.

And then fifthly, he particularly showed them, the constitution and jurisdiction of that court of admiralty sessions.

And lastly, the crimes cognizable therein; and particularly enlarged upon the crime of pyracy, which was then brought before them.

The indictments being found, a petit jury was sworn, and the following persons arraigned and tried.

Stede Bonnet, alias Edwards, alias Thomas, late of Barbados, mariner.
Robert Tucker, late of the island of Jamaica, mariner.
Edward Robinson, late of Newcastle upon Tyne, mariner.
Neal Paterson, late of Aberdeen, mariner.
William Scot, late of Aberdeen, mariner.
William Eddy, alias Neddy, late of Aberdeen, mariner.
Alexander Annand, late of Jamaica, mariner.
George Rose, late of Glasgow, mariner.
George Dunkin, late of Glasgow, mariner.
*Thomas Nicholas, late of London, mariner.
John Ridge, late of London, mariner.
Matthew King, late of Jamaica, mariner.
Daniel Perry, late of Guernsey, mariner.
Henry Virgin, late of Bristol, mariner.
James Robbins, alias Rattle, late of London, mariner.
James Mullet, alias Millet, late of London, mariner.
Thomas Price, late of Bristol, mariner.
James Wilson, late of Dublin, mariner.
John Lopez, late of Oporto, mariner.
Zachariah Long, late of the Province of Holland, mariner.
Job Bayly, late of London, mariner.
John-William Smith, late of Charles Town, Carolina, mariner.
Thomas Carman, late of Maidstone in Kent, mariner.
John Thomas, late of Jamaica, mariner.
William Morrison, late of Jamaica, mariner.
Samuel Booth, late of Charles Town, mariner.
William Hewet, late of Jamaica, mariner.
John Levit, late of North Carolina, mariner.
William Livers, alias Evis.
John Brierly, alias Timberhead, late of Bath Town, in North Carolina, mariner.
Robert Boyd, late of Bath Town aforesaid, mariner.
*Rowland Sharp, of Bath Town, mariner.
*Jonathan Clark, late of Charles Town, South Carolina, mariner.
*Thomas Gerrard, late of Antigua, mariner.

And all, except the last three, and Thomas Nicholas, were found guilty, and received sentence of death. They were most of them tried upon two indictments, as follows.

The Jurors for our Sovereign Lord the King, do upon their Oath, present that Stede Bonnet, late of Barbadoes, Mariner, Robert Tucker, &c. &c. The 2nd Day of August in the 5th Year of the Reign of our Sovereign Lord George, &c. By Force of Arms upon the High-Sea, in a certain Place called Cape James, &c. did pyratically and felloniously set upon, break, board, & enter, a certain Merchant Sloop, called the *Frances*, Peter Manwaring Commander, by Force, &c. upon the High-Sea, in a certain Place, called Cape James, alias Cape Inlopen, about two Miles distant from the Shore, in the Lattitude of 39, or thereabouts; and within the Jurisdiction of the Court of Vice-Admiralty, of South-Carolina, being a Sloop of certain Persons, (to the Jurors, unknown) and then, and there, pyratically and felloniously did make an Assault, in, & upon the said Peter Manwaring, & others his Mariners, (whose Names to the Jurors aforesaid, are unknown,) in the same Sloop, against the Peace of God, & of our said now Sovereign Lord the King, then, and there being, pyratically and felloniously, did put the aforesaid Peter Manwaring, and others, his Mariners, of the same Sloop, in the Sloop aforesaid, then being, in corporal Fear of their Lives, then & there, in the Sloop aforesaid, upon the High-Sea, in the Place aforesaid, called Cape James, alias Cape Inlopen, about two Miles from the Shore, in the Lattitude of 39, or thereabouts, as aforesaid, and within the Jurisdiction aforesaid; pyratically, & felloniously, did steal, take, & carry away the said Merchant Sloop, called the *Frances*, and also 26 Hogsheads, &c. &c. &c. being found in the aforesaid Sloop, in the Custody and Possession of the said Peter Manwaring, and others, his Mariners of the said Sloop, and from their Custody and Possession, then & there, upon the High-Sea aforesaid, called Cape James, alias Cape Inlopen, as aforesaid, & within the Jurisdiction aforesaid, against the Peace of our now Sovereign Lord the King, his Crown and Dignity.

This was the form of the indictments they were arraigned upon, and though they might have proved several more facts upon the major part of the crew, the court thought fit to prosecute but two; the other was for seizing in a piratical and felonious manner, the sloop *Fortune*, Thomas Read commander; which indictment running in the same form with the above-mentioned, it will be unnecessary to say more of it.

All the prisoners arraigned, pleaded not guilty, and put themselves upon their trials, except James Wilson, and John Levit, who pleaded guilty to both indictments, and Daniel Perry, to one only. The major would have gone through both the indictments at once, which the court not admitting, he pleaded not guilty to both indictments, but being convicted of one, he retracted his former plea to the second indictment, and pleaded guilty to it.

The prisoners made little or no defence, every one pretending only that they were taken off a maroon shore, and were shipped with Major Bonnet to go to St. Thomas's; but being out at sea, and wanting provisions, they were obliged to do what they did by others; and so did Major Bonnet himself, pretend that 'twas force, not inclination, that occasioned what had happened. However, the facts being plainly proved, and that they had all shared ten or eleven pounds a man, excepting the last three, and Thomas Nicholas, they were all but they, found guilty.

The judge made a very grave speech to them, setting forth the enormity of their crimes, the condition they were now in, and the nature and necessity of an unfeigned repentance; and then recommended them to the ministers of the province, for more ample directions, to fit them for eternity, "for" (concluded he) "the priest's lips shall keep knowledge, and you shall seek the law at their mouths; for they are the messengers of the Lord. Mat 11.57, and the ambassadors of Christ, and unto them is committed the word [or doctrine] of reconciliation, 2 Cor. V. 19. 20." And then pronounced sentence of death upon them.

On Saturday November the 8th 1711, Robert Tucker, Edward Robinson, Neal Paterson, William Scot, Job Bayley, John-William Smith, John Thomas, William Morrison, Samuel Booth, William Hewit, William Eddy, alias Neddy, Alexander Annand, George Ross, George Dunkin, Matthew King, Daniel Perry, Henry Virgin, James Robbins, James Mullet, alias Millet, Thomas Price, John Lopez, and Zachariah Long, were executed at the White Point near Charles Town, pursuant to their sentence.

As for the captain, his escape protracted his fate, and spun out his life a few days longer, for he was tried the 10th, and being found guilty, received sentence in like manner as the former;

before which Judge Trot, made a most excellent speech to him, rather somewhat too long to be taken into our history, yet I could not tell how to pass by so good and useful a piece of instruction, not knowing whose hands this book may happen to fall into.

THE LORD CHIEF JUSTICE'S SPEECH UPON HIS PRONOUNCING SENTENCE ON MAJOR STEDE BONNET

Major Stede Bonnet, you stand here convict'd upon 2 Indictments of Pyracy; one by the Verdict of the Jury, and the other by your own Confession. Altho' you were indicated but for two Facts, yet you know that at your Tryal it was fully proved even by an unwilling Witness, that you pyratically took and rifled no less than thirteen Vessels since you sailed from North-Carolina.

So that you might have been Indicted, and convicted of eleven more Acts of Piracy, since you took the Benefit of the King's Act of Grace, and pretended to leave that wicked Course of Life.

Not to mention the many Acts of Pyracy you committed before; for which if your Pardon from Man was never so authentick, yet you must expect to answer for them before God.

You know that the Crimes you have committed are evil in themselves, and contrary to the Light and Law of Nature, as well as the Law of God, by which you are commanded that you shall not steal, Exodus 20. 15. And the Apostle St. Paul expressly affirms, "That Thieves shall not inherit the Kingdom of God", I Cor. 6.10.

But to Theft, you have added a greater Sin, which is Murder. How many you may have killed of those that resist'd you in the committing your former Piracies, I know not: But this we all know, that besides the Wounded, you kill'd no less than eighteen Persons out of those that were sent by lawful Authority to suppress you, and put a stop to those Rapines that you daily acted.

And however you may fancy that that was killing Men fairly in open Fight, yet this know, that the Power of the Sword not being committ'd into your Hands by any lawful Authority, you were not impower'd to use any Force, or Fight any one; and therefore those Persons that fell in that

Action, in doing their Duty to their King & Country, were murder'd, and their Blood now cries out for Vengeance and Justice against you: For it is the Voice of Nature confirmed by the Law of God, "That whosoever sheddeth Man's Blood, by Man shall his Blood be shed". Gen. 9.6.

And consider that Death is not the only Punishment due to Murderers; for they are threatened to have "their Part in the Lake which burneth with Fire & Brimstone, which is the second Death", Rev. 21.8. See Chapter 22.15. Words which carry that Terror with them, that considering your Circumstances & your Guilt, surely the Sound of them must make you tremble; "for who can dwell with ever-lasting Burnings?" Chap. 33.14.

As the Testimony of your Conscience must convince you of the great & many evils you have committ'd, by which you have highly offend'd God, & provok'd most justly his Wrath and Indignation against you, so I suppose I need not tell you that the only Way of obtaining Pardon & Remission of your Sins from God, is by a true and un-feigned Repentance and Faith in Christ, by whose mer-itorious Death and Passion, you can only hope for Salvation.

You being a Gentleman that have had the Advantage of a liberal Education, and being generally esteemed a Man of Letters, I believe it will be needless for me to explain to you the Nature of Repentance and Faith in Christ, they being so fully and so often mentioned in the Scriptures, that you cannot but know them. And therefore, perhaps, for that Reason it might be thought by some improper for me to have said so much to you, as I have already on this Occa-sion; neither should I have done it, but that considering the Course of your Life and Actions, I have just Reason to fear, that the Principles of Religion that had been instilled into you by your Education, have been at least corrupted, if not entirely defaced, by the Scepticism and Infidelity of this wicked Age; and that what Time you allow'd for Study, was rather apply'd to the Polite Literature, & the vain Philo-sophy of the Times, than a serious Search after the Law & Will of God, as revealed unto us in the Holy Scriptures: "For had your Delight been in the Law of the Lord, & that you had meditated therein Day and Night", Psalms 1. 2. you would then have found that God's "Word was a Lamp unto your Feet, and a Light to your Path", Psalm. 119. 105, and that you would account all other Knowledge but Loss, in Comparison of "the Excellency of the Knowledge of Christ Jesus", Philistines 3. 8. "who to them that are called is the Power of God, and the Wisdom of God", I Cor. 1. 24. "even the hidden Wisdom which God ordained before the World", Chapters 2.7.

You would then have esteem'd the Scriptures as the Great Charter of Heaven, and which delivered to us not only the most perfect Laws and Rules of Life, but also discover'd to us the Acts of Pardon from God, wherein they have offended those righteous Laws: For in them only is to be found the great Mystery of fallen Man's "Redemption, which the Angels desire to look into", 1 Pet. 1. 12.

And they would have taught you that Sin is the debasing of Human Nature, as being a Derivation from that Purity, Rectitude and Holiness, in which God created us, and that Virtue and Religion, and walking by the Laws of God, were altogether preferable to the Ways of Sin and Satan; for that the Ways of Virtue are "Ways of Pleasantness, and all their Paths are Peace", Prov. 3.17.

But what you could not learn from God's Word, by reason of your carelessly, or but superficially considering the same, I hope the Course of his Providence, & the present Afflictions that he hath laid upon you, hath now convinc'd you of the same: For however in your seeming Prosperity you might make a "Mock of your Sins", Prov. 3. 17. yet now that you see that God's Hand hath reached you, and brought you to publick Justice, I hope your present unhappy Circumstances hath made you seriously reflect upon your past Actions and course of Life; and that you are now sensible of the Greatness of your Sins, and that you find the Burden of them is intolerable.

And that therefore being thus "labouring, & heavy laden with Sin", Mat. 11. 28. you will esteem that as the most valuable Knowledge, that can shew you how you can be reconciled to that Supreme God that you have so highly offended; and that can reveal to you Him who is not only the powerful "Advocate with the Father for you", I John 2. 1. but also who hath paid that Debt that is due for your Sins by his own Death upon the Cross for you; & thereby made full Satisfaction for the Justice of God. And this is to be found no where but in God's Word, which discovers to us that "Lamb of God which takes away the Sins of the world", John 1. 29. which is Christ the Son of God. For this know, & be assured, "that there is none other Name under Heaven given among Men, whereby we must be sav'd", Acts, 4, 12. but only by the Name of the Lord Jesus.

But then consider how he invites all Sinners to come unto him, and, "that he will give them rest", Matthew 11.28. for he assures us, "that he came to seek and to save that which was lost", Luke 19. 10. Matt. 18. 11. and hath promised, "that he that cometh unto him, he will in no wise cast out", John 6. 37.

So that if now you will sincerely turn to him, tho' late, even at the "eleventh Hour", Matthew 20. 6. 9. he will receive you.

But surely I need not tell you, that the Terms of his Mercy is Faith & Repentance.

And do not mistake the Nature of Repentance to be only a bare Sorrow for your Sins, arising from the consideration of the Evil and Punishment they have now brought upon you; but your Sorrow must arise from the Consideration of your having offended a gracious and merciful God.

But I shall not pretend to give you any particular Directions as to the Nature of Repentance: I consider that I speak to a Person, whose Offences have proceeded not so much from his not knowing, as his slighting & neglecting his Duty: Neither is it proper for me to give Advice out of the Way of my own Profession.

You may have that better delivered to you by those who have made Divinity their particular Study; and who, by their Knowledge, as well as their Office, as being the "Ambassadors of Christ", 2. Corinthians 5. 20. are best qualified to give you instructions therein.

I only heartily wish; that what, in Compassion to your Soul, I have now said to you upon this sad and solemn Occasion, by exhorting you in general to Faith & Repentance, may have that due Effect upon you, that thereby you may become a true Penitent.

And therefore having now discharg'd my Duty to you as a Christian, by giving you the best Counsel I can, with respect to the Salvation of your Soul, I must now do my Office as a Judge.

The Sentence that the Law hath appointed to pass upon you for your Offences, and which this Court doth therefore award, is:

That you, the said Stede Bonnet, shall go from hence to the Place from whence you came, & from thence to the Place of Execution, where you shall be hang'd by the Neck till you are dead.

And the God of infinite Mercy be merciful to your Soul.

*"In time of action, he . . . stuck lighted matches under his
hat which made him altogether such a figure that
imagination cannot form an idea of a Fury from hell to look
more frightful"*

BLACKBEARD

Captain Charles Johnson

*Blackbeard, aka Captain Teach, enjoyed only a fifteen-month
career as a pirate – yet it was enough to make him the most infamous
of all pirates.*

Edward Teach was a Bristol man born, but had sailed some time
out of Jamaica in privateers in the late French war; yet, though he
had often distinguished himself for his uncommon boldness and
personal courage, he was never raised to any command till he
went a-pirating, which I think was at the latter end of the year
1716, when Captain Benjamin Hornigold put him into a sloop
that he had made a prize of, and with whom he continued in
consortship till a little while before Hornigold surrendered.

In the spring of the year 1717 Teach and Hornigold sailed from
Providence for the Main of America, and took in their way a sloop
from the Havana, with 120 barrels of flour, as also a sloop from
Bermuda, Thurbar master, from whom they took only some
gallons of wine and then let him go; and a ship from Madeira
to South Carolina, out of which they got plunder to a considerable value. After cleaning on the coast of Virginia, they returned
to the West Indies, and in the latitude of 24 made prize of a large
French Guinea-man, bound to Martinique, which, by Hornigold's consent, Teach went aboard as of captain and took a cruise
in her. Hornigold returned with his sloop to Providence, where,
at the arrival of Captain Rogers, the Governor, he surrendered to
mercy, pursuant to the King's proclamation.

Aboard of this Guinea-man Teach mounted forty guns, and named her the *Queen Anne's Revenge*; and cruising near the island of St. Vincent took a large ship called the *Great Allen*, Christopher Taylor commander. The pirates plundered her of what they thought fit, put all the men ashore upon the island above mentioned, and then set fire to the ship.

A few days after, Teach fell in with the *Scarborough* man-of-war, of 30 guns, who engaged him for some hours; but she, finding the pirate well manned, and having tried her strength, gave over the engagement, and returned to Barbadoes, the place of her station, and Teach sailed towards Spanish America.

In his way he met with a pirate sloop of 10 guns, commanded by one Major Bonnet, lately a gentleman of good reputation and estate in the island of Barbadoes, whom he joined; but in a few days after, Teach, finding that Bonnet knew nothing of a maritime life, with the consent of his own men put in another captain, one Richards, to command Bonnet's sloop, and took the major on aboard his own ship; telling him that as he had not been used to the fatigues and care of such a post, it would be better for him to decline it and live easy, at his pleasure, in such a ship as his, where he should not be obliged to perform duty, but follow his own inclinations.

At Turneffe, ten leagues short of the Bay of Honduras, the pirates took in fresh water; and while they were at anchor there, they saw a sloop coming in. Whereupon Richards, in the sloop called the *Revenge*, slipped his cable and ran out to meet her; who, upon seeing the Black flag hoisted, struck her sail and came to, under the stern of Teach, the commodore. She was called the *Adventure* from Jamaica, David Harriot master. They took him and his men aboard the great ship, and sent a number of other hands with Israel Hands, master of Teach's ship, to man the sloop for the piratical account.

The 9th of April they weighed from Turneffe, having lain there about a week, and sailed to the Bay, where they found a ship and four sloops, three of the latter belonging to Jonathan Bernard, of Jamaica, and the other to Captain James. The ship was of Boston, called the *Protestant Caesar*, Captain Wyar commander. Teach hoisted his black colours and fired a gun, upon which Captain Wyar and all his men left their ship and got ashore in their boat. Teach's quartermaster and eight of his crew took possession of

Wyar's ship, and Richards secured all the sloops, one of which they burned, out of spite to the owner; the *Protestant Caesar* they also burned after they had plundered her, because she belonged to Boston where some men had been hanged for piracy. The three sloops belonging to Bernard they let go.

From hence the rovers sailed to Turkill [Trujillo?], and then to the Grand Cayman, a small island about thirty leagues to the westward of Jamaica, where they took a small turtler, and so to the Havana, and from thence to the Bahama wrecks. From the Bahama wrecks they sailed to Carolina (taking a brigantine and two sloops in their way), where they lay off the bar of Charleston for five or six days. They took here a ship as she was coming out, bound for London, commanded by Robert Clark, with some passengers aboard for England; the next day they took another vessel coming out of Charleston, and also two pinks coming into Charleston; likewise a brigantine with fourteen negroes aboard. All of which being done in the face of the town struck a great terror to the whole province of Carolina, having just before been visited by Vane, another notorious pirate, so that they abandoned themselves to despair, being in no condition to resist their force. There were eight sail in the harbour, ready for the sea, but none dared to venture out, it being almost impossible to escape their hands. The inward bound vessels were under the same unhappy dilemma, so that the trade of this place was totally interrupted. What made these misfortunes heavier to them was a long expensive war the colony had had with the natives, which was but just ended when these robbers infested them.

Teach detained all the ships and prisoners, and being in want of medicines, resolved to demand a chest from the government of the province. Accordingly Richards, the captain of the *Revenge* sloop, with two or three more pirates, were sent up along with Mr. Marks, one of the prisoners whom they had taken in Clark's ship, and very insolently made their demands; threatening that if they did not send immediately the chest of medicines, and let the pirate-ambassadors return without offering any violence to their persons, they would murder all their prisoners, send up their heads to the Governor, and set the sloops they had taken on fire.

Whilst Mr. Marks was making application to the council, Richards and the rest of the pirates walked the streets publicly in the sight of all people, who were fired with the utmost indignation, looking upon them as robbers and murderers and particularly the authors of their wrongs and oppressions; but durst not so much as think of executing their revenge, for fear of bringing more calamities upon themselves, and so they were forced to let the villains pass with impunity.

The government were not long in deliberating upon the message, though 'twas the greatest affront that could have been put upon them; yet for saving so many men's lives (among them Mr. Samuel Wragg, one of the council), they complied with the necessity and sent aboard a chest valued at between £300 and £400, and the pirates went back safe to their ships.

Blackbeard, for so Teach was generally called, as we shall hereafter show, as soon as he had received the medicines and his brother rogues, let go the ships and the prisoners; having first taken out of them in gold and silver about £1,500 sterling, besides provisions and other matters.

From the bar of Charleston, they sailed to North Carolina; Captain Teach in the ship which they called the man-of-war, Captain Richards and Captain Hands in the sloops, which they termed privateers, and another sloop serving them as a tender. Teach began now to think of breaking up the company, and securing the money and the best of the effects for himself and some others of his companions he had most friendship for, and to cheat the rest. Accordingly, on pretence of running into Topsail Inlet to clean, he grounded his ship, and then, as if it had been done undesignedly and by accident, he ordered Hands's sloop to come to his assistance and get him off again; which he endeavouring to do, ran the sloop on shore near the other, and so were both lost. This done, Teach goes into the tender sloop, with forty hands, and leaves the *Revenge* there; then takes seventeen others and maroons them upon a small sandy island, about a league from the Main, where there was neither bird, beast or herb for their subsistence, and where they must have perished if Major Bonnet had not two days after taken them off.

Teach goes up to the Governor of North Carolina with about twenty of his men, surrenders to His Majesty's Proclamation, and receives certificates thereof from His Excellency. But it did not appear that their submitting to this pardon was from any reformation of manners, but only to wait a more favourable opportunity to play the same game over again; which he soon after effected, with greater security to himself and with much better prospect of success, having in this time cultivated a very good understanding with Charles Eden, Esquire, the Governor above-mentioned.

The first piece of service this kind governor did to Blackbeard was to give him a right to the vessel which he had taken when he was a-pirating in the great ship called the *Queen Ann's Revenge*; for which purpose a court of Vice-Admiralty was held at Bath-Town and, though Teach had never any commission in his life, and the sloop belonged to the English merchants and was taken in time of peace, yet was she condemned as a prize taken from the Spaniards by the said Teach. These proceedings show that Governors are but men.

Before he sailed upon his adventures, he married a young creature of about sixteen years of age, the Governor performing the ceremony; as it is a custom here to marry by a priest, so it is there by a magistrate. And this, I have been informed, made Teach's fourteenth wife, whereof about a dozen might be still living. His behaviour in this state was something extraordinary; for, while his sloop lay in Ocracoke Inlet, he was ashore at a plantation where his wife lived, with whom, after he had lain all night, it was his custom to invite five or six of his brutal companions to come ashore, and he would force her to prostitute herself to them all, one after another, before his face.

In June, 1718, he went to sea upon another expedition, and steered his course towards Bermuda. He met with two or three English vessels in his way but robbed them only of provisions, stores and other necessaries, for his present expense; but near the island afore-mentioned, he fell in with two French ships, one of them was laden with sugar and cocoa, and the other light, both bound for Martinique. The ship that had no lading he let go, and putting all the men of the loaded ship aboard her he brought home the other with her cargo to North Carolina, where the Governor and the Pirates shared the plunder.

When Teach and his prize arrived, he and four of his crew went to His Excellency, and made affidavit that they found the French ship at sea without a soul on board her. And then a court was called and the ship condemned; the Governor had sixty hogs-heads of sugar for his dividend; and one Mr. Knight, who was his secretary and collector for the Province, twenty; and the rest was shared among the other Pirates.

The business was not done. The ship remained, and it was possible one or other might come into the river that might be acquainted with her, and so discover the roguery. But Teach thought of a contrivance to prevent this, for, upon a pretence that she was leaky, and that she might sink and so stop up the mouth of the inlet or cove where she lay, he obtained an order from the Governor to bring her out into the river, and set her on fire, which was accordingly executed, and she was burned down to the water's edge, her bottom sunk and with it, their fears of her ever rising in judgment against them.

Captain Teach, alias Blackbeard, passed three or four months in the river, sometimes lying at anchor in the coves, at other times sailing from one inlet to another, trading with such sloops as he met, for the plunder he had taken, and would often give them presents for stores and provisions taken from them, that is when he happened to be in a giving humour. At other times he made bold with them and took what he liked, without saying, by your leave, knowing well they dared not send him a bill for the payment. He often diverted himself with going ashore among the planters, where he revelled night and day. By these he was well received, but whether out of love or fear, I cannot say. Sometimes he used them courteously enough, and made them presents of rum and sugar, in recompense of what he took from them but as for liberties which, 'tis said, he and his companions often took with the wives and daughters of the planters, I cannot take upon me to say whether he paid them ad valorem or no. At other times he carried it in a lordly manner towards them, and would lay some of them under contribution; nay, he often proceeded to bully the Governor, not that I can discover the least cause or quarrel between them, but it seemed only to be done to show he dared do it.

The sloops trading up and down this river, being so frequently pillaged by Blackbeard, consulted with the traders and some of the best of the planters, what course to take. They saw plainly it would be in vain to make any application to the Governor of North Carolina, to whom it properly belonged to find some redress; so that if they could not be relieved from some other quarter, Blackbeard would be like to reign with impunity. Therefore, with as much secrecy as possible, they sent a deputation to Virginia, to lay the affair before the Governor of that Colony, and to solicit an armed force from the men-of-war lying there to take or destroy this Pirate.

This Governor consulted with the captains of the two men-of-war, viz. the *Pearl* and the *Lime*, who had lain in James's River about ten months. It was agreed that the Governor should hire a couple of small sloops, and the men-of-war should man them. This was accordingly done, and the command of them given to Mr. Robert Maynard, first lieutenant of the *Pearl*, an experienced officer and a gentleman of great bravery and resolution, as will appear by his gallant behaviour in this expedition. The sloops were well manned and furnished with ammunition and small arms, but had no guns mounted.

About the time of their going out, the Governor called an Assembly in which it was resolved to publish a proclamation offering certain rewards to any person or persons, who, within a year after that time, should take or destroy any Pirate. The original proclamation being in our hands is as follows:

By His Majesty's Lieutenant Governor and Commander in Chief of the Colony and Dominion of Virginia,
  A PROCLAMATION.
  Publishing the Rewards Given for Apprehending or Killing Pirates. WHEREAS, by an Act of Assembly, made at a Session of Assembly, begun at the Capital in Williamsburg, the eleventh day of November in the fifth year of His Majesty's Reign, entitled An Act to Encourage the Apprehending and Destroying of Pirates: It is amongst other things enacted, that all and every person or persons, who, from and after the fourteenth day of November, in the Year of Our Lord One Thousand Seven Hundred and Eighteen, and before the fourteenth day of November, which shall be in the Year of our Lord One Thousand Seven Hundred and Nineteen, shall take any Pirate or Pirates, on the sea or land, or in case of resistance, shall kill any such Pirate or Pirates, between the degrees of thirty four and thirty nine Northern latitude, and within one hundred leagues of the Continent of Virginia, or within the Provinces of Virginia, or North Carolina, upon the

conviction, or making due proof of the killing of all, and every such Pirate, and Pirates, before the Governor and Council, shall be entitled to have, and receive out of the public money, in the hands of the, Treasurer of this Colony, the several rewards following that is to say, for Edward Teach, commonly called Captain Teach or Blackbeard, one hundred pounds; for every other commander of a pirate ship, sloop or vessel, forty pounds; for every lieutenant, master or quartermaster, boatswain or carpenter, twenty pounds; for every other inferior officer, fifteen pounds, and for every private man taken aboard such ship, sloop, or vessel, ten pounds; and that for every Pirate which shall be taken by any ship, sloop or vessel, belonging to this colony, or North Carolina, within the time aforesaid, in any place whatsoever, the like rewards shall be paid according to the quality and condition of such pirates. Wherefore, for the encouragement of all such persons as shall be willing to serve His Majesty and their Country, in so just and hon-ourable undertaking, as the suppressing a sort of people, who may be truly called enemies to mankind: I have thought fit, with the advice and consent of His Majesty's Council to issue this Proclamation; hereby declaring, the said rewards shall be punctually and justly paid, in current money in Virginia, according to the directions of the said Act. And, I do order and appoint this Proclamation, to be published by the Sheriffs at their respective County houses, and by all Ministers and Readers in the several Churches and Chapels throughout this Colony.

Given at our Council Chamber at Williamsburg, this 24th day of November, 1718. In the Fifth year of His Majesty's Reign.

GOD SAVE THE KING.

A. Spotswood.

[Governor of Virginia, 1710–1722]

The 17th of November, 1718, the lieutenant sailed from Kicque-tan, in James River, in Virginia, and the 21st in the evening came to the mouth of the Ocracoke Inlet where he got sight of the pirate. This expedition was made with all imaginable secrecy, and the officer managed with all the prudence that was necessary, stopping all boats and vessels he met with in the river from going up, and therefore preventing any intelligence from reaching Blackbeard, and receiving at the same time an account from them all of the place where the pirate was lurking. But notwithstanding this caution, Blackbeard had information of the design from His Excellency of the province, whose secretary, Mr. Knight, wrote him a letter particularly concerning it, intimating that he had sent him four of his men, which were all he could meet with in or about town, and so bid him be upon his guard. These men belonged to Blackbeard, and were sent from Bath-Town to Ocracoke Inlet, where the sloop lay, which is about twenty leagues.

Blackbeard had heard several reports which happened not to be true, and so gave the less credit to this, nor was he convinced till he saw the sloops, whereupon he put his vessel in a posture of defence. He had no more than twenty-five men on board, so he gave out to all the vessels he spoke with that he had forty. When he had prepared for battle, he set down and spent the night in drinking with the master of a trading sloop who, 'twas thought, had more business with Teach than he should have had.

Lieutenant Maynard came to an anchor, for the place being shoal and the channel intricate, there was no getting in where Teach lay that night. But in the morning he weighed and sent his boat ahead of the sloops to sound, and coming within gunshot of the Pirate, received his fire. Whereupon Maynard hoisted the King's colours and stood directly towards him, with the best way that his sails and oars could make. Blackbeard cut his cable, and endeavoured to make a running fight, keeping a continual fire at his enemies with his guns. Mr. Maynard not having any, kept a constant fire with small arms, while some of his men laboured at their oars. In a little time Teach's sloop ran aground, and Mr. Maynard's drawing more water than that of the Pirate, he could not come near him; so he anchored within half a gunshot of the enemy, and in order to lighten his vessel, that he might run him aboard, the lieutenant ordered all his ballast to be thrown overboard, and all the water [i.e., watercasks] to be staved, and then weighed and stood for him. Upon which Blackbeard hailed him in this rude manner:

Damn you for villains, who are you? And from whence came you? The Lieutenant made him answer, You may see by our colours we are no pirates. Blackbeard bid him send his boat on board, that he might see who he was: but Mr. Maynard replied thus, I cannot spare my boat, but I will come aboard of you as soon as I can, with my sloop. Upon this, Blackbeard took a glass of liquor, and drank to him with these words: Damnation seize my soul if I give you quarter or take any from you. In answer to which Mr. Maynard told him that he expected no quarter from him, nor should he give any.

By this time Blackbeard's sloop floated, as Mr. Maynard's sloops were rowing towards him, which, being not above a foot high in the waist and consequently the men all exposed, as they came near together (there being hitherto little or no execution done on either side), the Pirate fired a broadside, charged with all manner of small shot – a fatal stroke to them – the sloop the lieutenant was in having twenty men killed and wounded and the other sloop nine. This could not be helped for, there being no wind, they were obliged to keep to their oars, otherwise the Pirate would have got away from him, which, it seems, the lieutenant was resolute to prevent.

After this unlucky blow Blackbeard's sloop fell broadside to the shore. Mr. Maynard's other sloop, which was called the *Ranger*, fell astern, being, for the present disabled. So the lieutenant finding his own sloop had way and would soon be on board of Teach, he ordered all his men down for fear of another broadside, which must have been their destruction and the loss of the expedition. Mr. Maynard was the only person that kept the deck, except the man at the helm, whom he directed to lie down snug, and the men in the hold were ordered to get their pistols and their swords ready for close fighting, and to come up at his command; in order to which, two ladders were placed in the hatchway for the more expedition. When the lieutenant's sloop boarded the other, Captain Teach's men threw in several new-fashioned sort of grenadoes, viz. case bottles filled with powder and small shot, slugs, and pieces of lead or iron, with a quick match at the end of it, which, being lighted outside, presently runs into the bottle to the powder. As it is instantly thrown on board, it generally does great execution, besides putting all the crew into a confusion; but by good providence, they had not that effect here, the men being in the hold. And Blackbeard, seeing few or no hands aboard, told his men that they were all knocked on the head except three or four; and therefore, says he, let's jump on board and cut them to pieces.

Whereupon, under the smoke of one of the bottles just mentioned, Blackbeard enters with fourteen men, over the bows of Maynard's sloop, and were not seen by him until the air cleared. However, he just then gave a signal to his men, who all rose in an instant and attacked the Pirates with as much bravery as ever was done upon such an occasion. Blackbeard and the lieutenant fired the first pistol at each other, by which the Pirate received a wound; and then engaged with swords, till the lieutenant's unluckily broke, and [he] stepping back to cock a pistol, Blackbeard, with his cutlass, was striking at that instant that one of Maynard's men gave him a terrible wound in the neck and throat; by which the lieutenant came off with a small cut over his fingers.

They were so closely and warmly engaged, the lieutenant and twelve men against Blackbeard and fourteen, till the sea was tinctured with blood round the vessel.

Blackbeard received a shot in his body from the pistol that Lieutenant Maynard, discharged, yet he stood his ground, and fought with great fury till he received five-and-twenty wounds, and five of them by shot. At length, as he was cocking another pistol, having fired several before, he fell down dead; by which time eight more out of the fourteen dropped, and all the rest, much wounded, jumped overboard and called out for quarter, which was granted; though it was only prolonging their lives for a few days. The sloop *Ranger* came up, and attacked the men that remained in Blackbeard's sloop, with equal bravery, till they likewise cried for quarter.

Here was an end of that courageous brute, who might have passed in the world for a hero had he been employed in a good cause. His destruction, which was of such consequence to the plantations, was entirely owing to the conduct and bravery of Lieutenant Maynard and his men, who might have destroyed him with much less loss had they had 1 vessel with great guns. But they were obliged to use small vessels, because the holes and places he lurked in would not admit of others of greater draught. And it was no small difficulty for this gentleman to get to him, having grounded his vessel at least a hundred times, in getting up the river, besides other discouragements enough to have turned back any gentleman without dishonour who was less resolute and bold than this lieutenant. The broadside that did so much mischief before they boarded, in all probability saved the rest from destruction; for before that, Teach had little or no hopes of escaping, and therefore had posted a resolute fellow, a negro whom he had bred up, with a lighted match in the powder room, with commands to blow up, when he should give him orders, which was as soon as the lieutenant and his men could have entered, that so he might have destroyed his conquerors; and when the negro found how it went with Blackbeard, he could hardly be persuaded from the rash action by two prisoners that were then in the hold of the sloop. What seems a little odd is that some of these men who behaved so bravely against Blackbeard went afterwards a-pirating themselves, and one of them was taken along with Roberts. But I do not find that any of them were provided for, except one that was hanged. But this is a digression.

The lieutenant caused Blackbeard's head to be severed from his body and hung up at the bowsprit end; then he sailed to Bath-Town, to get relief for his wounded men.

It must be observed, that in rummaging the Pirate's sloop they found several letters and written papers, which discovered the correspondence betwixt Governor Eden, the Secretary, Collector, also some traders at New York, and Blackbeard. It is likely he had regard enough for his friends to have destroyed these papers before the action, in order to hinder them from falling into such hands where the discovery would be of no use either to the interest or reputation of these fine gentlemen, if it had not been his fixed resolution to have blown all up together, when he found no possibility of escaping.

When the lieutenant came to Bath-Town he made bold to seize, in the Governor's store-house, the sixty hogsheads of sugar, and from honest Mr. Knight, twenty; which, it seems, was their dividend of the plunder taken in the French ship. The latter did not long survive this shameful discovery, for being apprehensive that he might be called to an account for these trifles, [he] fell sick with the fright, and died in a few days.

After the wounded men were pretty well recovered the lieutenant sailed back to the men-of-war in James River, in Virginia, with Black-beard's head still hanging at the bowsprit end, and fifteen prisoners, thirteen of whom were hanged. It appeared upon trial that one of them, viz. Samuel Odell, was taken out of the trading sloop but the night before the engagement. This poor fellow was a little unlucky at his first entering upon his new trade, there appearing no less than 70 wounds upon him after the action; notwithstanding which, he lived and was cured of them all. The other person that escaped the gallows was one Israel Hands, the master of Blackbeard's sloop, and formerly captain of the same, before the *Queen Ann's Revenge* was lost in Topsail Inlet.

The aforesaid Hands happened not to be in the fight, but was taken afterwards ashore at Bath-Town, having been some time before disabled by Blackbeard in one of his savage humours, after the following manner. One night, drinking in his cabin with Hands, the pilot, and another man, Blackbeard, without any provocation, privately draws out a small pair of pistols, and cocks them under the table. Which being perceived by the man, he withdrew and went upon deck, leaving Hands, the pilot, and the Captain together. When the pistols were ready, he blew out the candle and crossing his hands, discharged them at his company. Hands, the master, was shot through the knee and lamed for life; the other pistol did no execution. Being asked the meaning of this, he only answered by damning them, that if he did not now and then kill one of them, they would forget who he was.

Hands, being taken, was tried and condemned; but just as he was about to be executed, a ship arrived at Virginia with a Proclamation for prolonging the time of His Majesty's pardon to such of the Pirates as should surrender by a limited time therein expressed. Notwithstanding the sentence, Hands pleaded the pardon and was allowed the benefit of it, and is alive at this time in London, begging his bread.

Now that we have given some account of Teach's life and actions, it will not be amiss that we speak of his beard, since it did not a little contribute towards making his name so terrible in those parts. Plutarch and other grave historians have taken notice that several great men amongst the Romans took their surnames from certain odd marks in their countenances, as Cicero from a mark or vetch on his nose. So our hero, Captain Teach, assumed the cognomen of Black-beard, from that large quantity of hair which, like a frightful meteor, covered his whole face and frightened America more than any comet that has appeared there a long time.

This beard was black, which he suffered to grow of an extravagant length; as to breadth, it came up to his eyes. He was accustomed to twist it with ribbons, in small tails, after the manner of our Ramillies wigs, and turn them about his ears. In time of action he wore a sling over his shoulders, with three brace of pistols, hanging in holsters, like bandoliers; and stuck lighted matches under his hat, which, appearing on each side of his face, his eyes naturally looking fierce and wild, made him altogether such a figure that imagination cannot form an idea of a Fury from Hell to look more frightful.

If he had the look of a Fury, his humours and passions were suitable to it. We shall relate two or three more of his extravagances which we omitted in the body of his history, by which it will appear to what a pitch of wickedness human nature may arrive, if its passions are not checked.

In the commonwealth of Pirates he who goes the greatest length of wickedness is looked upon with a kind of envy amongst them, as a person of a more extraordinary gallantry, and is thereby entitled to be distinguished by some post. And if such a one has but courage, he must certainly be a great man. The hero of whom we are writing was thoroughly accomplished this way, and some of his frolics of wickedness were so extravagant as if he aimed at making his men believe he was a Devil incarnate. For being one day at sea, and a little flushed with drink, come, says he, let us make a hell of our own, and try how long we can bear it. Accordingly he, with two or three others went down into the hold and closing up all the hatches, filled several pots full of brimstone and other combustible matter, and set it on fire, and so continued until they were almost suffocated, when some of the men cried out for air. At length, he opened the hatches, not a little pleased that he held out the longest.

The night before he was killed he sat up and drank till the morning with some of his own men and the master of a merchant-man; and having had intelligence of the two sloops coming to attack him, as has been before observed, one of his men asked him in case anything should happen to him in the engagement with the sloops, whether his wife knew where he had buried his money? He answered, That nobody but himself and the Devil knew where it was, and the longest liver should take all.

Those of his crew who were taken alive told a story which may appear a little incredible; however, we think it will not be fair to omit it, since we had it from their own mouths. That once, upon a cruise, they found out that they had a man on board more than their crew. Such a one was seen several days amongst them, sometimes below, and sometimes upon deck; yet no man in the ship could give an account who he was, or from whence he came, but that he disappeared a little before they were cast away in their great ship. But, it seems, they verily believed it was the Devil.

One would think these things should induce them to reform their lives; but so many reprobates together encouraged and spirited one another up in their wickedness, to which a continual course of drinking did not a little contribute. For in Blackbeard's journal which was taken, there were several memorandums of the following nature, found writ with his own hand: Such a day, rum all out:-Our company somewhat sober:-A damn'd confusion amongst us!-Rogues a-plotting:-Great talk of separation-so I looked sharp for a prize:-Such a day took one, with a great deal of liquor on board, so kept the company hot, damned hot; then all things went well again.

Thus it was these wretches passed their lives, with very little pleasure or satisfaction in the possession of what they violently took away from others, and sure to pay for it at last by an ignominious death.

The Names of the Pirates killed in the engagement are as follows:

Edward Teach, Commander.
Phillip Morton, Gunner.
Garrat Gibbens, Boatswain.
Owen Roberts, Carpenter.
Thomas Miller, Quartermaster.
John Husk.
Joseph Curtice.
Joseph Brooks (1).
Nath. Jackson.

All the rest, except the two last, were wounded and afterwards hanged in Virginia:

John Carnes, Joseph Philips,
Joseph Brooks (2), James Robbins,
James Blake, John Martin,
John Gills, Edward Salter,

Thomas Gates, Stephen Daniel,
James White, Richard Greensail,
Richard Stiles, Israel Hands, pardoned.
Caesar, Samuel Odell, acquitted.

There were, in the Pirate sloops and ashore in a tent near where
the sloops lay, 25 hogsheads of sugar, 11 tierces [casks containing
about 304–330 1b), and 145 bags of cocoa, a barrel of indigo, and
a bale of cotton; which, with what was taken from the Governor
and Secretary, and the sale of the sloop, came to £2,500, besides
the rewards paid by the Governor of Virginia, pursuant to his
Proclamation. All which was divided among the companies of the
two ships, *Lime* and *Pearl*, that lay in James River; the brave
fellows that took them coming in for no more than their dividend
amongst the ruff, and was paid it within these three months.

We shall add here a few particulars of the famous Blackbeard,
relating to his taking the South Carolina ships and insulting that
Colony. This was at the time that the Pirates had obtained such
an acquisition of strength that they were in no concern about
preserving themselves from the justice of the laws, but of advancing their power, and maintaining their sovereignty, not over the
seas only, but to stretch their dominions to the plantations
themselves, and the Governors thereof; insomuch, that when
their prisoners came aboard their captors' ships, the Pirates freely
owned their acquaintance with them, and never endeavoured to
conceal their names, or habitations; as if they had been inhabitants of a legal commonwealth, and were resolved to treat with all
the world on the foot of a free state. And all judicial acts went in
the name of Teach, under the title of Commodore. All the
Carolina prisoners were lodged aboard the Commodore's ship,
after being strictly examined concerning the lading of their
vessels, and the number and condition of other traders in the
harbour; when they thought they would sail and whither bound.
And the enquiry was so solemnly carried on, that the Pirates
swore that it should be death for that man that told a lie or
otherwise shifted or evaded in his answers. At the same time all
their papers were perused with the same diligence as though it
had been at the Secretary's office, here in England. When this
business was gone through, word was given that all the prisoners
should be immediately turned aboard their own ship, out of

which they had already taken their provisions and stores. This was done with that hurry and precipitation that it struck a great terror in the unfortunate people, verily believing they were then going to their destruction; and what seemed to confirm them in this notion was, that no regard was had to the qualities of the prisoners, but merchants, gentlemen of rank, and even a child of Mr. Wragg's, were thrust aboard in a tumultuous and confused manner, and locked all under the hatches, where not so much as one Pirate stayed amongst them. In this melancholy situation were those innocent people left, bewailing their condition for several hours, expecting, every moment that passed either that a match would be laid to a train to blow them up, or that the ship was to be set on fire or sunk, nobody could tell which; but everyone supposed they were, one way or other, destined for a sacrifice to their brutal humours. But at length, a gleam of light shot in upon them, that recovered their drooping souls. The hatches were unlaid, and they were immediately ordered back on board the Commodore. They began then to think the Pirates had changed their savage resolution, and that God had inspired them with sentiments less shocking to nature and humanity. and they went aboard, as it were, with new life. The chief of them were brought before Blackbeard, the Pirates' General, who acquainted them with the occasion of that extraordinary procedure, and that they were only put out of the way while a general council was held, at which time they suffered no prisoner to be present. He told them, the Company was in want of medicines, and must be supplied from the Province; that their first surgeon had drawn up a catalogue, which he would send to the Governor and Council by two of his own officers, for whose safe return, as well as for the chest itself, they had come to a resolution of keeping all the prisoners as hostages, who would all be put to death, if such their demands were not complied with punctually.

Mr. Wragg answered that perhaps it might not be in their power to comply with every part of it, and, he feared, that some certain drugs in the surgeon's list were not to be had in the Province; and if it should prove so, he hoped they would be contented to have that want made up by substituting something else in the place. He likewise proposed that one of them might go with the two gentlemen that were to be sent on the embassy, who might truly represent the danger they were in, and induce them more readily to submit, in order to save the lives of so many of the King's subjects, and further, to prevent any insult from the common people (for whose conduct on such an occasion, they could not answer) on the persons of his envoys.

His Excellency Blackbeard thought this advice reasonable, and therefore called another council, who likewise approved of the amendment. Thereupon, Mr. Wragg, who was the first in authority and known to be a man of good understanding among the Carolinas, was offered, and the gentleman himself was willing, to leave a young son in the hands of the Pirates, till he should return, which he promised to do, though the Government should refuse the terms of the releasement. But Blackbeard positively denied this request, saying, he knew too well of what consequence he was in the Province, and he would be equally so to them, and therefore he should be the last man they would part with. After some debate, Mr. Marks was agreed upon to accompany the ambassadors, and accordingly they went off from the fleet in a canoe, and two days were appointed for their return. In the meanwhile the commodore lay to at five or six leagues distant from the land, expecting the conditions of peace. But the time expiring, and nothing appearing from the harbour, Mr. Wragg was sent for up before Teach, who putting on a terrible countenance, told him they were not to be trifled with, that he imagined some foul treachery was played them, and that nothing but immediate death to them all should be the consequence of it. Mr. Wragg begged to respite the dreadful execution one day longer, for that he was sure the Province regarded their lives so much that they would be solicitous to the last degree to redeem them; that, perhaps some misfortune might have befallen the canoe in going in, or it might be their own men that occasioned the delay, for either of which it would be hard for them to suffee.

Teach was pacified for the present, and allowed a day more for their coming back, but at the end of that time how was he enraged to find himself disappointed, calling them villains a thousand times, and swearing they should not live two hours. Mr. Wragg humoured him all he could, and desired a good look-out should be kept. Matters seemed now to be coming to extremities, and nobody thought their lives worth a day's purchase. The innocent people were under great agonies of mind, expecting that nothing but a miracle could preserve them from being crushed by the weight of the enemy's power, when word was given from the forecastle that a small boat appeared in sight. This raised their drooping spirits and revived their hopes. Blackbeard went forward himself with his spying-glass, and declared he could perceive his own scarlet cloak he lent Mr. Marks to go ashore in. This was thought to be a sure reprieve, till the boat came aboard, and then their fears returned, seeing neither the Pirates, Mr. Marks, nor the chest of medicines in the boat.

This boat, is seems, was sent off by Mr. Marks very discreetly, lest a misconstruction should be put upon the stay that an unfortunate accident had occasioned, and which the men that belonged to her acquainted the commodore of, viz. that the boat they had sent ashore was cast away, being overset by a sudden squall of Wind, and the men with great trouble had got ashore at an uninhabited island three or four leagues from the Main; that having stayed there some time till reduced to extremity, there being no provision of any kind, and fearing what disaster might befall the prisoners aboard, the persons belonging to their company set Mr. Marks upon a hatch and floated it upon the sea, after which they stripped and flung themselves in, and swimming after it, thrust the float forward, endeavouring by that means to get to town. This proved a very tedious venture and in all likelihood they had perished, had not this fishing boat sailed by in the morning, and perceived something in the water, made to it, and took them in, when they were near spent with their labour. When they were thus providentially preserved Mr. Marks hired a boat which carried them to Charleston. In the meantime he had sent this boat to give them an account of the accident.

Mr. Teach was pacified with this relation, and consented to stay two days longer, since there appeared no fault of theirs in causing this delay. At the end of two days they lost all patience, and the commodore could not be prevailed on to give them any longer time than the next morning to live, if the boat did not return by that time. Still expecting and still disappointed, the gentlemen knew not what to say, nor how to excuse their friends at land. Some of them told the Pirates that they had equal reason with them to blame their conduct; that they doubted not, by what had already happened, of Mr. Mark's doing his duty faithfully; and since they had received notice of the boat's going safe into Charleston, they could not conceive what should hinder the execution of the business, unless they put a greater value on the chest of medicines than on the lives of fourscore men now on the verge of destruction. Teach, for his part, believed they had imprisoned his men and refused the condition of the prisoner's enlargement, and swore a thousand times that they should not only die, but every Carolina man that hereafter should fall into his hands. The prisoners, at last petitioned to have this one favour granted, viz. that the fleet should weigh and stand off the harbour, and if they should not then see the boat coming out, that they, the prisoners, would pilot them in before the town, which, if they pleased to batter down, they would stand by them to the last man. This proposal of taking revenge for the supposed treachery (as the commodore was pleased to term it) suited well enough the savage temper of the general and his brutes, and he acquiesced at once. The project was likewise approved of by the myrmidons, and accordingly they weighed anchor, being in all eight sail of ships, which were the prizes they had in custody, and ranged along the town. The inhabitants then had their share of the fright, expecting nothing less than a general attack. The men were brought all under arms, but not in so regular a manner as might have been done had the surprise been less; but the women and children ran about the street like mad things. However, before matters came to extremities, the boat was seen coming out, which brought redemption to the poor captives and peace to all.

The chest was brought aboard, and accepted of, and it further appeared that Mr. Marks had done his duty, and the blame of the delay was deservedly thrown on the two Pirates that were sent on the embassy. For while the gentlemen attended the Governor and Council upon the business, the other fine gentlemen were visiting and drinking with their quondam friends and acquaintances, and going from house to house, so that they were not to be found when the medicines were ready to go on board; and Mr. Marks knew it were death to them all to go without them, for the Commodore would not easily have believed, had they not returned, that there had been no foul play acted by them. But now none but smiling countenances were seen aboard; the storm that threatened the prisoners so heavily blew over, and a day of sunshine succeeded. In short, Blackbeard released them as he had promised, and sent them away in the ships after he had done with them, and then sailed off the coast, as has been mentioned.

What follows, contains reflections on a gentleman now deceased, who was Governor of North Carolina, namely Charles Eden, Esq., which we apprehend, by accounts since received, to be without just grounds; therefore, it will be necessary to say something in this place, to take off the calumny thrown on his character by persons who have misjudged of his conduct by the height things appeared in at that time.

Upon a review of this part of Blackbeard's story, it does not seem, by any matters of fact candidly considered, that the said Governor held any private or criminal correspondence with this Pirate; and I have been informed since, by very good hands, that Mr. Eden always behaved, as far as he had power, in a manner suitable to his post, and bore the character of a good governor and an honest man.

But his misfortune was the weakness of the colony he commanded, wanting strength to punish the disorders of Teach, who lorded it at pleasure, not only in the plantation, but in the Governor's own habitation; threatening to destroy the town with fire and sword if any injury was offered to him or his companions. Insomuch that he sometimes drew up his vessel against the town, and once, when he suspected that there was a design of seizing him, he went ashore to the Governor, well armed, and left orders with his men on board, that in case he should not return in a hour's time (as he determined, if at liberty) to batter down the house about their ears without any more to do, notwithstanding he himself were to be in it. Such were the outrageous insolences of this villain, who was so big with mischief that he resolved to be revenged upon his enemies at all events, even though he should give up his own life, as a sacrifice, to obtain those wicked ends.

It is to be observed that Blackbeard, nevertheless, as to his Piracies, had complied with the Proclamation, and thereby satisfied the law, and having a certificate thereof from under the hand of His Excellency, he could not be prosecuted for any of those crimes committed heretofore, because they were wiped off by the said Proclamation of Pardon. And as to condemning the French Martinique-man that Blackbeard brought into North Carolina afterwards, the Governor proceeded judicially upon her. He called a court of Vice Admiralty, by virtue of his commission, at which four of the crew swore they found the ship at sea with no person on board her; so the Court condemned her, as any other court must have done, and the cargo was disposed of according to law. As to the secret expedition from Virginia, undertaken by the Governor and the two captains of men-of-war, they had their secret views in it. The men-of-war had lain up these ten months while the Pirates infested the coast and did great mischief, for which 'tis likely, they might have been called to an account. But the success of the enterprise against Teach, alias Blackbeard, perhaps prevented such enquiry, though I am at a loss to know what acts of Piracy he had committed after this surrender to the Proclamation. The French ship was lawfully condemned, as has been said before, and if he had committed any depredations amongst the planters, as they seemed to complain of, they were not upon the high sea, but either in the river, or on shore, and could not come within the jurisdiction of the Admiralty, nor under any laws of Piracy.

The Governor of Virginia found his interest in the affair, for he sent, at the same time, a force by land, and seized considerable effects of Blackbeard's in Eden's Province; which was certainly a new thing for the Governor of one Province, whose commission was limited to that jurisdiction, to exercise authority in another government, and the Governor himself upon the spot. Thus was poor Mr. Eden insulted and abused on all sides, without having the power of doing himself justice, and asserting his lawful rights.

In fine, to do justice to Governor Eden's character, who is since dead, there did not appear from any writings or letters found in Blackbeard's sloop or from any other evidence whatsoever, that the said Governor was concerned at all in any malpractice; but on the contrary that during his continuance in that post, he was honoured and beloved by his colony, for his uprightness, probity and prudent conduct in his administration. What affairs were carried on privately by his then Secretary I know not. He died a few days after Blackbeard's destruction and no enquiry was made; perhaps there might be no occasion for it.

PIRATES ON THE BOARDS

Five classic pirate plays and musicals.

1) James Cross, *Blackbeard; or, the Captive Princess*, 1798
2) Edward Fitzball, *The Red Rover*, 1829
3) Gilbert & Sullivan, *The Pirates of Penzance*, 1880
4) Verdi, *Le Corsaire*,
5) J.M. Barrie, *Peter Pan*, 1904

PURCHASE AND PREY:
THE EXPLOITS OF
"CALICO JACK" RACKAM

Captain Charles Johnson

Nicknamed "Calico Jack" for his Indian cotton clothing, the English pirate John Rackam (Rackham) was quartermaster to Charles Vane before the sea thieves fell out and Rackam took command.

The 24th of November 1718, was the first day of his [Rackam's] command, and his first cruize was among the Carribee Islands, where he took and plundered several vessels.

To windward of Jamaica, a Madeiraman fell into the pirates' way, which they detained two or three days till they had made their market out of her, and then gave her back to the master, and permitted one Hosea Tisdell, a tavern-keeper at Jamaica, who had been picked up in one of their prizes, to depart in her, she being then bound for that island.

After this cruize, they went into a small island and cleaned, and spent their Christmas ashore, drinking and carouzing as long as they had any liquor left, and then went to sea again for more, where they succeeded but too well, though they took no extraordinary prize, for above two months, except a ship laden with thieves from Newgate, bound for the plantations, which, in a few days, was retaken with all her cargo by an English man-of-war.

Rackam stood off towards the island of Bermuda, and took a ship bound to England from Carolina, and a small pink from New England, and brought 'em to the Bahama Islands, where with the pitch, tar, and stores, they cleaned again and refitted their own vessel; but staying too long in that neighbourhood, and Captain Rogers, who was Governor of Providence, hearing of these ships being taken, sent out a sloop well manned and armed, which retook both the prizes, and in the meanwhile the pirate had the good fortune to escape.

From hence they sailed to the back of Cuba, where Rackam kept a little kind of a family, at which place they stayed a considerable time, living ashore with their dalilahs till their money and provisions were expended, and then they concluded it time to look out. They repaired to their vessel, and were making ready to put to sea, when a Guarda del Costa came in with a small English sloop, which she had taken as an interloper on the coast. The Spanish guardship attacked the pirate, but Rackam being close in behind a little island, she could do but little execution where she lay, therefore the Spaniard warps into the channel that evening, in order to make sure of her the next morning. Rackam finding his case desperate, and hardly any possibility of escaping, resolved to attempt the following enterprize. The Spanish prize lying for better security close into the land, between the little island and the main, Rackham takes his crew into the boat, with their pistols and cutlasses, rounds the little island, and falls aboard their prize silently in the dead of night, without being discovered, telling the Spaniards that they were aboard of her, that if they spoke a word, or made the least noise, they were dead men, and so became master of her. When this was done, he slipped her cable and drove out to sea. The Spanish man-of-war was so intent upon their expected prize that they minded nothing else, and, as soon as day broke, made a furious fire upon the empty sloop, but 'twas not long before they were rightly appraized of the matter, and cursed themselves for fools, to be bit out of a good rich prize, as she proved to be, and to have nothing but an old crazy hull in the room of her.

Rackam and his crew had no occasion to be displeased at the exchange, that enabled them to continue some time longer in a way of life that suited their depraved tempers. In August 1720, we find him at sea again, scouring the harbours and inlets to north and west parts of Jamaica, where he took several small craft, which proved great booty to the rovers, but they had but few men and therefore they were obliged to run at low game, till they could increase their company.

In the beginning of September, they took seven or eight fishing boats in Harbour Island, stole their nets and other tackle, and then went off to the French part of Hispaniola, and landed, and took cattle away, with two or three French men they found near the waterside, hunting of wild hogs in the evening. The French men came on board, whether by consent or by compulsion, I cannot say. They afterwards plundered two sloops, and returned to Jamaica, on the north coast of which island, near Porto Maria Bay, they took a schooner, Thomas Spenlow master. 'Twas then the 19th of October. The next day, Rackam seeing a sloop in Dry Harbour Bay, he stood in and fired a gun; the men all ran ashore, and he took the sloop and lading, but when those ashore found them to be pirates, they hailed the sloop, and let them know they were all willing to come aboard of them.

Rackam's coasting the island in this manner, proved fatal to him, for intelligence came to the governor of his expedition, by a canoe which he had surprized ashore, in Ocho Bay; upon which a sloop was immediately fitted out, and sent round the island in quest of him, commanded by one Captain Barnet, with a good number of hands. Rackam rounding the island, and drawing near the westermost point, called Point Negril, saw a small pettiaga, which at sight of the sloop, run ashore and landed her men. When one of them hailed her, answer was made; they were English men, and desired the pettiaga's men to come on board, and drink a bowl of punch, which they were prevailed upon to do. Accordingly the company came all aboard of the pirate, consisting of nine persons, in an ill hour; they were armed with muskets and cutlasses. What was their real design by so doing, I shall not take upon me to say, but they had no sooner laid down their arms, and taken up their pipes, but Barnet's sloop, which was in pursuit of Rackam's, came in sight.

The pirates finding she stood directly towards her, feared the event, and weighed their anchor, which they but lately let go, and stood off. Captain Barnet gave them chase and having the advantage of little breezes of wind, which blew off the land, came up with her, and, after a very small dispute, took her, and brought her into Port Royal in Jamaica.

In about a fortnight after the prisoners were brought ashore, viz. November 16, 1720, a court of admiralty was held at Saint Jago de la Vega, before which the following persons were convicted, and sentence of death past upon 'em, by the president, Sir Nicholas Laws, viz. John Rackam, captain, George Fetherston, master, Richard Corner, quartermaster, John Davis, John Howell, Patrick Carty, Thomas Earl, James Dobbin and Noah Harwood. The five first were executed the next day at Gallows Point, at the town of Port Royal and the rest, the day after, at Kingston. Rackam, Feverston and Corner were afterwards taken down and hanged up in chains, one at Plumb Point, one at Bush Key, and the other at Gun Key.

But that which was very surprising, was the conviction of the nine men that came on board the sloop the same day she was taken. They were tried at an adjournment of the court, on the 24th of January, waiting all that time, 'tis supposed, for evidence, to prove the piratical intention of going aboard the sloop; for it seems there was no act of piracy committed by them, after their coming on board, as appeared by the witnesses against them, who were two French men taken by Rackam, off from the island of Hispaniola, and deposed in the following manner:

That the prisoners at the bar, viz. John Eaton, Edward Warner, Thomas Baker, Thomas Quick, John Cole, Benjamin Talmer, Walter Rouse, John Hanson, and John Howard, came aboard the pirate's sloop at Negril Point, Rackam sending his canoe ashore for that purpose. That they brought guns and cutlasses on board with them. That when Captain Barnet chased them, some were drinking, and others walking the deck. That there was a great gun and a small arm fired by the pirate sloop, at Captain Barnet's sloop, when he chased her; and that when Captain Barnet's sloop fired at Rackam's sloop, the prisoners at the bar went down under deck. That during the time Captain Barnet chased them, some of the prisoners at the bar (but which of 'em he could not tell) helped to row the sloop, in order to escape from Barnet. That they all seemed to be consorted together.

This was the substance of all that was evidenced against them, the prisoners answered in their defence, that they'd no witnesses; that they had bought a pettiaga in order to go aturtling; and being at Negril Point and just got on shore when they saw a sloop with a white pendant coming towards them, upon which they took their arms, and hid themselves in the bushes. That one of them hailed the sloop, who answered they were English men and desired them to come aboard and drink a bowl of punch, which they at first refused, but afterwards with much persuasion, they went on board, in the sloop's canoe, and left their own pettiaga at anchor; that they had been but a short time on board, when Captain Barnet's sloop heaved in sight; that Rackam ordered 'em to help weigh the sloop's anchor immediately, which they all refused; that Rackam used violent means to oblige them, and that when Captain Barnet came up with them they all readily and willingly submitted.

When the prisoners were taken from the bar, and the persons present being withdrawn, the court considered the prisoners' cases, and the majority of the commissioners being of opinion, that they were all guilty of the piracy and felony they were charged with, which was "the going over with a piratical and felonious intent to John Rackam, etc, then notorious pirates, and by them known to be so", they were all received sentence of death; which everybody must allow proved somewhat unlucky to the poor fellows.

On the 17th of February, John Eaton, Thomas Quick and Thomas Baker were executed at Gallows Point, at Port Royal, and the next day John Cole, John Howard and Benjamin Palmer, were executed at Kingston; whether the other three were executed afterwards, or not, I never heard.

Two other pirates were tried that belonged to Rackam's crew, and being convicted, were brought up, and asked if either or them had any thing to say why sentence of death should not pass upon them, in like manner as had been done to all the rest, and both of them pleaded their bellies, being quick with child, and prayed that execution might be stayed, whereupon the court passed sentence, as in cases of piracy, but ordered them back, till a proper jury should be appointed to enquire into the matter.

*"It was on the deck of the very brigantine on which Anne
sailed . . . that another woman, also disguised in man's
clothes, made a dramatic entrance"*

DEADLIER THAN THE MALE: ANNE BONNEY AND MARY READ

E.O. Hoppé

*Piracy has been overwhelmingly a male occupation; Jo Stanley in
Bold in Her Breeches: Women Pirates Across the Ages estimates
that in the "Golden Age" of eighteenth-century piracy only 0.5 per
cent of Anglo-American pirates were cross-dressed females. That is
perhaps fifty to a hundred individuals. Most ships had an injunction
against women aboard, for the simple reason that their sexual favours
(or the possibility thereof) would lead to dissension amongst the crew.
Even so, there have been exceptions to the male-only rule of piracy,
beginning with Queen Artemisia in the Persian Gulf in the fifth
century BC and ending with Lai Choi San in Macao in the 1920s.*

*The most celebrated of the female pirates across the ages and the
seas have been England's Anne Bonney and Mary Read.*

In the Public Record Office at Spanish Town, known in former
times as St. Iago de la Vega, Jamaica, there is preserved a rare and
quaintly worded record, entitled–

The TRYALS of Captain John Rackham, and other PI-
RATES who were all condemn'd for PIRACY, at the Town
of St. Iago de la Vega, in the island of JAMAICA, on
Wednesday and Thursday the Sixteenth and Seventeenth
Days of November 1720, as also the TRYALS of Mary

Read and Anne Bonney who were also condemn'd for
"PIRACY."

Lurid as are the chronicles of sea-robbers who followed the cult
of the Black Flag in the heyday of buccaneering, for sheer devilry
they pale beside the deeds of some of the women pirates of the
early eighteenth century whose audacious exploits add a highly
colored page to piratical romance.

Making all allowance for the probability that, in the passage of
time, such tales have acquired an historical patina, their glamor
makes them irresistible to such of us, who, by force of convention
and circumstances, must be content to indulge any subconscious
leanings to lawless adventure, at second hand, or equally to those
who merely like to be thrilled.

Whether or not women number largely in the great company of
readers of this class of literature is a matter for conjecture but that
members of "the weaker sex" have, in the past, and right up into
recent times, carried out the business of robbery by violence on the
high seas and inland waters with conspicuous success, is irrefutable.

Take the case of Anne Bonney, daughter of a notary or
solicitor, practising in County Cork, Ireland. There was nothing
in her antecedents to account for her latent propensities. Anne
was a pretty, vivacious child, idolized by her father, who, until his
liaison with his wife's maid came to light with the birth of Anne,
had a good standing in local professional circles, but the gradual
decline in prestige and revenue brought about a determination to
emigrate, and take the child with him, to America, to try his luck
there. Shortly after their arrival he changed his legal profession
for that of a planter and Anne grew to attractive girlhood in the
pleasant setting of a comfortable home in Carolina where her
father had become a prosperous estate owner. The old man had
ambitious plans for Anne's future, who kept house for him until
she reached the age of sixteen, but these plans were brought to an
abrupt termination when the girl announced that she had fallen in
love with a good-looking but penniless sailor whom she had met
and whom she was going to marry. She would not listen to her
father's earnest entreaties to give up this mad plan, and being
headstrong and possessing a violent temper, she eloped with her
betrothed, whereupon the irate parent refused to sanction the
match and cut Anne off with the proverbial shilling.

A bride with expensive tastes and no money was not to the bridegroom's liking, who had expected that his young wife would be well provided for by her father. Finding that her only fortune was her good looks and having no means to support himself and his wife, the pair sailed to the island of New Providence in the Bahamas, where he hoped to find employment. In the early eighteenth century this group of islands was one of the favorable "resting" places of the Caribbean pirates and buccaneers who retired there in the intervals between their nefarious exploits, and a more villainous riffraff of cutthroats it would have been hard to find. In this setting, then, appeared handsome John Rackham, famed and feared throughout the West Indies for his daredevil acts of piracy. He met Anne and swept her off her feet, and there started an alliance which carried her straight on to the stage where she was to play out her life's drama. Anne asked her sailor husband that he should give her her freedom in exchange for a liberal sum of money which her new, dashing lover offered to provide. As this proposal was indignantly refused, Anne jumped at Rackham's suggestion that she should go to sea with him in his ship, disguised in man's clothes, pledging herself that she would not reveal the secret of her sex to her shipmates.

Anne accompanied her pirate-lover on all his buccaneering cruises and eventually proved to be his equal with sword and pistol and his superior in audacity and reckless courage. She fought, pillaged and plundered with ruthless brutality, her only concession to her womanhood being an occasional retirement when a child was born to her. On these occasions she usually stayed in Cuba, living in the extravagance and luxury characteristic of the successful freebooter.

Whenever these incidents were over, Anne joined Rackham again, sailing under the skull and crossbones, and acting as his trusted lieutenant. Before the curtain was finally rung down on the amazing career of this sea-amazon, fate played one of those strange tricks which writers of fiction would be hesitant to introduce into the plots of their stories. It was on the deck of the very brigantine on which Anne sailed with her lover that another woman, also disguised in man's clothes, made a dramatic entrance.

So complete was the appearance of both that each took the other for what she appeared to be. In many ways the life of Mary

Read in her early womanhood had been singularly like that of Anne Bonney, as will be seen later. Mary's fair skin and beardless face gave her a boyish appearance, and her fine, sparkling eyes and cheerful manners were a challenge to Anne's susceptibilities. Unaware of each other's secret, Anne took an immediate liking to the dashing "young man" and finally confessed to Mary that she had fallen in love with her, revealing at the same time her sex, much to the latter's embarrassment. Under the circumstances Mary had no choice but in turn to divulge her womanhood, also. After the amorous Anne had recovered from her surprise and, it may be assumed, disappointment, the two girls became close friends. Rackham was greatly disturbed by the growing intimacy between his sweetheart and the young sailor and in a fit of violent jealousy threatened that he would cut the young man's throat. Therefore, to quiet her irate lover Anne was forced to let him into the secret, which Rackham never betrayed.

The recorded history of Mary Read suggests that her early environment, unlike that of Anne Bonney, may have had some influence in the shaping of her chosen career. Her mother, who seems to have had no scruples where self-interest was affected, was the wife of a merchant skipper and Mary was born during one of the voyages on which Mrs. Read usually accompanied her husband. For the first few years of her life the girl lived on board her father's ship and it is therefore little wonder that the sea was in her blood.

Mary had a brother, one year older than herself, and when her father died her mother set up home with the children in a small Devonshire village where she appears to have supported herself and son and daughter by her wits rather than by hard work. Her late husband's mother who lived in Plymouth was fairly well-to-do and it was presumed that her grandson might expect to be her heir but he, unfortunately, died shortly after the family had settled down. But Mary's mother had no intention to let a trifle such as this stand in the way of an inheritance, and conceived the bold plan that her daughter must cease to exist as a girl and must forthwith impersonate her dead brother. By dressing her in his clothes and coaching her in the ways of little boys Mary turned out to be a most apt pupil and entered enthusiastically into the spirit of what was to her mind an exciting adventure.

The ruse was entirely successful and when Mrs. Read presented her daughter to the old lady, who had never seen her grandson before, she was completely deceived. She was delighted with the bright and handsome "lad" and did not question his genuineness for one single moment. So pleased, indeed, was she, that she contributed a small sum each week towards "his" support.

However, when Mary was thirteen the grandmother died and despite all schemes and machinations it was discovered that she had left her money elsewhere and her "grandson" did not profit by a penny.

The girl continued masquerading and living as a boy and, when the time came to earn her living, a job as a pageboy at a small hotel was found for her. But Mary quickly tired of the monotony of the work and the restrictions it imposed upon her mercurial nature and obtained employment at one of the dockside taverns where she felt more at ease among the sailors and longshoremen who frequented them. Yet, her roving spirit would not let her rest and she ran away to sea, enlisting in the Queen's Navy and serving as a "powder monkey" on board a man-of-war. After a few years' service she became fed up with the hard life and, when the ship was at anchor at a Flemish port, deserted and joined a foot regiment as a cadet, or volunteer. She fought with daring and bravery in several actions and her courage and gallantry won her the notice and good opinion of her officers and comrades. To her disappointment, however, she was not promoted, in spite of her fine record, whereupon she quitted the service in disgust and enlisted in a cavalry regiment.

By this time Mary had grown into a dashing creature, lithe and supple of figure and with merry, laughing eyes. Fighting, swearing and drinking with the best of them, her high spirits soon made her a favorite among her messmates, none of whom ever suspected that the good-looking lad was in reality a woman. Fate, however, challenged her in the person of a handsome young cavalryman who joined the band with her and with whom she fell violently in love. To him she revealed the secret of her sex and the two lovers became inseparable companions.

When the campaign was drawing to a close and the regiment had gone into winter quarters Mary publicly made a clean breast of the situation, much to the amazement and delight of her comrades, and, for the first time since early babyhood, appeared dressed as a woman. Shortly afterwards the pair were married and the unusual circumstances so intrigued the commanding officer that he and his staff not only assisted at the marriage ceremony but made a gift of money to bride and groom. Mary and her husband then obtained their discharge and settled down at Breda where they opened a tavern, or eating house, at the sign of the "Three Horseshoes". Owing to the romantic nature of their adventurous past the young couple soon did a thriving business and numbered among their guests many of their former officers as well as not a few of the wealthy burghers of the town.

After a while, Mary's husband fell ill and died soon afterwards, which brought the one and only domestic interlude in Mary's life to a close. With the coming of the Peace of Ryswick most of the soldiery whose patronage of the tavern had proved so lucrative disbanded and trade decreased so rapidly that Mary was forced to sell out. But she had by no means sown all the wild oats of which she was capable and, deciding to become a young man once again, donned male attire and went back to army life, joining a regiment of foot garrisoned in one of the Dutch seaport towns. As was to be expected, after a life of independence spent in comparative luxury and having been made much of by her former associates Mary revolted against the strict military discipline and made up her mind to go to sea again. She watched her opportunity and when a Dutch West Indiaman was on the point of leaving port, she deserted and joined its crew.

The journey was uneventful until the Island of New Providence or the Bahamas, as they are now known, was almost sighted, when the vessel was assailed and seized by English pirates who ransacked it, but set the crew free and let them continue their journey with the exception of Mary, who was the only English sailor on board. Having been greatly impressed by her cool-headed behavior during the action they forced her to throw in her lot with them. For some time Mary sailed under the Black Flag, taking to the adventurous life as a duck takes to water and handling cutlass and pistol like any man; nobody ever realized she was a girl.

The Bahamas were at that time one of the resorts of pirates under the main leadership of Vane and Edward Teach, the infamous "Blackbeard", and their daring sea-robberies had become so intolerable that Captain Woodes Rogers was sent there by the British Government, charged to suppress piracy and stamp out the evils by every means at his disposal including persuasive charm – which he possessed in no small degree – the offer of a free pardon to all those pirates who surrendered by a given date, and by armed force to bring the recalcitrants to justice. Captain Rogers was the famous navigator who, nine years earlier, rescued Alexander Selkirk, the hero of "Robinson Crusoe's Island" while on an expedition against the Spaniards at Guayaquil. So well did he succeed through his commanding personality, no less than through his strategy, that not only did many of the pirates and buccaneers, who some reports claim to have numbered well over two thousand, surrender and receive their pardon but actually helped Captain Rogers with the trial and execution of some of those of their former companions in crime who reverted and were recaptured.

The crew of the pirate ship which captured the Dutch Indiaman had put into Nassau on New Providence Island and settled ashore, Mary among them. She lived there quietly when Captain Rogers arrived with his free pardon to all pirates, in 1718, but her money began to grow short and hearing of a privateering expedition being sent out by Captain Rogers to cruise against the Spaniards, Mary signed on as a member of the crew, which consisted in the main of converted freebooters.

The ship had hardly left port when these men mutinied, deciding to return to their old calling. They put the captain into irons and elected one of their number, John Rackham, as their leader. This man was a powerful, swashbuckling blackguard, nicknamed "Calico Jack", whose exploits as a seasoned member of the infamous "Brethren of the Coast" had earned him a sinister reputation. One of the first to express their willingness to sign on under pirate regulations was Mary. This, at last, she felt, was her opportunity to lead the kind of life for which she was really fitted and Rackham had no objection to adding the lively, courageous "lad" to his company.

Fate was ready to take a hand in shaping Mary's destiny. To her unbounded astonishment she was confronted on board by Anne Bonney, pattern of all women brigands, who always sailed with her sweetheart, John Rackham, wearing men's clothes, the same as Mary did.

For some turbulent months Rackham sailed the main taking

and looting several merchantmen homeward bound from Jamaica. In one of these successful raids an attractive youth with engaging manners was taken prisoner to whom Mary lost her heart. No doubt, this was the main reason why Mary did not fasten her affection on the captain resulting in amicable relations between the two women being maintained, and why no jealousy or rivalry arose between them. On the contrary, they fought valiantly side by side, using sword and musketoon with terrorizing effect on their victims.

In the course of the cruise Mary proved her devotion to her lover by an act of stoical heroism. Her sweetheart quarreled violently with a fellow pirate who challenged him to a duel. As the sloop lay at anchor at one of the islands the men appointed an hour for the following day when they would go ashore and fight. Desperate in her anxiety that the man whom she loved might be killed, Mary picked a quarrel with the fellow challenging him to a duel herself, the latter agreeing to fight it two hours earlier than his engagement with his other opponent. Unknown to her lover the two antagonists went ashore at the appointed time and both fighting with sword and pistol alike, in true pirate fashion, Mary outwitted the ferociously attacking ruffian by taking him off his guard and wounding him mortally.

For some time fortune was kind to Jack Rackham and several merchantmen were captured. But as was usual in a sea-robber's career, retribution overtook him. A big fast-sailing sloop which had been sent out by the Governor of Jamaica, manned by a detachment of marines, sighted the pirate ship and went at once in pursuit of it. Before the more cumbersome brigantine's anchor was weighed the sloop came up and the King's men boarded it.

In the ensuing skirmish none of the pirates, with the exception of Mary Read and Anne Bonney and one of the crew, kept the deck. All the others, including the captain, fled below deck in panic, upon which the two women ran after them and, cursing them as cowards, forced them at pistol's point to come up again and fight like men. However, the odds were heavy against the demoralized pirate crew and the only three who had shown courage and valor realized the hopelessness of their plight and surrendered.

All the prisoners were taken to Jamaica where Jack and his followers were given a quick trial and sentenced to be hanged.

Rackham was executed at Gallows Point, Port Royal and his body was later cut down and hung in chains on one of the quays, along with eight of his crew. Mary and Anne managed each to escape vengeance. As they were found to be expectant mothers at the time of their trials, execution was postponed but Mary died in prison of a fever at the age of only 27 years. Anne was reprieved after the birth of a child but no record can be found of what eventually became of her.

The last request of Rackham to be allowed to visit his sweetheart before his execution was granted as a special favor but it brought him instead of consolation, sneering taunts from the outraged Anne, whose parting words to him were: "I am sorry to see you here, Jack, but if you had fought like a man you would not now be hanged like a dog."

WOMEN PIRATES

Ten female pirates:

1) Queen Artemisia, active Persian Gulf, 480 BC
2) Queen Teuta, active Adriatic, third century BC
3) Alfhild, active North Sea, mid fifth century AD
4) Granuaile O'Malley, active Ireland, c 1560–80
5) Elizabeth Killigrew, active Atlantic, 1560–80
6) Anne Bonny (Bonney), active Caribbean, 1720
7) Mary Read, active Caribbean, 1720
8) Maria Cobham, active Atlantic, early eighteenth century
9) Ching Yih Saou, active China, 1807–10
10) Lai Choi San, active Macao, c 1920s

---

*"The pirates now divided their plunder,
receiving forty-two diamonds per man"*

THE LIFE AND ADVENTURES
OF CAPTAIN ENGLAND

Charles Ellms

This adventurer was mate of a sloop that sailed from Jamaica, and was taken by Captain Winter, a pirate, just before the settlement of the pirates at Providence island. After the pirates had surrendered to his Majesty's pardon, and Providence island was peopled by the English government, Captain England sailed to Africa. There he took several vessels, particularly the *Cadogan*, from Bristol, commanded by one Skinner. When the latter struck to the pirate, he was ordered to come on board in his boat. The person upon whom he first cast his eye proved to be his old boatswain, who stared him in the face, and accosted him in the following manner: "Ah, Captain Skinner, is it you? the only person I wished to see: I am much in your debt, and I shall pay you all in your own coin." The poor man trembled in every joint, and dreaded the event, as he well might. It happened that Skinner and his old boatswain, with some of his men, had quarrelled, so that he thought fit to remove them on board a man-of-war, while he refused to pay them their wages. Not long after, they found means to leave the man-of-war, and went on board a small ship in the West Indies. They were taken by a pirate, and brought to Providence, and from thence sailed as pirates with Captain England. Thus accidentally meeting their old captain, they severely revenged the treatment they had received.

After the rough salutation which has been related, the boatswain called to his comrades, laid hold of Skinner, tied him fast to the windlass, and pelted him with glass bottles until they cut him in a shocking manner, then whipped him about the deck until they were quite fatigued, remaining deaf to all his prayers and entreaties; and at last, in an insulting tone, observed that as he had been a good master to his men, he should have an easy death, and upon this shot him through the head.

Having taken such things out of the ship as they stood most in need of, she was given to Captain Davis in order to try his fortune with a few hands.

Captain England, some time after, took a ship called the *Pearl*, for which he exchanged his own sloop, fitted her up for piratical service, and called her the *Royal James*. In that vessel he was very fortunate, and took several ships of different sizes and different nations. In the spring of 1719, the pirates returned to Africa, and beginning at the River Gambia, sailed down the coast to Cape Corso, and captured several vessels. Some of them they pillaged, and allowed to proceed, some they fitted out for the pirate service, and others they burned.

Leaving our pirate upon this coast, the *Revenge* and the *Flying King*, two other pirate vessels, sailed for the West Indies, where they took several prizes, and then cleared and sailed for Brazil. There they captured some Portuguese vessels; but a large Portuguese man-of-war coming up to them, proved an unwelcome guest. The *Revenge* escaped, but was soon lost upon that coast. The *Flying King* in despair run ashore. There were then seventy on board, twelve of whom were slain, and the remainder taken prisoners. The Portuguese hanged thirty-eight of them.

Captain England, whilst cruising upon that coast, took the *Peterborough* of Bristol, and the *Victory*. The former they detained, the latter they plundered and dismissed. In the course of his voyage, England met with two ships, but these taking shelter under Cape Corso Castle, he unsuccessfully attempted to set them on fire. He next sailed down to Whydah road, where Captain La Bouche had been before England, and left him no spoil. He now went into the harbor, cleaned his own ship, and fitted up the *Peterborough*, which he called the *Victory*. During several weeks the pirates remained in this quarter, indulging in every species of riot and debauchery, until the natives, exasperated with their conduct, came to an open rupture, when several of the negroes were slain, and one of their towns set on fire by the pirates.

Leaving that port, the pirates, when at sea, determined by vote to sail for the East Indies, and arrived at Madagascar. After watering and taking in some provisions they sailed for the coast of Malabar. This place is situated in the Mogul Empire, and is one of its most beautiful and fertile districts. It extends from the coast of Canora to Cape Comorin. The original natives are negroes; but a mingled race of Mahometans, who are generally merchants, have been introduced in modern times. Having sailed almost round the one half of the globe, literally seeking whom they might devour, our pirates arrived in this hitherto untried and prolific field for their operations.

Not long after their settlement at Madagascar, they took a cruise, in which they captured two Indian vessels and a Dutchman. They exchanged the latter for one of their own, and directed their course again to Madagascar. Several of their hands were sent on shore with tents and ammunition, to kill such beasts and venison as the island afforded. They also formed the resolution to go in search of Avery's crew, which they knew had settled upon the island; but as their residence was upon the other side of the island, the loss of time and labour was the only fruit of their search.

They tarried here but a very short time, then steered their course to Johanna, and coming out of that harbor, fell in with two English vessels and an Ostend ship, all Indiamen, which, after a most desperate action, they captured. The particulars of this extraordinary action are related in the following letter from Captain Mackra.

"Bombay, November 16th, 1720.
"We arrived on the 25th of July last, in company with the *Greenwich*, at Johanna, an island not far from Madagascar. Putting in there to refresh our men, we found fourteen pirates who came in their canoes from the Mayotta, where the pirate ship to which they belonged, viz. the *Indian Queen*, two hundred and fifty tons, twenty-eight guns, and ninety men, commanded by Captain Oliver de la Bouche, bound from the Guinea coast to the East Indies, had been bulged and lost.

They said they left the captain and forty of their men building
a new vessel, to proceed on their wicked designs. Captain
Kirby and I concluding that it might be of great service to
the East India Company to destroy such a nest of rogues, were
ready to sail for that purpose on the 17th of August, about eight
o'clock in the morning, when we discovered two pirates standing into the bay Johanna, one of thirty-four, and the other of
thirty-six guns. I immediately went on board the *Greenwich*,
where they seemed very diligent in preparation for an engagement, and I left Captain Kirby with mutual promises of
standing by each other. I then unmoored, got under sail,
and brought two boats a-head to row me close to the *Greenwich*; but he being open to a valley and a breeze, made the best
of his way from me; which an Ostender in our company, of
twenty-two guns, seeing, did the same, though the captain had
promised heartily to engage with us, and I believe would have
been as good as his word, if Captain Kirby had kept his. About
half an hour after twelve, I called several times to the *Greenwich* to bear down to our assistance, and fired a shot at him, but
to no purpose; for though we did not doubt but he would join
us, because, when he got about a league from us he brought his
ship to and looked on, yet both he and the Ostender basely
deserted us, and left us engaged with barbarous and inhuman
enemies, with their black and bloody flags hanging over us,
without the least appearance of ever escaping, but to be cut to
pieces. But God in his good providence determined otherwise;
for, notwithstanding their superiority, we engaged them both
about three hours; during which time the biggest of them
received some shot betwixt wind and water, which made her
keep off a little to stop her leaks. The other endeavored all she
could to board us, by rowing with her oars, being within half a
ship's length of us above an hour; but by good fortune we shot
all her oars to pieces, which prevented them, and by consequence saved our lives.

"About four o'clock most of the officers and men posted on the
quarter-deck being killed and wounded, the largest ship making
up to us with diligence, being still within a cable's length of us,
often giving us a broadside; there being now no hopes of Captain
Kirby's coming to our assistance, we endeavored to run a-shore;
and though we drew four feet of water more than the pirate, it

pleased God that he stuck fast on a higher ground than happily we fell in with; so was disappointed a second time from boarding us. Here we had a more violent engagement than before: all my officers and most of my men behaved with unexpected courage; and, as we had a considerable advantage by having a broadside to his bow, we did him great damage; so that had Captain Kirby come in then, I believe we should have taken both the vessels, for we had one of them sure; but the other pirate (who was still firing at us) seeing the *Greenwich* did not offer to assist us, supplied his consort with three boats full of fresh men. About five in the evening the *Greenwich* stood clear away to sea, leaving us struggling hard for life, in the very jaws of death; which the other pirate that was afloat, seeing, got a warp out, and was hauling under our stern.

"By this time many of my men being killed and wounded, and no hopes left us of escaping being all murdered by enraged barbarous conquerors, I ordered all that could to get into the long-boat, under the cover of the smoke of our guns; so that, with what some did in boats, and others by swimming, most of us that were able, got ashore by seven o'clock. When the pirates came aboard, they cut three of our wounded men to pieces. I with some of my people made what haste I could to King's-town, twenty-five miles from us, where I arrived next day, almost dead with the fatigue and loss of blood, having been sorely wounded in the head by a musket-ball.

"At this town I heard that the pirates had offered ten thousand dollars to the country people to bring me in, which many of them would have accepted, only they knew the king and all his chief people were in my interest. Meantime, I caused a report to be spread that I was dead of my wounds, which much abated their fury. About ten days after, being pretty well recovered, and hoping the malice of our enemies was nigh over, I began to consider the dismal condition we were reduced to; being in a place where we had no hopes of getting a passage home, all of us in a manner naked, not having had time to bring with us either a shirt or a pair of shoes, except what we had on. Having obtained leave to go on board the pirates with a promise of safety, several of the chief of them knew me, and some of them had sailed with me, which I found to be of great advantage; because, notwithstanding their promise, some of them would have cut me to pieces, and all that would not enter with them, had it not been for their chief captain, Edward England, and some others whom I knew. They talked of burning one of their ships, which we had so entirely disabled as to be no farther useful to them, and to fit the *Cassandra* in her room; but in the end I managed the affair so well, that they made me a present of the said shattered ship, which was Dutch built, and called the *Fancy*; her burden was about three hundred tons. I procured also a hundred and twenty-nine bales of the Company's cloth, though they would not give me a rag of my own clothes.

"They sailed the 3rd of September; and I, with jury-masts, and such old sails as they left me, made a shift to do the like on the 8th, together with forty-three of my ship's crew, including two passengers and twelve soldiers; having no more than five tuns of water aboard. After a passage of forty-eight days, I arrived here on the 26th of October, almost naked and starved, having been reduced to a pint of water a-day, and almost in despair of ever seeing land, by reason of the calms we met with between the coast of Arabia and Malabar.

"We had in all thirteen men killed and twenty-four wounded; and we were told that we destroyed about ninety or a hundred of the pirates. When they left us, they were about three hundred whites, and eighty blacks, on both ships. I am persuaded, had our consort the *Greenwich* done his duty, we had destroyed both of them, and got two hundred thousand pounds for our owners and selves; whereas the loss of the *Cassandra* may justly be imputed to his deserting us. I have delivered all the bales that were given me into the Company's warehouse, for which the governor and council have ordered me a reward. Our governor, Mr. Boon, who is extremely kind and civil to me, had ordered me home with the packet; but Captain Harvey, who had a prior promise, being come in with the fleet, goes in my room. The governor had promised me a country voyage to help to make up my losses, and would have me stay and accompany him to England next year."

Captain Mackra was certainly in imminent danger, in trusting himself and his men on board the pirate ship, and unquestionably nothing but the desperate circumstances in which he was placed could have justified so hazardous a step. The honor and influence of Captain England, however, protected him and his men from the fury of the crew, who would willingly have wreaked their vengeance upon them.

It is pleasing to discover any instance of generosity or honor among such an abandoned race, who bid defiance to all the laws of honor, and, indeed, are regardless of all laws human and divine. Captain England was so steady to Captain Mackra, that he informed him, it would be with no small difficulty and address that he would be able to preserve him and his men from the fury of the crew, who were greatly enraged at the resistance which had been made. He likewise acquainted him, that his influence and authority among them was giving place to that of Captain Taylor, chiefly because the dispositions of the latter were more savage and brutal. They therefore consulted between them what was the best method to secure the favor of Taylor, and keep him in good humor. Mackra made the punch to flow in great abundance, and employed every artifice to soothe the mind of that ferocious villain.

A single incident was also very favorable to the unfortunate captain. It happened that a pirate, with a prodigious pair of whiskers, a wooden leg, and stuck round with pistols, came blustering and swearing upon the quarter deck, inquiring "where was Captain Mackra." He naturally supposed that this barbarous-looking fellow would be his executioner; but, as he approached, he took the captain by the hand, swearing "that he was an honest fellow, and that he had formerly sailed with him, and would stand by him; and let him see the man that would touch him." This terminated the dispute, and Captain Taylor's disposition was so ameliorated with punch, that he consented that the old pirate ship, and so many bales of cloth, should be given to Mackra, and then sank into the arms of intoxication. England now pressed Mackra to hasten away, lest the ruffian, upon his becoming sober, should not only retract his word, but give liberty to the crew to cut him and his men to pieces.

But the gentle temper of Captain England, and his generosity towards the unfortunate Mackra, proved the organ of much calamity to himself. The crew, in general, deeming the kind of usage which Mackra had received, inconsistent with piratical policy, they circulated a report that he was coming against them with the Company's force. The result of these invidious reports was to deprive England of his command, and to excite these cruel villains to put him on shore, with three others, upon the island of Mauritius. If England and his small company had not been destitute of every necessary, they might have made a comfortable subsistence here, as the island abounds with deer, hogs, and other animals. Dissatisfied, however, with their solitary situation, Captain England and his three men exerted their industry and ingenuity, and formed a small boat, with which they sailed to Madagascar, where they subsisted upon the generosity of some more fortunate piratical companions.

They proceeded to Calicut, and attempting to cut out a ship, were prevented by some guns placed upon the shore. One of Captain Mackra's officers was under deck at this time, and was commanded both by the captain and the quarter-master to tend the braces on the booms, in hopes that a shot would take him before they got clear. He was about to have excused himself, but they threatened to shoot him; and when he expostulated, and claimed their promise to put him on shore, he received an umerciful beating from the quarter-master; Captain Taylor, to whom that duty belonged, being lame in his hands.

The day following they met a Dutch galliot, laden with lime-stone, bound for Calicut, on board of which they put one Captain Fawkes; and some of the crew interceding for Mackra's officer, Taylor and his party replied, "If we let this dog go, who has overheard our designs and resolutions, he will overset all our well-advised resolutions, and particularly this supply we are seeking for at the hands of the Dutch."

When they arrived at Cochin, they sent a letter on shore by a fishing-boat, entered the road, and anchored, each ship saluting the fort with eleven guns, and receiving the same number in return. This was the token of their welcome reception, and at night a large boat was sent, deeply laden with liquors and all kinds of provisions, and in it a servant of John Trumpet, one of their friends, to inform them that it would be necessary for them to run farther south, where they would be supplied both with provisions and naval stores.

They had scarcely anchored at the appointed place, when several canoes, with white and black inhabitants, came on board, and continued without interruption to perform all the good offices in their power during their stay in that place. In particular, John Trumpet brought a large boat of arrack, and sixty bales of sugar, as a present from the governor and his daughter; the former receiving in return a table-clock, and the other a gold watch, the spoil of Captain Mackra's vessel. When their provisions were all on board, Trumpet was rewarded with about six or seven thousand pounds, was saluted with three cheers, and eleven guns; and several handsfull of silver were thrown into the boat, for the men to gather at pleasure.

There being little wind that night, they remained at anchor, and in the morning were surprised with the return of Trumpet, bringing another boat equally well stored with provisions, with chests of piece-goods and ready-made clothes, and along with him the fiscal of the place. At noon they espied a sail towards the south, and immediately gave chase, but she outsailed them, and sheltered under the fort of Cochin. Informed that they would not be molested in taking her from under the castle, they sailed towards her, but upon the fort firing two guns, they ran off for fear of more serious altercation, and returning, anchored in their former station. They were too welcome visitants to be permitted to depart, so long as John Trumpet could contrive to detain them. With this view he informed them, that in a few days a rich vessel, commanded by the Governor of Bombay's brother, was to pass that way.

That government is certainly in a wretched state, which is under the necessity of trading with pirates, in order to enrich itself; nor will such a government hesitate by what means an injury can be repaired, or a fortune gained. Neither can language describe the low and base principles of a government which could employ such a miscreant as John Trumpet in its service. He was a tool in the hands of the government of Cochin; and, as the dog said in the fable, "What is done by the master's orders, is the master's action," or, as the same sentiment is, perhaps, better expressed in the legal axiom: "Qui facit per alium facit per se."

While under the direction of Trumpet, some proposed to proceed directly to Madagascar, but others were disposed to wait until they should be provided with a store ship. The majority being of the latter opinion, they steered to the south, and seeing a ship on shore were desirous to get near her, but the wind preventing, they separated, the one sailing northward and the other southward, in hopes of securing her when she should come out, whatever direction she might take. They were now, however, almost entrapped in the snare laid for them. In the morning, to their astonishment and consternation, instead of being called to give chase, five large ships were near, which made a signal for the pirates to bear down. The pirates were in the greatest dread lest it should be Captain Mackra, of whose activity and courage they had formerly sufficient proof. The pirate ships, however, joined and fled with all speed from the fleet. In three hours' chase none of the fleet gained upon them, except one grab. The remainder of the day was calm, and, to their great consolation, the next day this dreaded fleet was entirely out of sight.

Their alarm being over, they resolved to spend the Christmas in feasting and mirth, in order to drown care, and to banish thought. Nor did one day suffice, but they continued their revelling for several days, and made so free with their fresh provisions, that in their next cruise they were put upon short allowance; and it was entirely owing to the sugar and other provisions that were in the leaky ship that they were preserved from absolute starvation.

In this condition they reached the island of Mauritius, re-fitted the *Victory*, and left that place with the following in-scription written upon one of the walls: "Left this place on the 5th of April, to go to Madagascar for Limos." This they did lest any visit should be paid to the place during their absence. They, however, did not sail directly for Madagascar, but the island of Mascarius, where they fortunately fell in with a Portuguese of seventy guns, lying at anchor. The greater part of her guns had been thrown overboard, her masts lost, and the whole vessel disabled by a storm; she therefore became an easy prey to the pirates. Conde de Ericeira, Viceroy of Goa, who went upon the fruitless expedition against Angria the Indian, and several passengers, were on board. Besides other valuable articles and specie, they found in her diamonds to the amount of four millions of dollars. Supposing that the ship was an Englishman, the Viceroy came on board next morning, was made prisoner, and obliged to pay two thousand dollars as a ransom for himself and the other prisoners. After this he was sent ashore, with an express engagement to leave a ship to convey him and his companions to another port.

Meanwhile, the pirates received intelligence that a vessel was to the leeward of the island, which they pursued and captured. But instead of performing their promise to the Viceroy, which they could easily have done, they sent the Ostender along with some of their men to Madagascar, to inform their friends of their success, with instructions to prepare masts for the prize; and they soon followed, carrying two thousand negroes in the Portuguese vessel.

Madagascar is an island larger than Great Britain, situated upon the eastern coast of Africa, abounding with all sorts of provisions, such as oxen, goats, sheep, poultry, fish, citrons, oranges, tamarinds, dates, cocoa-nuts, bananas, wax, honey, rice, cotton, indigo, and all other fruits common in that quarter of the globe; ebony of which lances are made, gums of several kinds, and many other valuable productions. Here, in St. Augustine's bay, the ships sometimes stop to take in water, when they make the inner passage to India, and do not intend to stop at Johanna.

When the Portuguese ship arrived there, they received intelligence that the Ostender had taken advantage of an hour when the men were intoxicated, had risen upon them, and carried the ship to Mozambique, from whence the governor ordered her to Goa.

The pirates now divided their plunder, receiving forty-two diamonds per man, or in smaller proportion according to their magnitude. A foolish jocular fellow, who had received a large diamond of the value of forty-two, was highly displeased, and so went and broke it in pieces, exclaiming, that he had many more shares than either of them. Some, contended with their treasure, and unwilling to run the risk of losing what they possessed, and perhaps their lives also, resolved to remain with their friends at Madagascar, under the stipulation that the longest livers should enjoy all the booty. The number of adventurers being now lessened, they burned the *Victory*, cleaned the *Cassandra*, and the remainder went on board her under the command of Taylor, whom we must leave for a little while, in order to give an account of the squadron which arrived in India in 1721.

When the commodore arrived at the Cape, he received a letter that had been written by the Governor of Pondicherry to the

Governor of Madras, informing him that the pirates were strong in the Indian seas; that they had eleven sail, and fifteen hundred men; but adding, that many of them retired about that time to Brazil and Guinea, while others fortified themselves at Madagascar, Mauritius, Johanna, and Mohilla; and that a crew under the command of Condin, in a ship called the *Dragon*, had captured a vessel with thirteen sacks of rupees on board, and having divided their plunder, had taken up their residence with their friends at Madagascar.

Upon receiving this intelligence, Commodore Matthews sailed for these islands, as the most probable place of success. He endeavored to prevail on England, at St. Mary's, to communicate to him what information he could give respecting the pirates; but England declined, thinking that this would be almost to surrender at discretion. He then took up the guns of the *Jubilee* sloop that were on board, and the men-of-war made several cruises in search of the pirates, but to no purpose. The squadron was then sent down to Bombay, was saluted by the fort, and after these exploits returned home.

The pirate, Captain Taylor, in the *Cassandra*, now fitted up the Portuguese man-of-war, and resolved upon another voyage to the Indies; but, informed that four men-of-war had been sent after the pirates in that quarter, he changed his determination, and sailed for Africa. Arrived there, they put in a place near the river Spirito Sancto, on the coast of Monomotapa. As there was no correspondence by land, nor any trade carried on by sea to this place, they thought that it would afford a safe retreat. To their astonishment, however, when they approached the shore, it being in the dusk of the evening, they were accosted by several shot. They immediately anchored, and in the morning saw that the shot had come from a small fort of six guns, which they attacked and destroyed.

This small fort was erected by the Dutch East India Company a few weeks before, and committed to the care of 150 men, the one half of whom had perished by sickness or other causes. Upon their petition, sixteen of these were admitted into the society of the pirates; and the rest would also have been received, had they not been Dutchmen, to whom they had a rooted aversion.

In this place they continued during four months, refitting their vessels, and amusing themselves with all manner of diversions, until the scarcity of their provisions awakened them to industry and exertion. They, however, left several parcels of goods to the starving Dutchmen, which Mynheer joyfully exchanged for provisions with the next vessel that touched at that fort.

Leaving that place, they were divided in opinion what course to steer; some went on board the Portuguese prize, and, sailing for Madagascar, abandoned the pirate life; and others going on board the *Cassandra*, sailed for the Spanish West Indies. The *Mermaid* man-of-war, returning from a convoy, got near the pirates, and would have attacked them, but a consultation being held, it was deemed inexpedient, and thus the pirates escaped. A sloop was, however, dispatched to Jamaica with the intelligence, and the *Lancaster* was sent after them; but they were some days too late, the pirates having, with all their riches, surrendered to the Governor of Portobello.

PIRATE FLAGS

The first seventeenth-century ensigns flown by West Indian privateers were personal standards, intended to supplement the different national flags under which each commander served, rather than be unfurled alone. Thus, for example, the mixed force of *flibustiers* and Jamaican buccaneers which devastated. Veracruz under Laurens de Graaf and the Sieur de Grammont in May 1683 were observed to march out of that smouldering city behind "five French flags, four English, a green and a flowered one", the latter two presumably being individual banners.

Red was the preferred colour background for such ensigns throughout much of this period, being the traditional banner displayed in any battle where no quarter was to be expected or given, and thus suiting the buccaneers' purpose of instilling fear in their enemies. One instance of this occurred after the sack of Granada (Nicaragua) in May 1686, when a *flibustier* force under Captains Francois Grogniet, Jean Rose and Francis Townley began fighting their way back towards their anchored ships off the Pacific coast. At the town of Masaya they found 500 Spanish militia barring their path, and the chronicler Ravenau de Lussan noted:

> They were flying the red flag, thus giving us to understand there would be no quarter. Upon seeing this we hauled down our white [French] colours and exposed a red flag like theirs.

Nevertheless such displays were more usually made in conjunction with national standards, such as when Captain Edward Stanley's Royal Naval warship *Bonito*, of four guns, was attacked off the south Cuban coast by a Spanish corsair in November 1684 "flying the Spanish flag with a red ensign".

Some privateer commanders apparently refined this practice even further, by deliberately devising personal banners on blood-red backgrounds, to add the appropriate touch of menace when displayed: Captain Edmond Cooke, for example, flew a red flag striped with yellow, and emblazoned with a white hand and sword, when he invaded the Pacific Ocean with John Coxon in 1680. It was precisely these latter banners which became known collectively as the "Jolly Roger", a euphemism believed to derive from the French expression *jolie rouge* ("pretty red"), itself an ironic reference to the bloodthirsty significance of red ensigns.

Flags with a black background were a later development, dating from the early eighteenth century. The first recorded use occurred in 1700, when Captain Cranby of HMS *Poole* described the French corsair Emmanuel Wynne as fighting under "a sable ensign with crossbones, a Death's head and an hour glass" [the latter to signify that his opponent's time was running out]. When the War of the Spanish Succession ended thirteen short years later, most pirates were using a black background for their personal standards, and red for battle flags.

Thus when the pirate Charles Vane was driven out of New Providence (Nassau) in the Bahamas by the arrival of the new Royal Governor Woodes Rogers in 1718, he set sail defiantly flying the cross of Saint George at his maintop masthead, and a black pirate flag at the mizzen; two years later Edward England engaged the East Indiaman *Cassandra* off Johanna Island (near

Madagascar) flying a black flag at his maintopmast, a red flag at the foretopmast, and a cross of Saint George at the ensign staff. The unfortunate master of *Cassandra* exclaimed that he was beset by "barbarous and inhuman enemies, with their black and bloody flags hanging over us".

From *Pirates: Adventurers of the High Seas*, David F. Marley, Arms & Armour Press, 1995. Copyright © 1995 David F. Marley

*"Roberts . . . made a gallant figure . . . two pair of pistols
hanging at the end of a silk sling flung over his shoulders"*

BLACK BART

Charles Ellms

Bartholomew Roberts was trained to a sea-faring life. Among
other voyages which he made during the time that he lawfully
procured his maintenance, he sailed for the Guinea coast, in
November, 1719, where he was taken by the pirate Davis. He was
at first very averse to that mode of life, and would certainly have
deserted, had an opportunity occurred. It happened to him,
however, as to many upon another element, that preferment
calmed his conscience, and reconciled him to that which he
formerly hated.

Davis having fallen in the manner related, those who had
assumed the title of Lords assembled to deliberate concerning
the choice of a new commander. There were several candidates,
who, by their services, had risen to eminence among their breath-
ren, and each of them thought themselves qualified to bear rule.
One addressed the assembled lords, saying, "that the good of the
whole, and the maintenance of order, demanded a head, but that
the proper authority was deposited in the community at large; so
that if one should be elected who did not act and govern for the
general good, he could be deposed, and another be substituted in
his place."

"We are the original," said he, "of this claim, and should a
captain be so saucy as to exceed prescription at any time, why,
down with him! It will be a caution, after he is dead, to his
successors, to what fatal results any undue assumption may lead;
however, it is my advice, while we are sober, to pitch upon a man
of courage, and one skilled in navigation, – one who, by his

prudence and bravery, seems best able to defend this common-wealth, and ward us from the dangers and tempests of an unstable element, and the fatal consequences of anarchy; and such a one I take Roberts to be: a fellow in all respects worthy of your esteem and favor."

This speech was applauded by all but Lord Simpson, who had himself strong expectations of obtaining the highest command. He at last, in a surly tone, said he did not regard whom they chose as a commander, provided he was not a papist, for he had conceived a mortal hatred to papists, because his father had been a sufferer in Monmouth's rebellion.

Thus, though Roberts had only been a few weeks among them, his election was confirmed by the Lords and Commons. He, with the best face he could, accepted of the dignity, saying, "that since he had dipped his hands in muddy water, and must be a pirate, it was better being a commander than a private man."

The governor being settled, and other officers chosen in the room of those who had fallen with Davis, it was resolved not to leave this place without revenging his death. Accordingly, thirty men, under the command of one Kennedy, a bold and profligate fellow, landed, and under cover of the fire of the ship, ascended the hill upon which the fort stood. They were no sooner discovered by the Portuguese, than they abandoned the fort, and took shelter in the town. The pirates then entered without opposition, set fire to the fort, and tumbled the guns into the sea.

Not satisfied with this injury, some proposed to land and set the town in flames. Roberts however, reminded them of the great danger to which this would inevitably expose them; that there was a thick wood at the back of the town, where the inhabitants could hide themselves, and that, when their all was at stake, they would make a bolder resistance: and that the burning or destroying of a few houses, would be a small return for their labor, and the loss that they might sustain. This prudent advice had the desired effect, and they contented themselves with lightening the French vessel, and battering down several houses of the town, to show their high displeasure.

Roberts sailed southward, captured a Dutch Guineaman, and, having emptied her of everything they thought proper, returned her to the commander. Two days after, he captured an English ship, and, as the men joined in pirating, emptied and burned the vessel, and then sailed for St. Thomas. Meeting with no prize, he sailed for Anamaboa, and there watered and repaired. Having again put to sea, a vote was taken whether they should sail for the East Indies or for Brazil. The latter place was decided upon, and they arrived there in twenty-eight days.

Upon this coast our rovers cruised for about nine weeks, keeping generally out of sight of land, but without seeing a sail; which discouraged them so, that they determined to leave the station, and steer for the West Indies; and, in order thereto, they stood in to make the land for the taking of their departure, by which means they fell in, unexpectedly, with a fleet of forty-two sail of Portuguese ships, off the Bay of Los Todos Santos, with all their lading in for Lisbon; several of them of good force, who lay there waiting for two men of war of seventy guns each for their convoy. However, Roberts thought it should go hard with him but he would make up his market among them, and thereupon he mixed with the fleet, and kept his men concealed till proper resolutions could be formed; that done, they came close up to one of the deepest, and ordered her to send the master on board quietly, threatening to give them no quarter, if any resistance or signal of distress was made. The Portuguese, being surprised at these threats, and the sudden flourish of cutlasses from the pirates, submitted without a word, and the captain came on board. Roberts saluted him in a friendly manner, telling him that they were gentlemen of fortune, and that their business with him was only to be informed which was the richest ship in that fleet; and if he directed them right, he should be restored to his ship without molestation, otherwise he must expect instant death.

He then pointed to a vessel of forty guns, and a hundred and fifty men; and though her strength was greatly superior to Roberts', yet he made towards her, taking the master of the captured vessel along with him. Coming alongside of her, Roberts ordered the prisoner to ask, "How Seignior Captain did?" and to invite him on board, as he had a matter of importance to impart to him. He was answered, "That he would wait upon him presently." Roberts, however, observing more than ordinary bustle on board, at once concluded they were discovered, and pouring a broadside into her, they immediately boarded, grappled, and took her. She was a very rich prize, laden with sugar, skins, and tobacco, with four thousand moidores of gold, besides other valuable articles.

In possession of so much riches, they now became solicitous to find a safe retreat in which to spend their time in mirth and wantonness. They determined upon a place called the Devil's Island upon the river Surinam, where they arrived in safety, and met with a kind reception from the governor and the inhabitants.

In this river they seized a sloop, which informed them that she had sailed in company with a brigantine loaded with provisions. This was welcome intelligence, as their provisions were nearly exhausted. Deeming this too important a business to trust to foreign hands, Roberts, with forty men in the sloop, gave chase to that sail. In the keenness of the moment, and trusting in his usual good fortune, Roberts supposed that he had only to take a short sail in order to bring in the vessel with her cargo; but to his sad disappointment, he pursued her during eight days, and instead of gaining, was losing way. Under these circumstances, he came to anchor, and sent off the boat to give intelligence of their distress to their companions.

In their extremity of want, they took up part of the floor of the cabin, and patched up a sort of tray with rope-yarns, to paddle on shore to get a little water to preserve their lives. When their patience was almost exhausted, the boat returned, but instead of provisions, brought the unpleasing information, that the lieutenant, one Kennedy, had run off with both the ships.

The misfortune and misery of Roberts were greatly aggravated by reflecting upon his own imprudence and want of foresight, as well as from the baseness of Kennedy and his crew. Impelled by the necessity of his situation, he now began to reflect upon the means he should employ for future support. Under the foolish supposition that any laws, oaths or regulations, could bind those who had bidden open defiance to all divine and human laws, he proceeded to form a code of regulations for the maintenance of order and unity in his little commonwealth.

But present necessity compelled them to action, and with their small sloop they sailed for the West Indies. They were not long before they captured two sloops, which supplied them with provisions, and a few days after, a brigantine, and then proceeded to Barbadoes. When off that island they met a vessel of ten guns, richly laden from Bristol; after plundering, and detaining her three days, they allowed her to prosecute her voyage. This vessel, however, informed the governor of what had befallen them, who sent a vessel of twenty guns and eighty men in quest of the pirates.

That vessel was commanded by one Rogers, who, on the second day of his cruise, discovered Roberts. Ignorant of any vessel being sent after them, they made towards each other. Roberts gave him a gun but instead of striking, the other returned a broadside, with three huzzas. A severe engagement ensued, and Roberts being hard put to it, lightened his vessel and ran off.

Roberts then sailed for the Island of Dominica, where he watered, and was supplied by the inhabitants with provisions, for which he gave them goods in return. Here he met with fifteen Englishmen left upon the island by a Frenchman who had made a prize of their vessel; and they, entering into his service, proved a seasonable addition to his strength.

Though he did not think this a proper place for cleaning, yet as it was absolutely necessary that it should be done, he directed his course to the Granada islands for that purpose. This, however, had well nigh proved fatal to him; for the Governor of Martinique fitted out two sloops to go in quest of the pirates. They, however, sailed to the above-mentioned place, cleaned with unusual despatch, and just left that place the night before the sloops in pursuit of them arrived.

They next sailed for Newfoundland, arriving upon the banks in June, 1720, and entered the harbor of Trepassi, with their black colors flying, drums beating, and trumpets sounding. In that harbor there were no less than twenty-two ships, which the men abandoned upon the sight of the pirates. It is impossible to describe the injury which they did at this place, by burning or sinking the ships, destroying the plantations, and pillaging the houses. Power in the hands of mean and ignorant men renders them wanton, insolent and cruel. They are literally like madmen, who cast firebrands, arrows and death, and say, "Are not we in sport?"

Roberts reserved a Bristol galley from his depredations in the harbor, which he fitted and manned for his own service. Upon the banks he met ten sail of French ships, and destroyed them all, except one of twenty-six guns, which he seized and carried off, and called her the *Fortune*. Then giving the Bristol galley to the

Frenchman, they sailed in quest of new adventures, and soon took several prizes, and out of them increased the number of their own hands. The *Samuel*, one of these, was a very rich vessel, having some respectable passengers on board, who were roughly used, and threatened with death if they did not deliver up their money and their goods. They stripped the vessel of every article, either necessary for their vessel or themselves, to the amount of eight or nine thousand pounds. They then deliberated whether to sink or burn the *Samuel*, but in the mean time they discovered a sail, so they left the empty *Samuel*, and gave the other chase. At midnight they overtook her, and she proved to be the *Snow* from Bristol; and, because he was an Englishman, they used the master in a cruel and barbarous manner. Two days after, they took the *Little York* of Virginia, and the *Love* of Liverpool, both of which they plundered and sent off. In three days they captured three other vessels, removing the goods out of them, sinking one, and sending off the other two.

They next sailed for the West Indies, but provisions growing short, proceeded to St. Christopher's, where, being denied provisions by the governor, they fired on the town, and burnt two ships in the roads. They then repaired to the island of St. Bartholomew, where the governor supplied them with every necessary, and caressed them in the kindest manner. Satiated with indulgence, and having taken in a large stock of everything necessary, they unanimously voted to hasten to the coast of Guinea. In their way they took a Frenchman, and as she was fitter for the pirate service than their own, they informed the captain, that, as "a fair exchange was no robbery," they would exchange sloops with him; accordingly, having shifted their men, they set sail. However, going by mistake out of the track of the trade winds, they were under the necessity of returning to the West Indies.

They now directed their course to Surinam but not having sufficient water for the voyage they were soon reduced to a mouthful of water in the day; their numbers daily diminished by thirst and famine and the few who survived were reduced to the greatest weakness. They at last had not one drop of water or any other liquid, when, to their inexpressible joy, they anchored in seven fathoms of water. This tended to revive exhausted nature and inspire them with new vigour, though as yet they had received no relief. In the morning they discovered land, but at such a distance that their hopes were greatly dampened. The boat was however sent off, and at night returned with plenty of that necessary element. But this remarkable deliverance produced no reformation in the manners of these unfeeling and obdurate men.

Steering their course from that place to Barbadoes, in their way they met with a vessel which supplied them with all necessaries. Not long after, they captured a brigantine, the mate of which joined their association. Having from these two obtained a large supply, they changed their course and watered at Tobago. Informed, however, that there were two vessels sent in pursuit of them, they went to return their compliments to the Governor of Martinique for this kindness.

It was the custom of the Dutch interlopers, when they approached this island to trade with the inhabitants, to hoist their jacks. Roberts knew the signal, and did so likewise. They, supposing that a good market was near, strove who could first reach Roberts. Determined to do them all possible mischief he destroyed them one by one as they came into his power. He only reserved one ship to send the men on shore, and burnt the remainder, to the number of twenty.

Roberts and his crew were so fortunate as to capture several vessels and to render their liquor so plentiful, that it was esteemed a crime against Providence not to be continually drunk. One man, remarkable for his sobriety, along with two others, found an opportunity to set off without taking leave of their friends. But a despatch being sent after them, they were brought back, and in a formal manner tried and sentenced, but one of them was saved by the humorous interference of one of the judges, whose speech was truly worthy of a pirate – while the other two suffered the punishment of death.

When necessity again compelled them, they renewed their cruising; and, dissatisfied with capturing vessels which only afforded them a temporary supply, directed their course to the Guinea coast to forage for gold. Intoxication rendered them unruly, and the brigantine at last embraced the cover of night to abandon the commodore. Unconcerned at the loss of his companion, Roberts pursued his voyage. He fell in with two French ships, the one of ten guns and sixty-five men, and the other of sixteen guns and seventy-five men. These dastards no sooner beheld the black flag than they surrendered. With these they went to Sierra Leone, constituting one of them a consort, by the name of the *Ranger*, and the other a store-ship. This port being frequented by the greater part of the traders to that quarter, they remained here six weeks, enjoying themselves in all the splendor and luxury of a piratical life.

After this they renewed their voyage, and having captured a vessel, the greater part of the men united their fortunes with the pirates. On board of one of the ships was a clergyman, whom some of them proposed taking along with them, for no other reason than that they had not a chaplain on board. They endeavored to gain his consent, and assured him that he should want for nothing, and his only work would be to make punch and say prayers. Depraved, however, as these men were, they did not choose to constrain him to go, but displayed their civility further, by permitting him to carry along with him whatever he called his own. After several cruises, they now went into a convenient harbor at Old Calabar, where they cleaned, refitted, divided their booty, and for a considerable time caroused, to banish care and sober reflection.

According to their usual custom, the time of festivity and mirth was prolonged until the want of means recalled them to reason and exertion. Leaving this port, they cruised from place to place with varied success; but in all their captures, either burning, sinking, or devoting their prizes to their own use, according to the whim of the moment. The *Swallow* and another man-of-war being sent out expressly to pursue and take Roberts and his fleet, he had frequent and certain intelligence of their destination; but having so often escaped their vigilance, he became rather too secure and fearless. It happened, however, that while he lay off Cape Lopez, the *Swallow* had information of his being in that place, and made towards him. Upon the appearance of a sail, one of Roberts' ships was sent to chase and take her. The pilot of the *Swallow* seeing her coming, manoeouvred his vessel so well, that though he fled at her approach, in order to draw her out of the reach of her associates, yet he at his own time allowed her to overtake the man-of-war.

Upon her coming up to the *Swallow*, the pirate hoisted the black flag, and fired upon her; but how greatly were her crew astonished, when they saw that they had to contend with a man-of-war, and seeing that all resistance was vain, they cried out for quarter, which was granted, and they were made prisoners, having ten men killed and twenty wounded, without the loss or hurt of one of the king's men.

On the 10th, in the morning, the man-of-war bore away to round the cape. Roberts' crew, discerning their masts over the land, went down into the cabin to acquaint him of it, he being then at breakfast with his new guest, Captain Hill, on a savoury dish of salmagundy and some of his own beer. He took no notice of it, and his men almost as little, some saying she was a Portuguese ship, others a French slave ship, but the major part swore it was the French *Ranger* returning; and they were merrily debating for some time on the manner of reception, whether they should salute her or not; but as the *Swallow* approached nearer, things appeared plainer; and though they who showed any apprehension of danger were stigmatized with the name of cowards, yet some of them, now undeceived, declared it to Roberts, especially one Armstrong, who had deserted from that ship, and knew her well. These Roberts swore at as cowards, who meant to dishearten the men, asking them, if it were so, whether they were afraid to fight or not? In short, he hardly refrained from blows. What his own apprehensions were, till she hauled up her ports and hoisted her proper colors, is uncertain; but then, being perfectly convinced, he slipped his cable, got under sail, ordered his men to arms without any show of timidity, dropping a first-rate oath, that it was a bite, but at the same time resolved, like a gallant rogue, to get clear or die.

There was one Armstrong, as was just mentioned, a deserter from the *Swallow*, of whom they enquired concerning the trim and sailing of that ship; he told them she sailed best upon the wind, and therefore, if they designed to leave her, they should go before it.

The danger was imminent, and the time very short, to consult about means to extricate himself; his resolution in this strait was as follows: to pass close to the *Swallow* with all their sails, and receive her broadside before they returned a shot; if disabled by this, or if they could not depend on sailing, then to run on shore at the point, and every one to shift for himself among the negroes; or failing these, to board, and blow up together, for he saw that the greatest part of his men were drunk, passively courageous, and unfit for service.

Roberts, himself, made a gallant figure at the time of the engagement, being dressed in a rich crimson damask waistcoat and breeches, a red feather in his hat, a gold chain round his neck, with a diamond cross hanging to it, a sword in his hand, and two pair of pistols hanging at the end of a silk sling flung over his shoulders, according to the custom of the pirates. He is said to have given his orders with boldness and spirit. Coming, according to what he had purposed, close to the man-of-war, he received her fire, and then hoisted his black flag and returned it, shooting away from her with all the sail he could pack; and had he taken Armstrong's advice to have gone before the wind, he had probably escaped; but keeping his tacks down, either by the wind's shifting, or ill steerage, or both, he was taken aback with his sails, and the *Swallow* came a second time very nigh to him. He had now, perhaps, finished the fight very desperately, if death, who took a swift passage in a grape shot, had not interposed, and struck him directly on the throat. He settled himself on the tackles of a gun; which one Stephenson, from the helm, observing, ran to his assistance, and not perceiving him wounded, swore at him, and bade him stand up and fight like a man; but when he found his mistake, and that his captain was certainly dead, he burst into tears, and wished the next shot might be his portion. They presently threw him overboard, with his arms and ornaments on, according to his repeated request in his life-time.

This extraordinary man and daring pirate was tall, of a dark complexion, about 40 years of age, and born in Pembrokeshire. His parents were honest and respectable, and his natural activity, courage, and invention, were superior to his education. At a very early period, he, in drinking, would imprecate vengeance upon "the head of him who ever lived to wear a halter." He went willingly into the pirate service, and served three years as a second man. It was not for want of employment, but from a roving, wild, and boisterous turn of mind. It was his usual declaration, that, "In an honest service, there are commonly low wages and hard labor; in this, – plenty, satiety, pleasure and ease, liberty, and power; and who would not balance creditor on this side, when all the hazard that is run for it at worst, is only a sour look or two at choking? No, – a merry life and a short one, shall be my motto!" But it was one favorable trait in his character, that he never forced any man into the pirate service.

The prisoners were strictly guarded while on board, and being conveyed to Cape Coast castle, they underwent a long and solemn trial. The generality of them remained daring and impenitent for some time, but when they found themselves confined within a castle, and their fate drawing near, they changed their course, and became serious, penitent, and fervent in their devotions. Though the judges found no small difficulty in explaining the law, and different acts of parliament, yet the facts were so numerous and flagrant which were proved against them, that there was no difficulty in bringing in a verdict of guilty.

"This was a warning to Ashton
that he was about to be marooned"

MAROONED

Edward Leslie

Philip Ashton's schooner was taken by the notorious sea-robber Edward "Ned" Low on 15 June 1722. Low demanded that Ashton sign the pirate ship's articles of agreement; Ashton refused and determined instead to escape.

The first time Ashton tried to escape, he climbed into a boat with two other captives who were going ashore to retrieve Low's dog – the animal had inadvertently been left behind. Before the craft could be pushed off, the quartermaster seized him by the shoulder and pulled him back on deck. When the other two men deserted, the quartermaster accused Ashton of being a party to their plot, and Ashton's denial so infuriated him that he aimed a pistol at the prisoner and snapped it, but it misfired. This only fueled the man's rage, and three more times the weapon misfired as he tried to kill his victim. When, in total frustration, he drew his cutlass, Ashton was able to save himself only by leaping into the hold.

While Low sailed about the Caribbean, taking nearly a dozen prizes in the process, Ashton watched for another chance. He thought it had come when the brigands talked of returning to New England for provisions and the recruitment of more men. He and seven others planned to seize the pirates' vessel when she was off the coast and the pirates were in drunken stupors. Francis Spriggs learned of the plot and informed Low of it. Luckily the captain discounted the accusation, but Spriggs was furious. He threatened to shoot the would-be mutineers, adding, "You dog, Ashton, you deserved to be hanged for designing to cut us off." Nothing came of these fulminations, despite their ferocity.

Philip Ashton would remain with this disreputable company for nine months before his opportunity finally came. They were visiting an island north of the Honduran coast when the cooper and six men went ashore to fetch water. At first they did not want to take him along, but he managed to talk them into it. On the beach he put them off guard by being very energetic in helping to get the casks out of the boat and rolling them to the stream.

He took a deep drink of water and then strolled along the sand, nonchalantly picking up stones and shells as he drifted away. Once, when he was nearly out of musket range, the cooper shouted after him asking where he was going. "For coconuts" was Ashton's reply, the he headed for the woods. As soon as he was out of sight, he began to run.

As the others were preparing to depart, they called out for him, but he "lay snug" and silent in a thicket. They said to each other, "The dog is lost in the woods and cannot find the way out again." They hallooed some more. The cooper said, "He has run away and won't come to us." They searched the nearby trees and bushes. The cooper, a man with some kindness in him, cried, "If you do not come away presently I shall go off and leave you alone." This was a warning to Ashton that he was about to be marooned, but he would not heed:

> Nothing . . . could induce me to discover myself, and my comrades, seeing it vain to wait any longer, put off without me.
>   Thus was I left on a desolate island, destitute of all help and remote from the track of navigators; but, compared with the state and society I had quitted, I considered the wilderness hospitable and the solitude interesting.

The foraging party having rowed away, Ashton came out of the thicket and sat down by a stream to keep a watch on the pirate vessels. Five days later, to his great joy, they departed, and only then did he examine his situation realistically. The cooper's implicit warning had had merit:

> I was on an island which I had no means of leaving; I knew of no human being within many miles; my clothing was scanty and it was impossible to procure a supply. I was

altogether destitute of provision, nor could tell how my life was to be supported. This melancholy prospect drew a copious flood of tears from my eyes; but as it had pleased God to grant my wishes in being liberated from those whose occupation was devising mischief against their neighbors, I resolved to account every hardship light. Yet Low would never suffer his men to work on the Sabbath, which was more devoted to play; and I have even seen some of them sit down to read in a good book.

He began exploring his new Caribbean home. It was known as Roatan, and he estimated it to be eleven leagues long and thought it lay at about 16° 30′ north latitude. No human beings lived on it, but he found shards of earthenware belonging to its former Indian inhabitants. It was very hilly and had numerous fig and coconut trees. Another tree he did not recognize bore an oval fruit with brownish skin and red pulp. He was afraid to eat these until he saw wild hogs feeding on them without being sickened, and then he found them to be quite delicious.

The hogs were plentiful, as were tortoise and deer, yet though the "store of provisions abounded", he could avail himself of "nothing but the fruit". This was because he lacked a knife or any other weapon, and he did not have the means of starting a cooking fire. He dreamed of trapping the hogs and deer by digging pits and covering them with branches but had no shovel. No matter what his desires, it seemed he would have to be satisfied with fruit.

Eventually Ashton managed to locate tortoise eggs that had been buried a foot or two down in the sand. He did this by poking a stick into the ground repeatedly until the end came out with part of an egg adhering to it. He scooped out the sand with his hands and found about 150 unspoiled eggs, some of which he ate immediately; the rest he strung up on a strip of palmetto. He hung them in the sun until the insides became "thick and somewhat hard, so that they were more palatable. After all they were not very savory food, though one who had nothing but what fell from the trees behoved to be content."

There were snakes on Roatan, too. The most intimidating grew to a length of twelve to fourteen feet and had a circumference as large as a man's waist. When lying stretched out, these serpents had the appearance of moss-covered tree trunks, and the first time Ashton came upon one of them unawares, it "opened its mouth wide enough to receive a hat and breathed on me". After that Ashton was at pains to avoid them.

The enormous numbers of small black flies were more of a problem. During his first months on the island he built several huts; the frames were constructed of branches bound together with split palmetto palms over which he laid coverings of larger leaves. Most of these shelters he built near the beach, facing the ocean, so that he could be cooled by the sea breeze and at the same time keep watch for ships. But if these open structures worked well to defend him "against the heat of the sun by day and the heavy dews at night", they afforded no protection from the pesky flies. The insects were such an annoyance that Ashton became determined to reach adjacent islands in the hope of finding some relief, even though he was a poor swimmer and lacked a canoe or raft or the means of building one.

The only life preserver he could find was a hollow piece of bamboo with which he experimented, sticking it under his arms and across his chest and kicking his feet in the water until he felt confident enough to make a try for a small key a gunshot's distance from Roatan.

Buoyed by the bamboo, he reached his destination without difficulty. He found that though it lacked trees and was less than four hundred feet in circumference, it had an overriding attraction: the wind passing unobstructed over it kept it free of flies. Even without food sources or shelter, it was for Ashton "a new world, where I lived infinitely more at ease. Hither I retired, therefore, when the heat of day rendered the insect tribe most obnoxious; yet I was obliged to be much on Roatan to procure food and water, and at night on account of my hut."

He swam back and forth between the two islands with his jersey and trousers tied to the top of his head. The journeys were not without danger, since alligators and shovel-nosed sharks hunted in these waters. At least once a shark attacked him, striking his thigh, but this occurred just as he had gotten close enough to shore to stand, and in the shallows his assailant became grounded and unable to make a second pass. Ashton had not been bitten, but his leg ached for some time afterward from the blow.

On another occasion the bamboo slipped from under his arms,

and he had to fight for his life in the powerful current. Gradually his swimming improved, however, to the point where he was able to visit still other islands in the archipelago.

His shoes having fallen apart, his feet were constantly being injured. The hot sand burned them, and sticks, stones, and broken shells cut them.

> Often, when treading with all possible caution, a stone or shell on the beach or a pointed stick in the woods would penetrate an old wound and the extreme anguish would strike me down suddenly as if I had been shot. Then I would remain for hours together with tears gushing from my eyes from the acuteness of the pain. I could travel no more than absolute necessity compelled me in quest of subsistence and I have sat, my back leaning against a tree, looking out for a vessel during a complete day.
>
> Once, while faint from such injuries, as well as smarting under the pain of them, a wild boar rushed towards me. I knew not what to do, for I had not the strength to resist his attack. Therefore as he drew nearer I caught the bough of a tree and half suspended myself by means of it. The boar tore away part of my ragged trousers with his tusks and then left me.

In his weakened condition, subsisting on little more than figs and grapes, he sometimes fell into a trancelike state from which "I thought I should never wake again, or rise in life. Under this affliction I first lost count of the days of the week. I could not distinguish Sunday, and as my illness became more aggravated I became ignorant of the month also."

He was depressed. He had no "healing balsam for my feet nor any cordial to revive my drooping spirits". He was unable to enlarge his diet, and although wood was plentiful on Roatan, he was still unable to start a fire: he rubbed sticks together without producing a spark until he was utterly weary.

Earlier in his marooning he had been able to accept his lot with a certain equanimity:

> One day after another was lingered out, I knew not how, void of occupation or amusement except collecting food,

rambling from hill to hill and from island to island and
gazing on sky and water. Although my mind was occupied
by many regrets I had the reflection that I was lawfully
employed when taken, so that I had no hand in bringing
misery on myself. I was also comforted to think that I had
the approbation and consent of my parents in going to sea,
and I trusted that it would please God in his own time and
manner to provide for my return to my father's house.
Therefore I resolved to submit patiently to my misfortune.

A few pages later in his narrative, however, we see Philip Ashton
losing his composure:

While passing nine months in this lonely, melancholy and
irksome condition my thoughts would sometimes wander
to my parents; and, I reflected that, notwithstanding it
would be consolatory to myself if they knew where I was,
it might be distressing to them. The nearer my prospect of
death, which I often expected, the greater my penitence
became.

One day in November his melancholia was interrupted by the
appearance of a man and a dog in a canoe. At first Ashton did not
react to the sight: he had no hope that the stranger would befriend
him, and if he had hostile intentions, Ashton had no means of
resisting him. While still in the water, the canoeist, who was
startled to see a man on what he thought would be an uninhabited
shore, cautiously called out to him. Ashton assured him it was
safe to land, "for I was alone and almost expiring. Coming close
up, he knew not what to make of me; my garb and countenance
seemed so singular that he looked wild with astonishment. He
started back a little and surveyed me more thoroughly; but,
recovering himself again, came forward and, taking me by the
hand, expressed his satisfaction at seeing me."

He was an elderly Englishman "of grave and venerable aspect
and of a reserved temper", who had lived for twenty-two years
among the Spanish. He was in flight from them now because for
an unspecified reason they had decided to burn him at the stake.
He had paddled twenty leagues in his canoe to Roatan, seeking
sanctuary, intending to live out his days there, subsisting on what

he could shoot; he had brought along his dog, a gun and ammunition, and a supply of pork.

For two days these men lived together, and on the third day the stranger announced that he was going to make a hunting expedition to other islands. Ashton could not go along; the condition of his feet would not allow it. This did not seem to matter because the Englishman would be gone only a short time, and there was no danger; the sky was clear, with no signs of a storm.

An hour after the old fellow had set off, a sudden, violent tempest arose, and Ashton never saw him again.

> Thus, after having the pleasure of a companion almost three days, I was reduced to my former lonely state as unexpectedly as I had been relieved from it. Yet, through God's goodness, I was myself preserved from having been unable to accompany him, and I was left in better circumstances than those in which he found me; for now I had about five pounds of pork, a knife, a bottle of gunpowder, tobacco, tongs, and flint, by which means my life could be rendered more comfortable. I was enabled to have fire, extremely requisite at this time, being the rainy months of winter. I could cut up a tortoise and have a delicate broiled meal. Thus, by the help of the fire and dressed provisions, through the blessing of God I began to recover strength, though the soreness of my feet remained. But I had, besides, the advantage of being able now and then to catch a dish of crayfish, which, when roasted, proved good eating. To accomplish this I made up a small bundle of broken sticks, nearly resembling pitch-pine or candle-wood; and having lighted one end, waded with it in my hand up to the waist in water. The crayfish, attracted by the light, would crawl to my feet and lie directly under it; when, by means of a forked stick, I could toss them ashore.

Three months later, Ashton found a small canoe at the water's edge. At first he thought it was the Englishman's, but a closer examination proved otherwise. The craft would, he thought, make him "admiral of the neighboring seas as well as sole possessor and chief commander of the islands". Laying in it a stock of figs, grapes, and tortoise, he set off for the isle of Bonacco, six leagues away.

Arriving there, he spied a sloop anchored near the eastern coast. Unable to tell whether or not she belonged to pirates, he paddled around to Bonacco's western side. He would creep overland until he was close enough to get a look. He dragged the canoe ashore and undertook a trek that, because of the condition of his feet, would take two days and two nights to complete. At the end of this painful journey, during which he had often crawled on his hands and knees through dense undergrowth, he eased himself up to the edge of the beach to study the vessel, while at the same time being careful to keep himself concealed from those on board her – and found that she had sailed away.

Utterly weary, Philip Ashton slumped against the stump of a tree and immediately fell asleep. He awoke to the sound of musket fire. Leaping up, he saw in the sea before him nine periaguas (long canoes) filled with Spaniards taking aim at him. He spun and hobbled into the bushes as bullets perforated leaves and severed twigs all around him. The marksmen bellowed, "O, Englishman, we will give you good quarter!"

He thought later that had he not been so startled, he might have accepted the offer. As it was, he lay out of range in a dense thicket for several hours until he heard the Spaniards leaving. Creeping to where he could observe the departure, he noted that the sloop was flying British colors. She had been just recently captured in the Bay of Honduras, he was certain.

The next day he returned to the stump where he had fallen asleep and found that it had been struck six or seven times by musket balls, all of which had landed within a foot of where his head had been resting. For a moment he had been an unmoving target, yet the marksmen had missed. It showed, he thought, the wonderful goodness of God.

The walk back to his canoe took three days. Though he felt quite exhausted, he was glad to push off for Roatan, with which he was now more contented. Bonacco had proved to have even less to offer in the way of food, and it harbored insects "infinitely more numerous and harassing than at my old habitation". In fact, Roatan was, he thought, "a royal palace to me compared to Bonacco".

For the next four months he occupied his time by hunting and visiting the adjacent islands. One day in June 1724, while on the small key, hiding from the flies and mosquitoes, Ashton saw two canoes heading for the harbor. When the occupants glimpsed the smoke of his fire, they paused. Ashton was also hesitant: the memory of the Spaniards' attack was still fresh in his mind. He chose to slip away to his canoe and paddle to Roatan, where he had "places of safety against an enemy and sufficient accommodation for any ordinary number of friends".

The sight of him racing for the island did not comfort the visitors. They were in flight from Spaniards, as it turned out, and were not anxious to run into a pirates' ambush. So they approached the shore with great caution.

Screwing up his courage, Ashton walked out into the open. The men stopped rowing and called out, asking who he was and where he had come from. His answer brought them closer to the beach. Now they wanted to know how many men were with him. Ashton replied that he was by himself, and then he asked questions of his own. At last he invited them ashore, and they accepted – although they landed a safe distance from him and sent only one of their company toward him. The maroon went to meet this delegate, who "started back at the sight of a poor, ragged, wild, forlorn, miserable object so near him. Collecting himself, however, he took me by the hand and we began embracing each other, he from surprise and wonder and I from a sort of ecstasy of joy. When this was over he took me in his arms and carried me down to the canoes, where all his comrades were struck with astonishment at my appearance; but they gladly received me and I experienced great tenderness from them."

Ashton told them of his adventures – his capture by Low and his escape and his sixteen months alone. His story amazed them.

Observing me very weak and depressed, they gave me about a spoonful of rum to recruit my fainting spirits. But even this small quantity, from my long disuse of strong liquors, threw me into violent agitation and produced a kind of stupor, which at last ended in [the] privation of sense. Some of the party, perceiving a state of insensibility come on, would have administered more rum, which those better skilled among them prevented; and, after lying a short time in a fit, I revived.

The leader of the group was John Hope, an elderly man known as Father Hope. He had come with seventeen men from the Bay of Honduras; they had left their homes after learning that a Spanish raid was imminent. They knew of Roatan because Hope and another of their number, John Ford, had once hidden themselves for four years on a neighboring island. On that isle, named Barbarat, Hope and these Baymen had just established two "plantations", having brought with them provisions, firearms, hunting dogs, nets for tortoises, and an Indian woman to prepare their food. Actually they would be spending much of their time on a key near Barbarat, which they called the Castle of Comfort because, since it had no trees or bushes, the wind swept over it unimpeded and drove away "pestiferous mosquitoes and other insects".

The barrenness of the Castle of Comfort forced them to travel to surrounding islands for water, firewood, and materials with which to build their huts. It was while on such an errand that they found Ashton.

They took him to Barbarat and fed and clothed him. They even gave him a large wrapping gown to protect him from the dew at night while they finished constructing their shelters. They treated him with "a great deal of civility in their way", Ashton admitted gratefully, although his puritanism qualified his admiration for them.

> Yet after all they were bad society; and, as to their common conversation, there was little difference between them and pirates. However, it did not appear that they were now engaged in any such evil design as rendered it unlawful to join them or be found in their company.

In any case, while among them he mended well enough to hunt with them. (Much of what they killed was smoked as a means of maintaining a "ready supply at all times".) Perhaps more important, being in the presence of so many constantly armed men gave Ashton a feeling of security. This confidence would soon prove to be misplaced.

The assault on the plantations came seven months after Ashton had been brought to Barbarat. He and three other men were returning to the island from a hunting trip one evening when, upon entering the mouth of the harbor, they saw a great flash and heard the boom of a swivel gun. It came from a large periagua floating close offshore and was followed by a volley from about twenty small arms. Hope's settlers fired back.

Ashton and the men with him, caught in the open, decided to try to slip away to another island. They took down their mast and sail and endeavored to row quietly out of the harbor. But the large periagua pursued them and was soon closing the distance between them. Ashton and the others rowed with all their might. The enemy fired, but the shot passed over their heads. When the canoe ground ashore, the Barbaratists leaped out and raced for cover while bullets cut the air around them. Their pursuers called out that they had nothing to fear – they were buccaneers, not Spaniards.

No attempt at reassurance could have been less comforting to Philip Ashton: "I had the utmost dread of a pirate; and my original aversion was now enhanced by the apprehension of being sacrificed [for] my former desertion." He and the others fled deeper into the woods.

The cutthroats contented themselves with taking the canoe and its contents and marooning the four men. This did not dismay Ashton, "who had known both want and solitude". At least this time he had companions, and they had weapons.

Ashton's fear proved to be well founded. These brigands had once held him prisoner. They were commanded by Spriggs, who had broken with Low and gone off on his own. The cause of their parting had been an argument over whether or not to hang a crewman who had murdered another man in cold blood. Low had been against the execution, and so Spriggs, who had wanted the killer to die, slipped away under the cover of darkness in the *Delight*. Eighteen men went along with him in the appropriated prize, which had formerly been the man-of-war *Squirrel*. They held an election and, not surprisingly, chose Spriggs to be their commander. They also made a Jolly Roger with the same design that Low used: a white skeleton in the middle of a black background, holding in one hand an hourglass and in the other a long dart that pierced a bleeding heart. "When this was finished and hoisted," Defoe tells us, "they fired all their guns to salute their captain and themselves and then looked out for prey."

In the West Indies they captured a Portuguese bark, and in her they found

> valuable plunder, but not contented with that alone, they said they would have a little game with the men, and so ordered them a sweat, more for the brutes' diversion than the poor men's healths; which operation is performed after this manner: they stick up lighted candles circularly round the mizzenmast, between decks, within which the patients one at a time enter; without the candles the pyrates post themselves, as many as can stand, forming another circle, armed with penknives, tucks [swords], forks, compasses, etc., and as he runs round and round, the musick playing at the same time, they prick him with those instruments. This usually lasts ten or twelve minutes, which is as long as the miserable man can support himself. When the sweating was over, they gave the Portuguese their boat with a small quantity of provisions and set their vessel on fire.

These blackguards then sailed about taking other ships, forcing sailors to sign their articles and administering beatings with cutlasses and whips whenever they felt the least inclination. The mate of one sloop, being a "grave, sober man", declined to join the band and asked to be cast away. They told him they would give him a discharge – but instead of issuing him papers, they would write it on his back. He was given ten lashes by every man on the ship, which amounted to a total of well over two hundred strokes.

The pirates continued on in this fashion – drinking, firing their cannons, and shouting huzzas when they were not engaged in bloodier work – until they arrived at Roatan. They came in two vessels (the largest of them being a well-armed ship with twenty-four guns), seeking to replenish their water supplies, but when they found the neighboring island populated, they sent some of their men in a periagua to capture the residents.

In the process of defeating the Englishmen, Spriggs and his men killed one of them, threw his body into a canoe containing tar, and then set fire to it. After this they "shamefully abused" the Indian woman. One of the settlers chose to join the ranks of the victors and immediately revealed to his new confederates that John Hope had hidden valuables somewhere in the woods. This intelligence resulted in the old man being beaten until he revealed the location of his treasure.

For five days Spriggs kept his prisoners aboard his ship before finally deciding to let them go. They were put into a flat, which they were welcome to try to sail the seventy leagues to the Bay of Honduras. Spriggs refused to give them any provisions and made them swear not to go near Ashton and the other marooned men.

As soon as Spriggs's vessels were out of sight, Father Hope, "little regarding the oath extorted from him", came to find his comrades in hiding. They had lived for the five days without lighting a fire, for fear of disclosing their whereabouts, and so had been subsisting on raw victuals.

All but one of Hope's company had had enough of island existence: they elected to return to their homes on the Bay. Ashton wanted to go with them, but the old leader counseled against it. The journey would be very risky in an overloaded flat that had not been designed to sail in rough seas. Then, too, the Spaniards might be waiting at the far end of the precarious voyage. Better that Ashton remain where he was – even in solitude – than gamble with his freedom and his life.

Besides, he would not be alone. One individual, a man named John Symonds, was not leaving. Symonds saw the opportunity to make money trading with the colonists on Jamaica, and he urged Ashton to stay and assist him. Ashton, he argued, was more likely to get passage for New England on a ship bound from Jamaica than any he could find in the Bay of Honduras. Since Ashton's only desire now was to get home, he allowed himself to be persuaded.

Hope gave them a canoe, firearms, and two dogs, and then he sailed away. For a few months the men "ranged" among the islands, eventually accumulating a supply of tortoise shells that could be used as trade goods.

When the "season for the Jamaica traders approached", they went to Bonacco. One day a number of vessels arrived, but a furious storm kept their crews from coming ashore. The weather eventually improved enough for some men from a brigantine to be dispatched in a boat to search for fresh water.

Ashton studied the three occupants of the cask-laden craft as she approached the beach. Concluding from their appearance that they were Englishmen, he stepped from his hiding place and walked onto the sand, where they could get a look at him. Symonds stayed out of the way so as not to make them fear an ambush.

As so often seems to have happened at these moments, they stopped rowing at the sight of him and demanded to know who he was. He answered and then asked the same question of them. They were indeed British, and their vessel was part of a convoy bound for Jamaica under the protection of a man-of-war named the *Diamond*. By chance the brigantine was commanded by a man Ashton knew, a Captain Dove, and her home port was Salem, which was just a few miles from the house of Ashton's father. Ashton assured the sailors that they could safely land, and they did so: "A happy meeting it was for me."

The next day, the water casks having been filled, the ships set sail. Symonds wept at Ashton's leaving.

Captain Dove treated Ashton with courtesy and kindness and not only promised to take him home but, being short-handed, took him on as a crewman. Thus Ashton would not be returning to his family utterly destitute.

They left the island at the end of March 1725 and reached Salem Harbor on the first of May. Ashton calculated the time he had been gone: it was "two years, ten months and fifteen days after I was first taken by pirates, and two years and nearly two months after making my escape from them on Roatan Island. That same evening I went to my father's house, where I was received as one risen from the dead."

By the time Ashton reached home, the insanely sadistic Low – he once made the captain of a Boston whaler eat his own ears – had met his end. Some report him as falling victim to Yellow Fever, although he was more probably marooned by his own crew in the West Indies.

BLACK PIRATES

There were also large numbers of blacks aboard pirate ships, these often being distinguished from their white shipmates in depositions, and one modern writer has suggested that as many as 30 per cent of pirate crews were of African descent. This is probably an exaggeration, though not a very great one. The problem is to determine the exact status of these black pirates. Some optimists claim they were treated by their white shipmates as equals and that this early form of black empowerment should be celebrated, an idea rejected by members of the modern black establishment in America who are not at all keen that free black history should "start with gangsters, which is what pirates were". Other writers more pessimistically suggest that the blacks were slaves forced by the white pirates to do the pumping and other dirty work of the ship. The truth, as usual, probably lies somewhere in between.

Black sailors were quite common in the merchant shipping of America and especially in the Caribbean, where many sloops and other vessels engaged in coastal waters were crewed almost entirely by blacks. These men were nearly always slaves, most of whose wages went to their shorebound masters, but simply working at sea gave them a taste of freedom denied to their brothers working in plantations ashore. Some of these slave sailors worked aboard privateer or pirate ships on the same conditions. Juan Silvester, a Cuban slave, was ordered by his master to serve on the pirate ship commanded by Augustino Blanco, or at least that was what he claimed at his trial in the Bahamas for piracy. "His master was to have his share except jewels and rings, his master having often sent him out on privateering upon shares." Such men, with their seafaring and fighting skills, would be welcome aboard any pirate ship which captured them, though whether they would be treated as equals is another matter. "Black sailors knew full well that race rarely disappeared, even among shipmates," as a recent historian of black mariners points out.

Pirates also captured large numbers of slavers, but they certainly did not free all the slaves on board and welcome them as brothers. Most were sold as booty, while the female slaves were often abused and raped, a fate shared only rarely by white female captives. Nevertheless, pirates did take many freed slaves aboard as crew. Some of these were exploited simply for their labour, but others were trained up in the seafaring and fighting skills of the pirate. The pirate John Bowen, whose ship the *Speaking Trumpet* was wrecked on Mauritius in 1702, had several black men in his crew, "very cunning and well trained in the use of arms", useful-sounding men, but he still sold four of them to pay for food and other necessities.

From *The Pirate Wars*, Peter Earle, 2003. Copyright © Peter Earle 2003

CAPTAIN BLOOD

Daniel Defoe

Defoe's account of the piratical career of John Gow (aka John Smith) begins in November 1724 with Gow mutinying against the captain of a merchantman bound for France.

It was the Captain's constant Custom to call all the Ship's Company every Night, at Eight a-Clock, into the great Cabbin to Prayers; and then the Watch being set, one Watch went upon Deck, and the other turn'd in (as the Seamen call it) – that is, went to their Hammocks to Sleep. And here they concerted their devilish Plot. It was the Turn of five of the Conspirators to go to Sleep, and of these, Gow and Williams were two; the three who were to be upon the Deck were Winter, Rolson, and Melvin, a Scotchman.

The Persons they had immediately Design'd for Destruction were four – viz., the Captain, the Mate, the Super Cargo, and the Surgeon, whereof all but the Captain were gone to Sleep, the Captain himself being upon the Quarter-deck.

Between Nine and Ten at Night, all being quiet and secure, and the poor Gentlemen that were to be Murther'd, fast asleep, the Villains that were below gave the Watch-Word, which was, who Fires next? at which they all got out of their Hammocks with as little Noise as they could, and going, in the Dark, to the Hammocks of the Chief Mate, Super Cargo, and Surgeon, they cut all their Throats; the Surgeon's Throat was cut so effectually that he could struggle very little with them, but leaping out of his Hammock, ran up to get upon the Deck, holding his Hand upon his Throat, but stumbled at the Tiller, and falling down, had no Breath, and consequently no Strength, to raise himself, but dyed where he lay.

The Mate, whose Throat was cut, but not his Windpipe, had strugled so Vigorously with the Villain that attempted him that he got from him and got into the Hold; and the Super Cargo, in the same Condition, got forward between Decks, under some Deals, and both of them begg'd, with the most moving Cries and Intreaties, for their Lives; and when nothing could prevail, they beg'd, with the same Earnestness, but for a few Moments to pray to God, and Recommend their Souls to his Mercy; but alike, in vain, for the wretched Murtherers, heated with Blood, were pass'd all Pitty; and not being able to come at them with their Knives, with which they had begun the Execution, they shot them with their Pistols, Firing several times upon each of them, till they found they were quite dead.

As all this, before the Firings, could not be done without some Noise, the Captain, who was walking alone upon the Quarter-Deck, call'd out and ask'd what was the matter? The Boatswain, who, sat on the After Bits, and was not of the Party, answer'd, He could not tell, but was afraid there was some Body Over-board, upon which the Captain step'd towards the ship's side to look over, when Winter, Rowlinson, and Melvin, coming that Moment behind him, attempted to throw him Over-board into the Sea; but he being a nimble, strong Man, got hold of the shrouds, and strugled so hard with them that they could not break his Hold; but turning his Head to look behind him to see who he had to deal with, one of them cut his Throat with a broad Dutch Knife, but neither was that wound mortal. And the Captain still strugled with them, tho' seeing he should undoubtedly be murther'd, he constantly cry'd out to God for Mercy, for he found there was no Mercy to be expected from them. During this Struggle, another of the Murtherers stab'd him with a Knife in the Back, and that with such Force that the Villain could not draw the Knife out again to repeat his Blow, which he would otherwise have done.

At this Moment Gow came up from the Butchery he had been at between Decks, and seeing the Captain still alive, he went close up to him, and shot him (as he confess'd) with a Brace of Bullets.

What Part he shot him into could not be known, tho' they said he shot him into the Head; however, he had yet Life enough, tho' they threw him Over-board, to take hold of a Rope, and would still have saved himself, but they cut that Rope, and he fell into the Sea, and was seen no more. Thus they finished the Tragedy, having murther'd four of the principal Men of Command in the Ship, so that there was now no Body to Oppose them; for Gow being Second Mate and Gunner, the Command fell to him, of course, and the rest of the Men having no Arms ready, nor knowing how to get at any, were in the utmost Consternation, expecting they would go on with the Work, and cut all their Throats.

In this Fright, every one shifted for himself. As for those who were upon Deck, some got into the Ship's Head, resolving to throw themselves into the Sea, rather than to be mangled with Knives, and murther'd in Cold Blood, as the Captain and Mate, &c., had been. Those who were below, not knowing what to do, or whose Turn it should be next, lay still in their Hammocks, expecting Death every Moment, and not daring to stir, least the Villains should think they did it in order to make Resistance, which, however, they were no way capable of doing, having no Concert one with another, nor knowing any Thing in Particular of one another, as who was Alive or who was Dead; whereas had the Captain, who was himself a bold and stout Man, been in his Great Cabbin with three or four Men with him, and his Fire-Arms, as he intended to have had, those eight Fellows had never been Able to have done their Work, but every Man was taken Unprovided, and in the utmost Surprise, so that the Murtherers met with no Resistance. And as for those that were left, they were less Able to make Resistance than the other; so that, as I have said, they were in the utmost Terror and Amazement, expecting every Minute to be Murthered as the rest had been.

But the Villains had done. The Persons who had any Command were Dispatch'd, so they Cool'd a little as to Blood. The first Thing they did afterward was to call up all the Eight upon the Quarter-Deck, where they Congratulated one another, and shook Hands together, engaging to proceed, by unanimous Consent, in their resolved Design – that is to say, of turning Pirates, in Order to which they, with a Nem. Con., chose Gow to Command the Ship, promising all Subjection and Obedience to his Orders (so that now we must call him Captain Gow), and he, by the same Consent of the rest, named Williams to be his Lieutenant. Other Officers they appointed afterwards.

The first Order they Issued was to let all the rest of the Men

know, That if they continued Quiet, and offer'd not to Meddle
with any of their affairs, they should receive no Hurt. But strictly
forbid any Man among them to set a Foot Abaft the Main-mast,
except they were call'd to the Helm, upon Pain of being immediately Cut in Pieces, keeping, for that Purpose, one Man at
the Steerage-door, and one upon the Quarter-deck, with drawn
Cutlashes in their Hands; but there was no need for it, for the
Men were so terrified with the bloody Doings they had seen that
they never offer'd to come in sight till they were call'd.

Their next Work was to throw the three dead Bodies of the
Mate, the Surgeon, and the Super Cargo over Board, which, they
said, lay in their Way, and that was soon done, their Pockets first
Search'd and rifled. From thence they went to work with the
Great Cabbin, and with all the Lockers, Chests, Boxes, and
Trunks. These they Broke open and Rifled — that is, such of
them as belong'd to the murthered Persons; and whatever they
found there, they shar'd among themselves. When they had done
this, they call'd for Liquor, and sat down to Drinking till
Morning, leaving the Men (as above) to keep Guard, and particularly to Guard the Arms, but Relieved them from Time to
Time, as they saw Occasion. By this Time they had drawn in four
more of the Men to approve of what they had done, and promise
to Joyn with them, so that now they were twelve in Number, and
being but 24 at first, whereof four were Murthered, they had but
eight Men to be Apprehensive, and those they could easily look
after; so for the next Day they sent for them all to appear before
their new Captain; where they were told by Gow what his
Resolution was, viz., to go a Cruising, or to go upon the Account
(as above), that if they were willling to joyn with them, and go
into their Measures, they should be well used, and there should
be no Distinction among them, but they should all fare alike; that
they had been forced by the barbarous Usage of Ferneau to do
what they had done, but that now there was no looking back; and
therefore, as they had not been concern'd in what was past, they
had nothing to do but to act in Concert, do their Duty as Sailors,
and obey Orders for the good of the Ship, and no Harm should he
do to any of them. As they all look'd like condemn'd Prisoners
brought up to the Bar to receive Sentence of Death, so they all
answer'd by a profound Silence; not one Word being said by any
of them, which Gow took, as they meant it, viz., for a Consent,

because they durst not refuse; so they were then permitted to go up and down every where as they used to do. Tho' such of them as sometimes afterwards shewed any Reluctance to act as Principals, were never Trusted, always Suspected, and often severely Beaten, and some of them were many ways inhumanly Treated, and that particularly by Williams, the Lieutenant, who was, in his Nature, a merciless, cruel, and inexorable Wretch, as we shall have occasion to take Notice of again in its Place.

They were now in a new Circumstance of Life, and acting upon a different Stage of Business, tho' upon the same stage as to the Element, the Water; before, they were a Merchant Ship, loaden, upon a good Account, with Merchant Goods from the Coast of Barbary, and bound to the Coast of Italy: But they were now a Crew of Pirates, or as they call them in the Levant, Corsaires, Bound no where, but to look out for Purchase and Spoil wherever they could find it.

In persuit of this wicked Trade, they first chang'd the Name of the Ship, which was before call'd the *George Gally*, and which they call now the *Revenge*, a Name indeed suitable to the bloody steps they had taken. In the next place they made the best of the Ship's Forces. The Ship had but twelve Guns mounted when they came out of Holland; but as they had six more good Guns in the Hold, with Carriages and every Thing proper for Service, which they had in Store, because being Freighted for the Dutch Merchants, and the Algerines being at War with the Dutch, they suppos'd they might want them for Defence. Now they took care to Mount them for a much worse Design; so that now they had 18 Guns, tho' too many for the number of Hands they had on Board.

In the third Place, instead of persuing their Voyage to Genoa with the Ship's Cargo, they took a clear contrary Course, and resolv'd to station themselves upon the Coasts of Spain and Portugal, and to cruise upon all Nations; but what they chiefly aim'd at was a Ship with Wine, if possible, for that they wanted Extreamly.

The first Prize they took was an English Sloop, belonging to Pool, Thomas Wise, Commander, bound from Newfoundland with Fish, for Cadiz. This was a Prize of no Value to them, for they knew not what to do with the Fish; so they took out the Master, Mr Wise, and his Men, who were but Five in Number, with their Anchors, and Cables, and Sails, and what else they found worth taking out, and sunk the Vessel.

N.B, Here it is to be observ'd, they found a Man very fit for their Turn, one James Belvin; he was Boatswain of the Sloop, a stout, brisk Fellow, and a very good Sailor; but otherways wicked enough to suit with their Occasion, and as soon as he came among them, he discover'd it; for tho' he was not in the first bloody Contrivance, nor in the terrible execution of which I have given a Relation, that is to say, he was not guilty of running away with the Ship, *George Gally*, nor of murthering the four innocent Men, which we have given an Account of above; yet, 'tis evident he joyn'd Heartily in all the Villanies which follow'd. And, indeed, this Man's Fate is a just and needful Caution to all those Sailors, who, being taken in other Ships by the Pirates, think that is a sufficient Plea for them to act as real Pirates afterwards; and that the Plea, or Pretence of being forced, will be a sufficient Protection to them, however Guilty they may have been afterward, and however Volunteir they may have Acted when they come among the Pirates.

Doubtless 'tis possible for a man to prove a hearty Rogue after he is forced into the Service of the Pirates, however Honest he was before, and however Undesignedly or against his Consent he at first come among them. Therefore those who expect to be Acquitted in a Court of Justice afterward, on Pretence of their being at first forced into the Company of Rogues, must take care not to act any thing in Concert with them, while they are Embark'd together, but what they really cannot Avoid, and are apparently under a constraint in the doing.

But this Man, 'twas plain, acted a quite different Part; for after he took on with them, he took all Occasions to engage their Confidence, and to convince them that he was hearty in his joyning them. In a Word, he was the most active and vigorous Fellow of any that were, as it may be said, forced into their Service; for many of the others, tho' they acted with them, and were apparently Assisting, yet there was always a kind of Backwardness and Disgust at the Villainy, for which they were often maltreated, and always suspected by their Masters.

The next Prize they took was a Scotch Vessel, bound from Glassgow, with Herrings and Salmon, from thence to Genoa, and commanded by one Mr John Somerville, of Port Patrick; this

Vessel was likewise of very little Value to them, except that they took out, as they had done from the other, their Arms, Ammunition, Cloths, Provisions, Sails, Anchors, Cables, &c., and every Thing of Value, and therefore they sunk her too, as they had done the Sloop. The Reason they gave for sinking these two Vessels was, to prevent their being Discover'd; for, as they were now Cruising on the Coast of Portugal, had they let the Ships have gone with several of their Men on Board, they would presently have stood in for the Shore, and have given the Alarm; and the Men of War, of which there were several, as well Dutch as English, in the River of Lisbon, would presently have put out to Sea in Quest of them. And they were very unwilling to leave the Coast of Portugal, till they had got a Ship with Wine, which they very much wanted.

They Cruised eight or ten days after this, without seeing so much as one Vessel upon the Seas, and were just resolving to stand more to the Norward, to the Coast of Gallitia, when they descryed a Sail to the Southward, being a Ship about as big as their own. tho' they could not perceive what Force she had; however, they gave Chase, and the Vessel perceiving it, crowded from them with all the Sail they could make, hoisting up French Colours, and standing away to the Southward.

They continued the Chase three Days and three Nights; and tho' they did not gain much upon her, the Frenchman sailing very well, yet they kept her in sight all the while, and for the most part within Gunshot. But the third Night, the Weather proving a little Haizy, the Frenchman chang'd his Course in the Night, and so got clear of them, and good reason they had to bless themselves in the Escape they had made: If they had but known what a dreadful crew of Rogues they had fallen among, if they had been taken.

They were now gotten a long way to the Southward, and being greatly Disappointed, and in want of Water, as well as Wine, they resolved to stand away for the Maderas, which they knew was not far off, so they accordingly made the Island in two Days more; and keeping a large Offing, they cruis'd for three or four Days more, expecting to meet with some Portuguese Vessel going in or coming out; but 'twas in vain, for nothing stirr'd. So, tir'd with Expecting, they stood in for the Road, and came to an Anchor, tho' at a great Distance; then they sent their Boat towards the Shore with seven Men, all well Arm'd, to see whether it might not be Practicable to Board one of the Ships in the Road, and, cutting her away from her Anchors, bring her off; or, if they found that could not be done, then their Orders were to Intercept some of the Boats, belonging to the Place, which carry Wines off on Board the Ships in the Road, or from one Place to another on the Coast; but they came back again disappointed in both; every Body being alarm'd and aware of them, knowing by their Posture what they were.

Having thus spent several days to no Purpose, and finding themselves Discovered (at length being apparently under a Necessity to make an Attempt some where), they stood away for Porto Santa, about ten Leagues to the Windward of Maderas, and belonging also to the Portuguese; here putting up British Colours, they sent their Boat ashore with Captain Somerville's Bill of Health, and a Present to the Governor of three Barrels of Salmon, and six Barrels of Herrings, and a very civil Message, desiring leave to Water, and to buy some Refreshments, pretending to be Bound to—

The Governor very courteously granted their Desire; but with more Courtesie than Discretion, went off himself, with about nine or ten of his principal people, to pay the English Captain a visit, little thinking what kind of a Captain it was they were going to Compliment, and what price it might have cost them.

However, Gow, handsomely dress'd, received them with some ceremony, and entertain'd them tollerably well for a while; but the Governor having been kept by Civillity as they could, and the Refreshments from the Shore not appearing, he was forced to Unmask; and when the Governor and his Company rose up to take their leave, they were, to their great surprise, suddenly surrounded with a gang of Fellows with Musquets and an Officer at the Head of them, who told them, in so many words, they were the Captain's Prisoners, and must not think of going on shore any more, till the water and Provisions, which were promised, should come on Board.

It is impossible to conceive the Consternation and Surprize the Portuguese Gentry were in; nor is it very Decently to be express'd; the poor Governour was so much more than half-dead with the Fright, that he really Befoul'd himself in a piteous Manner, and the rest were in no much better Condition; they trembl'd, cry'd, begg'd, cross'd themselves, and said their

Prayers as Men going to Execution; but 'twas all one; they were told flatly the Captain was not to be Trifled with, that the Ship was in want of Provisions, and they would have them, or they would carry them all away. They were, however, well enough treated, except the Restraint of their Persons, and were often ask'd to Refresh themselves, but they would neither Eat or Drink any more all the while they stay'd on Board, which was till the next Day in the Evening, when to their great Satisfaction they saw a great Boat come off from the Fort, and which came directly on Board with seven Buts of Water, and a Cow and a Calf, and a good number of Fowls.

When the Boat came on Board, and had delivered the Stores, Captain Gow complimented the Governour and his Gentlemen, and Discharg'd them to their great Joy; and besides Discharging them, he gave them, in return for the Provisions they brought, two Cerons of Bees Wax, and fir'd them three Guns at their going away. I suppose, however, they will have a care how they go on Board of any Ship again in Compliment to their Captain, unless they are very sure who they are.

Having had no better Success in this out of the way run, to the Maderas, they resolved to make the best of their way back again to the Coast of Spain or Portugal; they accordingly left Porto Santa the next Morning, with a fair Wind, standing directly for Cape St Vincent, or the Southward Cape.

They had not been upon the Coast of Spain above two or three Days before they met with a New England Ship, — Cross, Commander, laden with staves, and bound for Lisbon, and being to Load there with Wine for London; this was a Prize also of no Value to them, and they began to be very much discouraged with their bad Fortune. However, they took out Captain Cross and his men, which were seven or eight in Number, with most of the Provisions and some of the Sails, and gave the Ship to Captain Wise, the Poor Man who they took at first in a Sloop from Newfoundland; and in order to pay Wise and his Men for what he took from them, and made them satisfaction, as he call'd it, he gave to Captain Wise and his Mate 24 Cerons of Bees Wax, and to each of his Men, who were four in Number, two Cerons of Wax each; thus he pretended Honestly, and to make Reperation of Damages by giving them the Goods which he had robb'd the Dutch Merchants of, whose Super-Cargo he had Murdered.

After this, Cruising some Days off the Bay, they met with a French Ship from Cadiz, laden with Wine, Oyl, and Fruit; this was in some respect the very Thing they wanted; so they mann'd her with their own men, and stood off to Sea, that they might divide the spoil of her with more Safety, for they were too near the Land.

And first they took out the French Master and all his Men, which were twelve in Number; then they shifted great Part of the Cargo, especially of the Wine, with some Oyl, and a large quantity of Almonds, out of the French Ship into their own; with five of his best Guns, and their Carriages, all their Ammunition and small Arms, and all the best of their Sails, and then he gave that ship to Captain Somerville, the Glasgow Captain, whose ship they had sunk, and to Captain Cross, the New England Captain, who they had taken but just before; and to do Justice, as they call'd it, here also, they gave half the Ship and Cargo to Somerville, one quarter to his Mate, and the other quarter to Capt. Cross, and 16 Cerons of Wax to the Men to be shar'd among them.

It is to be observ'd here, that Captain Somerville carryed all his Men along with him; except one who chose to enter among the Pirates, so that he could never pretend he was forced into their service; but Cross's Men were all detain'd, whether by Force, or by their own Consent, does not appear at present.

The Day before this Division of the Spoil, they saw a large Ship to Windward, which at first put them into some Surprise, for she came bearing down directly upon them, and they thought she had been a Portuguese Man-of-War, but they found soon after that it was a Merchant Ship, had French Colours, and bound Home, as they suppos'd, from the West Indies, and it was so; for, as we afterwards learn'd, she was loaden at Martinico, and bound for Rochelle.

The Frenchman, not fearing them, came on large to the Wind, being a Ship of much greater Force than Gow's Ship, and carrying 32 Guns and 80 Men, besides a great many Passengers; however, Gow at first made as if he would lye by for them, but seeing plainly what a Ship it was, and that they should have their Hands full of her, he began to consider, and calling his Men all together upon the Deck, told them his Mind – viz., That the Frenchman was apparently superior in Force every way, that they were but ill mann'd, and had a great many Prisoners on Board, and that some of their own People were not very well to be trusted, that six of their best Hands were on Board the Prize, and that all they had left were not sufficient to ply their Guns and stand by the Sails; and that therefore, as they were under no Necessity to engage, so he thought it would be next to Madness to think of it, the French Ship being so very much Superior to them in Force.

The generality of the Men were of Gow's Mind, and agreed to decline the Fight, but Williams, his Lieut, strenuously oppos'd it, and being not to be appeas'd by all that Gow could say to him, or any one else, flew out in a Rage at Gow, upbraiding him with being a Coward, and not fit to command a Ship of Force.

The Truth is, Gow's Reasoning was Good, and the Thing was Just, considering their own Condition. But Williams was a Fellow uncapable of any solid Thinking, had a kind of a savage, brutal Courage, but nothing of true Bravery in him; and this made him the most desperate and outrageous Villain in the World, and the most cruel and inhumane to those whose Disaster it was to fall into his Hands, as had frequently appear'd in his Usage of the Prisoners, under his Power, in this very Voyage.

Gow was a man of Temper, and notwithstanding all the ill Language Williams gave him, said little or nothing, but by way of Argument, against attacking the French Ship, which would certainly have been too strong for them. But this provok'd Williams the more; and he grew to such an extravagant height, that he demanded boldly of Gow to give his Orders for Fighting, which Gow declined still, Williams presented his Pistol at him, and snapt it, but it did not go off, which enrag'd him the more.

Winter and Peterson standing nearest to Williams, and seeing him so furious, flew at him immediately, and each of them fir'd a Pistol at him, one shot him thro' the Arm, and the other into his Belly, at which he fell, and the men about him laid hold of him to throw him Overboard, believing he was dead; but as they lifted him up, he started violently out of their Hands, and leaped directly into the Hold, and from thence run desperately into the Powder-Room, with his Pistol cock'd in his Hand, swearing he would blow them all up; and had certainly done it, if they had not seiz'd him just as he had gotten the Scuttle open, and was that Moment going in to put his hellish Resolution in practice.

Having thus secur'd the demented raving Creature, they car-ryed him forward to the Place which they had made on Purpose, between Decks, to secure their Prisoners, and put him in amongst them, having first loaded him with Irons, and particularly Hand-cuffed him with his Hands behind him, to the great satisfaction of the other Prisoners, who knowing what a butcherly, furious Fellow he was, were terrified, to the last Degree, to see him come in among them; till they saw the Condition he came in. He was, indeed, the Terror of all the Prisoners, for he usually treated them in a barbarous manner, without the least Provocation, and merely for his Humour; presenting Pistols to their Breasts, swearing he would shoot them that Moment, and then would beat them unmercifully, and all for his Diversion, as he call'd it.

Having thus laid him fast, they presently resolv'd to stand away to the Westward, by which they quitted the Martinico Ship, who by that time was come nearer to them, and farther convinc'd them they were in no Condition to have Engag'd her, for she was a stout Ship and full of Men.

All this happen'd Just the Day before they shar'd their last Prize among the Prisoners (as I have said), in which they put on such a Mock-face of doing Justice to the several Captains and Mates, and other Men, their Prisoners, whose Ships they had taken away, and who now they made a Reparation to, by giving them what they had taken Violently from another, that it was a strange Medly of Mock-Justice made up of Rapine and Gener-osity blended together.

Two Days after this they took a Bristol Ship, bound from Newfoundland to Oporto with Fish; they let her Cargo alone, for they had no occasion for Fish, but they took out also almost all their Provisions, all the Ammunition, Arms, &c., all her good Sails, also her best Cables, and forced two of her Men to go away with them, and then put 10 of the French Men on Board her, and let her go.

But just as they were parting with her, they consulted together what to do with Williams, their Lieutenant, who was then among their Prisoners, and in Irons; and after a short Debate, they resolved to put him on Board the Bristol Man and send him away too, which accordingly was done; with Directions to the Master to deliver him on Board the first English Man of War they should meet with, in order to his being hang'd for a Pirate (so they jeeringly call'd him) as soon as he came to England, giving them also an Account of some of his Villanies.

The Truth is, this Williams was a Monster, rather than a Man; he was the most inhuman, bloody, and desperate Creature that the World could produce; he was even too wicked for Gow and all his Crew, tho' they were Pirates and Murtherers, as has been said; his Temper was so Savage, so Villainous, so Merciless, that even the Pirates themselves told him it was Time he was hang'd out of the Way.

One Instance of this Barbarity in Williams can not be omitted, and will be sufficient to justify all that can be said of him, namely, that when Gow gave it as a Reason against engaging with the Martinico Ship, that he had a great many Prisoners on Board (as above), and some of their own. Men they could not depend upon; Williams propos'd to have them all call'd up, one by one, and to cut their Throats, and throw them Overboard; A Proposal so Horrid, that the worst of the Crew shook their Heads at it; yet Gow answer'd him very handsomly, That there had been too much Blood spilt already; yet the refusing this highten'd the Quarrel, and was the chief Occasion of his offering to Pistol Gow himself, as has been said at large. After which, his Behaviour was such as made all the Ship's Crew resolve to be rid of him. And 'twas thought, if they had not had an Opportunity to send him away, as they did by the Bristol Ship, they would have been oblig'd to have hang'd him themselves.

This cruel and butcherly Temper of Williams being carry'd to such a height, so near to the ruine of them all, shock'd some of them, and as they acknowledged gave them some check in the heat of their wicked Progress, and had they had a fair Opportunity to have gone on Shore at the Time, without falling into the Hands of Justice, 'tis believ'd the greatest Part of them would have abandon'd the Ship, and perhaps the very Trade of a Pirate too. But they had dipt their Hands in Blood, and Heaven had no doubt determin'd to bring them, that is to say, the Chief of them, to the Gallows for it, as indeed they all deserv'd, so they went on.

When they put Williams on board the Bristol Man, and he was told what Directions they gave with him, he began to resent, and made all the Intercession he could to Captain Gow for Pardon, or at least not to be put on board the Ship, knowing if he was carried to Lisbon, he should meet with his Due from the Portuguese, if not from the English; for it seems he had been concern'd in some Villanies among the Portuguese, before he came on Board the *George Galley*; what they were he did not confess, nor indeed did his own Ship's Crew trouble themselves to examine him about it. He had been wicked enough among them, and it was sufficient to make them use him as they did; it was more to be wonder'd, indeed, they did not cut him in pieces upon the Spot, and throw him into the Sea, half on one side of the Ship, and half on the other; for there was scarce a Man in the Ship, but on one Occasion or other, had some apprehensions of him, and might be said to go in danger of his life from him.

But they chose to shift their Hands of him this bloodless way; so they double fetter'd him and brought him up. When they brought him out among the Men, he begg'd they would throw him into the Sea and drown him; then entreated for his Life with a meanness which made them despise him, and with Tears, so that one Time they began to relent; but then the devilish Temper of the Fellow overrul'd it again; so at last they resolv'd to let him go, and did accordingly put him on Board, and gave him a hearty Curse at parting, wishing him a good Voyage to the Gallows, as was made good afterwards, tho' in such Company as they little thought of at that Time.

The Bristol Captain was very just to them, for according to their Orders, as soon as they came to Lisbon, they put him on board the *Argyle*, one of His Majesty's Ships, Captain Bowler, Commander, then lying in the Tagus, and bound Home for England, who accordingly brought him Home; tho', as it happen'd, Heaven brought the Captain and the rest of the Crew so quickly to the end of their Villanies, that they all came Home time enough to be hang'd with their Lieutenant. But I return to Gow and his Crew. Having thus dismiss'd the Bristol Man, and clear'd his Hands of most of his Prisoners, he, with the same wicked Generosity, gave the Bristol Captain 13 Cerons of Bees Wax, as a Gratuity for his Trouble and Charge with the Prisoners, and in Recompense, as he call'd it, for the Goods he had taken from him, and so they parted.

What these several Captains did, to whom they thus divided the spoil of poor Ferneau's Cargo, or as I ought rather to call it, of the Merchants Cargo, which was loaded in Africa; I say, what was done with the Bees-Wax, and other Things which they distributed to the Captains, and their Crews, who they thus transpos'd from Ship to Ship, that we cannot tell, nor indeed could these people either well known how to keep it, or how to part with it.

It was certainly a Gift they had no power to give, nor had the other any Right to it by their Donation; but as the Owners were unknown, and the several Persons possessing it are not easily known, I do not see which way the poor Dutchmen can come at their Goods again.

It is true, indeed, the Ships which they exchang'd may, and ought to be restored, and the honest Owners put in Possession of them again, and I suppose will be so in a legal Manner; but the Goods were so dispers'd that it was impossible.

This was the last Prize they took, not only on the Coast of Portugal, but any where else.

In February 1725 Gow made for the Orkney Islands, where he was born and where his girlfriend still lived. Unfortunately for the luckless Gow, his ship ran aground and he, along with eight of his crew, was captured. Tried in London Gow and his cohorts "stepped off" at Execution Dock on 11 June 1725.

*"The Joassamees . . . having tasted the sweets of plunder
. . . determined to attempt more promising victories"*

THE JOASSAMEE
PIRATES OF THE GULF

Charles Ellms

The line of coast from Cape Mussenndom to Bahrain, on the Arabian side of the Persian Gulf, had been from time immemorial occupied by a tribe of Arabs called Joassamees. These, from local position, were all engaged in maritime pursuits. Some traded in their own small vessels to Bussorah, Bushire, Muscat, and even India; others annually fished in their own boats on the pearl banks of Bahrain; and a still greater number hired themselves out as sailors to navigate the coasting small craft of the Persian Gulf. The Joassamees at length perceiving that their local position enabled them to reap a rich harvest by plundering vessels in passing this great highway of nations, commenced their piratical career. The small coasting vessels of the gulf, from their defence-less state, were the first object of their pursuit, and these soon fell an easy prey; until, emboldened by success, they directed their views to more arduous enterprises, and having tasted the sweets of plunder in the increase of their wealth, had determined to attempt more promising victories.

About the year 1797, one of the East India Company's vessels of war, the *Viper*, of ten guns, was lying at anchor in the inner roads of Bushire. Some dows of the Joassames were at the same moment anchored in the harbor; but as their warfare had hitherto been waged only against what are called native vessels, and they had either feared or respected the British flag, no hostile measures were ever pursued against them by the British ships. The commanders of these dows had applied to the Persian agent of the East India Company there, for a supply of gunpowder and cannon shot for their cruise: and as this man had no suspicions of their intentions, he furnished them with an order to the commanding officer on board for the quantity required. The captain of the *Viper* was on shore at the time, in the agent's house, but the order being produced to the officer on board, the powder and shot were delivered, and the dows weighed and made sail. The crew of the *Viper* were at this moment taking their breakfast on deck, and the officers below; when on a sudden, a cannonading was opened on them by two of the dows, who attempted also to board.

The officers, leaping on deck, called the crew to quarters, and cutting their cable, got sail upon the ship, so as to have the advantage of manoeuvring. A regular engagement now took place between this small cruiser and four dows, all armed with great guns, and full of men. In the contest Lieut. Carruthers, the commanding officer, was once wounded by a ball in the loins; but after girding a handkerchief round his waist, he still kept the deck, till a ball entering his forehead, he fell. Mr. Salter, the midshipman on whom the command devolved, continued the fight with determined bravery, and after a stout resistance, beat them off, chased them from distance out to sea, and subsequently regained the anchorage in safety.

Several years elapsed before the wounds of the first defeat were sufficiently healed to induce a second attempt on vessels under the British flag, though a constant state of warfare was still kept up against the small craft of the gulf. In 1804, the East India Company's cruiser, *Fly*, was taken by a French privateer, off the Island of Kenn, in the Persian Gulf; but before the enemy boarded her, she ran into shoal water, near that island, and sunk the government dispatches, and some treasure with which they were charged, in about two and a half fathoms of water, taking marks for the recovery of them, if possible, at some future period. The passengers and crew were taken to Bushire where they were set at liberty, and having purchased a country dow by subscription, they fitted her out and commenced their voyage down the gulf, bound for Bombay. On their passage down, as they thought it would be practicable to recover the government packet and treasure sunk off Kenn, they repaired to that island, and were successful, after much exertion, in recovering the former, which being in their estimation of the first importance, as the dispatches were from England to Bombay, they sailed with them on their way thither, without loss of time.

Near the mouth of the gulf, they were captured by a fleet of Joassamee boats, after some resistance, in which several were wounded and taken into their chief port at Ras-el-Khyma. Here they were detained in hope of ransom, and during their stay were shown to the people of the town as curiosities, no similar beings having been before seen there within the memory of man. The Joassamee ladies were so minute in their enquiries, indeed, that they were not satisfied without determining in what respect an uncircumcised infidel differed from a true believer.

When these unfortunate Englishmen had remained for several months in the possession of the Arabs, and no hope of their ransom appeared, it was determined to put them to death, and thus rid themselves of unprofitable enemies. An anxiety to preserve life, however, induced the suggestion, on their parts, of a plan for the temporary prolongation of it, at least. With this view they communicated to the chief of the pirates the fact of their having sunk a quantity of treasure near the island of Kenn, and of their knowing the marks of the spot, by the bearings of objects on shore, with sufficient accuracy to recover it, if furnished with good divers. They offered, therefore, to purchase their own liberty, by a recovery of this money for their captors; and on the fulfillment of their engagement it was solemnly promised to be granted to them.

They soon sailed for the spot, accompanied by divers accustomed to that occupation on the pearl banks of Bahrain; and, on their anchoring at the precise points of bearing taken, they commenced their labors. The first divers who went down were so successful, that all the crew followed in their turns, so that the vessel was at one time almost entirely abandoned at anchor. As the men, too, were all so busily occupied in their golden harvest, the moment appeared favorable for escape; and the still captive Englishmen were already at their stations to overpower the few on board, cut the cable, and make sail. Their motions were either seen or suspected, as the divers repaired on board in haste, and the scheme was thus frustrated. They were now given their liberty as promised, by being landed on the island of Kenn, where, however, no means offered for their immediate escape. The pirates, having at the same time landed themselves on the island, commenced a general massacre of the inhabitants, in which their released prisoners, fearing they might be included, fled for shelter to clefts and hiding places in the rocks. During their refuge here, they lived on such food as chance threw in their way; going out under cover of the night to steal a goat and drag it to their haunts. When the pirates had at length completed their work of blood, and either murdered or driven off every former inhabitant of the island, they quitted it themselves, with the treasure which they had thus collected from the sea and shore. The Englishmen now ventured to come out from their hiding places, and to think of devising some means of escape. Their good fortune in a moment of despair, threw them on the wreck of a boat, near the beach, which was still capable of repair. In searching about the now deserted town, other materials were found, which were of use to them, and sufficient plank and logs of wood for the construction of a raft. These were both completed in a few days, and the party embarked on them in two divisions, to effect a passage to the Persian shore. One of these rafts was lost in the attempt, and all on board her perished; while the raft, with the remainder of the party reached land.

Having gained the main land they now set out on foot towards Bushire, following the line of the coast for the sake of the villages and water. In this they are said to have suffered incredible hardships and privations of every kind. No one knew the language of the country perfectly, and the roads and places of refreshment still less; they were in general destitute of clothes and money, and constantly subject to plunder and imposition, poor as they were. Their food was therefore often scanty, and always of the worst kind; and they had neither shelter from the burning sun of the day, nor from the chilling dews of night.

The Indian sailors, sipakees, and servants, of whom a few were still remaining when they set out, had all dropped off by turns; and even Europeans had been abandoned on the road, in the most affecting way, taking a last adieu of their comrades, who had little else to expect but soon to follow their fate. One instance is mentioned of their having left one who could march no further, at the distance of only a mile from a village; and on returning to the spot on the morrow, to bring him in, nothing was found but his mangled bones, as he had been devoured in the night by jackals. The packet being light was still, however, carried by turns, and preserved through all obstacles and difficulties; and with it they reached at length the island of Busheap, to which they crossed over in a boat from the main. Here they were detained by the Sheikh, but at length he provided them with a boat for the conveyance of themselves and dispatches to Bushire. From this place they proceeded to Bombay, but of all the company only two survived. A Mr. Jowl, an officer of a merchant ship, and an English sailor named Penmel together with the bag of letters and dispatches.

In the following year, two English brigs, the *Shannon*, Capt. Babcock, and the *Trimmer*, Capt. Cummings, were on their voyage from Bombay to Bussorah. These were both attacked, near the Islands of Polior and Kenn, by several boats, and after a slight resistance on the part of the *Shannon* only, were taken possession of, and a part of the crew of each, cruelly put to the sword. Capt. Babcock, having been seen by one of the Arabs to discharge a musket during the contest, was taken by them on shore; and after a consultation on his fate, it was determined that he should forfeit the arm by which this act of resistance was committed. It was accordingly severed from his body by one stroke of a sabre, and no steps were taken either to bind up the wound, or to prevent his bleeding to death. The captain, himself, had yet sufficient presence of mind left, however, to think of his own safety, and there being near him some clarified butter, he procured this to be heated, and while yet warm, thrust the bleeding stump of his arm into it. It had the effect of lessening the effusion of blood, and ultimately of saving a life that would otherwise most probably have been lost. The crew were then all made prisoners, and taken to a port of Arabia, from whence they gradually dispersed and escaped. The vessels themselves were additionally armed, one of them mounting twenty guns, manned with Arab crews, and sent from Ras-el-Khyma to cruise in the gulf, where they committed many piracies.

In the year 1808, the force of the Joassamees having gradually increased, and becoming flushed with the pride of victory, their insulting attacks on the British flag were more numerous and more desperate than ever. The first of these was on the ship *Minerva*, of Bombay, on her voyage to Bussorah. The attack was commenced by several boats, (for they never cruize singly,) and a spirited resistance in a running fight was kept up at intervals for several days in succession. A favorable moment offered, however, for boarding; the ship was overpowered by numbers, and carried amidst a general massacre. The captain was said to have been cut up into separate pieces, and thrown overboard by fragments; the second mate and carpenter alone were spared, probably to make use of their services; and an Armenian lady, the wife of Lieut. Taylor, then at Bushire, was reserved perhaps for still greater sufferings. But was subsequently ransomed for a large sum.

A few weeks after this, the *Sylph*, one of the East India Company's cruisers, of sixty tons and mounting eight guns, was accompanying the mission under Sir Hartford Jones, from Bombay, to Persia; when being separated from the rest of the squadron, she was attacked in the gulf by a fleet of dows. These bore down with all the menacing attitude of hostility; but as the commander, Lieut. Graham had received orders from the Bombay government, not to open his fire on any of these vessels until he had been first fired on himself, the ship was hardly prepared for battle, and the colors were not even hoisted to apprise them to what nation she belonged. The dows approached, threw their long overhanging prows across the *Sylph*'s beam, and pouring in a shower of stones on her deck, beat down and wounded almost every one who stood on it. They then boarded, and made the ship an easy prize, before more than a single shot had been fired, and in their usual way, put every one whom they found alive to the sword. Lieut. Graham fell, covered with wounds, down the fore hatchway of his own vessel, where he was dragged by some of the crew into a store room, in which they had secreted themselves, and barricaded the door with a crow-bar from within. The cruiser was thus completely in the possession of the enemy, who made sail on her, and were bearing her off in triumph to their own port, in company with their boats. Soon after, however, the commodore of the squadron in the *Neried* frigate hove in sight, and perceiving this vessel in company with the dows, judged her to be a prize to the pirates. She accordingly gave them all chase, and coming up with the brig, the Arabs took to their boats and abandoned her. The chase was continued after the dows, but without success.

These repeated aggressions at length opened the eyes of the

East India Government, and an expedition was accordingly assembled at Bombay. The naval force consisted of *La Chiffone*, frigate, Capt. Wainwright, as commodore. The *Caroline* of thirty-eight guns; and eight of the East India Company's cruisers, namely, the *Mornington*, *Ternate*, *Aurora*, *Prince of Wales*, *Ariel*, *Nautilus*, *Vestal* and *Fury*, with four large transports, and the *Stromboli* bomb-ketch. The fleet sailed from Bombay in September, and after a long passage they reached Muscat, where it remained for many days to refresh and arrange their future plans; they sailed and soon reached Ras-el-Khyma, the chief port of the pirates within the gulf. Here the squadron anchored abreast of the town, and the troops were landed under cover of the ships and boats. The inhabitants of the town assembled in crowds to repel the invaders; but the firm line, the regular volleys, and the steady charge of the troops at the point of the bayonet, overcome every obstacle, and multiplied the heaps of the slain. A general conflagration was then ordered, and a general plunder to the troops was permitted. The town was set on fire in all parts, and about sixty sail of boats and dows, with the *Minerva*, a ship which they had taken, then lying in the roads were all burnt and destroyed.

The complete conquest of the place was thus effected with very trifling loss on the part of the besiegers, and some plunder collected; though it was thought that most of the treasure and valuables had been removed into the interior. This career of victory was suddenly damped by the report of the approach of a large body of troops from the interior, and although none of these were seen, this ideal reinforcement induced the besiegers to withdraw. The embarkation took place at daylight in the morning; and while the fleet remained at anchor during the whole of the day, parties were still seen assembling on the shore, displaying their colors, brandishing their spears, and firing muskets from all points; so that the conquest was scarcely as complete as could be wished, since no formal act of submission had yet been shown. The expedition now sailed to Linga, a small port of the Joassamees, and burnt it to the ground. The force had now become separated, the greater portion of the troops being sent to Muscat for supplies, or being deemed unnecessary, and some of the vessels sent on separate services of blockading passages, &c. The remaining portion of the blockading squadron consisting of *La Chiffone*, frigate, and four of the cruisers, the *Mornington*, *Ternate*, *Nautilus*, and *Fury*, and two transports, with five hundred troops from Linga, then proceeded to Luft, another port of the Joassamees. As the channel here was narrow and difficult of approach, the ships were warped into their stations of anchorage, and a summons sent on shore, as the people had not here abandoned their town, but were found at their posts of defence, in a large and strong castle with many batteries, redoubts, &c. The summons being treated with disdain, the troops were landed with Col. Smith at their head; and while forming on the beach a slight skirmish took place with such of the inhabitants of the town, as fled for shelter to the castle. The troops then advanced towards the fortress, which is described to have had walls fourteen feet thick, pierced with loop holes, and only one entrance through a small gate, well cased with iron bars and bolts, in the strongest manner. With a howitzer taken for the occasion, it was intended to have blown this gate open, and to have taken the place by storm; but on reaching it while the ranks opened, and the men sought to surround the castle to seek for some other entrance at the same time, they were picked off so rapidly and unexpectedly from the loop holes above, that a general flight took place, the howitzer was abandoned, even before it had been fired, and both the officers and the troops sought shelter by lying down behind the ridges of sand and little hillocks immediately underneath the castle walls. An Irish officer, jumping up from his hiding place, and calling on some of his comrades to follow him in an attempt to rescue the howitzer, was killed in the enterprise. Such others as even raised their heads to look around them, were picked off by the musketry from above; and the whole of the troops lay therefore hidden in this way, until the darkness of the night favored their escape to the beach, where they embarked after sunset, the enemy having made no sally on them from the fort. A second summons was sent to the chief in the castle, threatening to bombard the town from a nearer anchorage if he did not submit, and no quarter afterwards shown. With the dawn of morning, all eyes were directed to the fortress, when, to the surprise of the whole squadron, a man was seen waving the British Union flag on the summit of its walls. It was lieutenant Hall, who commanded the *Fury* which was one of the vessels nearest the shore. During the night he had gone on shore alone, taking an union-jack in his hand, and advanced singly to the castle gate. The fortress had already been abandoned by the greater number of the inhabitants, but some few still remained there. These fled at the approach of an individual supposing him to be the herald of those who were to follow. Be this as it may, the castle was entirely abandoned, and the British flag waved on its walls by this daring officer, to the surprise and admiration of all the fleet. The town and fortifications were then taken possession of. After sweeping round the bottom of the gulf, the expedition returned to Muscat.

On the sailing of the fleet from hence, the forces were augmented by a body of troops belonging to the Imaun of Muscat, destined to assist in the recovery of a place called Shenaz, on the coast, taken by the Joassamees. On their arrival at this place, a summons was sent, commanding the fort to surrender, which being refused, a bombardment was opened from the ships and boats, but without producing much effect. On the following morning, the whole of the troops were landed, and a regular encampment formed on the shore, with sand batteries, and other necessary works for a siege. After several days bombardment, in which about four thousand shot and shells were discharged against the fortress, to which the people had fled for refuge after burning down the town, a breach was reported to be practicable, and the castle was accordingly stormed. The resistance still made was desperate; the Arabs fighting as long as they could wield the sword, and even thrusting their spears up through the fragments of towers, in whose ruins they remained irrevocably buried. The loss in killed and wounded was upwards of a thousand men. Notwithstanding that the object of this expedition might be said to be incomplete, inasmuch as nothing less than a total extirpation of their race could secure the tranquility of these seas, yet the effect produced by this expedition was such, as to make them reverence or dread the British flag for several years afterwards.

At length in 1815, their boats began to infest the entrance to the Red Sea; and in 1816, their numbers had so increased on that coast, that a squadron of them commanded by a chief called Ameer Ibrahim, captured within sight of Mocha, four vessels bound from surat to that port, richly laden and navigating under the British flag, and the crews were massacred.

A squadron consisting of His Majesty's ship *Challenger*, Captain Brydges, and the East India Company's cruisers, *Mercury*, *Ariel*, and *Vestal*, were despatched to the chief port of the Joassamees, Ras-el-Khyma. Mr. Buckingham the Great Oriental traveller, accompanied the expedition from Bushire. Upon their arrival at Ras-el-Khyma, a demand was made for the restoration of the four Surat vessels and their cargoes; or in lieu thereof twelve lacks of rupees. Also that the commander of the piratical squadron, Ameer Ibrahim, should be delivered up for punishment. The demand was made by letter, and answer being received, Captain Brydges determined to go on shore and have an interview with the Pirate Chieftain. Mr. Buckingham (says,)

He requested me to accompany him on shore as an interpreter. I readily assented. We quitted the ship together about 9 o'clock, and pulled straight to the shore, sounding all the way as we went, and gradually shoaling our water from six to two fathoms, within a quarter of a mile of the beach, where four large dows lay at anchor, ranged in a line, with their heads seaward, each of them mounting several pieces of cannon, and being full of men. On landing on the beach, we found its whole length guarded by a line of armed men, some bearing muskets, but the greater part armed with swords, shields, and spears; most of them were negroes, whom the Joassamees spare in their wars, looking on them rather as property and merchandise, than in the light of enemies. We were permitted to pass this line, and upon our communicating our wish to see the chief, we were conducted to the gate of the principal building, nearly in the centre of the town, and were met by the Pirate Chieftain attended by fifty armed men. I offered him the Mahometan salutation of peace, which he returned without hesitation.

The chief, Hassan ben Rahma, whom we had seen, was a small man, apparently about forty years of age, with an expression of cunning in his looks, and something particularly sarcastic in his smile. He was dressed in the usual Arab garments, with a cashmeer shawl, turban, and a scarlet benish, of the Persian form, to distinguish him from his followers. They were habited in the plainest garments. One of his eyes had been wounded, but his other features were good, his teeth beautifully white and regular, and his complexion very dark.

The town of Ras-el-Khyma stands on a narrow tongue of sandy land, pointing to the northeastward, presenting its northwest edge to the open sea, and its southeast one to a creek, which runs up within it to the southwestward, and affords a safe harbor for boats. There appeared to be no continued wall of defence around it, though round towers and portions of walls were seen in several parts, probably once connected in line, but not yet repaired since their destruction. The strongest points of defence appear to be in a fortress at the northeast angle, and a double round tower, near the centre of the town; in each of which, guns are mounted; but all the other towers appear to afford only shelter for musketeers. The rest of the town is composed of ordinary buildings of unhewn stone, and huts of rushes and long grass, with narrow avenues winding between them. The present number of inhabitants may be computed at ten thousand at least. They are thought to have at present (1816), sixty large boats out from their own port, manned with crews of from eighty, to three hundred men each, and forty other boats that belong to other ports. Their force concentrated, would probably amount to at least one hundred boats and eight thousand fighting men. After several fruitless negotiations, the signal was now made to weigh, and stand closer in towards the town. It was then followed by the signal to engage the enemy. The squadron bore down nearly in line, under easy sail, and with the wind right aft, or on shore; the *Mercury* being on the starboard bow, the *Challenger* next in order, in the centre, the *Vestal* following in the same line, and the *Ariel* completing the division.

A large fleet of small boats were seen standing in from Cape Mussundum, at the same time; but these escaped by keeping closer along shore, and at length passing over the bar and getting into the back water behind the town. The squadron continued to stand on in a direct line towards the four anchored dows, gradually shoaling from the depth of our anchorage to two and a half fathoms, where stream anchors were dropped under foot, with springs on the cables, so that each vessel lay with her broadside to the shore. A fire was now opened by the whole squadron, directed to the four dows. These boats were full of men, brandishing their weapons in the air, their whole number exceeding, probably, six hundred. Some of the shot from the few long guns of the squadron reached the shore, and were buried in the sand; others fell across the bows and near the hulls of the dows to which they were directed; but the cannonades all fell short, as we were then fully a mile from the beach.

The Arab colors were displayed on all the forts; crowds of armed men were assembled on the beach, bearing large banners on poles, and dancing around them with their arms, as if rallying around a sacred standard, so that no sign of submission or conquest was witnessed throughout. The *Ariel* continued to discharge about fifty shot after all the others had desisted, but with as little avail as before, and thus ended this wordy negotiation, and the bloodless battle to which it eventually led.

In 1818, these pirates grew so daring that they made an irruption into the Indian Ocean, and plundered vessels and towns on the islands and coasts. A fleet was sent against them, and intercepted them off Ashlola Island, proceeding to the westward in three divisions; and drove them back into the gulf. The *Eden* and *Psyche* fell in with two trankies, and these were so closely pursued that they were obliged to drop a small captured boat they had in tow. The *Thetes* one day kept in close chase of seventeen vessels, but they were enabled to get away owing to their superior sailing. The cruisers met with the Joassamees seventeen times and were constantly employed in hunting them from place to place.

At length, in 1819, they became such a scourge to commerce that a formidable expedition under the command of Major General Sir W. Grant Keir, sailed against them. It arrived before the chief town in December, and commenced operations. In his despatches Gen. Keir says—

I have the satisfaction to report the town of Ras-el Khyma, after a resistance of six days, was taken possession of this morning by the force under my command.

On the 18th, after completing my arrangements at Muscat, the *Liverpool* sailed for the rendezvous at Kishme; on the 21st, we fell in with the fleet of the Persian Gulf and anchored off the island of Larrack on the 24th November.

As it appeared probable that a considerable period would elapse before the junction of the ships which were detained at Bombay, I conceived it would prove highly advantageous to avail myself of all the information that could be procured respecting the strength and resources of the pirates we had to deal with.

No time was lost in making the necessary preparations for landing, which was effected the following morning without opposition, at a spot which had been previously selected for that purpose, about two miles to the westward of the town. The troops were formed across the isthmus connecting the peninsula on which the town is situated with the neighboring country, and the whole of the day was occupied in getting the tents on shore, to shelter the men from rain, landing engineers, tools, sand bags, &c., and making arrangements preparatory to commencing our approaches the next day. On the morning of the 4th, our light troops were ordered in advance, supported by the pickets, to dislodge the enemy from a bank within nine hundred yards of the outer fort, which was expected to afford good cover for the men. The whole of the light companies of the force under Capt. Backhouse, moved forward, and drove the Arabs with great gallantry from a date grove, and over the bank close under the walls of the fort, followed by the pickets under Major Molesworth, who took post at the sand banks, whilst the European light troops were skirmishing in front. The enemy kept up a sharp fire of musketry and cannon; during these movements, Major Molesworth, a gallant officer was here killed. The troops kept their position during the day, and in the night effected a lodgment within three hundred yards of the southernmost tower, and erected a battery of four guns, together with a mortar battery.

The weather having become rather unfavorable for the disembarkation of the stores required for the siege, but this important object being effected on the morning of the 6th, we were enabled to open three eighteen pounders on the fort, a couple of howitzers, and six pounders were also placed in the battery on the right, which played on the defences of the towers and nearly silenced the enemy's fire, who, during the whole of our progress exhibited a considerable degree of resolution in withstanding, and ingenuity in counteracting our attacks, sallied out at 8 o'clock this evening along the whole front of our entrenchments, crept close up to the mortar battery without being perceived, and entered it over the parapet, after spearing the advance sentries. The party which occupied it were obliged to retire, but being immediately reinforced charged the assailants, who were driven out of the battery with great loss. The enemy repeated his attacks towards morning but was vigorously repulsed. During the seventh every exertion was made to land and bring up the remaining guns and mortars, which was accomplished during the night. They were immediately placed in the battery, together with two twenty-four pounders which were landed from the *Liverpool*, and in the morning the whole of the ordnance opened on the fort and fired with scarcely any intermission till sunset, when the breach on the curtain was reported nearly practicable and the towers almost untenable. Immediate arrangements were made for the assault, and the troops ordered to move down to the entrenchments by daylight the next morning. The party moved forward about 8 o'clock, and entered the fort through the breaches without firing a shot, and it soon appeared the enemy had evacuated the place. The town was taken possession of and found almost entirely deserted, only eighteen or twenty men, and a few women remaining in their houses.

The expedition next proceeded against Rumps, a piratical town, eight miles north of Ras-el-Khyma, but the inhabitants abandoned the town and took refuse in the hill fort of Zyah, which is situated at the head of a navigable creek nearly two miles from the sea coast. This place was the residence of Hussein Bin Alley, a sheikh of considerable importance among the Joassamee tribes, and a person who from his talents and lawless habits, as well as from the strength and advantageous situation of the fort, was likely to attempt the revival of the piratical system upon the first occasion. It became a desirable object to reduce the power of this chieftain.

On the 18th December, the troops embarked at Ras-el-Khyma, at day break in the boats of the fleet under command of Major Warren, with the 65th regiment and the flank companies of the first and second regiment, and at noon arrived within four miles of their destination. This operation was attended with considerable difficulty and risk, owing to the heavy surf that beat on the shore; and which was the occasion of some loss of ammunition, and of a few boats being upset and stove in.

At half past three p.m., having refreshed the men, (says Major Warren) we commenced our march, and fording the creek or back water, took up our position at sunset, to the northeastward of the fort, the enemy firing at us as we passed, notwithstanding that our messenger, whom we had previously sent in to summon the Sheikh, was still in the place; and I lost no time in pushing our riflemen and pickets as far forward as I could without exposing them too much to the firing of the enemy, whom I found strongly posted under secure cover in the date three groves in front of the town. Captain Cocke, with the light company of his battalion, was at the same time sent to the westward, to cut off the retreat of the enemy on that side.

At day break the next morning, finding it necessary to drive the enemy still further in, to get a nearer view of his defences, I moved forward the rifle company of the 65th regiment, and after a considerable opposition from the enemy, I succeeded in forcing him to retire some distance; but not without disputing every inch of ground, which was well calculated for resistance, being intersected at every few yards, by banks and water courses raised for the purpose of irrigation, and covered with date trees. The next morning the riflemen, supported by the pickets, were again called into play, and soon established their position within three and four hundred yards of the town, which with the base of the hill, was so completely surrounded, as to render the escape of any of the garrison now almost impossible. This advantage was gained by a severe loss. Two twenty-four pounders and the two twelves, the landing of which had been retarded by the difficulty of communication with the fleet from which we derived all our supplies, having been now brought on shore, we broke ground in the evening, and notwithstanding the rocky soil, had them to play next morning at daylight.

Aware, however, that the families of the enemy were still in the town, and humanity dictating that some effort should be made to save the innocent from the fate that awaited the guilty; an opportunity was afforded for that purpose by an offer to the garrison of security to their women and children, should they be sent out within the hour; but the infatuated chief, either from an idea that his fort on the hill was not to be reached by our shot, or with the vain hope to gain time by procrastination, returning no answer to our communication, while he detained our messenger; we opened our fire at half past eight in the morning, and such was the precision of the practice, that in two hours we perceived the breach would soon be practicable. I was in the act of ordering the assault, when a white flag was displayed; and the enemy, after some little delay in assembling from the different quarters of the place, marched out without their arms, with Hussein Bin Alley at their head, to the number of three hundred and ninety-eight; and at half past one P.M., the British flags were hoisted on the hill fort and at the Sheikh's house. The women and children to the number of four hundred, were at the same time collected together in a place of security, and sent on board the fleet, together with the men. The service has been short but arduous; the enemy defended themselves with great obstinacy and ability worthy of a better cause.

From two prisoners retaken from the Joassamees, they learnt that the plunder is made a general stock, and distributed by the chief, but in what proportions the deponents cannot say; water is generally very scarce. There is a quantity of fish caught on the bank, upon which and dates they live. There were a few horses, camels, cows, sheep, and goats; the greatest part of which they took with them; they were in general lean, as the sandy plain produces little or no vegetation, except a few dates and cocoa-nut trees. The pirates who abandoned Ras-el-Khyma, encamped about three miles in the interior, ready to retreat into the desert at a moment's warning. The Sheikh of Rumps is an old man, but looks intelligent, and is said to be the man who advises upon all occasions the movements of the different tribes of pirates on the coast, and when he was told that it was the wish of the Company to put a stop to their piracy, and make an honest people of them by encouraging them to trade, seemed to regret much that those intentions were not made known, as they would have been most readily embraced. Rumps is the key to Ras-el-Khyma, and by its strength is defended from a strong banditti infesting the mountains, as also the Bedouin Arabs who are their enemies. A British garrison of twelve hundred men was stationed at Ras-el-Khyma, and a guard-ship. The other places sent in tokens of submission, as driven out of their fortresses on the margin of the sea, they had to contend within with the interior hostile tribes.

THE DEATH OF THE JOASSAMEE CHIEF, RAMAH-BEN-JABIR

The town of Bushire, on the Persian Gulf is seated in a low peninsula of sand, extending out of the general line of the coast, so as to form a bay on both sides. One of these bays was in 1816, occupied by the fleet of a certain Arab, named Rahmah-ben-Jabir, who has been for more than twenty years the terror of the gulf, and who was the most successful and the most generally tolerated pirate, perhaps, that ever infested any sea. This man by birth was a native of Grain, on the opposite coast, and nephew of the governor of that place. His fellow citizens had all the honesty, however, to declare him an outlaw, from abhorrence of his profession; but he found that aid and protection at Bushire, which his own townsmen denied him. With five or six vessels, most of which were very large, and manned with crews of from two to three hundred each, he sallied forth, and captured whatever he thought himself strong enough to carry off as a prize. His followers, to the number of two thousand, were maintained by the plunder of his prizes; and as the most of these were his own bought African slaves, and the remainder equally subject to his authority, he was sometimes as prodigal of their lives in a fit of anger as he was of his enemies, whom he was not content to slay in battle only, but basely murdered in cold blood, after they had submitted. An instance is related of his having put a great number of his own crew, who used mutinous expressions, into a tank on board, in which they usually kept their water, and this being shut close at the top, the poor wretches were all suffocated, and afterwards thrown overboard. This butcher chief, like the celebrated Djezzar of Acre, affecting great simplicity of dress, manners, and living; and whenever he went out, could not be distinguished by a stranger from the crowd of his attendants. He carried this simplicity to a degree of filthiness, which was disgusting, as his usual dress was a shirt, which was never taken off to be washed, from the time it was first put on till worn out; no drawers or coverings for the legs of any kind, and a large black goat's hair cloak, wrapped over all with a greasy and dirty handkerchief, called the keffeea, thrown loosely over his head. Infamous as was this man's life and character, he was not only cherished and courted by the people of Bushire, who dreaded him, but was courteously received and respectfully entertained whenever he visited the British Factory.

On one occasion (says Mr. Buckingham), at which I was present, he was sent for to give some medical gentlemen of the navy and company's cruisers an opportunity of inspecting his arm, which had been severely wounded. The wound was at first made by grape-shot and splinters, and the arm was one mass of blood about the part for several days, while the man himself was with difficulty known to be alive. He gradually recovered, however, without surgical aid, and the bone of the arm between the shoulder and elbow being completely shivered to pieces, the fragments progressively worked out, and the singular appearance was left of the fore arm and elbow connected to the shoulder by flesh and skin, and tendons, without the least vestige of bone. This man when invited to the factory for the purpose of making an exhibition of his arm, was himself admitted to sit at the table and take some tea, as it was breakfast time, and some of his followers took chairs around him. They were all as disgustingly filthy in appearance as could well be imagined; and some of them did not scruple to hunt for vermin on their skins, of which there was an abundance, and throw them on the floor. Rahmah-ben-Jabir's figure presented a meagre trunk, with four lank members, all of them cut and hacked, and pierced with wounds of sabres, spears and bullets, in every part, to the number, perhaps of more than twenty different wounds. He had, besides, a face naturally ferocious and ugly, and now rendered still more so by several scars there, and by the loss of one eye. When asked by one of the English gentlemen present, with a tone of encouragement and familiarity, whether he could not still dispatch an enemy with his boneless arm, he drew a crooked dagger, or yambeah, from the girdle round his shirt, and placing his left hand, which was sound, to support the elbow of the right, which was the one that was wounded, he grasped the dagger firmly with his clenched fist, and drew it backward and forward, twirling it at the same time, and saying that he desired nothing better than to have the cutting of as many throats as he could effectually open with his lame hand. Instead of being shocked at the uttering of such a brutal wish, and such a savage triumph at still possessing the power to murder unoffending victims, I knew not how to describe my feelings of shame and sorrow when a loud roar of laughter burst from the whole assembly, when I ventured to express my dissent from the general feeling of admiration for such a man.

This barbarous pirate in the year 1827, at last experienced a fate characteristic of the whole course of his life. His violent aggressions having united the Arabs of Bahrene and Ratiffe against him they blockaded his port of Daman from which Rahmah-ben-Jabir, having left a garrison in the fort under his son, had sailed in a well appointed bungalow, for the purpose of endeavoring to raise a confederacy of his friends in his support. Having failed in this object he returned to Daman, and in spite of the boats blockading the port, succeeded in visiting his garrison, and immediately re-embarked, taking with him his youngest son. On arriving on board his bungalow, he was received by his followers with a salute, which decisive indication of his presence immediately attracted the attention of his opponents, one of whose boats, commanded by the nephew of the Sheikh of Bahrene, proceeded to attack him. A desperate struggle ensued, and the Sheikh finding after some time that he had lost nearly the whole of his crew by the firing of Rahmah's boat, retired for reinforcements. These being obtained, he immediately returned singly to the contest. The fight was renewed with redoubled fury; when at last, Rahmah, being informed (for he had been long blind) that his men were falling fast around him, mustered the remainder of the crew, and issued orders to close and grapple with his opponent. When this was effected, and after embracing his son, he was led with a lighted torch to the magazine, which instantly exploded, blowing his own boat to atoms and setting fire to the Sheikh's, which immediately afterwards shared the same fate. Sheikh Ahmed and few of his followers escaped to the other boats; but only one of Rahmah's brave crew was saved; and it is supposed that upwards of three hundred men were killed in this heroic contest.

From *The Pirates Own Book*, Charles Ellms, Marine Research Society, 1924

"Log: Chased a French privateer with a prize in tow"

FIGHTING THE PRIVATEERS

Thomas Cochrane

The gamekeeper's view of privateering. In 1800 Captain Lord Cochrane, commander of the Royal Navy sloop Speedy, *was charged with patrolling the Mediterranean against the depredations of French privateers there.*

The *Speedy* was little more than a burlesque on a vessel of war, even sixty years ago. She was about the size of an average coasting brig, her burden being 158 tons. She was crowded, rather than manned, with a crew of eighty-four men and six officers, myself included. Her armament consisted of fourteen 4-*pounders!*, a species of gun little larger than a blunderbuss, and formerly known in the service under the name of "minion", an appellation which it certainly merited. Being dissatisfied with her armament, I applied for and obtained a couple of 12-pounders, intending them as bow and stern chasers, but was compelled to return them to the ordnance wharf, there not being room on deck to work them; besides which, the timbers of the little craft were found on trial to be too weak to withstand the concussion of anything heavier than the guns with which she was previously armed.

With her rig I was more fortunate. Having carried away her mainyard, it became necessary to apply for another to the senior officer, who, examining the list of spare spars, ordered the *foretopgallant-yard* of the *Généreux* to be hauled out *as a mainyard for the Speedy!*

The spar was accordingly sent on board and rigged, but even this appearing too large for the vessel, an order was issued to cut off the yard-arms and thus reduce it to its proper dimensions. This order was neutralized by getting down and planing the yardarms as though they had been cut, an evasion which, with some alteration in the rigging, passed undetected on its being again swayed up; and thus a greater spread of canvas was secured. The fact of the foretopgallant-yard of a second-rate ship being considered too large for the mainyard of my "man-of-war" will give a tolerable idea of her insignificance.

Despite her unformidable character and the personal discomfort to which all on board were subjected, I was very proud of my little vessel, caring nothing for her want of accommodation, though in this respect her cabin merits passing notice. It had not so much as room for a chair, the floor being entirely occupied by a small table surrounded with lockers, answering the double purpose of storechests and seats. The difficulty was to get seated, the ceiling being only five feet high, so that the object could only be accomplished by rolling on the locker, a movement sometimes attended with unpleasant failure. The most singular discomfort, however, was that my only practicable mode of shaving consisted in removing the skylight and putting my head through to make a toilet-table of the quarterdeck.

In the following enumeration of the various cruises in which the *Speedy* was engaged, the boarding and searching innumerable neutral vessels will be passed over, and the narrative will be strictly confined – as in most cases throughout this work – to log extracts, where captures were made, or other occurrences took place worthy of record.

May 10. – Sailed from Cagliari, from which port we had been ordered to convoy fourteen sail of merchantmen to Leghorn. At 9 a.m. observed a strange sail take possession of a Danish brig under our escort. At 11:30 a.m. rescued the brig and captured the assailant. This prize – my first piece of luck – was the *Intrépide*, French privateer of six guns and forty-eight men.

May 14. – Saw five armed boats pulling towards us from Monte Cristo. Out sweeps to protect convoy. At 4 p.m. the boats boarded and took possession of the two sternmost ships. A light breeze springing up, made all sail towards the captured vessels, ordering the remainder of the convoy to make the best of their way to Longona. The breeze freshening we came up with and recaptured the vessels with the prize crews on board, but during the operation the armed boats escaped.

May 21. – At anchor in Leghorn Roads. Convoy all safe.

25. – Off Genoa. Joined Lord Keith's squadron of five sail of the line, four frigates and a brig.

26, 27, 28. – Ordered by his lordship to cruise in the offing, to intercept supplies destined for the French army under Massena, then in possession of Genoa.

29. – At Genoa some of the gun-boats bombarded the town for two hours.

30. – All the gun-boats bombarded the town. A partial bombardment had been going on for an hour a day, during the past fortnight, Lord Keith humanely refraining from continued bombardment, out of consideration for the inhabitants, who were in a state of absolute famine.

This was one of the *crises* of the war. The French, about a month previous, had defeated the Austrians with great slaughter in an attempt, on the part of the latter, to retake Genoa; but the Austrians, being in possession of Savona, were nevertheless able to intercept provisions on the land side, whilst the vigilance of Lord Keith rendered it impossible to obtain supplies by sea.

It having come to Lord Keith's knowledge that the French in Genoa had consumed their last horses and dogs, whilst the Genoese themselves were perishing by famine, and on the eve of revolt against the usurping force – in order to save the carnage which would ensue, his lordship caused it to be intimated to Massena that a defence so heroic would command honourable terms of capitulation. Massena was said to have replied that if the word "capitulation" were mentioned his army should perish with the city; but, as he could no longer defend himself, he had no objection to "treat". Lord Keith, therefore, proposed a treaty, viz, that the army might return to France, but that Massena himself must remain a prisoner in his hands. To this the French general demurred; but Lord Keith insisting – with the complimentary observation to Massena that "he was worth 20,000 men" – the latter reluctantly gave in, and on the 4th of June, 1800, a definite treaty to the above effect was agreed upon, and ratified on the 5th, when the Austrians took possession of the city, and Lord Keith of the harbour, the squadron anchoring within the mole.

This affair being ended, his lordship ordered the *Speedy* to cruise off the Spanish coast, and on the 14th of June we parted company with the squadron.

June 16. – Captured a tartan off Elba. Sent her to Leghorn, in the charge of an officer and four men.

22. – Off Bastia. Chased a French privateer with a prize in tow. The Frenchman abandoned the prize, Sardinian vessel laden with oil and wool, and we took possession. Made all sail in chase of the privateer; but on our commencing to fire she ran under the fort of Caprea, where we did not think proper to pursue her. Took prize in tow, and on the following day left her at Leghorn, where we found Lord Nelson, and several ships at anchor.

25. – Quitted Leghorn, and on the 26th were again off Bastia, in chase of a ship which ran for that place, and anchored under a fort three miles to the southward. Made at and brought her away. Proved to be the Spanish letter of marque *Assuncion*, of ten guns and thirty-three men, bound from Tunis to Barcelona. On taking possession, five gunboats left Bastia in chase of us; took the prize in tow, and kept up a running fight with the gun-boats till after midnight, when they left us.

29. – Cast off the prize in chase of a French privateer off Sardinia. On commencing our fire she set all sail and ran off. Returned and took the prize in tow; and the 4th of July anchored with her in Port Mahon.

July 9. – Off Cape Sebastian. Gave chase to two Spanish ships standing along shore. They anchored under the protection of the forts. Saw another vessel lying just within range of the forts; – out boats and cut her out, the forts firing on the boats without inflicting damage.

July 19. – Off Caprea. Several French privateers in sight. Chased, and on the following morning captured one, the *Constitution*, of one gun and nineteen men. Whilst we were securing the privateer, a prize which she had taken made sail in the direction of Gorgona and escaped.

27. – Off Planosa, in chase of a privateer. On the following morning saw three others lying in a small creek. On making preparations to cut them out, a military force made

its appearance, and commenced a heavy fire of musketry, to which it would have answered no purpose to reply. Fired several broadsides at one of the privateers, and sunk her.

31. – Off Porto Ferraio in chase of a French privateer, with a prize in tow. The Frenchman abandoned his prize, of which we took possession, and whilst so doing the privateer got away.

August 3. – Anchored with our prizes in Leghorn Roads, where we found Lord Keith in the *Minotaur*.

Lord Keith received me very kindly, and directed the *Speedy* to run down the Spanish coast, pointing out the importance of harassing the enemy there as much as possible, but cautioning me against engaging anything beyond our capacity. During our stay at Leghorn, his lordship frequently invited me ashore to participate in the gaieties of the place.

Having filled up with provisions and water, we sailed on the 16th of August, and on the 21st captured a French privateer bound from Corsica to Toulon. Shortly afterwards we fell in with HMS *Mutine* and *Salamine*, which, to suit their convenience, gave into our charge a number of French prisoners, with whom and our prize we consequently returned to Leghorn.

On the 14th of September we again put to sea, the interval being occupied by a thorough overhaul of the sloop. On the 22nd, when off Caprea, fell in with a Neapolitan vessel having a French prize crew on board. Recaptured the vessel, and took the crew prisoners.

On the 5th of October, the *Speedy* anchored in Port Mahon, where information was received that the Spaniards had several armed vessels on the look-out for us, should we again appear on their coast. I therefore applied to the authorities to exchange our 4-pounders for 6-pounders, but the latter being too large for the *Speedy*'s ports, we were again compelled to forego the change as impracticable.

October 12. – Sailed from Port Mahon, cruising for some time off Cape Sebastian, Villa Nova, Oropesa, and Barcelona; occasionally visiting the enemy's coast for water, of which the *Speedy* carried only ten tons. Nothing material occurred till November 18th, when we narrowly escaped being swamped in a gale of wind, the sea breaking over our quarter, and clearing our deck, spars, &c., otherwise inflicting such damage as to compel our return to Port Mahon, where we were detained till the 12th of December.

December 15. – Off Majorca. Several strange vessels being in sight, singled out the largest and made sail in chase; shortly after which a French bombard bore up, hoisting the national colours. We now cleared for action, altering our course to meet her, when she bore up between Dragon Island and the Main. Commenced firing at the bombard, which returned our fire; but shortly afterwards getting closer in shore she drove on the rocks. Three other vessels being in the passage, we left her, and captured one of them, the *La Liza* of ten guns and thirty-three men, bound from Alicant to Marseilles. Took nineteen of our prisoners on board the *Speedy*. As it was evident that the bombard would become a wreck, we paid no further attention to her, but made all sail after the others.

December 18. – Suspecting the passage between Dragon Island and the Main to be a lurking-place for privateers, we ran in again, but found nothing. Seeing a number of troops lining the beach, we opened fire and dispersed them, afterwards engaging a tower, which fired upon us. The prisoners we had taken proving an incumbrance, we put them on shore.

December 19. – Stood off and on the harbour of Palamos, where we saw several vessels at anchor. Hoisted Danish colours and made the signal for a pilot. Our real character being evidently known, none came off, and we did not think it prudent to venture in.

It has been said that the *Speedy* had become the marked object of the Spanish naval authorities. Not that there was much danger of being caught, for they confined their search to the coast only, and that in the daytime, when we were usually away in the offing; it being our practice to keep out of sight during the day, and run in before dawn on the next morning.

On the 21st, however, when off Plane Island, we were very near "catching a Tartar". Seeing a large ship in shore, having all the appearance of a well-laden merchantman, we forthwith gave chase. On nearing her she raised her ports, which had been closed to deceive us, the act discovering a heavy broadside, a clear demonstration that we had fallen into the jaws of a formidable Spanish frigate, now crowded with men, who had before remained concealed below.

That the frigate was in search of us there could be no doubt, from the deception practised. To have encountered her with our insignificant armament would have been exceedingly imprudent, whilst escape was out of the question, for she would have outsailed us, and could have run us down by her mere weight. There was, therefore, nothing left but to try the effect of a *ruse*, prepared beforehand for such an emergency. After receiving at Mahon information that unusual measures were about to be taken by the Spaniards for our capture, I had the *Speedy* painted in imitation of the Danish brig *Clomer*; the appearance of this vessel being well known on the Spanish coast. We also shipped a Danish quartermaster, taking the further precaution of providing him with the uniform of an officer of that nation.

On discovering the real character of our neighbour, the *Speedy* hoisted Danish colours, and spoke her. At first this failed to satisfy the Spaniard, who sent a boat to board us. It was now time to bring the Danish quartermaster into play in his officer's uniform; and to add force to his explanations, we ran the quarantine flag up to the fore, calculating on the Spanish horror of the plague, then prevalent along the Barbary coast.

On the boat coming within hail – for the yellow flag effectually repressed the enemy's desire to board us – our mock officer informed the Spaniards that we were two days from Algiers, where at the time the plague was violently raging. This was enough. The boat returned to the frigate, which, wishing us a good voyage, filled, and made sail, whilst we did the same.

I have noted this circumstance more minutely than it merits, because it has been misrepresented. By some of my officers blame was cast on me for not attacking the frigate after she had been put off her guard by our false colours, as her hands – being then employed at their ordinary avocations in the rigging and elsewhere – presented a prominent mark for our shot. There is no doubt but that we might have poured in a murderous fire before the crew could have recovered from their confusion, and perhaps have taken her, but feeling averse to so cruel a destruction of human life, I chose to refrain from an attack, which might not, even with that advantage in our favour, have been successful.

It has been stated by some naval writers that this frigate was the *Gamo*, which we subsequently captured. To the best of my knowledge this is an error.

December 24. – Off Carthagena. At daylight fell in with a convoy in charge of two Spanish privateers, which came up and fired at us; but being to windward we ran for the convoy, and singling out two, captured the nearest, laden with wine. The other ran in shore under the fort of Port Genoese, where we left her.

25. – Stood for Cape St Martin, in hope of intercepting the privateers. At 8 a.m. saw a privateer and one of the convoy under Cape Lanar. Made sail in chase. They parted company; when, on our singling out the nearest privateer, she took refuge under a battery, on which we left off pursuit.

30. – Off Cape Oropesa. Seeing some vessels in shore, out boats in chase. At noon they returned pursued by two Spanish gunboats, which kept up a smart fire on them. Made sail to intercept the gun-boats, on which they ran in under the batteries.

January 10, 1801. – Anchored in Port Mahon, and having refitted, sailed again on the 12th.

16. – Off Barcelona. Just before daylight chased two vessels standing towards that port. Seeing themselves pursued, they made for the battery at the entrance. Bore up and set steering sails in chase. The wind falling calm, one of the chase drifted in shore and took the ground under Castel De Ferro. On commencing our fire, the crew abandoned her, and we sent boats with anchors and hawsers to warp her off, in which they succeeded. She proved to be the Genoese ship *Ns. Señora de Gratia*, of ten guns.

22. – Before daylight, stood in again for Barcelona. Saw several sail close in with the land. Out boats and boarded one, which turned out a Dane. Cruising off the port till 3 a.m., we saw two strange vessels coming from the westward. Made sail to cut them off. At 6 p.m. one of them hoisted Spanish colours and the other French. At 9 p.m. came up

with them, when after an engagement of half an hour both
struck. The Spaniard was the *Ecce Homo*, of eight guns and
nineteen men, the Frenchman, *L'Amitié*, of one gun and
thirty-one men. Took all the prisoners on board the *Speedy*.

23. – Still off Barcelona. Having sent most of our crew to
man the prizes, the number of prisoners on board the
Speedy became dangerous; we therefore put twenty-five
of the Frenchmen into one of their own launches and told
them to make the best of their way to Barcelona. As the
prizes were a good deal cut up about the rigging, repaired
their damages and made sail for Port Mahon, where we
arrived on the 24th, with our convoy in company.

28th. – Quitted Port Mahon for Malta, not being able to
procure at Minorca various things of which we stood in
need; and on the 1st of February, came to an anchor at
Valetta, where we obtained anchors and sweeps.

An absurd affair took place during our short stay at Malta, which
would not have been worthy of notice, had it not been made the
subject of comment.

The officers of a French royalist regiment, then at Malta,
patronized a fancy ball, for which I amongst others purchased
a ticket. The dress chosen was that of a sailor – in fact, my
costume was a tolerable imitation of that of my worthy friend,
Jack Larmour; in one of his relaxing moods, and personated in
my estimation as honourable a character as were Greek, Turkish,
or other kinds of Oriental disguises in vogue at such reunions. My
costume was, however, too much to the life to please French
royalist taste, not even the marlinspike and the lump of grease in
the hat being omitted.

On entering the ball-room, further passage was immediately
barred, with an intimation that my presence could not be permitted in such a dress. Good-humouredly expostulating that, as
the choice of costume was left to the wearer, my own taste – which
was decidedly nautical – had selected that of a British seaman, a
character which, though by no means imaginary, was quite as
picturesque as were the habiliments of an Arcadian shepherd;
further insisting that as no rule had been infringed, I must be
permitted to exercise my discretion. Expostulation being of no
avail, a brusque answer was returned that such a dress was not

admissible, whereupon I as brusquely replied that having purchased my ticket, and chosen my own costume in accordance with the regulations, no one had any right to prevent me from sustaining the character assumed.

Upon this a French officer, who appeared to act as master of the ceremonies, came up, and without waiting for further explanation, rudely seized me by the collar with the intention of putting me out; in return for which insult he received a substantial mark of British indignation, and at the same time an uncomplimentary remark in his own language. In an instant all was uproar; a French picket was called, which in a short time overpowered and carried me off to the guard-house of the regiment.

I was, however, promptly freed from detention on announcing my name, but the officer who had collared me demanded an apology for the portion of the *fracas* concerning him personally. This being of course refused, a challenge was the consequence; and on the following morning we met behind the ramparts and exchanged shots, my ball passing through the poor fellow's thigh, and dropping him. My escape, too, was a narrow one – his ball perforating my coat, waistcoat, and shirt, and bruising my side. Seeing my adversary fall, I stepped up to him – imagining his wound to be serious – and expressed a hope that he had not been hit in a vital part. His reply – uttered with all the politeness of his nation – was, that "he was not materially hurt." I, however, was not at ease, for it was impossible not to regret this, to him, serious *dénouement* of a trumpery affair, though arising from his own intemperate conduct. It was a lesson to me in future never to do anything in frolic which might give even unintentional offence.

On the 3rd of February we sailed under orders for Tripoli, to make arrangements for fresh provisions for the fleet. This being effected, the *Speedy* returned to Malta, and on the 20th again left port in charge of a convoy for Tunis.

24th. – At the entrance of Tunis Bay we gave chase to a strange sail, which wore and stood in towards the town, anchoring at about the distance of three miles. Suspecting some reason for this movement, I dispatched an officer to examine her, when the suspicion was confirmed by his ascertaining her to be *La Belle Caroline*, French brig of four guns, bound for Alexandria with field-pieces, ammunition, and wine for the use of the French army in Egypt.

Our position was one of delicacy, the vessel being in a neutral port, where, if we remained to watch her, she might prolong our stay for an indefinite period or escape in the night; whilst, from the warlike nature of the cargo, it was an object of national importance to effect her capture. The latter appearing the most beneficial course under all circumstances, we neared her so as to prevent escape, and soon after midnight boarded her, and having weighed her anchor, brought her close to the *Speedy*, before she had an opportunity of holding any communication with the shore.

The following day was employed in examining her stores, a portion of her ammunition being transferred to our magazine, to replace some damaged by leakage. Her crew, now on board the *Speedy* as prisoners, becoming clamorous at what they considered an illegal seizure, and being, moreover, in our way, an expedient was adopted to get rid of them, by purposely leaving their own launch within reach during the following night, with a caution to the watch not to prevent their desertion should they attempt it. The hint was taken, for before daylight on the 27th they seized the boat, and pulled out of the bay without molestation, not venturing to go to Tunis lest they should be retaken. We thus got rid of the prisoners, and at the same time of what might have turned out their reasonable complaint to the Tunisian authorities, for that we had exceeded the bounds of neutrality there could be no doubt.

On the 28th we weighed anchor, and proceeded to sea with our prize. After cruising for some days off Cape Bon, we made sail for Cagliari, where we arrived on the 8th of March, and put to sea on the 11th with the prize in tow. On the 16th, anchored in Port Mahon.

On the 18th we again put to sea, and towards evening observed a large frigate in chase of us. As she did not answer the private signal, it was evident that the stranger was one of our Spanish friends on the look-out. To cope with a vessel of her size and armament would have been folly, so we made all sail away from her, but she gave instant chase, and evidently gained upon us. To add to our embarrassment, the *Speedy* sprung her main-topgal-lant-yard, and lost ground whilst fishing it.

At daylight the following morning the strange frigate was still in chase, though by crowding all sail during the night we had gained a little upon her; but during the day she again recovered her advantage, the more so, as the breeze freshening, we were compelled to take in our royals, whilst she was still carrying on with everything set. After dark, we lowered a tub overboard with a light in it, and altering our course thus fortunately evaded her. On the 1st of April we returned to Port Mahon, and again put to sea on the 6th.

April 11. – Observing a vessel near the shoal of Tortosa, gave chase. On the following morning her crew deserted her, and we took possession. In the evening anchored under the land.

13. – Saw three vessels at anchor in a bay to the westward of Oropesa. Made sail up to them and anchored on the flank of a ten-gun fort. Whilst the firing was going on, the boats were sent in to board and bring out the vessels, which immediately weighed and got under the fort. At 5:30 p.m. the boats returned with one of them; the other two being hauled close in shore, we did not make any further attempt to capture them. As the prize, the *Ave Maria*, of four guns, was in ballast, we took the sails and spars out of her, and set her on fire.

On the following morning at daybreak, several vessels appeared to the eastward. Made all sail to intercept them, but before we could come up, they succeeded in anchoring under a fort. On standing towards them, they turned out to be Spanish gun-boats, which commenced firing at us. At 10 a.m. anchored within musket-shot, so as to keep an angle of the tower on our beam, thus neutralising its effect. Commenced firing broadsides alternately at the tower and the gunboats, with visible advantage. Shortly before noon made preparation to cut out the gun-boats, but a fresh breeze setting in dead on shore, rendered it impossible to get at them without placing ourselves in peril. We thereupon worked out of the bay.

15. – Two strange sail in sight. Gave chase, and in a couple of hours came up with and captured them. Made sail after a convoy in the offing, but the wind falling light at dusk, lost sight of them.

On the 26th we anchored in Mahon, remaining a week to

refit and procure fresh hands, many having been sent away in prizes. On the 2nd of May put to sea with a reduced crew, some of whom had to be taken out of HM's prison.

We again ran along the Spanish coast, and on the 4th of May were off Barcelona, where the *Speedy* captured a vessel which reported herself as Ragusan, though in reality a Spanish four-gun tartan. Soon after detaining her we heard firing in the WN–W and steering for that quarter fell in with a Spanish privateer, which we also captured, the *San Carlos*, of seven guns. On this a swarm of gun-boats came out of Barcelona, seven of them giving chase to us and the prizes, with which we made off shore, the gun-boats returning to Barcelona.

On the following morning the prizes were sent to Port Mahon, and keeping out of sight for the rest of the day, the *Speedy* returned at midnight off Barcelona, where we found the gun-boats on the watch; but on our approach they ran in shore, firing at us occasionally. Suspecting that the object was to decoy us within reach of some larger vessel, we singled out one of them and made at her, the others, however, supporting her so well that some of our rigging being shot away, we made off shore to repair, the gun-boats following. Having thus got them to some distance, and repaired damages, we set all sail, and again ran in shore, in the hope of getting between them and the land, so as to cut off some of their number. Perceiving our intention, they all made for the port as before, keeping up a smart fight, in which our foretopgallant-yard was so much injured, that we had to shift it, and were thus left astern. The remainder of the day was employed in repairing damages, and the gun-boats not venturing out again, at 9 p.m. we again made off shore.

Convinced that something more than ordinary had actuated the gun-boats to decoy us – just before daylight on the 6th we again ran in for Barcelona, when the trap manifested itself in the form of a large ship, running under the land, and bearing ES–E. On hauling towards her, she changed her course in chase of us, and was shortly made out to be a Spanish xebec frigate.

As some of my officers had expressed dissatisfaction at not having been permitted to attack the frigate fallen in with on the 21st of December, after her suspicions had been lulled by our device of hoisting Danish colours, &c., I told them they should

now have a fair fight, notwithstanding that, by manning the two
prizes sent to Mahon, our numbers had been reduced to fifty-
four, officers and boys included. Orders were then given to pipe
all hands, and prepare for action.

Accordingly we made towards the frigate, which was now
coming down under steering sails. At 9:30 a.m., she fired a
gun and hoisted Spanish colours, which the *Speedy* acknowledged by hoisting American colours, our object being, as we were
now exposed to her full broadside, to puzzle her, till we got on the
other tack, when we ran up the English ensign, and immediately
afterwards encountered her broadside without damage.

Shortly afterwards she gave us another broadside, also without
effect. My orders were not to fire a gun till we were close to her;
when, running under her lee, we locked our yards amongst her
rigging, and in this position returned our broadside, such as it
was.

To have fired our popgun 4-pounders at a distance would have
been to throw away the ammunition; but the guns being doubly,
and, as I afterwards learned, trebly, shotted, and being elevated,
they told admirably upon her main deck; the first discharge, as
was subsequently ascertained, killing the Spanish captain and the
boatswain.

My reason for locking our small craft in the enemy's rigging
was the one upon which I mainly relied for victory, viz that from
the height of the frigate out of the water, the whole of her shot
must necessarily go over our heads, whilst our guns, being
elevated, would blow up her main-deck.

The Spaniards speedily found out the disadvantage under
which they were fighting, and gave the order to board the
Speedy; but as this order was as distinctly heard by us as by
them, we avoided it at the moment of execution by sheering off
sufficiently to prevent the movement, giving them a volley of
musketry and a broadside before they could recover themselves.

Twice was this manoeuvre repeated, and twice thus averted.
The Spaniards finding that they were only punishing themselves,
gave up further attempts to board and stood to their guns, which
were cutting up our rigging from stem to stern, but doing little
farther damage; for after the lapse of an hour the loss to the
Speedy was only two men killed and four wounded.

This kind of combat, however, could not last. Our rigging being cut up and the *Speedy*'s sails riddled with shot, I told the men that they must either take the frigate or be themselves taken, in which case the Spaniards would give no quarter – whilst a few minutes energetically employed on their part would decide the matter in their own favour.

The doctor, Mr Guthrie, who, I am happy to say, is still living to peruse this record of his gallantry, volunteered to take the helm; leaving him therefore for the time both commander and crew of the *Speedy*, the order was given to board, and in a few seconds every man was on the enemy's deck – a feat rendered the more easy as the doctor placed the *Speedy* close alongside with admirable skill.

For a moment the Spaniards seemed taken by surprise, as though unwilling to believe that so small a crew would have the audacity to board them; but soon recovering themselves, they made a rush to the waist of the frigate, where the fight was for some minutes gallantly carried on. Observing the enemy's colours still flying, I directed one of our men immediately to haul them down, when the Spanish crew, without pausing to consider by whose orders the colours had been struck, and naturally believing it the act of their own officers, gave in, and we were in possession of the *Gamo* frigate, of thirty-two heavy guns and 319 men, who an hour and a half before had looked upon us as a certain if not an easy prey.

Our loss in boarding was Lieutenant Parker, severely wounded in several places, one seaman killed and three wounded, which with those previously killed and wounded gave a total of three seamen killed, and one officer and seventeen men wounded.

The *Gamo*'s loss was Captain de Torres – the boatswain – and thirteen seamen killed, together with forty-one wounded; her casualties thus exceeding the whole number of officers and crew on board the *Speedy*.

Some time after the surrender of the *Gamo*, and when we were in quiet possession, the officer who had succeeded the deceased Captain Don Francisco de Torres, not in command, but in rank, applied to me for a certificate that he had done his duty during the action; whereupon he received from me a certificate that he had "conducted himself like a true Spaniard", with which document he appeared highly gratified, and I had afterwards the satisfaction of learning that it procured him further promotion in the Spanish service.

Shortly before boarding, an incident occurred which, by those who have never been placed in similar circumstances, may be thought too absurd for notice. Knowing that the final struggle would be a desperate one, and calculating on the superstitious wonder which forms an element in the Spanish character, a portion of our crew were ordered to blacken their faces, and what with this and the excitement of combat, more ferocious looking objects could scarcely be imagined. The fellows thus disguised were directed to board by the head, and the effect produced was precisely that calculated on. The greater portion of the Spaniard's crew was prepared to repel boarders in that direction, but stood for a few moments as it were transfixed to the deck by the apparition of so many diabolical looking figures emerging from the white smoke of the bow guns; whilst our other men, who boarded by the waist, rushed on them from behind, before they could recover from their surprise at the unexpected phenomenon.

In difficult or doubtful attacks by sea – and the odds of 50 men to 320 comes within this description – no device can be too minute, even if apparently absurd, provided it have the effect of diverting the enemy's attention whilst you are concentrating your own. In this, and other successes against odds, I have no hesitation in saying that success in no slight degree depended on out-of-the-way devices, which the enemy not suspecting, were in some measure thrown off their guard.

The subjoined tabular view of the respective force of the two vessels will best show the nature of the contest.

Gamo	Speedy
Main-deck guns. –	
Twenty-two long 12-pounders.	Fourteen 4-pounders.
Quarter-deck. – Eight long 5-pounders,	
and two 24-pounder carronades.	None.
No. of crew, 319.	No. of crew, 54.
Broadside weight of shot, 190 lbs.	Broadside weight of shot,
Tonnage, 600 and upwards.	28 lbs. Tonnage, 158.

It became a puzzle what to do with 263 unhurt prisoners now we had taken them, the *Speedy* having only forty-two men left.

Promptness was however necessary; so driving the prisoners into the hold, with guns pointing down the hatchway, and leaving thirty of our men on board the prize – which was placed under the command of my brother, the Hon. Archibald Cochrane, then a midshipman – we shaped our course to Port Mahon – not Gibraltar, as has been recorded – and arrived there in safety; the Barcelona gun-boats, though spectators of the action, not venturing to rescue the frigate. Had they made the attempt, we should have had some difficulty in evading them and securing the prize, the prisoners manifesting every disposition to rescue themselves, and only being deterred by their own main deck guns loaded with cannister, and pointing down the hatchways, whilst our men stood over them with lighted matches.

Our success hitherto had procured us some prize-money, notwithstanding the peculations of the Mediterranean Admiralty Courts, by which the greater portion of our captures was absorbed.

Despite this drawback, which generally disinclined officers and crews from making extraordinary exertions, my own share of the twelvemonth's zealous endeavours in our little sloop was considerable, and even the crew were in receipt of larger sums than those constituting the ordinary pay of officers; a result chiefly owing to our nocturnal mode of warfare, together with our refraining from meddling with vessels ascertained to be loading in the Spanish ports, and then lying in wait for them as they proceeded on their voyage.

One effect of our success was no slight amount of ill-concealed jealousy on the part of officers senior to myself, though there were some amongst these who, being in command of small squadrons instead of single vessels, might, had they adopted the same means, have effected far more than the *Speedy*, with an armament so insignificant, was calculated to accomplish.

After remaining some days at Port Mahon to refit, we prepared to return to our cruising ground, where, from private information, we knew that other prizes were at hand. In place of being permitted so to do, the *Speedy* received an order to proceed to Algiers, for the purpose of representing to the Dey the illegality of his cruisers having taken a British vessel in retaliation for an Algerine captured whilst violating the law of blockade.

The mission was a singular one to be entrusted to the captain of one of the smallest and worst-armed vessels in the British service. Remonstrance, to be effectual with a piratical government, ought to have been committed to an officer armed with sufficient force at least to induce respect. There was, however, no alternative but to obey, and a short time saw us at anchor off the mole of the predatory potentate.

The request for an interview with his highness occasioned no little dissatisfaction amongst his ministers, if those who were quite as much his masters as his subordinates could be so termed. After some consultation the interview was, however, granted, and a day was appointed to deliver my message.

The invariable Moslem preliminary of taking coffee having been gone through, I was ushered through a series of galleries lined with men, each bearing on his shoulder a formidable-looking axe, and eyeing me with an insolent scowl, evidently meant to convey the satisfaction with which they would apply its edge to my vertebræ should the caprice of their chief so will.

On reaching the presence of the Dey – a dignified-looking and gorgeously-attired person, seated cross-legged on an elevated couch in one corner of the gallery, and surrounded by armed people of most unprepossessing appearance – I was marched up between two janizaries, and ordered to make three salaams to his highness.

This formality being complied with, he rudely demanded, through the medium of an interpreter, "What brought me there?" The reply was that "I was the commander of an English vessel of war in the roads, and had been deputed, on behalf of my Government, respectfully to remonstrate with his highness concerning a vessel which his cruisers had taken contrary to the laws of nations." On this being interpreted, the ferocious scowls of the bystanders were exchanged for expressions of injured innocence; but the Dey got in a great passion, and told the interpreter to inform me that "remonstrance came with an ill grace from us, the British vessels being the greatest pirates in the world, and mine one of the worst amongst them", which complimentary statement was acknowledged by me with a formal bow.

"If I did right," continued the Dey, through his interpreter, "I should put you and your crew in prison till" (naming a captured Algerine vessel) "she was restored; and but for my great respect for the English Government, and my impression that her seizure was unauthorized, you should go there. However, you may go, with a demand from me that the vessel unjustly taken from us shall be immediately restored."

This decision appeared to be anything but satisfactory to the oligarchy of which his court was composed, as savouring of a clemency to which they were little inclined. From the boisterous conversation which ensued, they were evidently desirous of prolonging my stay to an indefinite period, or perhaps of terminating it summarily through the instrumentality of the axe-men who lined the galleries, as a few years afterwards they terminated the existence of the Dey himself.

To confess the truth, there was some room for self-congratulation on quitting the presence of such barbarians, to whom I was not fairly accredited for such a mission. However, the remonstrance confided to me being duly delivered, we returned to Minorca to report progress, though not without being chased by an Algerine cruiser on our way. As the *Speedy* outsailed her, and as there was no beneficial object to be gained by interfering with her, we stood on without further notice.

On arriving at our former cruising ground we encountered a Spanish privateer of six guns, which was captured. This vessel was fitted out at my own private expense, and my brother appointed to command her, as a tender to the *Speedy*, several enemy's vessels having previously escaped for want of such aid.

In a few days after this we fell in with the *Kangaroo*, Captain Pulling, who, being senior to me, was therefore my commanding officer. Running down the coast in company, we attacked the fort of Almanara, and after silencing it, brought off a Spanish privateer of seven guns.

On the 8th of June the *Speedy* ran into Oropesa, where, on the 13th and 14th of April, we had fought an action with the fort and gunboats. Perceiving several vessels at anchor under the fort, it was deemed advisable to make offshore, with the intention of running in again at midnight and cutting some of them out.

We had not proceeded far before we again fell in with the *Kangaroo*, when informing Captain Pulling of what we had seen, he declined the night attack, preferring to postpone operations till the following day. Accordingly, at noon on the 9th, we went in, and made out a twenty-gun xebec and three gunboats, with ten sail of merchantmen under three convoy. It was determined to attack them as they lay; the *Kangaroo* anchoring well up to and engaging the fort, whilst the *Speedy* and her tender under my brother's orders encountered the xebec and the gunboats – the *Speedy* anchoring in a line between those vessels and the *Kangaroo*.

For some hours an incessant cannonade was kept up on both sides, the *Kangaroo*'s fire flanking the fort, whilst the slackened fire of the Spanish vessels showed that our shot had told. At this juncture, a twelve-gun felucca and two more gunboats having arrived from Valentia to their assistance, the Spaniards took heart, and the action became nearly as brisk as before.

The felucca and the newly-arrived gunboats were, however, for a time beat off, and after an hour's additional firing the xebec, two gunboats, and some of the convoy were sunk, the remaining gunboats shortly afterwards sharing the same fate.

The action had now continued for upwards of nine hours, during which the *Speedy* had expended nearly all her ammunition – namely, fourteen hundred shot – and the *Kangaroo* was much in the same predicament. As the felucca and gunboats had again come up, it was necessary to effect something decisive. Captain Pulling, therefore, slipping his cable, shifted close to the fort, which was soon afterwards abandoned, and the *Speedy* closed with the felucca and her consorts, which forthwith fled. Had they remained, we had not half a dozen rounds left to continue the action.

Both vessels now hoisted out boats and made for the merchantmen. Three of these had been sunk, and four others driven on shore; we, however, brought away the three still afloat. By this time a number of Spanish troops lined the beach for the protection of the vessels ashore, and as we had scarcely a shot left, it was impracticable to reply to the musketry, within range of which the boats must necessarily have been placed had the attempt been made. We therefore relinquished the endeavour to get off the stranded vessels.

It may be useful here to remark that on board the *Kangaroo* were some guns fitted on the non-recoil principle, and that during the action these broke from their breechings, one, if not more, endangering the vessel by bounding down the hatchways into the hold.

On our return to Port Mahon with the prizes, the *Gamo* had not been purchased by the Government; but, to my regret, this useful cruiser had been sold for a trifle to the Algerines, whilst I was condemned to continue in the pigmy and now battered craft by which she had been taken. To have obtained command of the *Gamo*, even as a means of deception on the enemy's coast, I would scarcely have changed place with an admiral.

But a more cruel thing still was in store for me. The commandant lived in the house of a Spanish merchant who had a contract for carrying the mails to Gibraltar. The vessel employed for this purpose was a notoriously bad sailer, and when the *Speedy* was ready for sea, instead of being permitted to return to our cruising ground, she was ordered to convoy this tub of a packet to Gibraltar, with further instructions to take the letter-bag on board the *Speedy*, protect the packet, put the mail on board her as soon as we arrived off the Rock, and return without holding any communication with the shore! – the evident object of the last injunction being that the service which had been thrust upon us should not become known!

The expectation of the packet-master, doubtless, was that we should put to sea out of privateer reach. In place of this, we ran along the Spanish coast, our superior sailing enabling us, without delay, to scrutinize every creek as we passed. Nothing, however, occurred till we were close in with a bay, or rather indentation of the shore, near Alicant, where, seeing some vessels at anchor, we made towards them, on which they weighed and deliberately ran ashore. To have stopped to get them off would have been in excess of our instructions. To set fire to them was not; and as one was laden with oil, and the night following very dark, the result was a blaze which illumined the sky for many miles round.

Unluckily for us, three French line-of-battle ships, which afterwards turned out to be the *Indomitable*, the *Dessaix*, and the *Formidable*, were in the vicinity, and being attracted by the light of the burning vessels, ran inshore to see what was the matter.

At daybreak on the morning of July 3rd these large ships were observed in the distance, calling up to our imaginations visions of Spanish galleons from South America, and accordingly the *Speedy* prepared for chase. It was not till day dawned that we found out our mistake, the vessels between us and the offing being clearly line-of-battle ships, forbidding all reasonable hope of escape.

It was about four o'clock in the morning when we made out the French ships, which immediately on discovering us gave chase. Being to windward, we endeavoured to escape by making all sail, and, as the wind fell light, by using our sweeps. This proving unavailing, we threw the guns overboard, and put the brig before the wind; but notwithstanding every effort, the enemy gained fast upon us, and, in order to prevent our slipping past, separated on different tacks, so as to keep us constantly within reach of one or the other; the *Dessaix*, being nearest, firing broadsides at us as she passed when tacking, at other times firing from her bow-chasers and cutting up our rigging.

For upwards of three hours we were thus within gunshot of the *Dessaix*, when, finding it impossible to escape by the wind, I ordered all the stores to be thrown overboard, in the hope of being able, when thus further lightened, to run the gauntlet between the ships, which continued to gain upon us.

Watching an opportunity when the nearest line-of-battle ship was before our beam, we bore up, set the studding-sails, and attempted to run between them, the French honouring us with a broadside for this unexpected movement. The *Dessaix*, however, immediately tacked in pursuit, and in less than an hour got within musket-shot. At this short distance she let fly at us a complete broadside of round and grape, the object evidently being to sink us at a blow, in retaliation for thus attempting to slip past, though almost without hope of escape.

Fortunately for us, in yawing to bring her broadside to bear, the rapidity with which she answered her helm carried her a little too far, and her round shot plunged in the water under our bows, or the discharge must have sunk us; the scattered grape, however, took effect in the rigging, cutting up a great part of it, riddling the sails, and doing material damage to the masts and yards, though not a man was hurt. To have delayed for another broadside would have been to expose all on board to certain destruction, and as further effort to escape was impotent, the *Speedy*'s colours were hauled down.

On going aboard the *Dessaix* and presenting my sword to the captain, Christie Palliere, he politely declined taking it, with the complimentary remark that "he would not accept the sword of an officer who had for so many hours struggled against impossibility," at the same time paying me the further compliment of requesting that "I would continue to wear my sword, though a prisoner" – a request with which I complied; Captain Palliere at the same time good-naturedly expressing his satisfaction at having terminated our exploits in the cruising line, they having, in fact, special instructions to look out for us. After this reception it is scarcely necessary to add that I was treated with great kindness by my captors.

Thus ended the thirteen months' cruise of the *Speedy*, during which we had taken and retaken upwards of fifty vessels, one hundred and twenty-two guns, and five hundred and thirty-four prisoners.

After the capture of the *Speedy* the French line-of-battle ships stood along the coast, and proceeded with her and the unlucky packet which had been the primary cause of the disaster to Algeciras. During this passage I had ample opportunity of observing the superior manner in which the sails of the *Dessaix* were cut, and the consequent flat surface exposed to the wind, this contrasting strongly with the bag reefs, bellying sails, and bread-bag canvas of English ships of war at that period.

As there was no force at Gibraltar adequate to an attack of the French squadron, the authorities lost no time in transmitting intelligence of their arrival to Sir James Saumarez, then blockading the Spanish squadron in Cadiz. The French meanwhile proceeded to water and refit, evidently with the intention of passing the Straits with the first fair wind.

Quitting Cadiz, Sir James Saumarez immediately sailed for Algeciras with his squadron, consisting of the *Cæsar*, *Venerable*, *Audacious*, *Hannibal*, *Superb*, *Pompée*, *Spencer*, *Calpe*, and *Thames*, these reaching the bay on the 6th of July.

At the time of their first appearance I was conversing with Captain Palliere in his cabin, when a lieutenant reported a British flag over Cabritta Point, and soon afterwards the topgallant masts and pendants of a British squadron became visible. We at once adjourned to the poop, when the surprise of the French at the sight of a more numerous squadron became not unreasonably apparent. Captain Palliere asked me "if I thought an attack would be made, or whether the British force would anchor off Gibraltar?" My reply was "that an attack would certainly be made, and that before night both British and French ships would be at Gibraltar", at the same time adding that when there, it would give me great pleasure to make him and his officers a return for the kindness I had experienced on board the *Dessaix*!

The French admiral, however, determined that his ships should not be carried across the bay if he could help it. Before the British squadron had rounded the point the French out boats, with kedges and stream anchors, for the purpose of warping inshore, so as to prevent the approaching squadron from cutting them out; but the order was so hurriedly executed that all three ships were hauled aground, with their sterns presented to the approaching British force – a position which could not have been taken by choice, for nothing could apparently be more easy than to destroy the French ships, which, lying aground stern on, could only use their stern-chasers.

To employ their consequently useless hands to some purpose, the French landed a considerable portion of their crews to man the Spanish batteries on the island, as the ships' guns could not be brought to bear. Two of the British ships anchored, and opened upon the French ships aground; but being exposed to the fire of some of the newly-manned forts higher up the bay, the heavy guns of which were admirably handled by the French seamen, both the British vessels slipped their cables, and, together with the remainder of the squadron, which did not anchor at all, backed their maintop-sails for the purpose of maintaining their position. The wind, however, blowing from the westward, with a rapid current sweeping round the bay, thwarted this intention, and the British squadron quickly drifted past the enemy, firing as they went.

Perhaps I ought previously to have mentioned an incident demonstrative of the *sang froid* of my captor. After having satisfied himself that an action with a superior force was inevitable, Captain Palliere remarked "that it should not spoil our breakfast", in which he had invited me to join him. Before the meal was ended a round shot crashed through the stern of the *Dessaix*, driving before it a shower of broken glass, the *débris* of a wine bin under the sofa.

We forthwith jumped up from table and went on the quarter-deck; but a raking shot from Sir James Saumarez's ship sweeping a file of marines from the poop not far from me, I considered further exposure on my part unnecessary, and went below to a position whence I could nevertheless at times see what was going on.

The *Hannibal*, having with the others forged past the enemy, gallantly filled and tacked with a view to get between the French ships and the shore being evidently unaware of their having been hauled aground. The consequence was that she ran upon a shoal, and remained fast, nearly bow on to the broadsides of the French line-of-battle ships, which, with the shore batteries and several gunboats, opened upon her a concentrated fire. This, from her position, she was unable to return. The result was that her guns were speedily dismounted, her rigging shot away, and a third of her crew killed or wounded; Captain Ferris, who commanded her, having now no alternative but to strike his colours – though not before he had displayed an amount of endurance which excited the admiration of the enemy.

A circumstance now occurred which is entitled to rank amongst the curiosities of war. On the French taking possession of the *Hannibal* they had neglected to provide themselves with their national ensign, and, either from necessity or bravado, rehoisted the English flag upside down. This being a well-known signal of distress, was so understood by the authorities at Gibraltar, who, manning all government and other boats with dockyard artificers and seamen, sent them, as it was mistakenly considered, to the assistance of the *Hannibal*.

On the approach of the launches I was summoned on deck by the captain of the *Dessaix*, who seemed doubtful what measures to adopt as regarded the boats now approaching to board the *Hannibal*, and asked my opinion as to whether they would attempt to retake the ship. As there could be no doubt in my mind about the nature of their mission or its result, it was evident that if they were allowed to board nothing could prevent the seizure of the whole. My advice, therefore, to Captain Palliere was to warn them off by a shot, hoping they would thereby be driven back and saved from capture. Captain Palliere seemed at first inclined to take the advice, but on reflection – either doubting its sincerity, or seeing the real state of the case – he decided to capture the whole by permitting them to board unmolested. Thus boat by boat was captured, until all the artificers necessary for the repair of the British squadron, and nearly all the sailors at that time in Gibraltar, were taken prisoners!

In this action the French and Spaniards suffered severely both as regarded ships and men, their masts and hulls being much knocked about, whilst several Spanish gunboats were sunk. The wonder to me was that the British squadron did not anchor; for the French ships being aground, stern on, could have offered little resistance, and must have been destroyed. It is true that the batteries on shore were admirably served, and thus constituted a formidable obstacle; but had not the squadron drifted past the French ships, the latter might have been interposed between the batteries and the British force, when the fire of the former would have been neutralized, and the enemy's ships aground destroyed with comparatively little loss. It is not, however, my purpose or province to criticize the action, but simply to give the details, as personally witnessed from that extraordinary place for a British officer, the deck of a French ship!

Neither the imprisonment of the captured crews nor my own was of long duration. The day after the action Sir James Saumarez sent Captain Brenton into Algeciras Bay with a flag of truce, to endeavour to effect an exchange of the gallant Captain Ferris, his officers, and crew. At that time there was no regulated system of exchange between the belligerent powers, but Captain Brenton succeeded in procuring the release of the crew of the *Hannibal* and the entrapped artificers, together with the officers and men of the *Speedy*. Admiral Linois would not at first give me up, but on further consideration allowed me to go with the other officers to Gibraltar on *parole*. My complete release was eventually effected for the second captain of the *San Antonio*, taken shortly afterwards.

The French ships having lost no time in communicating with the Spanish admiral at Cadiz, he promptly appeared off Algeciras with a reinforcement of six ships of the line, several frigates, and gunboats. The enemy having by this time warped off their grounded ships, as well as the *Hannibal*, and having by the 12th got them in seagoing order, the whole sailed from Algeciras, followed by the British squadron, which, by great exertions, had been got in readiness for pursuit.

Of the action which subsequently took place I have no personal knowledge, other than that of a scene witnessed by myself from the garden of the commissioner's house, in which I was staying.

The enemy were overtaken at dusk, soon after leaving the bay, and when it had become dark Captain Keats, in the *Superb*, gallantly dashed in between the two sternmost ships, firing right and left, and passed on. Of course I do not assert myself to have been personally cognizant of the way in which the attack was made, the firing only being visible from the Rock, but that this is the correct version of the affair rests upon indisputable authority. The movement was so rapidly executed that the *Superb* shot ahead before the smoke cleared away, and the Spanish ships, the *Real Carlos* (112) and the *San Hermenegildo* (112), mistaking each other for the aggressor, began a mutual attack, resulting in the *Real Carlos* losing her fore-top-mast, the sails of which, falling over her own guns, caught fire. While in this condition the *Hermenegildo* – still engaging the *Real Carlos* as an enemy – in the confusion fell on board her, and caught fire also. Both ships burned till they blew up, and nearly all on board perished, a few survivors only escaping on board the *Superb*, as Captain Keats was taking possession of a *third* Spanish line-of-battle ship, the *San Antonio* – for whose second captain, as has been said, I was exchanged.

A SHORT HISTORY OF NEW ENGLAND PRIVATEERING

David Mitchell

In Britain's American colonies, the cliques which had organized the Pirate Round and bought the loot of the New Providence men continued to profit from smuggling and privateering. Until the war of independence, French shipping was the main target. From 1776 to 1783, and again during the war of 1812–14, the prizes were British. The rebel navy consisted of thirteen mouldering frigates, whereas Britain already had more than a hundred naval vessels in American waters. The Continental Congress therefore sanctioned one of the largest and most effective corsair extra-

vaganzas of modern times. Anything that would float was commissioned – merchantmen, pilot boats, ferries, whalers, long-
boats, fishing smacks. "The people have gone mad a-
privateering," wrote one observer: and in some areas, especially
off Halifax and in the Gulf of St Lawrence, the concentration of
corsairs was such that they sometimes attacked each other.
Thanks to the hospitality of France, American or American-
commissioned French privateers roamed from the Shetlands to
Gibraltar.

Minor epics of daring were common. A Chesapeake barque
crusing in the Irish Sea was so tiny that the captain of a prize
mistook it for a pinnace and asked the crew where they had left
their ship. John Paul, the seafaring son of a gardener on Lord
Selkirk's estate near Kirkcudbright, changed his name to John
Paul Jones and emerged as one of the most impudent of rebel
"pirates", raiding the coasts of England, Scotland and Ireland
and sailing up the River Dee to loot Lord Selkirk's castle. His
recklessnesss is celebrated in a ballad:

> Our carpenter being frightened unto Paul Jones did say,
> "Our ship she leaks water since fighting today."
> Paul Jones then made answer in the height of his pride,
> "If we can't do no better we'll sink alongside."

In many New England ports privateering was the principal
business. Everyone invested in the corsair industry – including
George Washington, who dined off china that had once belonged to the Solicitor-General of the British West Indies.
Supply-ships to the British army were regularly intercepted,
and the West India trade was disrupted by corsairs sailing
from Martinique with French crews and French papers. Linen
ships from Dublin had to sail under convoy, 10 per cent
insurance was charged from Dover to Calais, in Portsmouth
and Plymouth receipts from harbour dues were cut by half, the
Liverpool trade fell off so steeply that ten thousand men were
thrown out of work, and the *Annual Register* for 1778 reported
that "the Thames presented the unusual and melancholy
spectacle of numbers of foreign ships, particularly French,
taking in cargoes of English commodities for various parts of
Europe."

The 1812 war was also fought almost entirely by corsairs and to almost equally devastating effect – despite fears that the British navy could establish a blockade three or four vessels deep and still have a reserve. American shipwrights came up with a secret weapon in the form of the Baltimore clippers. Long, low in the water, with tall, raked masts and a glorious spire of canvas, they tormented British ships of the line as mercilessly as Hawkins's new-model ships had plagued the Spanish Armada. Once again, in the opening months scores of pilot boats armed with one or two small guns went into action. *The Times* reported that in the West Indies American privateers were "so daring as even to cut vessels out of harbours and send raiding parties to carry off cattle from the plantations".

New York alone fitted out 120 cruisers which brought in 275 prizes and destroyed many more. One crew came back with 300,000 dollars' worth of booty after dodging seventeen pursuers. Profits were so regular and handsome that the New York legislature passed an "Act to encourage Privateering Associations". In August 1814 the London *Morning Chronicle* commented that "the whole coast of Ireland from Wexford round to Carrickfergus is virtually blockaded by a few petty fly-by-nights." Despite the presence of three frigates and fourteen sloops in Irish waters, the insurance rate rose to nearly 15 per cent. At Halifax it was 35½ per cent if you could insure at all. The *True-Blooded Yankee* accounted for twenty-seven vessels in thirty-seven days, and her crew realized three million dollars in prize money, including substantial government bounties (one half the estimated value of any armed vessel destroyed).

Jefferson, whose humanitarian ideals had been sadly battered, supported the "burn, sink or destroy" bounty policy with some misgiving but not without a certain aggressive relish. "Encourage these privateers to burn their prizes and let the public pay for them," he wrote to Monroe. "They will cheat us enormously. No matter, they will make the merchants of England feel and squeal and cry out for peace." He was right on both counts. The corsairs did cheat, and in London, Liverpool and Glasgow merchants did meet to deplore the depredations of "a horde of American cruisers" and urge an end to the war. As a last face-saving device, editorial writers and MPs attributed the success of the corsairs to the fact that they were of English descent and had "the blood of Drake" in their veins.

The end of the French and American wars was followed by a sharp explosion of lawlessness. Tens of thousands of seamen were discharged from the British navy and faced with unemployment. Reports came from the Caribbean, the Atlantic, the Gulf of Guinea and the Arabian Sea of crews mutinying, killing their officers, electing their own leaders and turning pirate. The London reaches of the Thames were infested with robbers. Eight men in a cutter held up the *Lady Campbell*, an East Indiaman, at Greenwich and got away with two chests of coins.

The West Indies, which had been swarming with French, British, Spanish and American privateers for the best part of forty years, now swarmed with about ten thousand ex-privateers. Some found employment in the improvised navies of the rebellious Spanish colonies during their wars of liberation. Others entered the service of Spain. Many simply scavenged a living, encouraged by the connivance of the authorities in Cuba and Puerto Rico. Using small, swift brigantines, schooners and sloops similar to those of the buccaneers, they produced a crop of pirate captains – Diabolito, Charles Gibbs and Benito de Soto were the most notorious – who revived on a miniature scale the Montbars-Lolonois tradition of ruthlessness. Perhaps they were conscious, like Ali Khoja, that time was running out and that restraint would serve no purpose.

Gibbs, a Rhode Islander, was one of the prime villains of *The Pirates' Own Book*. He had served with distinction on privateers during the 1812–14 war, and had no mind to join the ranks of the unemployed. Enlisting in an Argentinian privateer, he seized the ship and plundered in the Caribbean, offering the crews of his prizes a choice of joining his company or being killed, and sometimes, it was said, killing for the hell of it. But the cruise of the *Black Joke*, captained by a Spaniard, Benito de Soto, was the great pirate event of the time. Taken on as mate in the *Defensor de Pedro*, a Portuguese slaver which sailed from Buenos Aires in 1827, de Soto gained control while the captain was ashore, turned non-mutineers adrift in a small boat, renamed the ship the *Black Joke*, and lurked in the Atlantic. Within weeks he and his company captured the *Morning Star*, an East Indiaman, raping the wives and daughters of soldiers and officials coming home on furlough and leaving those passengers and seamen who had not been killed to drown in the hold as water seeped through holes bored in the hull.

From *Pirates*, David Mitchell, Thames & Hudson, 1976

CRUISING AND CANNIBALS: LIFE ABOARD A YANKEE PRIVATEER IN 1812

George Little

Little, born in Massachusetts, served aboard a US privateer in the War of 1812 against the British.

I now sailed on my sixth voyage, and arrived safely in Buenos Ayres. After having been there a few days another vessel arrived from Rio, having persons on board with powers to attach my vessel and cargo from under me. I soon learned that the house at Rio, in whose employment I sailed, had failed for a large amount, and that these persons were their creditors.

I was now left without a vessel, and fearing that I should lose the funds placed in their hands, lost no time in getting back to Rio, and when there I found the condition of the house even worse than I had anticipated; for all my two years' hard earnings were gone, with the exception of about five hundred dollars.

With this small sum I took passage in the ship *Scioto*, bound for Baltimore. I was induced to do this because little doubt was then entertained that there would be a war between the United States and England, and I was anxious to get home, if possible, before it was declared. We were fortunate enough to arrive in safety, although the war had been actually declared fifteen days before we got inside of the Capes of Virginia.

When we arrived in Baltimore, I found the most active preparations were in progress to prosecute the war. A number of privateers were fitting out, and everywhere the American flag might be seen flying, denoting the places of rendezvous: in a word, the most intense excitement prevailed throughout the city, and the position of a man was not at all enviable if it were ascertained that he was in any degree favourably disposed towards the British. It happened to fall to my lot to be an eyewitness to the unpleasant affair of tarring and feathering a certain Mr T., and also to the demolishing of the Federal Republican printing office by the mob.

Once more I returned to Boston to see my friends, whom I found pretty much in the same situation as when I left them. Two years had made but little alteration, except that my sister was married, and my father, being aged, had retired from the navy and taken up his residence in Marshfield. Every persuasion was now used to induce me to change my vocation, backed by the strong reasoning that the war would destroy commerce, and that no alternative would be left for seamen but the unhallowed pursuit of privateering.

These arguments had great weight, and I began to think seriously of entering into some business on shore, but then most insuperable difficulties arose in my mind as to the nature of the business I should pursue. My means were limited, quite too much so to enter into the mercantile line, and the only branch of it with which I was acquainted was the "commission"; another obstacle presented itself, which was to fix upon an eligible location. These difficulties, however, soon vanished, for a wealthy relative offered me the use of his credit, and a young friend with whom I was acquainted, having just returned from the south, informed me that there was a fine opening in Richmond, Virginia. Whereupon we immediately entered into a mutual arrangement to establish a commission house in that place. The necessary preparations were made, and we started for the south.

To my great surprise and mortification, however, when we reached Norfolk, I ascertained that my partner was without funds; neither had he the expectation of receiving any. This changed the current of my fortunes altogether. I was deceived by him, consequently all intercourse was broken off between us.

As my prospects were now blasted in reference to establishing myself in business on shore, I resolved once more to embark on my favourite element and try my luck there again. Here too, in

Norfolk, all was bustle and excitement, drums beating, colours flying, soldiers enlisting, men shipping in the States' service, and many privateers fitting out, creating such a scene of confusion as I had never before witnessed.

Young and of an ardent temperament, I could not look upon all these stirring movements an unmoved spectator; accordingly I entered on board the *George Washington* privateer, in the capacity of first lieutenant. She mounted one twelve-pounder on a pivot, and two long nines, with a complement of eighty men. She was in all respects a beautiful schooner of the most exact symmetrical proportions, about one hundred and twenty tons burden, and said to be as swift as anything that floated the ocean.

In reference to this enterprise, I must confess, in my cooler moments, that I had some qualms; to be sure here was an opportunity of making a fortune, but then it was counterbalanced by the possibility of getting my head knocked off, or a chance of being thrown into prison for two or three years; however, I had gone too far to recede, and I determined to make the best of it. Accordingly I placed what little funds I had in the hands of Mr G., of Norfolk, and repaired on board the privateer with my dunnage contained in a small trunk and clothes bag. On the morning of July 20th, 1812, the officers and crew being all on board, we weighed anchor, made sail, and stood down the river, with the stars and stripes floating in the breeze, and were saluted with a tremendous cheering from the shore.

I now was on board of a description of craft with which I was entirely unacquainted; I had, therefore, much to learn. The lieutenants and prize-masters, however, were a set of clever fellows, but the captain was a rough, uncouth sort of a chap, and appeared to me to be fit for little else than fighting and plunder. The crew were a motley set indeed, composed of all nations: they appeared to have been scraped together from the lowest dens of wretchedness and vice, and only wanted a leader to induce them to any act of daring and desperation.

Our destination, in the first place, was to cruise on the Spanish main, to intercept the English traders between the West India islands and the ports on the main. This cruising ground was chosen because, in case of need, we might run into Carthagena to refit and water. When we had run down as far as Lynnhaven Bay, information was received from a pilot boat that the British frigate

Belvidere was cruising off the Capes. This induced our captain to put to sea with the wind from the southward, as the privateer's best sailing was on the wind.

On the morning of the 22nd of July, we got under way from Lynnhaven Bay, and stood to sea. At 9 a.m., when about 10 miles outside of Cape Henry light-house, a sail was discovered directly in the wind's eye of us, bearing down under a press of canvas. Soon ascertaining she was a frigate, supposed to be the *Belvidere*, we stood on upon a wind until she came within short gunshot. Our foresail was now brailed up and the topsail lowered on the cap; at the same time the frigate took in all her light sails and hauled up her courses. As the privateer lay nearer the wind than the frigate, the latter soon dropped in our wake, and when within half-gunshot, we being under cover of her guns, she furled her topgallant-sails: at the same moment we hauled aft the foresheet, hoisted away the topsail, and tacked. By this manœuvre the frigate was under our lee. We took her fire and continued to make short boards, and in one hour were out of the reach of her guns without receiving any damage.

This was our first adventure, and we hailed it as a good omen. The crew were all in high spirits, because the frigate was considered to be as fast as anything on our coast at that time. And, furthermore, the captain had not only gained the confidence of the crew by this daring manœuvre, but we found we could rely upon our heels for safety.

Nothing material occurred until we got into the Mona passage, when we fell in with the *Black Joke* privateer, of New York, and, being unable to ascertain her character in consequence of a thick fog, we came into collision and exchanged a few shots before we found out we both wore the same national colours. This vessel was a sloop of not very prepossessing appearance, but as she had obtained some celebrity for sailing in smooth water, having previously been an Albany packet, she was fitted out as a privateer. In a seaway, however, being very short, she could not make much more headway than a tub.

It was agreed between the respective captains of the two vessels to cruise in company, and, in the event of a separation, to make a rendezvous at Carthagena. We soon ascertained that our craft would sail nearly two knots to the *Black Joke*'s one, and it may well be supposed that our company-keeping was of short duration.

In two days after parting with her the long wished for cry of "Sail ho!" was sung out from the mast-head, and we made all sail in chase. When within short gunshot we let her have our midship gun, when she immediately rounded to, took in the sail, hoisted English colours, and seemed to be preparing to make a gallant defence. In this we were not mistaken, for, as we ranged up, she opened a brisk cannonading upon us.

I now witnessed the daring intrepidity of Captain S., for while the brig was pouring a destructive fire into us, with the greatest coolness he observed to the crew, "That vessel, my lads, must be ours in ten minutes after I run this craft under her lee quarter."

By this time we had sheered up under her stern and received the fire of her stern-chasers, which did us no other damage than cutting away some of our ropes and making wind holes through the sails. It was the work of a moment; the schooner luffed up under the lee of the brig, and, with almost the rapidity of thought, we were made fast to her main chains.

"Boarders away!" shouted Captain S. We clambered up the sides of the brig and dropped on board of her like so many locusts, not, however, till two of our lads were run through with boarding-pikes.

The enemy made a brave defence, but were soon over-powered by superior numbers, and the captain of the brig was mortally wounded. In twenty minutes after we got alongside, the stars and stripes were waving triumphantly over the British flag.

In this affair we had two killed and seven slightly wounded, besides having some of our rigging cut away and sails somewhat riddled. The brig was from Jamaica, bound to the Gulf of Maracaibo; her cargo consisted of sugar, fruit, and other produce. She was two hundred tons burden, mounted six six-pounders, with a complement of fifteen men all told. She was manned with a prize master and crew, and ordered to any port in the United States wherever she could get in.

This affair very much disgusted me with privateering, especially when I saw so much loss of life, and beheld a band of ruthless desperadoes, for such I must call our crew, robbing and plundering a few defenceless beings who were pursuing both a lawful and peaceable calling. It induced me to form a resolve that I would relinquish what, to my mind, appeared to be an unjustifiable and outrageous pursuit, for I could not help believing that no conscientious man could be engaged in privateering, and certainly there was no honour to be gained by it. The second lieutenant came to the same determination as myself, and both of us most cordially despised our commander, because it was with his permission that those most outrageous scenes of robbing and plundering were committed on board the brig.

After repairing damages, we steered away for Carthagena to fill up the water casks and provision the privateer, so that we might extend the cruise.

Caught by Cannibals

In a few days we arrived at our destination without falling in with any other vessel, and, on entering the port, we found our comrade, the *Black Joke* privateer, who had arrived a day or two previously. It is well known that, at this time, all the provinces of Spain had shaken off their allegiance to the mother country, and declared themselves independent. Carthagena, the most prominent of the provinces, was a place of considerable commerce, and about this time a few men-of-war and a number of privateers were fitted out there.

The Carthagenian flag now presented a chance of gain to the cupidity of the avaricious and desperate, among whom was our commander, Captain S. As soon, therefore, as we had filled up our water, a proposition was made by him to the second lieutenant and myself, to cruise under both flags, the American and Carthagenian, and this to be kept a profound secret from the crew until we had sailed from port. Of course we rejected the proposition with disdain, and told him the consequence of such a measure in the event of being taken by a man-of-war of any nation: that it was a piracy to all intents and purposes, according to the law of nations. We refused to go out in the privateer if he persisted in this most nefarious act, and we heard no more of it while we lay in port.

In a few days we were ready for sea, and sailed in company with our companion, her force being rather more than ours, but the vessel very inferior, as stated before, in point of sailing. While together we captured several small British schooners, the cargoes of which, together with some specie, were divided between the two privateers. Into one of the prizes we put all the prisoners, gave them plenty of water and provisions, and let them pursue their course. The remainder of the prizes were burned. We then parted company, and, being short of water, ran in towards the land in order to ascertain if any could be procured.

In approaching the shore, the wind died away to a perfect calm, and at 4 p.m. a small schooner was seen in shore of us. As we had not steerage-way upon our craft, of course it would be impossible to ascertain her character before dark; it was therefore determined by our commander to board her with the boats under cover of the night. This was a dangerous piece of service, but there was no backing out. Volunteers being called for, I stepped forward, and very soon a sufficient number of men to man two boats offered their services to back me. Every disposition was made for the attack. The men were strongly armed, oars muffled, and a grappling placed in each boat.

The bearings of the strange sail were taken, and night came on perfectly clear and cloudless. I took command of the expedition, the second lieutenant having charge of one boat. The arrangement was to keep close together until we got sight of the vessel; the second lieutenant was to board on the bow and I on the quarter. We proceeded in the most profound silence; nothing was heard save now and then a slight splash of the oars in the water, and before we obtained sight of the vessel I had sufficient time to reflect on this most perilous enterprise.

My reflections were not of the most pleasant description, and I found myself inwardly shrinking, when I was aroused by the voice of the bow-man, saying, "There she is, sir, two points on the starboard bow." There she lay sure enough, with every sail hoisted, and a light was distinctly seen, as we supposed from her deck, it being too high for the cabin windows. We now held a consultation, and saw no good reason to change the disposition of attack, except that we agreed to board simultaneously.

It may be well to observe here, that any number of men on a vessel's deck in the night have double the advantage to repel boarders, because they may secrete themselves in such a position as to fall upon an enemy unawares, and thereby cut them off with little difficulty. Being fully aware of this, I ordered the men, as soon as we gained the deck of the schooner, to proceed with great caution, and keep close together till every hazard of the enterprise was ascertained.

The boats now separated and pulled for their respective stations, observing the most profound silence. When we had reached within a few yards of the schooner, we laid upon our oars for some moments but could neither hear nor see anything. We then pulled away cheerily, and the next minute were under her counter, grappled to her, and every man leaped on deck without opposition.

The other boat boarded nearly at the same moment, and we proceeded in a body, with great caution, to examine the decks. A large fire was in the caboose, and we soon ascertained that her deck was entirely deserted, and that she neither had any boat on deck nor to her stern.

We then proceeded to examine the cabin, leaving an armed force on deck. The cabin, like the deck, being deserted, the mystery was easily unravelled. Probably concluding that we should board them under cover of the night, they, no doubt, as soon as it was dark, took to their boats and deserted the vessel. On the floor of the cabin was a part of an English ensign, and some papers which showed that she belonged to Jamaica. The little cargo on board consisted of Jamaica rum, sugar, and fruit.

The breeze now springing up and the privateer showing lights, we were enabled to get alongside of her in a couple of hours. A prizemaster and crew were put on board, with orders to keep company. During the night we ran ashore, and in the morning took on board the privateer the greater part of the prize's cargo.

Being close in shore in the afternoon, we descried a settlement of huts, and supposing that water might be obtained there, the two vessels were run in and anchored about two miles distant from the beach. A proposition was made to me by Captain S. to get the water casks on board the prize schooner, and, as she drew a light draught of water, I was to run her in and anchor her near the beach, taking with me the two boats and twenty men. I observed to Captain S. that this was probably an Indian settlement, and it was well known that all the Indian tribes on the coast of Rio de la Hache were exceedingly ferocious, and said to be cannibals; and it was also well known that whoever fell into their hands never escaped with their lives; so that it was necessary, before any attempt was made to land, that some of the Indians should be decoyed on board and detained as hostages for our safety.

At the conclusion of this statement a very illiberal allusion was thrown out by Captain S., and some doubts expressed in reference to my courage; he remarking that if I was afraid to undertake the expedition, he would go himself. This was enough for me; I immediately resolved to proceed if I sacrificed my life in the attempt.

The next morning twenty water casks were put on board the prize, together with the two boats and twenty men, well armed with muskets, pistols, and cutlasses, and a supply of ammunition; I repaired on board, got the prize under way, ran in, and anchored about one hundred yards from the beach. The boats were got in readiness, and the men were well armed and the water casks slung ready to proceed on shore. I had examined my pistols narrowly that morning, and had put them in complete order, and, as I believed, had taken every precaution for our future operations so as to prevent surprise.

There were about a dozen of ill-constructed huts or wigwams, but no spot of grass or shrub was visible to the eye, and only here and there the trunk of an old tree. One solitary Indian was seen stalking on the beach, and the whole scene presented the most wild and savage appearance, and to my mind augured very unfavourably.

We pulled in with the casks in tow, seven men being in each boat; when within a short distance of the beach, the boats' heads were put to seaward, and the Indian came abreast of us. Addressing him in Spanish, I inquired if water could be procured, to which he replied in the affirmative. I then displayed to his view some gew-gaws and trinkets, at which he appeared perfectly delighted, and with many signs and gestures invited me on shore. Thrusting my pistols into my belt, and buckling on my cartridge-box, I gave orders to the boat's crew that in case they discovered anything like treachery or surprise after I had gotten on shore, to cut the water casks adrift and make the best of their way on board the prize.

As soon as I had jumped on shore, I enquired if there were any live stock, such as fowls, to be had? Pointing to a hut about thirty yards from the boats, he said that the stock was there, and invited me to go and see it. I hesitated, suspecting some treachery;

however, after repeating my order to the boats' crews, I proceeded with the Indian, and when within about a half-dozen yards of the hut, at a pre-concerted signal (as I suppose), as if by magic, at least one hundred Indians rushed out with the rapidity of thought.

I was knocked down, stripped of all my clothing except an inside flannel shirt, tied hand and foot, and then taken and secured to the trunk of a large tree, surrounded by about twenty squaws as a guard, who, with the exception of two or three, bore a most wild and hideous look in their appearance.

The capture of the boats' crews was simultaneous with my own, they being so much surprised and confounded at the stratagem of the Indians, that they had not the power, or presence of mind to pull off.

After they had secured our men, a number of them jumped into the boats, pulled off and captured the prize without meeting with any resistance from those on board, they being only six in number. Her cable was then cut and she was run on the beach, when they proceeded to dismantle her, by cutting the sails from the bolt-ropes, and taking out what little cargo there was, consisting of Jamaica rum and sugar. This being done, they led ropes on shore from the schooner, when about one hundred of them hauled her up nearly high and dry.

By this time the privateer had seen our disaster, stood boldly in and anchored within less than gunshot of the beach; they then very foolishly opened a brisk cannonade, but every shot was spent in vain. This exasperated the Indians, and particularly the one who had taken possession of my pistols. Casting my eye around, I saw him creeping toward me with one pistol presented, and when about five yards off, he pulled the trigger. But as Providence had no doubt ordered it, the pistol snapped; at the same moment a shot from the privateer fell a few yards from us, when the Indian rose upon his feet, cocked the pistol and fired it at the privateer; turning round with a most savage yell, he threw the pistol with great violence, which grazed my head, and then with a large stick beat and cut me until I was perfectly senseless.

This was about 10 o'clock, and I did not recover my consciousness until, as I supposed, about 4 o'clock in the afternoon. I perceived there were four squaws sitting around me, one of whom from her appearance, having on many gew-gaws and trinkets, was the wife of a chief. As soon as she discovered signs of returning consciousness, she presented me with a gourd, the contents of which appeared to be Indian meal mixed with water; she first drank and then gave it to me, and I can safely aver that I never drank any beverage before or since which produced such relief.

Night was now coming on, the privateer had got under way, and was standing off and on, with a flag of truce flying at her mast-head. The treacherous Indian with whom I had first conversed, came and, with a malignant smile, gave me the dreadful intelligence that at 12 o'clock that night we were to be roasted and eaten.

Accordingly at sunset I was unloosed and conducted by a band of about half a dozen savages to the spot where I found the remainder of our men firmly secured by having their hands tied behind them, their legs lashed together, and each man fastened to a stake that had been driven into the ground for that purpose. There was no possibility to elude the vigilance of these miscreants.

As soon as night shut in, a large quantity of brush wood was piled around us, and nothing now was wanting but the fire to complete this horrible tragedy. The same malicious savage approached us once more, and with the deepest malignity taunted us with our coming fate. Having some knowledge of the Indian character, I summoned up all the fortitude of which I was capable, and in terms of defiance told him that twenty Indians would be sacrificed for each one of us sacrificed by him. I knew very well that it would not do to exhibit any signs of fear or cowardice, and having heard much of the cupidity of the Indian character, I offered the savage a large ransom if he would use his influence to procure our release.

Here the conversation was abruptly broken off by a most hideous yell from the whole tribe, occasioned by their having taken large draughts of the rum, which now began to operate very sensibly upon them; and as it will be seen operated very much to our advantage. This thirst for rum caused them to relax their vigilance, and we were left alone to pursue our reflections, which were not of the most enviable or pleasant character. A thousand melancholy thoughts rushed over my mind. Here I was, and in all probability in a few hours I should be in eternity, and my death one of the most horrible description. Oh! thought I, how many were the entreaties and arguments used by my friends to deter me from pursuing an avocation so full of hazard and peril. If I had taken their advice, and acceded to their solicitations, in all probability. I should at this time have been in the enjoyment of much happiness.

I was aroused from this reverie by the most direful screams from the united voices of the whole tribe, they having drunk largely of the rum, and become so much intoxicated that a general fight ensued. Many of them lay stretched on the ground with tomahawks deeply implanted in their skulls, and many others, as the common phrase is, were dead drunk. This was an exceedingly fortunate circumstance for us. With their senses benumbed, of course they had forgotten their avowal to roast us, or, it may be, the Indian to whom I proposed ransom had conferred with the others, and they no doubt agreed to spare our lives until the morning.

It was a night however of pain and terror, as well as of the most anxious suspense, and when the morning dawn broke upon my vision, I felt an indescribable emotion of gratitude, as I had fully made up my mind the night previous that long before this time I should have been sleeping the sleep of death.

It was a pitiable sight, when the morning light broke forth, to see twenty human beings stripped naked, with their bodies cut and lacerated, and the blood issuing from their wounds, with their hands and feet tied, and their bodies fastened to stakes with brush wood piled around them, expecting every moment to be their last. My feelings on this occasion can be better imagined than described; suffice it to say, that I had given up all hopes of escape, and gloomily resigned myself to death.

When the fumes of the liquor had in some degree worn off from the benumbed senses of the savages, they arose and approached us, and for the first time the wily Indian informed me that the tribe had agreed to ransom us. They then cast off the lashings from our bodies and feet, and with our hands still secured drove us before them to the beach.

Then another difficulty arose: the privateer was out of sight, and the Indians became furious. To satiate their hellish malice they obliged us to run on the beach while they let fly their poisoned arrows after us. For my own part my limbs were so benumbed that I could scarcely walk, and I firmly resolved to stand still and take the worst of it, which was the best plan I could have adopted, for when they perceived that I exhibited no signs of fear, not a single arrow was discharged at me. Fortunately before they grew weary of this sport, to my great joy the privateer hove in sight. She stood boldly in with the flag of truce flying, and the savages consented to let one man of their own choosing go off in the boat to procure the stipulated ransom.

The boat returned loaded with articles of various descriptions, and two of our men were released. The boat kept plying to and from the privateer bringing with them such articles as they demanded, until all were released except myself.

Here it may be proper to observe, that the mulatto man who had been selected by the Indians performed all this duty himself, not one of the privateer's crew daring to hazard his life with him in the boat. I, then, was left alone, and for my release they required a double ransom. I began now seriously to think that they intended to detain me altogether. My mulatto friend, however, pledged himself that he would never leave me.

Again, for the last time, he sculled the boat off. She quickly returned with a larger amount of articles than previously. It was a moment of the deepest anxiety, for there had now arrived from the interior another tribe, apparently superior in point of numbers, and elated with the booty which had been obtained. They demanded a share, and expressed a determination to detain me for a larger ransom. These demands were refused, and a conflict ensued of the most frightful and terrific character. Tomahawks, knives, and arrows, were used indiscriminately, and many an Indian fell in that bloody contest. The tomahawks were thrown with the swiftness of arrows, and were generally buried in the skull or the breast; and whenever two came in contact with the famous "Indian hug", the strife was soon over with either one or the other, by one plunging the deadly knife up to the hilt in the body of his opponent; nor were the poisoned arrows of less swift execution, for wherever they struck, the wretched victim was quickly in eternity.

I shall never forget the frightful barbarity of that hour; although years have elapsed since its occurrence still the whole scene in imagination is before me – the savage yell of the war whoop, and the direful screams of the squaws still ring afresh in my ears.

In the height of this conflict, a tall Indian chief, who I knew belonged to the same tribe with the young squaw who gave me the drink, came down to the beach where I was. The boat had been discharged and was lying with her head off. At a signal given by the squaw to the chief, he caught me up in his arms with as much ease as if I had been a child, waded to the boat, threw me in, and then with a most expressive gesture, urged us off. Fortunately, there were two oars in the boat, and feeble as I was I threw all the remaining strength I had to the oar. It was the last effort, as life or death hung upon the next fifteen minutes.

Disappointed of a share of the booty, the savages were frantic with rage, especially when they saw I had eluded their grasp. Rushing to the beach, about a dozen threw themselves into the other boat which had been captured and pulled after us; but fortunately, in their hurry, they had forgotten their muskets, and being unacquainted with the method of rowing, of course they made but little progress, which enabled us to increase our distance.

The privateer having narrowly watched all these movements, and seeing our imminent danger, stood boldly on toward the beach, and in the next five minutes she lay between us and the Indians, discharging a heavy fire of musketry among them. Such was the high excitement of my feelings that I scarcely recollected how I gained the privateer's deck. But I was saved, nevertheless, though I was weak with the loss of blood and savage treatment, my limbs benumbed, and body scorched with the piercing rays of the sun: the whole scene rushing through my mind with the celerity of electricity, it unmanned and quite overpowered me; I fainted and fell senseless on the deck.

The usual restoratives and care were administered and I soon recovered from the effects of my capture. Some of the others were not so fortunate; two of them especially were cut in a shocking manner, and the others were so dreadfully beaten and mangled by clubs, that the greatest care was necessary to save their lives.

My dislike for the captain had been very much increased since that unhappy, disastrous affair; it never would have occurred if he had taken my advice, as his illiberality, and the hints he threw out in reference to my want of courage, were the causes of my suffering, and the sad result of the enterprise. I determined, therefore, in conjunction with the second lieutenant, to leave the privateer as soon as we arrived in Carthagena, to which port we were bound.

LAFITTE

Charles Ellms

Jean Lafitte was born at St. Maloes in France, in 1781, and went to sea at the age of thirteen; after several voyages in Europe, and to the coast of Africa, he was appointed mate of a French East Indiaman, bound to Madras. On the outward passage they encountered a heavy gale off the Cape of Good Hope, which sprung the mainmast and otherwise injured the ship, which determined the captain to bear up for the Mauritius, where he arrived in safety; a quarrel having taken place on the passage out between Lafitte and the captain, he abandoned the ship and refused to continue the voyage. Several privateers were at this time fitting out at this island, and Lafitte was appointed captain of one of these vessels; after a cruise during which he robbed the vessels of other nations, besides those of England, and thus committing piracy, he stopped at the Seychelles, and took in a load of slaves for the Mauritius; but being chased by an English frigate as far north as the equator, he found himself in a very awkward condition; not having provisions enough on board his ship to carry him back to the French Colony. He therefore conceived the bold project of proceeding to the Bay of Bengal, in order to get provisions from on board some English ships. In his ship of two hundred tons, with only two guns and twenty-six men, he attacked and took an English armed schooner with a numerous crew. After putting nineteen of his own crew on board the schooner, he took the command of her and proceeded to cruise upon the coast of Bengal. He there fell in with the *Pagoda*, a vessel belonging to the English East India Company, armed with twenty-six twelve pounders and manned with one hundred and fifty men. Expecting that the enemy would take him for a pilot of the Ganges, he manoeuvred accordingly. The *Pagoda* manifested no suspicions, whereupon he suddenly darted with his brave followers upon her decks, overturned all who opposed them, and speedily took the ship. After a very successful cruise he arrived safe at the Mauritius, and took the command of *La Confiance* of twenty-six guns and two hundred and fifty men, and sailed for the coast of British India. Off the Sand Heads in October, 1807, Lafitte fell in with the *Queen* East Indiaman, with a crew of near four hundred men, and carrying forty guns; he conceived the bold project of getting possession of her. Never was there beheld a more unequal conflict; even the height of the vessel compared to the feeble privateer augmented the chances against Lafitte; but the difficulty and danger far from discouraging this intrepid sailor, acted as an additional spur to his brilliant valor. After electrifying his crew with a few words of hope and ardor, he manoeuvred and ran on board of the enemy. In this position he received a broadside when close too; but he expected this, and made his men lay flat upon the deck. After the first fire they all rose, and from the yards and tops, threw bombs and grenades into the forecastle of the Indiaman. This sudden and unforeseen attack caused a great havoc. In an instant, death and terror made them abandon a part of the vessel near the mizen-mast. Lafitte, who observed every thing, seized the decisive moment, beat to arms, and forty of his crew prepared to board, with pistols in their hands and daggers held between their teeth. As soon as they got on deck, they rushed upon the affrighted crowd, who retreated to the steerage, and endeavored to defend themselves there. Lafitte thereupon ordered a second division to board, which he headed himself; the captain of the Indiaman was killed, and all were swept away in a moment. Lafitte caused a gun to be loaded with grape, which he pointed towards the place where the crowd was assembled, threatening to exterminate them. The English deeming resistance fruitless, surrendered, and Lafitte hastened to put a stop to the slaughter. This exploit, hitherto unparalleled, resounded through India, and the name of Lafitte became the terror of English commerce in these latitudes.

*   *   *

As British vessels now traversed the Indian Ocean under strong convoys, game became scarce, and Lafitte determined to visit France; and after doubling the Cape of Good Hope, he coasted up to the Gulf of Guinea, and in the Bight of Benin, took two valuable prizes loaded with gold dust, ivory, and Palm oil; with this booty he reached St. Maloes in safety. After a short stay at his native place he fitted out a brigantine, mounting twenty guns and one hundred and fifty men, and sailed for Gaudaloupe; amongst the West India Islands, he made several valuable prizes; but during his absence on a cruise the island having been taken by the British, he proceeded to Carthagena, and from thence to Barrataria. After this period, the conduct of Lafitte at Barrataria does not appear to be characterized by the audacity and boldness of his former career; but he had amassed immense sums of booty, and as he was obliged to have dealings with the merchants of the United States, and the West Indies, who frequently owed him large sums, and the cautious dealings necessary to found and conduct a colony of Pirates and smugglers in the very teeth of a civilized nation, obliged Lafitte to cloak as much as possible his real character.

As we have said before, at the period of the taking of Gaudaloupe by the British, most of the privateers commissioned by the government of that island, and which were then on a cruise, not being able to return to any of the West India Islands, made for Barrataria, there to take in a supply of water and provisions, recruit the health of their crews, and dispose of their prizes, which could not be admitted into any of the ports of the United States, we being at that time in peace with Great Britain. Most of the commissions granted to privateers by the French government at Gaudaloupe, having expired sometime after the declaration of the independence of Carthagena, many of the privateers repaired to that port, for the purpose of obtaining from the new government commissions for cruising against Spanish vessels. Having duly obtained their commissions, they in a manner blockaded for a long time all the ports belonging to the royalists, and made numerous captives, which they carried into Barrataria. Under this denomination is comprised part of the coast of Louisiana to the west of the mouths of the Mississippi, comprehended between Bastien bay on the east, and the mouths of the river or bayou la Fourche on the west. Not far from the sea are lakes called the great and little lakes of Barrataria, communicating with one another by several large bayous with a great number of branches. There is also the island of Barrataria, at the extremity of which is a place called the Temple, which denomination it owes to several mounds of shells thrown up there by the Indians. The name of Barrataria is also given to a large basin which extends the whole length of the cypress swamps, from the Gulf of Mexico to three miles above New Orleans. These waters disembogue into the gulf by two entrances of the bayou Barrataria, between which lies an island called Grand Terre, six miles in length, and from two to three miles in breadth, running parallel with the coast. In the western entrance is the great pass of Barrataria, which has from nine to ten feet of water. Within this pass about two leagues from the open sea, lies the only secure harbor on the coast, and accordingly this was the harbor frequented by the Pirates, so well known by the name of Barratarians.

At Grand Jerre, the privateers publicly made sale by auction, of the cargoes of their prizes. From all parts of Lower Louisiana, people resorted to Barrataria, without being at all solicitous to conceal the object of their journey. The most respectable inhabitants of the state, especially those living in the country, were in the habit of purchasing smuggled goods coming from Barrataria.

The government of the United States sent an expedition under Commodore Patterson, to disperse the settlement of marauders at Barrataria; the following is an extract of his letter to the secretary of war.

Sir – I have the honor to inform you that I departed from this city on the 11th June, accompanied by Col. Ross, with a detachment of seventy of the 44th regiment of infantry. On the 12th, reached the schooner *Carolina*, of Plaquemine, and formed a junction with the gun vessels at the Balize on the 13th, sailed from the southwest pass on the evening of the 15th, and at half past 8 o'clock, A.M. on the 16th, made the Island of Barrataria, and discovered a number of vessels in the harbor, some of which shewed Carthagenian colors. At 2 o'clock, perceived the pirates forming their vessels, ten in number, including prizes, into a line of battle near the entrance of the harbor, and making every preparation to offer me battle. At 10 o'clock, wind light and variable, formed the order of battle with six gun boats and the *Sea Horse* tender, mounting one six pounder and fifteen men, and a launch mounting one twelve pound carronade; the schooner *Carolina*, drawing too much water to cross the bar. At half past 10 o'clock, perceived several smokes along the coasts as signals, and at the same time a white flag hoisted on board a schooner at the fort, an American flag at the mainmast head and a Carthagenian flag (under which the pirates cruise) at her topping lift; replied with a white flag at my main; at 11 o'clock, discovered that the pirates had fired two of their best schooners; hauled down my white flag and made the signal for battle; hoisting with a large white flag bearing the words "Pardon for Deserters"; having heard there was a number on shore from the army and navy. At a quarter past 11 o'clock, two gun boats grounded and were passed agreeably to my previous orders, by the other four which entered the harbor, manned by my barge and the boats belonging to the grounded vessels, and proceeded in to my great disappointment. I perceived that the pirates abandoned their vessels, and were flying in all directions. I immediately sent the launch and two barges with small boats in pursuit of them. At meridian, took possession of all their vessels in the harbor consisting of six schooners and one felucca, cruisers, and prizes of the pirates, one brig, a prize, and two armed schooners under the Carthagenian flag, both in the line of battle, with the armed vessels of the pirates, and apparently with an intention to aid them in any resistance they might make against me, as their crews were at quarters, tompions out of their guns, and matches lighted. Col. Ross at the same time landed, and with his command took possession of their establishment on shore, consisting of about forty houses of different sizes, badly constructed, and thatched with palmetto leaves.

When I perceived the enemy forming their vessels into a line of battle I felt confident from their number and very advantageous position, and their number of men, that they would have fought me; their not doing so I regret; for had they, I should have been enabled more effectually to destroy or make prisoners of them and their leaders; but it is a subject of great satisfaction to me, to have effected the object of my enterprise, without the loss of a man.

The enemy had mounted on their vessels twenty pieces of cannon of different calibre; and as I have since learnt, from eight hundred, to one thousand men of all nations and colors.

Early in the morning of the 20th, the *Carolina* at anchor, about five miles distant, made the signal of a "strange sail in sight to eastward"; immediately after she weighed anchor, and gave chase the strange sail, standing for Grand Terre, with all sail; at half past 8 o'clock, the chase hauled her wind off shore to escape; sent acting Lieut. Spedding with four boats manned and armed to prevent her passing the harbor; at 9 o'clock A.M., the chase fired upon the *Carolina*, which was returned; each vessel continued firing during the chase, when their long guns could reach. At 10 o'clock, the chase grounded outside of the bar, at which time the *Carolina* was from the shoalness of the water obliged to haul her wind off shore and give up the chase; opened a fire upon the chase across the island from the gun vessels. At half past 10 o'clock, she hauled down her colors and was taken possession of. She proved to be the armed schooner *Gen. Boliver*; by grounding she broke both her rudder pintles and made water; took from her her armament, consisting of one long brass eighteen pounder, one long brass six pounder, two twelve pounders, small arms, &c., and twenty-one packages of dry goods. On the afternoon of the 23d, got underway with the whole squadron, in all seventeen vessels, but during the night one escaped, and the next day arrived at New Orleans with my whole squadron.

At different times the English had sought to attack the pirates at Barrataria, in hopes of taking their prizes, and even their armed vessels. Of these attempts of the British, suffice it to instance that of June 23d, 1813, when two privateers being at anchor off Cat Island, a British sloop of war anchored at the entrance of the pass, and sent her boats to endeavor to take the privateers; but they were repulsed with considerable loss.

Such was the state of affairs, when on the 2d Sept., 1814, there appeared an armed brig on the coast opposite the pass. She fired a gun at a vessel about to enter, and forced her to run aground; she then tacked and shortly after came to an anchor at the entrance of the pass. It was not easy to understand the intentions of this vessel, who, having commenced with hostilities on her first appearance now seemed to announce an amicable disposition. Mr. Lafitte then went off in a boat to examine her, venturing so far that he could not escape from the pinnace sent from the brig, and making towards the shore, bearing British colors and a flag of truce. In this pinnace were two naval officers. One was Capt. Lockyer, commander of the brig. The first question they asked was, where was Mr. Lafitte? he not choosing to make himself known to them, replied that the person they inquired for was on shore. They then delivered to him a packet directed to Mr. Lafitte, Barrataria, requesting him to take particular care of it, and to deliver it into Mr. Lafitte's hands. He prevailed on them to make for the shore, and as soon as they got near enough to be in his power, he made himself known, recommending to them at the same time to conceal the business on which they had come. Upwards of two hundred persons lined the shore, and it was a general cry amongst the crews of the privateers at Grand Terre, that those British officers should be made prisoners and sent to New Orleans as spies. It was with much difficulty that Lafitte dissuaded the multitude from this intent, and led the officers in safety to his dwelling. He thought very prudently that the papers contained in the packet might be of importance towards the safety of the country and that the officers if well watched could obtain no intelligence that might turn to the detriment of Louisiana. He now examined the contents of the packet, in which he found a proclamation addressed by Col. Edward Nichalls, in the service of his Brittanic Majesty, and commander of the land forces on the coast of Florida, to the inhabitants of Louisiana. A letter from the same to Mr. Lafitte, the commander of Barrataria; an official letter from the honorable W.H. Percy, captain of the sloop of war *Hermes*, directed to Lafitte. When he had perused these letters, Capt. Lockyer enlarged on the subject of them and proposed to him to enter into the service of his Brittanic Majesty with the rank of post captain and to receive the command of a 44 gun frigate. Also all those under his command, or over whom he had sufficient influence. He was also offered thirty thousand dollars, payable at Pensacola, and urged him not to let slip this opportunity of acquiring fortune and consideration. On Lafitte's requiring a few days to reflect upon these proposals, Capt. Lockyer observed to him that no reflection could be necessary, respecting proposals that obviously precluded hesitation, as he was a Frenchman and proscribed by the American government. But to all his splendid promises and daring insinuations, Lafitte replied that in a few days he would give a final answer; his object in this procrastination being to gain time to inform the officers of the state government of this nefarious project. Having occasion to go to some distance for a short time, the persons who had proposed to send the British officers prisoners to New Orleans, went and seized them in his absence, and confined both them and the crew of the pinnace, in a secure place, leaving a guard at the door. The British officers sent for Lafitte; but he, fearing an insurrection of the crews of the privateers, thought it advisable not to see them until he had first persuaded their captains and officers to desist from the measures on which they seemed bent. With this view he represented to the latter that, besides the infamy that would attach to them if they treated as prisoners people who had come with a flag of truce, they would lose the opportunity of discovering the projects of the British against Louisiana.

Early the next morning Lafitte caused them to be released from their confinement and saw them safe on board their pinnace, apologizing the detention. He now wrote to Capt. Lockyer the following letter.

To CAPTAIN LOCKYER.
Barrataria, 4th Sept. 1814.
Sir – The confusion which prevailed in our camp yesterday and this morning, and of which you have a complete knowledge, has prevented me from answering in a precise manner to the object of your mission; nor even at this moment can I give you all the satisfaction that you desire; however, if you could grant me a fortnight, I would be entirely at your disposal at the end of that time. This delay is indispensable to enable me to put my affairs in order. You may communicate with me by sending a boat to the eastern

point of the pass, where I will be found. You have inspired
me with more confidence than the admiral, your superior
officer, could have done himself; with you alone, I wish to
deal, and from you also I will claim, in due time the reward
of the services, which I may render to you. Yours, &c.

    J. LAFITTE.

His object in writing that letter was, by appearing disposed to
accede to their proposals, to give time to communicate the affair
to the officers of the state government, and to receive from them
instructions how to act, under circumstances so critical and
important to the country. He accordingly wrote on the 4th
September to Mr. Blanque, one of the representatives of the
state, sending him all the papers delivered to him by the British
officers with a letter addressed to his excellency, Gov. Claiborne
of the state of Louisiana.

To Gov. CLAIBORNE.
Barrataria, Sept. 4th, 1814.
Sir – In the firm persuasion that the choice made of you to
fill the office of first magistrate of this state, was dictated by
the esteem of your fellow citizens, and was conferred on
merit, I confidently address you on an affair on which may
depend the safety of this country. I offer to you to restore to
this state several citizens, who perhaps in your eyes have
lost that sacred title. I offer you them, however, such as you
could wish to find them, ready to exert their utmost efforts
in defence of the country. This point of Louisiana, which I
occupy, is of great importance in the present crisis. I tender
my services to defend it; and the only reward I ask is that a
stop be put to the proscription against me and my adherents, by an act of oblivion, for all that has been done
hitherto. I am the stray sheep wishing to return to the fold.
If you are thoroughly acquainted with the nature of my
offences, I should appear to you much less quilty, and still
worthy to discharge the duties of a good citizen. I have
never sailed under any flag but that of the republic of
Carthagena, and my vessels are perfectly regular in that
respect. If I could have brought my lawful prizes into the
ports of this state, I should not have employed the illicit

means that have caused me to be proscribed. I decline saying more on the subject, until I have the honor of your excellency's answer, which I am persuaded can be dictated only by wisdom. Should your answer not be favourable to my ardent desires, I declare to you that I will instantly leave the country, to avoid the imputation of having cooperated towards an invasion on this point, which cannot fail to take place, and to rest secure in the acquittal of my conscience.

I have the honor to be

your excellency's, &c.

J. LAFITTE.

The contents of these letters do honor to Lafitte's judgment, and evince his sincere attachment to the American cause. On the receipt of this packet from Lafitte, Mr. Blanque immediately laid its contents before the governor, who convened the committee of defence lately formed of which he was president; and Mr. Rancher the bearer of Lafitte's packet, was sent back with a verbal answer to desire Lafitte to take no steps until it should be determined what was expedient to be done; the message also contained an assurance that, in the meantime no steps should be taken against him for his past offences against the laws of the United States.

At the expiration of the time agreed on with Captain Lockyer, his ship appeared again on the coast with two others, and continued standing off and on before the pass for several days. But he pretended not to perceive the return of the sloop of war, who tired of waiting to no purpose, put out to sea and disappeared.

Lafitte having received a guarantee from General Jackson for his safe passage from Barrataria to New Orleans and back, he proceeded forthwith to the city where he had an interview with Gov. Claiborne and the General. After the usual formalities and courtesies had taken place between these gentlemen, Lafitte addressed the Governor of Louisiana nearly as follows. "I have offered to defend for you that part of Louisiana I now hold. But not as an outlaw, would I be its defender. In that confidence, with which you have inspired me, I offer to restore to the state many citizens, now under my command. As I have remarked before, the point I occupy is of great importance in the present crisis. I tender not only my own services to defend it, but those of all I command; and the only reward I ask, is, that a stop be put to the proscription against me and my adherents, by an act of oblivion for all that has been done hitherto."

"My dear sir," said the Governor, who together with General Jackson, was impressed with admiration of his sentiments, "your praiseworthy wishes shall be laid before the council of the state, and I will confer with my August friend here present, upon this important affair, and send you an answer to-morrow." At Lafitte withdrew, the General said farewell: "When we meet again, I trust it will be in the ranks of the American army." The result of the conference was the issuing the following order.

> The Governor of Louisiana, informed that many individuals implicated in the offences heretofore committed against the United States at Barrataria, express a willingness at the present crisis to enroll themselves and march against the enemy.
>
> He does hereby invite them to join the standard of the United States and is authorised to say, should their conduct in the field meet the approbation of the Major General, that that officer will unite with the governor in a request to the president of the United States, to extend to each and every individual, so marching and acting, a free and full pardon.

These general orders were placed in the hands of Lafitte, who circulated them among his dispersed followers, most of whom readily embraced the conditions of pardon they held out. In a few days many brave men and skillful artillerists, whose services contributed greatly to the safety of the invaded state, flocked to the standard of the United States, and by their conduct, received the highest approbation of General Jackson.

BY THE PRESIDENT OF THE UNITED STATES OF AMERICA.
A PROCLAMATION.

Among the many evils produced by the wars, which, with little intermission, have afflicted Europe, and extended their ravages into other quarters of the globe, for a period exceeding twenty years, the dispersion of a considerable portion of the inhabitants of different countries, in sorrow and in want, has not been the least injurious to human happiness, nor the least severe in the trial of human virtue.

It had been long ascertained that many foreigners, flying from the dangers of their own home, and that some citizens, forgetful of their duty, had co-operated in forming an establishment on the island of Barrataria, near the mouth of the river Mississippi, for the purpose of a clandestine and lawless trade. The government of the United States caused the establishment to be broken up and destroyed; and, having obtained the means of designating the offenders of every description, it only remained to answer the demands of justice by inflicting an exemplary punishment.

But it has since been represented that the offenders have manifested a sincere penitence; that they have abandoned the prosecution of the worst cause for the support of the best, and, particularly, that they have exhibited, in the defence of New Orleans, unequivocal traits of courage and fidelity. Offenders, who have refused to become the associates of the enemy in the war, upon the most seducing terms of invitation; and who have aided to repel his hostile invasion of the territory of the United States, can no longer be considered as objects of punishment, but as objects of a generous forgiveness.

It has therefore been seen, with great satisfaction, that the General Assembly of the State of Louisiana earnestly recommend those offenders to the benefit of a full pardon; And in compliance with that recommendation, as well as in consideration of all the other extraordinary circumstances in the case, I, James Madison, President of the United States of America, do issue this proclamation, hereby granting, publishing and declaring, a free and full pardon of all offences committed in violation of any act or acts of the Congress of the said United States, touching the revenue, trade and navigation thereof, or touching the intercourse and commerce of the United States with foreign nations, at any time before the eighth day of January, in the present year one thousand eight hundred and fifteen, by any person or persons whatsoever, being inhabitants of New Orleans and the adjacent country, or being inhabitants of the said island of Barrataria, and the places adjacent; Provided, that every person, claiming the benefit of this full pardon, in order to entitle himself thereto, shall produce a certificate in writing from the governor of the State of Louisiana, stating that such person has aided in the defence of New Orleans and the adjacent country, during the invasion thereof as aforesaid.

And I do hereby further authorize and direct all suits, indictments, and prosecutions, for fines, penalties, and forfeitures, against any person or persons, who shall be entitled to the benefit of this full pardon, forthwith to be stayed, discontinued and released: All civil officers are hereby required, according to the duties of their respective stations, to carry this proclamation into immediate and faithful execution.

Done at the City of Washington, the sixth day of February, in the year one thousand eight hundred and fifteen, and of the independence of the United States the thirty-ninth.

By the President,
JAMES MADISON
JAMES MONROE,
Acting Secretary of State.

The morning of the eighth of January, was ushered in with the discharge of rockets, the sound of cannon, and the cheers of the British soldiers advancing to the attack. The Americans, behind the breastwork, awaited in calm intrepidity their approach. The enemy advanced in close column of sixty men in front, shouldering their muskets and carrying fascines and ladders. A storm of rockets preceded them, and an incessant fire opened from the battery, which commanded the advanced column. The musketry and rifles from the Kentuckians and Tennesseans, joined the fire of the artillery, and in a few moments was heard along the line a ceaseless, rolling fire, whose tremendous noise resembled the continued reverberation of thunder. One of these guns, a twenty-four pounder, placed upon the breastwork in the third embrasure from the river, drew, from the fatal skill and activity with which it was managed, even in the heat of battle, the admiration of both Americans and British; and became one of the points most dreaded by the advancing foe.

Here was stationed Lafitte and his lieutenant Dominique and a large band of his men, who during the continuance of the battle, fought with unparalleled bravery. The British already had been twice driven back in the utmost confusion, with the loss of their commander-in-chief, and two general officers.

Two other batteries were manned by the Barratarians, who served their pieces with the steadiness and precision of veteran gunners. In the first attack of the enemy, a column pushed forward between the levee and river; and so precipitate was their charge that the outposts were forced to retire, closely pressed by the enemy. Before the batteries could meet the charge, clearing the ditch, they gained the redoubt through the embrasures, leaping over the parapet, and overwhelming by their superior force the small party stationed there.

Lafitte, who was commanding in conjunction with his officers, at one of the guns, no sooner saw the bold movement of the enemy, than calling a few of his best men by his side, he sprung forward to the point of danger, and clearing the breastwork of the entrenchments, leaped, cutlass in hand, into the midst of the enemy, followed by a score of his men, who in many a hard fought battle upon his own deck, had been well tried.

Astonished at the intrepidity which could lead men to leave their entrenchments and meet them hand to hand, and pressed by the suddenness of the charge, which was made with the reck-lessness, skill and rapidity of practised boarders bounding upon the deck of an enemy's vessel, they began to give way, while one after another, two British officers fell before the cutlass of the pirate, as they were bravely encouraging their men. All the energies of the British were now concentrated to scale the breast-work, which one daring officer had already mounted. While Lafitte and his followers, seconding a gallant band of volunteer riflemen, formed a phalanx which they in vain assayed to pene-trate.

The British finding it impossible to take the city and the havoc in their ranks being dreadful, made a precipitate retreat, leaving the field covered with their dead and wounded.

General Jackson, in his correspondence with the secretary of war did not fail to notice the conduct of the "Corsairs of Barrataria", who were, as we have already seen, employed in the artillery service. In the course of the campaign they proved, in an unequivocal manner, that they had been misjudged by the enemy, who a short time previous to the invasion of Louisiana, had hoped to enlist them in his cause. Many of them were killed or wounded in the defence of the country. Their zeal, their courage, and their skill, were remarked by the whole army, who could no longer consider such brave men as criminals. In a few days peace was declared between Great Britain and the United States.

The piratical establishment of Barrataria having been broken up and Lafitte not being content with leading an honest, peaceful life, procured some fast sailing vessels, and with a great number of his followers, proceeded to Galvezton Bay, in Texas, during the year 1819; where he received a commission from General Long; and had five vessels generally cruising and about 300 men. Two open boats bearing commissions from General Humbert, of Galvezton, having robbed a plantation on the Marmento river, of negroes, money, &c., were captured in the Sabine river, by the boats of the United States schooner *Lynx*. One of the men was hung by Lafitte, who dreaded the vengeance of the American government. The *Lynx* also captured one of his schooners, and her prize that had been for a length of time smuggling in the Carmento. One of his cruisers, named the *Jupiter*, returned safe to Galvezton after a short cruise with a valuable cargo, principally specie; she was the first vessel that sailed under the authority of Texas. The American government well knowing that where Lafitte was, piracy and smuggling would be the order of the day, sent a vessel of war to cruise in the Gulf of Mexico, and scour the coasts of Texas. Lafitte having been appointed governor of Galvezton and one of the cruisers being stationed off the port to watch his motions, it so annoyed him that he wrote the following letter to her commander, Lieutenant Madison.

To the commandant of the American cruiser, off the port of Galvezton. Sir – I am convinced that you are a cruiser of the navy, ordered by your government. I have therefore deemed it proper to inquire into the cause of your living before this port without communicating your intention. I shall by this message inform you, that the port of Galvezton belongs to and is in the possession of the republic of Texas, and was made a port of entry the 9th October last. And whereas the supreme congress of said republic have thought proper to appoint me as governor of this place, in consequence of which, if you have any demands on said government, or persons belonging to or residing in the same, you will please to send an officer with such demands, whom you may be assured will be treated with the greatest politeness, and receive every satisfaction required. But if you are ordered, or should attempt to enter this port in a hostile manner, my oath and duty to the government compels me to rebut your intentions at the expense of my life.

To prove to you my intentions towards the welfare and harmony of your government I send enclosed the declaration of several prisoners, who were taken in custody yesterday, and by a court of inquiry appointed for that purpose, were found guilty of robbing the inhabitants of the United States of a number of slaves and specie. The gentlemen bearing this message will give you any reasonable information relating to this place, that may be required.

Yours, &c.

J. LAFITTE.

About this time one Mitchell, who had formerly belonged to Lafitte's gang, collected upwards of one hundred and fifty desperadoes and fortified himself on an island near Barrataria, with several pieces of cannon; and swore that he and all his comrades would perish within their trenches before they would surrender to any man. Four of this gang having gone to New Orleans on a frolic, information was given to the city watch, and the house surrounded, when the whole four with cocked pistols in both hands sallied out and marched through the crowd which made way for them and no person dared to make an attempt to arrest them.

The United States cutter, *Alabama*, on her way to the station off the mouth of the Mississippi, captured a piratical schooner belonging to Lafitte; she carried two guns and twenty-five men, and was fitted out at New Orleans, and commanded by one of Lafitte's lieutenants, named Le Fage; the schooner had a prize in company and being hailed by the cutter, poured into her a volley of musketry; the cutter then opened upon the privateer and a smart action ensued which terminated in favor of the cutter, which had four men wounded and two of them dangerously; but the pirate had six men killed; both vessels were captured and brought into the bayou St. John. An expedition was now sent to dislodge Mitchell and his comrades from the island he had taken possession of; after coming to anchor, a summons was sent for him to surrender, which was answered by a brisk cannonade from his breastwork. The vessels were warped close in shore; and the boats manned and sent on shore whilst the vessels opened upon the pirates; the boat's crews landed under a galling fire of grape shot and formed in the most undaunted manner; and although a severe loss was sustained they entered the breastwork at the point of the bayonet; after a desperate fight the pirates gave way, many were taken prisoners but Mitchell and the greatest part escaped to the cypress swamps where it was impossible to arrest them. A large quantity of dry goods and specie together with other booty was taken. Twenty of the pirates were taken and brought to New Orleans, and tried before Judge Hall, of the Circuit Court of the United States, sixteen were brought in guilty; and after the Judge had finished pronouncing sentence of death upon the hardened wretches, several of them cried out in open court, "Murder – by God".

Accounts of these transactions having reached Lafitte, he plainly perceived there was a determination to sweep all his cruisers from the sea; and a war of extermination appeared to be waged against him.

In a fit of desperation he procured a large and fast sailing brigantine mounting sixteen guns and having selected a crew of one hundred and sixty men he started without any commission as a regular pirate determined to rob all nations and neither to give or receive quarter. A British sloop of war which was cruising in the Gulf of Mexico, having heard that Lafitte himself was at sea, kept a sharp look out from the mast head; when one morning as an officer was sweeping the horizon with his glass he discovered a long dark looking vessel, low in the water, but having very tall masts, with sails white as the driven snow. As the sloop of war had the weather gage of the pirate and could outsail her before the wind, she set her studding sails and crowded every inch of canvas in chase; as soon as Lafitte ascertained the character of his opponent, he ordered the awnings to be furled and set his big square-sail and shot rapidly through the water; but as the breeze freshened the sloop of war came up rapidly with the pirate, who, finding no chance of escaping, determined to sell his life as dearly as possible; the guns were cast loose and the shot handed up; and a fire opened upon the ship which killed a number of men and carried away her foretopmast, but she reserved her fire until within a cable's distance of the pirate; when she fired a general discharge from her broadside, and a volley of small arms; the broadside was too much elevated to hit the low hull of the brigantine, but was not without effect; the foretopmast fell, the jaws of the main gaff were severed and a large proportion of the rigging came rattling down on deck; ten of the pirates were killed, but Lafitte remained unhurt. The sloop of war entered her men over the starboard bow and a terrific contest with pistols and cutlasses ensued; Lafitte received two wounds at this time which disabled him, a grape shot broke the bone of his right leg and he received a cut in the abdomen, but his crew fought like tigers and the deck was ankle deep with blood and gore; the captain of the boarders received such a tremendous blow on the head from the butt end of a musket, as stretched him senseless on the deck near Lafitte, who raised his dagger to stab him to the heart. But the tide of his existence was ebbing like a torrent, his brain was giddy, his aim faltered and the point descended in the Captain's right thigh; dragging away the blade with the last convulsive energy of a death struggle, he lacerated the wound. Again the reeking steel was upheld, and Lafitte placed his left hand near the Captain's heart, to make his aim more sure; again the dizziness of dissolution spread over his sight, down came the dagger into the captain's left thigh and Lafitte was a corpse.

The upper deck was cleared, and the boarders rushed below on the main deck to complete their conquest. Here the slaughter was dreadful, till the pirates called out for quarter, and the carnage ceased; all the pirates that surrendered were taken to Jamaica and tried before the Admiralty court where sixteen were condemned to die, six were subsequently pardoned and ten executed.

*   *   *

Thus perished Lafitte, a man superior in talent, in knowledge of his profession, in courage, and moreover in physical strength; but unfortunately his reckless career was marked with crimes of the darkest dye.

THE STRANGE CASE OF
CAPTAIN SCARFIELD

Howard Pyle

Eleazer Cooper, or Captain Cooper, as was his better-known title in Philadelphia, was a prominent member of the Society of Friends. He was an overseer of the meeting and an occasional speaker upon particular occasions. When at home from one of his many voyages he never failed to occupy his seat in the meeting both on First Day and Fifth Day, and he was regarded by his fellow townsmen as a model of business integrity and of domestic responsibility.

More incidental to this history, however, it is to be narrated that Captain Cooper was one of those trading skippers who carried their own merchandise in their own vessels which they sailed themselves, and on whose decks they did their own bartering. His vessel was a swift, large schooner, the *Eliza Cooper*, of Philadelphia, named for his wife. His cruising grounds were the West India Islands, and his merchandise was flour and corn meal ground at the Brandywine Mills at Wilmington, Delaware.

During the War of 1812 he had earned, as was very well known, an extraordinary fortune in this trading; for flour and corn meal sold at fabulous prices in the French, Spanish, Dutch, and Danish islands, cut off, as they were, from the rest of the world by the British blockade.

The running of this blockade was one of the most hazardous maritime ventures possible, but Captain Cooper had met with such unvaried success, and had sold his merchandise at such

incredible profit that, at the end of the war, he found himself to
have become one of the wealthiest merchants of his native city.

It was known at one time that his balance in the Mechanics'
Bank was greater than that of any other individual depositor upon
the books, and it was told of him that he had once deposited in the
bank a chest of foreign silver coin, the exchanged value of which,
when translated into American currency, was upward of forty-
two thousand dollars – a prodigious sum of money in those days.

In person, Captain Cooper was tall and angular of frame. His
face was thin and severe, wearing continually an unsmiling,
mask-like expression of continent and unruffled sobriety. His
manner was dry and taciturn, and his conduct and life were
measured to the most absolute accord with the teachings of his
religious belief.

He lived in an old-fashioned house on Front Street below
Spruce – as pleasant, cheerful a house as ever a trading captain
could return to. At the back of the house a lawn sloped steeply
down toward the river. To the south stood the wharf and store-
houses; to the north an orchard and kitchen garden bloomed with
abundant verdure. Two large chestnut trees sheltered the porch
and the little space of lawn, and when you sat under them in the
shade you looked down the slope between two rows of box bushes
directly across the shining river to the Jersey shore.

At the time of our story – that is, about the year 1820 – this
property had increased very greatly in value, but it was the old
home of the Coopers, as Eleazer Cooper was entirely rich enough
to indulge his fancy in such matters. Accordingly, as he chose to
live in the same house where his father and his grandfather had
dwelt before him, he peremptorily, if quietly, refused all offers
looking toward the purchase of the lot of ground – though it was
now worth five or six times its former value.

As was said, it was a cheerful, pleasant home, impressing you
when you entered it with the feeling of spotless and all-pervading
cleanliness – a cleanliness that greeted you in the shining brass
door-knocker; that entertained you in the sitting room with its
stiff, leather-covered furniture, the brass-headed tacks whereof
sparkled like so many stars – a cleanliness that bade you farewell
in the spotless stretch of sand-sprinkled hallway, the wooden
floor of which was worn into knobs around the nail heads by the
countless scourings and scrubbings to which it had been sub-

jected and which left behind them an all-pervading faint, fragrant odor of soap and warm water.

Eleazer Cooper and his wife were childless, but one inmate made the great, silent, shady house bright with life. Lucinda Fairbanks, a niece of Captain Cooper's by his only sister, was a handsome, sprightly girl of eighteen or twenty, and a great favorite in the Quaker society of the city.

It remains only to introduce the final and, perhaps, the most important actor of the narrative, Lieut. James Mainwaring. During the past twelve months or so he had been a frequent visitor at the Cooper house. At this time he was a broad-shouldered, red-cheeked, stalwart fellow of twenty-six or twenty-eight. He was a great social favorite, and possessed the added romantic interest of having been aboard the *Constitution* when she fought the *Guerriere,* and of having, with his own hands, touched the match that fired the first gun of that great battle.

Mainwaring's mother and Eliza Cooper had always been intimate friends, and the coming and going of the young man during his leave of absence were looked upon in the house as quite a matter of course. Half a dozen times a week he would drop in to execute some little commission for the ladies, or, if Captain Cooper was at home, to smoke a pipe of tobacco with him, to sip a dram of his famous old Jamaica rum, or to play a rubber of checkers of an evening. It is not likely that either of the older people was the least aware of the real cause of his visits; still less did they suspect that any passages of sentiment had passed between the young people.

The truth was that Mainwaring and the young lady were very deeply in love. It was a love that they were obliged to keep a profound secret, for not only had Eleazer Cooper held the strictest sort of testimony against the late war – a testimony so rigorous as to render it altogether unlikely that one of so military a profession as Mainwaring practised could hope for his consent to a suit for marriage, but Lucinda could not have married one not a member of the Society of Friends without losing her own birthright membership therein. She herself might not attach much weight to such a loss of membership in the Society, but her fear of, and her respect for, her uncle led her to walk very closely in her path of duty in this respect. Accordingly she and Mainwaring met as they could – clandestinely – and the stolen moments were very sweet. With equal secrecy Lucinda had, at the request of her lover, sat for a miniature portrait to Mrs. Gregory, which miniature, set in a gold medallion, Mainwaring, with a mild, sentimental pleasure, wore hung around his neck and beneath his shirt frill next his heart.

In the month of April of the year 1820 Mainwaring received orders to report at Washington. During the preceding autumn the West India pirates, and notably Capt. Jack Scarfield, had been more than usually active, and the loss of the packet *Marblehead* (which, sailing from Charleston, South Carolina, was never heard of more) was attributed to them. Two other coasting vessels off the coast of Georgia had been looted and burned by Scarfield, and the government had at last aroused itself to the necessity of active measures for repressing these pests of the West India waters.

Mainwaring received orders to take command of the *Yankee*, a swift, light-draught, heavily armed brig of war, and to cruise about the Bahama Islands and to capture and destroy all the pirates' vessels he could there discover.

On his way from Washington to New York, where the *Yankee* was then waiting orders, Mainwaring stopped in Philadelphia to bid good-by to his many friends in that city. He called at the old Cooper house. It was on a Sunday afternoon. The spring was early and the weather extremely pleasant that day, being filled with a warmth almost as of summer. The apple trees were already in full bloom and filled all the air with their fragrance. Everywhere there seemed to be the pervading hum of bees, and the drowsy, tepid sunshine was very delightful.

At that time Eleazer was just home from an unusually successful voyage to Antigua. Mainwaring found the family sitting under one of the still leafless chestnut trees, Captain Cooper smoking his long clay pipe and lazily perusing a copy of the National Gazette. Eleazer listened with a great deal of interest to what Mainwaring had to say of his proposed cruise. He himself knew a great deal about the pirates, and, singularly unbending from his normal, stiff taciturnity, he began telling of what he knew, particularly of Captain Scarfield – in whom he appeared to take an extraordinary interest.

Vastly to Mainwaring's surprise, the old Quaker assumed the position of a defendant of the pirates, protesting that the wickedness of the accused was enormously exaggerated. He declared that he knew some of the freebooters very well and that at the most they were poor, misdirected wretches who had, by easy gradation, slid into their present evil ways, from having been tempted by the government authorities to enter into privateering in the days of the late war. He conceded that Captain Scarfield had done many cruel and wicked deeds, but he averred that he had also performed many kind and benevolent actions. The world made no note of these latter, but took care only to condemn the evil that had been done. He acknowledged that it was true that the pirate had allowed his crew to cast lots for the wife and the daughter of the skipper of the *Northern Rose*, but there were none of his accusers who told how, at the risk of his own life and the lives of all his crew, he had given succor to the schooner *Halifax*, found adrift with all hands down with yellow fever. There was no defender of his actions to tell how he and his crew of pirates had sailed the pest-stricken vessel almost into the rescuing waters of Kingston harbor. Eleazer confessed that he could not deny that when Scarfield had tied the skipper of the *Baltimore Belle* naked to the foremast of his own brig he had permitted his crew of cutthroats (who were drunk at the time) to throw bottles at the helpless captive, who died that night of the wounds he had received. For this he was doubtless very justly condemned, but who was there to praise him when he had, at the risk of his life and in the face of the authorities, carried a cargo of provisions which he himself had purchased at Tampa Bay to the Island of Bella Vista after the great hurricane of 1818? In this notable adventure he had barely escaped, after a two days' chase, the British frigate *Ceres*, whose captain, had a capture been effected, would instantly have hung the unfortunate man to the yardarm in spite of the beneficent mission he was in the act of conducting.

In all this Eleazer had the air of conducting the case for the defendant. As he talked he became more and more animated and voluble. The light went out in his tobacco pipe, and a hectic spot appeared in either thin and sallow cheek. Mainwaring sat wondering to hear the severely peaceful Quaker preacher defending so notoriously bloody and cruel a cutthroat pirate as Capt. Jack Scarfield. The warm and innocent surroundings, the old brick house looking down upon them, the odor of apple blossoms and the hum of bees seemed to make it all the more incongruous. And still the elderly Quaker skipper talked on and on with hardly an interruption, till the warm sun slanted to the west and the day began to decline.

That evening Mainwaring stayed to tea and when he parted from Lucinda Fairbanks it was after nightfall, with a clear, round moon shining in the milky sky and a radiance pallid and unreal enveloping the old house, the blooming apple trees, the sloping lawn and the shining river beyond. He implored his sweetheart to let him tell her uncle and aunt of their acknowledged love and to ask the old man's consent to it, but she would not permit him to do so. They were so happy as they were. Who knew but what her uncle might forbid their fondness? Would he not wait a little longer? Maybe it would all come right after a while. She was so fond, so tender, so tearful at the nearness of their parting that he had not the heart to insist. At the same time it was with a feeling almost of despair that he realized that he must now be gone – maybe for the space of two years – without in all that time possessing the right to call her his before the world.

When he bade farewell to the older people it was with a choking feeling of bitter disappointment. He yet felt the pressure of her cheek against his shoulder, the touch of soft and velvet lips to his own. But what were such clandestine endearments compared to what might, perchance, be his – the right of calling her his own when he was far away and upon the distant sea? And, besides, he felt like a coward who had shirked his duty.

But he was very much in love. The next morning appeared in a drizzle of rain that followed the beautiful warmth of the day before. He had the coach all to himself, and in the damp and leathery solitude he drew out the little oval picture from beneath his shirt frill and looked long and fixedly with a fond and foolish joy at the innocent face, the blue eyes, the red, smiling lips depicted upon the satinlike, ivory surface.

For the better part of five months Mainwaring cruised about in the waters surrounding the Bahama Islands. In that time he ran to earth and dispersed a dozen nests of pirates. He destroyed no less than fifteen piratical crafts of all sizes, from a large half-decked whaleboat to a three-hundred-ton barkentine. The name of the *Yankee* became a terror to every sea wolf in the western tropics, and the waters of the Bahama Islands became swept almost clean of the bloody wretches who had so lately infested it.

But the one freebooter of all others whom he sought – Capt. Jack Scarfield – seemed to evade him like a shadow, to slip through his fingers like magic. Twice he came almost within touch of the famous marauder, both times in the ominous wrecks that the pirate captain had left behind him. The first of these was the water-logged remains of a burned and still smoking wreck that he found adrift in the great Bahama channel. It was the *Water Witch*, of Salem, but he did not learn her tragic story until, two weeks later, he discovered a part of her crew at Port Maria, on the north coast of Jamaica. It was, indeed, a dreadful story to which he listened. The castaways said that they of all the vessel's crew had been spared so that they might tell the commander of the *Yankee*, should they meet him, that he might keep what he found, with Captain Scarfield's compliments, who served it up to him hot cooked.

Three weeks later he rescued what remained of the crew of the shattered, bloody hulk of the *Baltimore Belle*, eight of whose crew, headed by the captain, had been tied hand and foot and heaved overboard. Again, there was a message from Captain Scarfield to the commander of the *Yankee* that he might season what he found to suit his own taste.

Mainwaring was of a sanguine disposition, with fiery temper. He swore, with the utmost vehemence, that either he or John Scarfield would have to leave the earth.

He had little suspicion of how soon was to befall the ominous realization of his angry prophecy.

At that time one of the chief rendezvous of the pirates was the little island of San Jose, one of the southernmost of the Bahama group. Here, in the days before the coming of the *Yankee*, they were wont to put in to careen and clean their vessels and to take in a fresh supply of provisions, gunpowder, and rum, preparatory to renewing their attacks upon the peaceful commerce circulating up and down outside the islands, or through the wide stretches of the Bahama channel.

Mainwaring had made several descents upon this nest of freebooters. He had already made two notable captures, and it was here he hoped eventually to capture Captain Scarfield himself.

A brief description of this one-time notorious rendezvous of freebooters might not be out of place. It consisted of a little settlement of those wattled and mud-smeared houses such as you find through the West Indies. There were only three houses of a more pretentious sort, built of wood. One of these was a store-house, another was a rum shop, and a third a house in which dwelt a mulatto woman, who was reputed to be a sort of left-handed wife of Captain Scarfield's. The population was almost entirely black and brown. One or two Jews and a half dozen Yankee traders, of hardly dubious honesty, comprised the entire white population. The rest consisted of a mongrel accumulation of negroes and mulattoes and half-caste Spaniards, and of a multitude of black or yellow women and children. The settlement stood in a bight of the beach forming a small harbor and affording a fair anchorage for small vessels, excepting it were against the beating of a southeasterly gale. The houses, or cabins, were surrounded by clusters of coco palms and growths of bananas, and a long curve of white beach, sheltered from the large Atlantic breakers that burst and exploded upon an outer bar, was drawn like a necklace around the semi-circle of emerald-green water.

Such was the famous pirates' settlement of San Jose – a paradise of nature and a hell of human depravity and wickedness – and it was to this spot that Mainwaring paid another visit a few days after rescuing the crew of the *Baltimore Belle* from her shattered and sinking wreck.

As the little bay with its fringe of palms and its cluster of wattle huts opened up to view, Mainwaring discovered a vessel lying at anchor in the little harbor. It was a large and well-rigged schooner of two hundred and fifty or three hundred tons burden. As the *Yankee* rounded to under the stern of the stranger and dropped anchor in such a position as to bring her broadside battery to bear should the occasion require, Mainwaring set his glass to his eye to read the name he could distinguish beneath the overhang of her stern. It is impossible to describe his infinite surprise when, the white lettering starting out in the circle of the glass, he read, the *Eliza Cooper*, of Philadelphia. He could not believe the evidence of his senses. Certainly this sink of iniquity was the last place in the world he would have expected to have fallen in with Eleazer Cooper.

He ordered out the gig and had himself immediately rowed

over to the schooner. Whatever lingering doubts he might have entertained as to the identity of the vessel were quickly dispelled when he beheld Captain Cooper himself standing at the gangway to meet him. The impassive face of the friend showed neither surprise nor confusion at what must have been to him a most unexpected encounter.

But when he stepped upon the deck of the *Eliza Cooper* and looked about him, Mainwaring could hardly believe the evidence of his senses at the transformation that he beheld. Upon the main deck were eight twelve-pound carronade neatly covered with tarpaulin; in the bow a Long Tom, also snugly stowed away and covered, directed a veiled and muzzled snout out over the bowsprit.

It was entirely impossible for Mainwaring to conceal his astonishment at so unexpected a sight, and whether or not his own thoughts lent color to his imagination, it seemed to him that Eleazer Cooper concealed under the immobility of his countenance no small degree of confusion.

After Captain Cooper had led the way into the cabin and he and the younger man were seated over a pipe of tobacco and the invariable bottle of fine old Jamaica rum, Mainwaring made no attempt to refrain from questioning him as to the reason for this singular and ominous transformation.

"I am a man of peace, James Mainwaring," Eleazer replied, "but there are men of blood in these waters, and an appearance of great strength is of use to protect the innocent from the wicked. If I remained in appearance the peaceful trader I really am, how long does thee suppose I could remain unassailed in this place?"

It occurred to Mainwaring that the powerful armament he had beheld was rather extreme to be used merely as a preventive. He smoked for a while in silence and then he suddenly asked the other point-blank whether, if it came to blows with such a one as Captain Scarfield, would he make a fight of it?

The Quaker trading captain regarded him for a while in silence. His look, it seemed to Mainwaring, appeared to be dubitative as to how far he dared to be frank. "Friend James," he said at last, "I may as well acknowledge that my officers and crew are somewhat worldly. Of a truth they do not hold the same testimony as I. I am inclined to think that if it came to the point of a broil with those men of iniquity, my individual voice cast for peace would not be sufficient to keep my crew from meeting violence with violence. As for myself, thee knows who I am and what is my testimony in these matters."

Mainwaring made no comment as to the extremely questionable manner in which the Quaker proposed to beat the devil about the stump. Presently he asked his second question:

"And might I inquire," he said, "what you are doing here and why you find it necessary to come at all into such a wicked, dangerous place as this?"

"Indeed, I knew thee would ask that question of me," said the Friend, "and I will be entirely frank with thee. These men of blood are, after all, but human beings, and as human beings they need food. I have at present upon this vessel upward of two hundred and fifty barrels of flour which will bring a higher price here than anywhere else in the West Indies. To be entirely frank with thee, I will tell thee that I was engaged in making a bargain for the sale of the greater part of my merchandise when the news of thy approach drove away my best customer."

Mainwaring sat for a while in smoking silence. What the other had told him explained many things he had not before understood. It explained why Captain Cooper got almost as much for his flour and corn meal now that peace had been declared as he had obtained when the war and the blockade were in full swing. It explained why he had been so strong a defender of Captain Scarfield and the pirates that afternoon in the garden. Meantime, what was to be done? Eleazer confessed openly that he dealt with the pirates. What now was his – Mainwaring's – duty in the case? Was the cargo of the *Eliza Cooper* contraband and subject to confiscation? And then another question framed itself in his mind: Who was this customer whom his approach had driven away?

As though he had formulated the inquiry into speech the other began directly to speak of it. "I know," he said, "that in a moment thee will ask me who was this customer of whom I have just now spoken. I have no desire to conceal his name from thee. It was the man who is known as Captain Jack or Captain John Scarfield."

Mainwaring fairly started from his seat. "The devil you say!" he cried. "And how long has it been," he asked, "since he left you?"

The Quaker skipper carefully refilled his pipe, which he had by now smoked out. "I would judge," he said, "that it is a matter of four or five hours since news was brought overland by means of swift runners of thy approach. Immediately the man of wickedness disappeared." Here Eleazer set the bowl of his pipe to the candle flame and began puffing out voluminous clouds of smoke. "I would have thee understand, James Mainwaring," he resumed, "that I am no friend of this wicked and sinful man. His safety is nothing to me. It is only a question of buying upon his part and of selling upon mine. If it is any satisfaction to thee I will heartily promise to bring thee news if I hear anything of the man of Belial. I may furthermore say that I think it is likely thee will have news more or less directly of him within the space of a day. If this should happen, however, thee will have to do thy own fighting without help from me, for I am no man of combat nor of blood and will take no hand in it either way."

It struck Mainwaring that the words contained some meaning that did not appear upon the surface. This significance struck him as so ambiguous that when he went aboard the *Yankee* he confided as much of his suspicions as he saw fit to his second in command, Lieutenant Underwood. As night descended he had a double watch set and had everything prepared to repel any attack or surprise that might be attempted.

Nighttime in the tropics descends with a surprising rapidity. At one moment the earth is shining with the brightness of the twilight; the next, as it were, all things are suddenly swallowed into a gulf of darkness. The particular night of which this story treats was not entirely clear; the time of year was about the approach of the rainy season, and the tepid, tropical clouds added obscurity to the darkness of the sky, so that the night fell with even more startling quickness than usual. The blackness was very dense. Now and then a group of drifting stars swam out of a rift in the vapors, but the night was curiously silent and of a velvety darkness.

As the obscurity had deepened, Mainwaring had ordered lanthorns to be lighted and slung to the shrouds and to the stays, and the faint yellow of their illumination lighted the level white of the snug little war vessel, gleaming here and there in a starlike spark upon the brass trimmings and causing the rows of cannons to assume curiously gigantic proportions.

For some reason Mainwaring was possessed by a strange, uneasy feeling. He walked restlessly up and down the deck for a time, and then, still full of anxieties for he knew not what, went into his cabin to finish writing up his log for the day. He unstrapped his cutlass and laid it upon the table, lighted his pipe at the lanthorn and was about preparing to lay aside his coat when word was brought to him that the captain of the trading schooner was come alongside and had some private information to communicate to him.

Mainwaring surmised in an instant that the trader's visit related somehow to news of Captain Scarfield, and as immediately, in the relief of something positive to face, all of his feeling of restlessness vanished like a shadow of mist. He gave orders that Captain Cooper should be immediately shown into the cabin, and in a few moments the tall, angular form of the Quaker skipper appeared in the narrow, lanthorn-lighted space.

Mainwaring at once saw that his visitor was strangely agitated and disturbed. He had taken off his hat, and shining beads of perspiration had gathered and stood clustered upon his forehead. He did not reply to Mainwaring's greeting; he did not, indeed, seem to hear it; but he came directly forward to the table and stood leaning with one hand upon the open log book in which the lieutenant had just been writing. Mainwaring had reseated himself at the head of the table, and the tall figure of the skipper stood looking down at him as from a considerable height.

"James Mainwaring," he said, "I promised thee to report if I had news of the pirate. Is thee ready now to hear my news?"

There was something so strange in his agitation that it began to infect Mainwaring with a feeling somewhat akin to that which appeared to disturb his visitor. "I know not what you mean, sir!" he cried, "by asking if I care to hear your news. At this moment I would rather have news of that scoundrel than to have anything I know of in the world."

"Thou would? Thou would?" cried the other, with mounting agitation. "Is thee in such haste to meet him as all that? Very well; very well, then. Suppose I could bring thee face to face with him – what then? Hey? Hey? Face to face with him, James Mainwaring!"

The thought instantly flashed into Mainwaring's mind that the pirate had returned to the island; that perhaps at that moment he was somewhere near at hand.

"I do not understand you, sir," he cried. "Do you mean to tell me that you know where the villain is? If so, lose no time in informing me, for every instant of delay may mean his chance of again escaping."

"No danger of that!" the other declared, vehemently. "No danger of that! I'll tell thee where he is and I'll bring thee to him quick enough!" And as he spoke he thumped his fist against the open log book. In the vehemence of his growing excitement his eyes appeared to shine green in the lanthorn light, and the sweat that had stood in beads upon his forehead was now running in streams down his face. One drop hung like a jewel to the tip of his beaklike nose. He came a step nearer to Mainwaring and bent forward toward him, and there was something so strange and ominous in his bearing that the lieutenant instinctively drew back a little where he sat.

"Captain Scarfield sent something to you," said Eleazer, almost in a raucous voice, "something that you will be surprised to see." And the lapse in his speech from the Quaker "thee" to the plural "you" struck Mainwaring as singularly strange.

As he was speaking Eleazer was fumbling in a pocket of his long-tailed drab coat, and presently he brought something forth that gleamed in the lanthorn light.

The next moment Mainwaring saw leveled directly in his face the round and hollow nozzle of a pistol.

There was an instant of dead silence and then, "I am the man you seek!" said Eleazer Cooper, in a tense and breathless voice.

The whole thing had happened so instantaneously and unexpectedly that for the moment Mainwaring sat like one petrified. Had a thunderbolt fallen from the silent sky and burst at his feet he could not have been more stunned. He was like one held in the meshes of a horrid nightmare, and he gazed as through a mist of impossibility into the lineaments of the well-known, sober face now transformed as from within into the aspect of a devil. That face, now ashy white, was distorted into a diabolical grin. The teeth glistened in the lamplight. The brows, twisted into a tense and convulsed frown, were drawn down into black shadows, through which the eyes burned a baleful green like the eyes of a wild animal driven to bay. Again he spoke in the same breathless voice. "I am John Scarfield! Look at me, then, if you want to see a pirate!" Again there was a little time of silence, through which Mainwaring heard his watch ticking loudly from where it hung against the bulkhead. Then once more the other began speaking. "You would chase me out of the West Indies, would you? G————you! What are you come to now? You are caught in your own trap, and you'll squeal loud enough before you get out of it. Speak a word or make a movement and I'll blow your brains out against the partition behind you! Listen to what I say or you are a dead man. Sing out an order instantly for my mate and my bos'n to come here to the cabin, and be quick about it, for my finger's on the trigger, and it's only a pull to shut your mouth forever."

It was astonishing to Mainwaring, in afterward thinking about it all, how quickly his mind began to recover its steadiness after that first stunning shock. Even as the other was speaking he discovered that his brain was becoming clarified to a wonderful lucidity; his thoughts were becoming rearranged, and with a marvelous activity and an alertness he had never before experienced. He knew that if he moved to escape or uttered any outcry he would be instantly a dead man, for the circle of the pistol barrel was directed full against his forehead and with the steadiness of a rock. If he could but for an instant divert that fixed and deadly attention he might still have a chance for life. With the thought an inspiration burst into his mind and he instantly put it into execution; thought, inspiration, and action, as in a flash, were one. He must make the other turn aside his deadly gaze, and instantly he roared out in a voice that stunned his own ears: "Strike, bos'n! Strike, quick!"

Taken by surprise, and thinking, doubtless, that another enemy stood behind him, the pirate swung around like a flash with his pistol leveled against the blank boarding. Equally upon the instant he saw the trick that had been played upon him and in a second flash had turned again. The turn and return had occupied but a moment of time, but that moment, thanks to the readiness of his own invention, had undoubtedly saved Mainwaring's life. As the other turned away his gaze for that brief instant Mainwaring leaped forward and upon him. There was a flashing flame of fire as the pistol was discharged and a deafening detonation that seemed to split his brain. For a moment, with reeling senses, he supposed himself to have been shot, the next he knew he had escaped. With the energy of despair he swung his enemy around and drove him with prodigious violence against the corner of the table. The pirate emitted a grunting cry and then they fell together, Mainwaring upon the top, and the pistol clattered with them to the floor in their fall. Even as he fell, Mainwaring roared in a voice of thunder, "All hands repel boarders!" And then again, "All hands repel boarders!"

Whether hurt by the table edge or not, the fallen pirate struggled as though possessed of forty devils, and in a moment or two Mainwaring saw the shine of a long, keen knife that he had drawn from somewhere about his person. The lieutenant caught him by the wrist, but the other's muscles were as though made of steel. They both fought in despairing silence, the one to carry out his frustrated purposes to kill, the other to save his life. Again and again Mainwaring felt that the knife had been thrust against him, piercing once his arm, once his shoulder, and again his neck. He felt the warm blood streaming down his arm and body and looked about him in despair. The pistol lay near upon the deck of the cabin. Still holding the other by the wrist as he could, Mainwaring snatched up the empty weapon and struck once and again at the bald, narrow forehead beneath him. A third blow he delivered with all the force he could command, and then with a violent and convulsive throe the straining muscles beneath him relaxed and grew limp and the fight was won.

Through all the struggle he had been aware of the shouts of voices, of trampling of feet and discharge of firearms, and the thought came to him, even through his own danger, that the *Yankee* was being assaulted by the pirates. As he felt the struggling form beneath him loosen and dissolve into quietude, he leaped up, and snatching his cutlass, which still lay upon the table, rushed out upon the deck, leaving the stricken form lying twitching upon the floor behind him.

It was a fortunate thing that he had set double watches and prepared himself for some attack from the pirates, otherwise the *Yankee* would certainly have been lost. As it was, the surprise was so overwhelming that the pirates, who had been concealed in the large whaleboat that had come alongside, were not only able to gain a foothold upon the deck, but for a time it seemed as though they would drive the crew of the brig below the hatches.

But as Mainwaring, streaming with blood, rushed out upon the deck, the pirates became immediately aware that their own captain must have been overpowered, and in an instant their desperate energy began to evaporate. One or two jumped overboard; one, who seemed to be the mate, fell dead from a pistol shot, and then, in the turn of a hand, there was a rush of a retreat and a vision of leaping forms in the dusky light of the lanthorns and a sound of splashing in the water below.

The crew of the *Yankee* continued firing at the phosphorescent wakes of the swimming bodies, but whether with effect it was impossible at the time to tell.

The pirate captain did not die immediately. He lingered for three or four days, now and then unconscious, now and then semi-conscious, but always deliriously wandering. All the while he thus lay dying, the mulatto woman, with whom he lived in this part of his extraordinary dual existence, nursed and cared for him with such rude attentions as the surroundings afforded. In the wanderings of his mind the same duality of life followed him. Now and then he would appear the calm, sober, self-contained, well-ordered member of a peaceful society that his friends in his faraway home knew him to be; at other times the nether part of his nature would leap up into life like a wild beast, furious and gnashing. At the one time he talked evenly and clearly of peaceful things; at the other time he blasphemed and hooted with fury.

Several times Mainwaring, though racked by his own wounds, sat beside the dying man through the silent watches of the tropical nights. Oftentimes upon these occasions as he looked at the thin, lean face babbling and talking so aimlessly, he wondered what it all meant. Could it have been madness – madness in which the separate entities of good and bad each had, in its turn, a perfect and distinct existence? He chose to think that this was the case. Who, within his inner consciousness, does not feel that same ferine, savage man struggling against the stern, adamantine bonds of morality and decorum? Were those bonds burst asunder, as it was with this man, might not the wild beast rush forth, as it had rushed forth in him, to rend and to tear? Such were the questions that Mainwaring asked himself. And how had it all come about? By what easy gradations had the respectable Quaker skipper descended from the decorum of his home life, step by step, into such a gulf of iniquity? Many such thoughts passed through Mainwaring's mind, and he pondered them through the still reaches of the tropical nights while he sat watching the pirate captain struggle out of the world he had so long burdened. At last the poor wretch died, and the earth was well quit of one of its torments.

A systematic search was made through the island for the scattered crew, but none was captured. Either there were some secret hiding places upon the island (which was not very likely) or else they had escaped in boats hidden somewhere among the tropical foliage. At any rate they were gone.

Nor, search as he would, could Mainwaring find a trace of any of the pirate treasure. After the pirate's death and under close questioning, the weeping mulatto woman so far broke down as to confess in broken English that Captain Scarfield had taken a quantity of silver money aboard his vessel, but either she was mistaken or else the pirates had taken it thence again and had hidden it somewhere else.

Nor would the treasure ever have been found but for a most fortuitous accident. Mainwaring had given orders that the *Eliza Cooper* was to be burned, and a party was detailed to carry the order into execution. At this the cook of the *Yankee* came petitioning for some of the Wilmington and Brandywine flour to make some plum duff upon the morrow, and Mainwaring granted his request in so far that he ordered one of the men to knock open one of the barrels of flour and to supply the cook's demands.

The crew detailed to execute this modest order in connection with the destruction of the pirate vessel had not been gone a quarter of an hour when word came back that the hidden treasure had been found.

Mainwaring hurried aboard the *Eliza Cooper*, and there in the midst of the open flour barrel he beheld a great quantity of silver coin buried in and partly covered by the white meal. A systematic search was now made. One by one the flour barrels were heaved up from below and burst open on the deck and their contents searched, and if nothing but the meal was found it was swept overboard. The breeze was whitened with clouds of flour, and the white meal covered the surface of the ocean for yards around.

In all, upward of one hundred and fifty thousand dollars was found concealed beneath the innocent flour and meal. It was no wonder the pirate captain was so successful, when he could upon an instant's notice transform himself from a wolf of the ocean to a peaceful Quaker trader selling flour to the hungry towns and settlements among the scattered islands of the West Indies, and so carrying his bloody treasure safely into his quiet Northern home.

In concluding this part of the narrative it may be added that a wide strip of canvas painted black was discovered in the hold of the *Eliza Cooper*. Upon it, in great white letters, was painted the name, "The Bloodhound". Undoubtedly this was used upon occasions to cover the real and peaceful title of the trading schooner, just as its captain had, in reverse, covered his sanguine and cruel life by a thin sheet of morality and respectability.

This is the true story of the death of Capt. Jack Scarfield.

The Newburyport chap-book, of which I have already spoken, speaks only of how the pirate disguised himself upon the ocean as a Quaker trader.

Nor is it likely that anyone ever identified Eleazer Cooper with the pirate, for only Mainwaring of all the crew of the *Yankee* was exactly aware of the true identity of Captain Scarfield. All that was ever known to the world was that Eleazer Cooper had been killed in a fight with the pirates.

In a little less than a year Mainwaring was married to Lucinda Fairbanks. As to Eleazer Cooper's fortune, which eventually came into the possession of Mainwaring through his wife, it was many times a subject of speculation to the lieutenant how it had been earned. There were times when he felt well assured that a part of it at least was the fruit of piracy, but it was entirely impossible to guess how much more was the result of legitimate trading.

For a little time it seemed to Mainwaring that he should give it all up, but this was at once so impracticable and so quixotic that he presently abandoned it, and in time his qualms and misdoubts faded away and he settled himself down to enjoy that which had come to him through his marriage.

In time the Mainwarings removed to New York, and ultimately the fortune that the pirate Scarfield had left behind him was used in part to found the great shipping house of Mainwaring & Bigot, whose famous transatlantic packet ships were in their time the admiration of the whole world.

AMERICAN PIRATE: THE BLOODY CAREER OF CAPTAIN GIBBS

Charles Ellms

This atrocious and cruel pirate, when very young became addicted to vices uncommon in youths of his age, and so far from the gentle reproof and friendly admonition, or the more severe chastisement of a fond parent, having its intended effect, it seemed to render him still worse, and to incline him to repay those whom he ought to have esteemed as his best friends and who had manifested so much regard for his welfare, with ingratitude and neglect. His infamous career and ignominious death on the gallows brought down the "grey hairs of his parents in sorrow to the grave". The poignant affliction which the infamous crimes of children bring upon their relatives ought to be one of the most effective persuasions for them to refrain from vice.

Charles Gibbs was born in the state of Rhode Island, in 1794; his parents and connexions were of the first respectability. When at school, he was very apt to learn, but so refractory and sulky, that neither the birch nor good counsel made any impression on him, and he was expelled from the school.

He was now made to labor on a farm; but having a great antipathy to work, when about fifteen years of age, feeling a great inclination to roam, and like too many unreflecting youths of that age, a great fondness for the sea, he in opposition to the friendly counsel of his parents, privately left them and entered on board the United States sloop-of-war, *Hornet*, and was in the action when she captured the British sloop-of-war *Peacock*, off the coast of Pernambuco. Upon the return of the *Hornet* to the United States, her brave commander, Capt. Lawrence, was promoted for his gallantry to the command of the unfortunate *Chesapeake*, and to which he was followed by young Gibbs, who took a very distinguished part in the engagement with the *Shannon*, which resulted in the death of Lawrence and the capture of the *Chesapeake*. Gibbs states that while on board the *Chesapeake* the crew previous to the action, were almost in a state of mutiny, growing out of the non payment of the prize money, and that the address of Capt. Lawrence was received by them with coldness and murmurs.

After the engagement, Gibbs became with the survivors of the crew a prisoner of war, and as such was confined in Dartmoor prison until exchanged.

After his exchange, he returned to Boston, where having determined to abandon the sea, he applied to his friends in Rhode Island, to assist him in commencing business; they accordingly lent him one thousand dollars as a capital to begin with. He opened a grocery in Ann Street, near what was then called the Tin Pot, a place full of abandoned women and dissolute fellows. As he dealt chiefly in liquor, and had a "License to retail Spirits", his drunkery was thronged with customers. But he sold his groceries chiefly to loose girls who paid him in their coin, which, although it answered his purpose, would neither buy him goods or pay his rent, and he found his stock rapidly dwindling away without his receiving any cash to replenish it. By dissipation and inattention his new business proved unsuccessful to him. He resolved to abandon it and again try the sea for a subsistence. With a hundred dollars in his pocket, the remnant of his property, he embarked in the ship *John*, for Buenos Ayres, and his means being exhausted soon after his arrival there, he entered on board a Buenos Ayrean privateer and sailed on a cruise. A quarrel between the officers and crew in regard to the division of prize money, led eventually to a mutiny; and the mutineers gained the ascendancy, took possession of the vessel, landed the crew on the coast of Florida, and steered for the West Indies, with hearts resolved to make their fortunes at all hazards, and where in a short time, more than twenty vessels were captured by them and nearly four hundred human beings murdered!

Havana was the resort of these pirates to dispose of their plunder; and Gibbs sauntered about this place with impunity and was acquainted in all the out of the way and bye places of that hot bed of pirates the Regla. He and his comrades even lodged in the very houses with many of the American officers who were sent out to take them. He was acquainted with many of the officers and was apprised of all their intended movements before they left the harbor. On one occasion, the American ship *Caroline*, was captured by two of their piratical vessels off Cape Antonio. They were busily engaged in landing the cargo, when the British sloop-of-war, *Jearus*, hove in sight and sent her barges to attack them. The pirates defended themselves for some time behind a small four gun battery which they had erected, but in the end were forced to abandon their own vessel and the prize and fly to the mountains for safety. The *Jearus* found here twelve vessels burnt to the water's edge, and it was satisfactorily ascertained that their crews, amounting to one hundred and fifty persons had been murdered. The crews, if it was thought not necessary otherways to dispose of them were sent adrift in their boats, and frequently without any thing on which they could subsist a single day; nor were all so fortunate thus to escape. "Dead men can tell no tales," was a common saying among them; and as soon as a ship's crew were taken, a short consultation was held; and if it was the opinion of a majority that it would be better to take life than to spare it, a single nod or wink from the captain was sufficient; regardless of age or sex, all entreaties for mercy were then made in vain; they possessed not the tender feelings, to be operated upon by the shrieks and expiring groans of the devoted victims! there was a strife among them, who with his own hands could despatch the greatest number, and in the shortest period of time.

Without any other motives than to gratify their hellish propensities (in their intoxicated moments), blood was not unfrequently and unnecessarily shed, and many widows and orphans probably made, when the lives of the unfortunate victims might have been spared, and without the most distant prospect of any evil consequences (as regarded themselves), resulting therefrom.

Gibbs states that sometime in the course of the year 1819, he left Havana and came to the United States, bringing with him about $30,000. He passed several weeks in the city of New York, and then went to Boston, whence he took passage for Liverpool in the ship *Emerald*. Before he sailed, however, he had squandered a large part of his money by dissipation and gambling. He remained in Liverpool a few months, and then returned to Boston. His residence in Liverpool at that time is satisfactorily ascertained from another source besides his own confession. A female now in New York was well acquainted with him there, where, she says, he lived like a gentleman, with apparently abundant means of support. In speaking of his acquaintance with this female he says, "I fell in with a woman, who I thought was all virtue, but she deceived me, and I am sorry to say that a heart that never felt abashed at scenes of carnage and blood, was made a child of for a time by her, and I gave way to dissipation to drown the torment. How often when the fumes of liquor have subsided, have I thought of my good and affectionate parents, and of their Godlike advice! But when the little monitor began to move within me, I immediately seized the cup to hide myself from myself, and drank until the sense of intoxication was renewed. My friends advised me to behave myself like a man, and promised me their assistance, but the demon still haunted me, and I spurned their advice."

In 1826, he revisited the United States, and hearing of the war between Brazil and the Republic of Buenos Ayres, sailed from Boston in the brig *Hitty*, of Portsmouth, with a determination, as he states, of trying his fortune in defence of a republican government. Upon his arrival he made himself known to Admiral Brown, and communicated his desire to join their navy. The admiral accompanied him to the Governor, and a Lieutenant's commission being given him, he joined a ship of 34 guns, called the *Twenty Fifth of May*. "Here," says Gibbs, "I found Lieutenant Dodge, an old acquaintance, and a number of other persons with whom I had sailed. When the Governor gave me the commission he told me they wanted no cowards in their navy, to which I replied that I thought he would have no apprehension of my cowardice or skill when he became acquainted with me. He thanked me, and said he hoped he should not be deceived; upon which we drank to his health and to the success of the Republic. He then presented me with a sword, and told me to wear that as my companion through the doubtful struggle in which the republic was engaged. I told him I never would disgrace it, so long as I had a nerve in my arm. I remained no board the ship in the capacity of 5th Lieutenant, for about four months, during which time we had a number of skirmishes with the enemy. Having succeeded in gaining the confidence of Admiral Brown, he put me in command of a privateer schooner, mounting two long 24 pounders and 46 men. I sailed from Buenos Ayres, made two good cruises, and returned safely to port. I then bought one half of a new Baltimore schooner, and sailed again, but was captured seven days out, and carried into Rio Janeiro, where the Brazilians paid me my change. I remained there until peace took place, then returned to Buenos Ayres, and thence to New York.

"After the lapse of about a year, which I passed in travelling from place to place, the war between France and Algiers attracted my attention. Knowing that the French commerce presented a fine opportunity for plunder, I determined to embark for Algiers and offer my services to the Dey. I accordingly took passage from New York, in the *Sally Ann*, belonging to Bath, landed at Barcelona, crossed to Port Mahon, and endeavored to make my way to Algiers. The vigilance of the French fleet prevented the accomplishment of my design, and I proceeded to Tunis. There finding it unsafe to attempt a journey to Algiers across the desert, I amused myself with contemplating the ruins of Carthage, and reviving my recollections of her war with the Romans. I afterwards took passage to Marseilles, and thence to Boston."

An instance of the most barbarous and cold blooded murder of which the wretched Gibbs gives an account in the course of his confessions, is that of an innocent and beautiful female of about 17 or 18 years of age! She was with her parents a passenger on board a Dutch ship, bound from Curracoa to Holland; there were a number of other passengers, male and female, on board, all of whom except the young lady above-mentioned were put to death; her unfortunate parents were inhumanly butchered before her eyes, and she was doomed to witness the agonies and to hear the expiring, heart-piercing groans of those whom she held most dear, and on whom she depended for protection! The life of their wretched daughter was spared for the most nefarious purposes – she was taken by the pirates to the west end of Cuba, where they had a rendezvous, with a small fort that mounted four guns – here she was confined about two months, and where, as has been said by the murderer Gibbs, "she received such treatment, the bare recollection of which causes me to shudder!" At the expiration of the two months she was taken by the pirates on board of one of their vessels, and among whom a consultation was soon after held, which resulted in the conclusion that it would be necessary for their own personal safety, to put her to death! and to her a fatal dose of poison was accordingly administered, which soon proved fatal! when her pure and immortal spirit took its flight to that God, whom, we believe, will avenge her wrongs! Her lifeless body was then committed to the deep by two of the merciless wretches with as much unconcern, as if it had been that of the meanest brute! Gibbs persists in the declaration that in this horrid transaction he took no part, that such was his pity for this poor ill-fated female, that he interceded for her life so long as he could do it with safety to his own!

Gibbs in his last visit to Boston remained there but a few days, when he took passage to New Orleans, and there entered as one of the crew on board the brig *Vineyard*; and for assisting in the murder of the unfortunate captain and mate of which, he was justly condemned, and the awful sentence of death passed upon him! The particulars of the bloody transaction (agreeable to the testimony of Dawes and Brownrigg, the two principal witnesses) are as follows: The brig *Vineyard*, Capt. William Thornby, sailed from New Orleans about the 9th of November, for Philadelphia, with a cargo of 112 bales of cotton, 113 hhds. sugar, 54 casks of molasses and 54,000 dollars in specie. Besides the captain there were on board the brig, William Roberts, mate, six seamen shipped at New Orleans, and the cook. Robert Dawes, one of the crew, states on examination, that when, about five days out, he was told that there was money on board, Charles Gibbs, E. Church and the steward then determined to take possession of the brig. They asked James Talbot, another of the crew, to join them. He said no, as he did not believe there was money in the vessel. They concluded to kill the captain and mate, and if Talbot and John Brownrigg would not join them, to kill them also. The next night they talked of doing it, and got their clubs ready. Dawes dared not say a word, as they declared they would kill him if he did; as they did not agree about killing Talbot and Brownrigg, two shipmates, it was put off. They next concluded to kill the captain and mate on the night of November 22, but did not get ready; but, on the night of the 23d, between twelve and one o'clock, as Dawes was at the helm, saw the steward come up with a light and a knife in his hand; he dropt the light and seizing the pump break, struck the captain with it over the head or back of the neck; the captain was sent forward by the blow, and halloed, oh! and murder! once; he was then seized by Gibbs and the cook, one by the head and the other by the heels, and thrown overboard. Atwell and Church stood at the companion way, to strike down the mate when he should come up. As he came up and enquired what was the matter they struck him over the head – he ran back into the cabin, and Charles Gibbs followed him down; but as it was dark, he could not find him – Gibbs came on deck for the light, with which he returned. Dawes' light being taken from him, he could not see to steer, and he in consequence left the helm, to see what was going on below. Gibbs found the mate and seized him, while Atwell and Church came down and struck him with a pump break and a club; he was then dragged upon deck; they called for Dawes to come to them, and as he came up the mate seized his hand, and gave him a death gripe! three of them then hove him overboard, but which three Dawes does not know; the mate when cast overboard was not dead, but called after them twice while in the water! Dawes says he was so frightened that he hardly knew what to do. They then requested him to call Talbot, who was in the forecastle, saying his prayers; he came up and said it would be his turn next! but they gave him some grog, and told him not to be afraid, as they would not hurt him; if he was true to them, he should fare as well as they did. One of those who had been engaged in the bloody deed got drunk, and another became crazy!

After killing the captain and mate, they set about overhauling the vessel, and got up one keg of Mexican dollars. They then divided the captain's clothes, and money – about 40 dollars, and a gold watch. Dawes, Talbot and Brownrigg (who were all innocent of the murder) were obliged to do as they were commanded – the former, who was placed at the helm, was ordered to steer for Long Island. On the day following, they divided several kegs of the specie, amounting to five thousand dollars each – they made bags and sewed the money up. After this division, they divided the remainder of the money without counting it. On Sunday, when about 15 miles S.S.E. of Southampton Light, they got the boats out and put half the money in each – they then scuttled the vessel and set fire to it in the cabin, and took to the boats. Gibbs, after the murder, took charge of the vessel as captain. From the papers they learnt that the money belonged to Stephen Girard. With the boats they made the land about daylight. Dawes and his three companions were in the long boat; the others, with Atwell, were in the jolly boat – on coming to the bar the boats struck – in the long boat, they threw overboard a trunk of clothes and a great deal of money, in all about 5000 dollars – the jolly boat foundered; they saw the boat fill, and heard them cry out, and saw them clinging to the masts – they went ashore on Barron Island, and buried the money in the sand, but very lightly. Soon after they met with a gunner, whom they requested to conduct them where they could get some refreshments. They were by him conducted to Johnson's (the only man living on the island,) where they staid all night – Dawes went to bed at about 10 o'clock – Jack Brownrigg sat up with Johnson, and in the morning told Dawes that he had told Johnson all about the murder. Johnson went in the morning with the steward for the clothes, which were left on the top of the place where they buried the money, but does not believe they took away the money.

The prisoners (Gibbs and Wansley) were brought to trial at the February term of the United States Court, holden in the city of New York; when the foregoing facts being satisfactorily proved, they were pronounced guilty, and on the 11th March last, the awful sentence of the law was passed upon them in the following affecting and impressive manner: The Court opened at 11 o'clock, Judge Betts presiding. A few minutes after that hour, Mr. Hamilton, District Attorney, rose and said – May it please the Court, Thomas J. Wansley, the prisoner at the bar, having been tried by a jury of his country, and found guilty of the murder of Captain Thornby, I now move that the sentence of the Court be pronounced upon that verdict.

By the Court. Thomas J. Wansley, you have heard what has been said by the District Attorney – by the Grand Jury of the South District of New York, you have been arraigned for the wilful murder of Captain Thornby, of the brig *Vineyard*; you have been put upon your trial, and after a patient and impartial hearing, you have been found Guilty. The public prosecutor now moves for judgment on that verdict; have you any thing to say, why the sentence of the law should not be passed upon you?

Thomas J. Wansley. I will say a few words, but it is perhaps of no use. I have often understood that there is a great deal of difference in respect of color, and I have seen it in this Court. Dawes and Brownrigg were as guilty as I am, and these witnesses have tried to fasten upon me greater guilt than is just, for their life has been given to them. You have taken the blacks from their own country, to bring them here to treat them ill. I have seen this. The witnesses, the jury, and the prosecuting Attorney consider me more guilty than Dawes, to condemn me – for otherwise the law must have punished him; he should have had the same verdict, for he was a perpetrator in the conspiracy. Notwithstanding my participating, they have sworn falsely for the purpose of taking my life; they would not even inform the Court, how I gave information of money being on board; they had the biggest part of the money, and have sworn falsely. I have said enough. I will say no more.

By the Court. The Court will wait patiently and hear all you have to say; if you have any thing further to add, proceed.

Wansley then proceeded. In the first place, I was the first to ship on board the *Vineyard* at New Orleans, I knew nobody; I saw the money come on board. The judge that first examined me, did not take my deposition down correctly. When talking with the crew on board, said the brig was an old craft, and when we arrived at Philadelphia, we all agreed to leave her. It was mentioned to me that there was plenty of money on board. Henry Atwell said "let's have it." I knew no more of this for some days. Atwell came to me again and asked "what think you of taking the money." I thought it was a joke, and paid no attention to it. The next day he said they had determined to take the brig and money, and that they were the strongest party, and would murder the officers, and he that informed should suffer with them. I knew Church in Boston, and in a joke asked him how it was made up in the ship's company; his reply, that it was he and Dawes. There was no arms on board as was ascertained; the conspiracy was known to the whole company, and had I informed, my life would have been taken, and though I knew if I was found out my life would be taken by law, which is the same thing, so I did not inform. I have committed murder and I know I must die for it.

By the Court. If you wish to add any thing further you will still be heard.

Wansley. No sir, I believe I have said enough.

The District Attorney rose and moved for judgment on Gibbs, in the same manner as in the case of Wansley, and the Court having addressed Gibbs, in similar terms, concluded by asking what he had to say why the sentence of the law should not now be passed upon him.

Charles Gibbs said, I wish to state to the Court, how far I am guilty and how far I am innocent in this transaction. When I left New Orleans, I was a stranger to all on board, except Dawes and Church. It was off Tortugas that Atwell first told me there was money on board, and proposed to me to take possession of the brig. I refused at that time. The conspiracy was talked of for some days, and at last I agreed that I would join. Brownrigg, Dawes, Church, and the whole agreed that they would. A few days after, however, having thought of the affair, I mentioned to Atwell, what a dreadful thing it was to take a man's life, and commit piracy, and recommended him to "abolish" their plan. Atwell and Dawes remonstrated with me; I told Atwell that if ever he would speak of the subject again, I would break his nose. Had I kept to my resolution I would not have been brought here to receive my sentence. It was three days afterwards that the murder was committed. Brownrigg agreed to call up the captain from the cabin, and this man (pointing to Wansley) agreed to strike the first blow. The captain was struck and I suppose killed, and I lent a hand to throw him overboard. But for the murder of the mate, of which I have been found guilty, I am innocent – I had nothing to do with that. The mate was murdered by Dawes and Church; that I am innocent of this I commit my soul to that God who will judge all flesh – who will judge all murderers and false swearers, and the wicked who deprive the innocent of his right. I have nothing more to say.

★   ★   ★

By the Court. Thomas J. Wansley and Charles Gibbs, the Court has listened to you patiently and attentively; and although you have said something in your own behalf, yet the Court has heard nothing to affect the deepest and most painful duty that he who presides over a public tribunal has to perform.

You, Thomas J. Wansley, conceive that a different measure of justice has been meted out to you, because of your color. Look back upon your whole course of life; think of the laws under which you have lived, and you will find that to white or black, to free or bond, there is no ground for your allegations; that they are not supported by truth or justice. Admit that Brownrigg and Dawes have sworn falsely; admit that Dawes was concerned with you; admit that Brownrigg is not innocent; admit, in relation to both, that they are guilty, the whole evidence has proved beyond a doubt that you are guilty; and your own words admit that you were an active agent in perpetrating this horrid crime. Two fellow beings who confided in you, and in their perilous voyage called in your assistance, yet you, without reason or provocation, have maliciously taken their lives.

If, peradventure, there was the slightest foundation for a doubt of your guilt, in the mind of the Court, judgment would be arrested, but there is none; and it now remains to the Court to pronounce the most painful duty that devolves upon a civil magistrate. The Court is persuaded of your guilt; it can form no other opinion. Testimony has been heard before the Court and Jury – from that we must form our opinion. We must proceed upon testimony, ascertain facts by evidence of witnesses, on which we must inquire, judge and determine as to guilt or innocence, by that evidence alone. You have been found guilty. You now stand for the last time before an earthly tribunal, and by your own acknowledgments, the sentence of the law falls just on your heads. When men in ordinary cases come under the penalty of the law there is generally some palliative – something to warm the sympathy of the Court and Jury. Men may be led astray, and under the influence of passion have acted under some long smothered resentment, suddenly awakened by the force of circumstances, depriving him of reason, and then they may take the life of a fellow being. Killing, under that kind of excitement, might possibly awaken some sympathy, but that was not your case; you had no provocation. What offence had Thornby or

Roberts committed against you? They entrusted themselves with you, as able and trustworthy citizens; confiding implicitly in you; no one act of theirs, after a full examination, appears to have been offensive to you; yet for the purpose of securing the money you coolly determined to take their lives – you slept and deliberated over the act; you were tempted on, and yielded; you entered into the conspiracy, with cool and determined calculation to deprive two human beings of their lives, and it was done.

You, Charles Gibbs, have said that you are not guilty of the murder of Roberts; but were you not there, strongly instigating the murderers on, and without stretching out a hand to save him? – It is murder as much to stand by and encourage the deed, as to stab with a knife, strike with a hatchet, or shoot with a pistol. It is not only murder in law, but in your own feelings and in your own conscience. Notwithstanding all this, I cannot believe that your feelings are so callous, so wholly callous, that your own minds do not melt when you look back upon the unprovoked deeds of yourselves, and those confederated with you.

You are American citizens – this country affords means of instruction to all: your appearance and your remarks have added evidence that you are more than ordinarily intelligent; that your education has enabled you to participate in the advantages of information open to all classes. The Court will believe that when you were young you looked with strong aversion on the course of life of the wicked. In early life, in boyhood, when you heard of the conduct of men, who engaged in robbery – nay more, when you heard of cold blooded murder – how you must have shrunk from the recital. Yet now, after having participated in the advantages of education, after having arrived at full maturity, you stand here as robbers and murderers.

It is a perilous employment of life that you have followed; in this way of life the most enormous crimes that man can commit, are MURDER AND PIRACY. With what detestation would you in early life have looked upon the man who would have raised his hand against his officer, or have committed piracy! Yet now you both stand here murderers and pirates, tried and found guilty – you Wansley of the murder of your Captain, and you, Gibbs, of the murder of your Mate. The evidence has convicted you of rising in mutiny against the master of the vessel, for that alone, the law is DEATH! – of murder and robbery on the high seas, for that crime, the law adjudges DEATH – of destroying the vessel and embezzling the cargo, even for scuttling and burning the vessel alone the law is DEATH; yet of all these the evidence has convicted you, and it only remains now for the Court to pass the sentence of the law. It is, that you, Thomas J. Wansley and Charles Gibbs be taken hence to the place of confinement, there to remain in close custody, that thence you be taken to the place of execution, and on the 22d April next, between the hours of 10 and 4 o'clock, you be both publicly hanged by the neck until you are DEAD – and that your bodies be given to the College of Physicians and Surgeons for dissection.

The Court added, that the only thing discretionary with it, was the time of execution; it might have ordered that you should instantly have been taken from the stand to the scaffold, but the sentence has been deferred to as distant a period as prudent – six weeks. But this time has not been granted for the purpose of giving you any hope for pardon or commutation of the sentence; – just as sure as you live till the twenty-second of April, as surely you will suffer death – therefore indulge not a hope that this sentence will be changed!

The Court then spoke of the terror in all men of death! – how they cling to life whether in youth, manhood or old age. What an awful thing it is to die! how in the perils of the sea, when rocks or storms threaten the loss of the vessel, and the lives of all on board, how the crew will labor, night and day, in the hope of escaping shipwreck and death! alluded to the tumult, bustle and confusion of battle – yet even there the hero clings to life. The Court adverted not only to the certainty of their coming doom on earth, but to THINK OF HEREAFTER – that they should seriously think and reflect of their FUTURE STATE! that they would be assisted in their devotions no doubt, by many pious men.

When the Court closed, Charles Gibbs asked, if during his imprisonment, his friends would be permitted to see him. The Court answered that that lay with the Marshal, who then said that no difficulty would exist on that score. The remarks of the Prisoners were delivered in a strong, full-toned and unwavering voice, and they both seemed perfectly resigned to the fate which inevitably awaited them. While Judge Betts was delivering his address to them, Wansley was deeply affected and shed tears –

but Gibbs gazed with a steady and unwavering eye, and no sign betrayed the least emotion of his heart. After his condemnation, and during his confinement, his frame became somewhat enfeebled, his face paler, and his eyes more sunken; but the air of his bold, enterprising and desperate mind still remained. In his narrow cell, he seemed more like an object of pity than vengeance – was affable and communicative, and when he smiled, exhibited so mild and gentle a countenance, that no one would take him to be a villain. His conversation was concise and pertinent, and his style of illustration quite original.

Gibbs was married in Buenos Ayres, where he has a child now living. His wife is dead. By a singular concurrence of circumstances, the woman with whom he became acquainted in Liverpool, and who is said at that time to have borne a decent character, was lodged in the same prison with himself. During his confinement he wrote her two letters – one of them is subjoined, to gratify the perhaps innocent curiosity which is naturally felt to know the peculiarities of a man's mind and feelings under such circumstances, and not for the purpose of intimating a belief that he was truly penitent. The reader will be surprised with the apparent readiness with which he made quotations from Scripture.

BELLEVUE PRISON, March 20, 1831.

It is with regret that I take my pen in hand to address you with these few lines, under the great embarrassment of my feelings placed within these gloomy walls, my body bound with chains, and under the awful sentence of death! It is enough to throw the strongest mind into gloomy prospects! but I find that Jesus Christ is sufficient to give consolation to the most despairing soul. For he saith, that he that cometh to me I will in no ways cast out. But it is impossible to describe unto you the horror of my feelings. My breast is like the tempestuous ocean, raging in its own shame, harrowing up the bottom of my soul! But I look forward to that serene calm when I shall sleep with Kings and Counsellors of the earth. There the wicked cease from troubling – and there the weary are at rest! – There the prisoners rest together – they hear not the voice of the oppressor; and I trust that there my breast will not be ruffled by the storm of sin – for the thing which I greatly feared has come upon me. I was not in safety, neither had I rest; yet trouble came. It is the Lord, let him do what seemeth to him good. When I saw you in Liverpool, and a peaceful calm wafted across both our breasts, and justice no claim upon us, little did I think to meet you in the gloomy walls of a strong prison, and the arm of justice stretched out with the sword of law, awaiting the appointed period to execute the dreadful sentence. I have had a fair prospect in the world, at last it budded, and brought forth the gallows. I am shortly to mount that scaffold, and to bid adieu to this world, and all that was ever dear to my breast. But I trust when my body is mounted on the gallows high, the heavens above will smile and pity me. I hope that you will reflect on your past, and fly to that Jesus who stands with open arms to receive you. Your character is lost, it is true. When the wicked turneth from the wickedness that they have committed, they shall save their soul alive.

Let us imagine for a moment that we see the souls standing before the awful tribunal, and we hear its dreadful sentence, depart ye cursed into everlasting fire. Imagine you hear the awful lamentations of a soul in hell. It would be enough to melt your heart, if it was as hard as adamant. You would fall upon your knees and plead for God's mercy, as a famished person would for food, or as a dying criminal would for a pardon. We soon, very soon, must go the way whence we shall ne'er return. Our names will be struck off the records of the living, and enrolled in the vast catalogues of the dead. But may it ne'er be numbered with the damned. – I hope it will please God to set you at your liberty, and that you may see the sins and follies of your life past. I shall now close my letter with a few words which I hope you will receive as from a dying man; and I hope that every important truth of this letter may sink deep in your heart, and be a lesson to you through life.

Rising griefs distress my soul,
And tears on tears successive roll–
For many an evil voice is near,
To chide my woes and mock my fear–

And silent memory weeps alone,
O'er hours of peace and gladness known.
    I still remain your sincere friend, CHARLES GIBBS.

In another letter which the wretched Gibbs wrote after his condemnation to one who had been his early friend, he writes as follows: "Alas! it is now, and not until now, that I have become sensible of my wicked life, from my childhood, and the enormity of the crime, for which I must shortly suffer an ignominious death! – I would to God that I never had been born, or that I had died in my infancy! – the hour of reflection has indeed come, but come too late to prevent justice from cutting me off – my mind recoils with horror at the thoughts of the unnatural deeds of which I have been guilty! – my repose rather prevents than affords me relief, as my mind, while I slumber, is constantly disturbed by frightful dreams of my approaching awful dissolution!"

On Friday, April twenty-second, Gibbs and Wansley paid the penalty of their crimes. Both prisoners arrived at the gallows about twelve o'clock, accompanied by the marshal, his aids, and some twenty or thirty United States' marines. Two clergymen attended them to the fatal spot, where everything being in readiness, and the ropes adjusted about their necks, the Throne of Mercy was fervently addressed in their behalf. Wansley then prayed earnestly himself, and afterwards joined in singing a hymn. These exercises concluded, Gibbs addressed the spectators nearly as follows:

MY DEAR FRIENDS,

    My crimes have been heinous – and although I am now about to suffer for the murder of Mr. Roberts, I solemnly declare my innocence of the transaction. It is true, I stood by and saw the fatal deed done, and stretched not forth my arm to save him; the technicalities of the law believe me guilty of the charge – but in the presence of my God – before whom I shall be in a few minutes – I declare I did not murder him.

    I have made a full and frank confession to Mr. Hopson, which probably most of my hearers present have already read; and should any of the friends of those whom I have been accessary to, or engaged in the murder of, be now present, before my Maker I beg their forgiveness – it is the only boon I ask – and as I hope for pardon through the blood of Christ, surely this request will not be withheld by man, to a worm like myself, standing as I do, on the very verge of eternity! Another moment, and I cease to exist – and could I find in my bosom room to imagine that the spectators now assembled had forgiven me, the scaffold would have no terrors, nor could the precept which my much respected friend, the marshal of the district, is about to execute. Let me then, in this public manner, return my sincere thanks to him, for his kind and gentlemanly deportment during my confinement. He was to me like a father, and his humanity to a dying man I hope will be duly appreciated by an enlightened community.

My first crime was piracy, for which my life would pay for forfeit on conviction; no punishment could be inflicted on me further than that, and therefore I had nothing to fear but detection, for had my offences been millions of times more aggravated than they are now, death must have satisfied all.

Gibbs having concluded, Wansley began. He said he might be called a pirate, a robber, and a murderer, and he was all of these, but he hoped and trusted God would, through Christ, wash away his aggravated crimes and offences, and not cast him entirely out. His feelings, he said, were so overpowered that he hardly knew how to address those about him, but he frankly admitted the justness of the sentence, and concluded by declaring that he had no hope of pardon except through the atoning blood of his Redeemer, and wished that his sad fate might teach others to shun the broad road to ruin, and travel in that of virtue, which would lead to honor and happiness in this world, and an immortal crown of glory in that to come.

He then shook hands with Gibbs, the officers, and clergymen – their caps were drawn over their faces, a handkerchief dropped by Gibbs as a signal to the executioner caused the cord to be severed, and in an instant they were suspended in air. Wansley folded his hands before him, soon died with very trifling struggles. Gibbs died hard; before he was run up, and did not again remove them, but after being near two minutes suspended, he raised his right hand and partially removed his cap, and in the course of another minute, raised the same hand to his mouth. His dress was a blue round-about jacket and trousers, with a foul anchor in white on his right arm. Wansley wore a white frock coat, trimmed with black, with trousers of the same color.

After the bodies had remained on the gallows the usual time, they were taken down and given to the surgeons for dissection.

Gibbs was rather below the middle stature, thick set and powerful. The form of Wansley was a perfect model of manly beauty.

"the poor wretch was now exposed
naked to the full heat of the sun"

THE ATROCITIES OF THE PIRATES

Aaron Smith

*Aaron Smith was captured by Cuban pirates in 1822, when his ship
was boarded en route to England from Jamaica. The pirates forcibly
employed him as navigator, doctor and sail-maker. Smith found
little honour among these thieves of the sea. Here Smith recounts the
pirate captain's put down of a suspected mutiny.*

In the afternoon a boat full of men appeared coming towards the
schooner, which, upon examination, was found to contain some
of the chief mate's party. No sooner was this known than the
captain declared he would kill them all, and ordered thirty
muskets to be loaded and brought on deck. When the boat
was about two hundred yards from the schooner, the men ceased
rowing, and held up a white handkerchief for a signal, as if
doubtful of their safety, which was answered by a similar one
from on board, and they again advanced. When within reach of
the musketry, the dreadful order of "fire" was given. Five of the
men fell in the boat, the sixth leaped over and began to swim,
after whom a boat was despatched. On his being brought on
board, the captain told him the accusation that was against him
and his party, and threatened him with a cruel and lingering
death, if he did not confess the whole truth. In vain did he declare
his innocence, and ignorance of any plot; the ruffian was resolved
to glut his vengeance, and ordered him to be stripped and
exposed, naked, wounded, and bleeding as he was, to the scorching fervour of a July sun; the July sun of a tropical climate!

The feelings of humanity got the better of my caution, and I
entreated the captain not to torture the poor wretch in that

dreadful manner, declaring that I firmly believed him innocent; for, had he been guilty, torture and terror would have wrung a confession from him. In vain I pleaded, in vain I represented the inhumanity of punishing a poor wretch, in all probability innocent of the crime laid to his charge. He was deaf to my entreaties, & threatened me with vengeance for my interference, declaring that he had not done half that he intended to do.

Having said this, he turned to the man, told him that he should be killed, and therefore advised him to prepare for death, or confess himself to any of the crew whom I chose to call aside for that purpose.

The man persisted in his plea of innocence, declared that he had nothing to confess, and entreated them all to spare his life. They paid no attention to his assertions, but, by the order of the captain, the man was put into the boat, pinioned, and lashed in the stern, and five of the crew were directed to arm themselves with pistols and muskets and to go in her. The captain then ordered me to go with them, savagely remarking that I should now see how he punished such rascals, and giving directions to the boat's crew to row for three hours backwards and forwards through a narrow creek formed by a desert island and the island of Cuba. "I will see," cried he, exultingly, "whether the musquitoes & the sandflies will not make him confess." Prior to our leaving the schooner, the thermometer was above ninety degrees in the shade, and the poor wretch was now exposed naked to the full heat of the sun. In this state we took him to the channel, one side of which was bordered by swamps full of mangrove trees, and swarming with the venomous insects before mentioned.

We had scarcely been half an hour in this place when the miserable victim was distracted with pain; his body began to swell, and he appeared one complete blister from head to foot. Often in the agony of his torments did he implore them to end his existence and release him from his misery; but the inhuman wretches only imitated his cries, and mocked and laughed at him. In a very short time, from the effects of the solar heat and the stings of the musquitoes and sandflies, his face had become so swollen that not a feature was distinguishable; his voice began to fail, & his articulation was no longer distinct.

I had long suspected that the whole story of the conspiracy was a wicked and artful fabrication; and the constancy with which this unfortunate being underwent these tortures, served to confirm my suspicions. I resolved, therefore, to hazard my interference, and, after much entreaty and persuasion, prevailed upon them to endeavour to mitigate his sufferings, and to let the poor wretch die in peace, as the injuries which he had already sustained were sufficient of themselves to occasion death. At first they hesitated; but, after consulting for some time among themselves, they consented to go to the other side of the island where they would be secured from observation, and untie him and put something over him. When we had reached that place, we lay upon our oars and set him loose; but the moment he felt the fresh sea breeze, he fainted away. His appearance at this time was no longer human, and my heart bled at seeing a fellow creature thus tormented. When our time was expired, we again tied him as before, to prevent the fury of the Captain for our lenity, and once more pulled for the passage on our way to the vessel. On our arrival, his appearance was the source of merriment to all on board; and the captain asked if he had made any confession. An answer in the negative gave him evident disappointment, and he enquired of me whether I could cure him. I told him he was dying; "then he shall have some more of it before he dies," cried the monster, and directed the boat to be moored within musquet shot in the bay. This having been done, he ordered six of the crew to fire at him. The man fell, and the boat was ordered along-side. The poor wretch had only fainted; and when they perceived that he breathed, a pig of iron was fastened round his neck, & he was thrown into the sea. Thus ended a tragedy, which, for the miseries inflicted on the victim, and for the wanton and barbarous depravity of his fiend-like tormenters, never, perhaps, had its equal.

The inhuman wretches who had been the chief participaters in this horrid deed, seemed to regard it as an everyday occurrence: the guitar tinkled and the song went round, as if nothing had happened; and the torments which their victim had just undergone, and the cries that he had uttered, seemed to form the subject of their jests, and to be echoed in their barbarous mirth.

At nine o'clock at night I was ordered below, as usual; but the image of what had occurred haunted my slumbers, and my sleep was broken by constant apprehensions of assassination. Morning brought round my appointed task of attending the sick; after which I was ordered to make a new gaff top-sail. I went aloft and took the measure of the sail, and then informed the captain that it would be necessary to take the canvas on shore to cut it out. The very mention of the shore excited his fury, & he immediately accused me of intending to escape, observing that any endeavour would be fruitless, as he could have me apprehended in less than two hours after I should go. I told him I had merely said so with a view of expediting the work, and then proceeded to cut out the canvas upon deck in the best manner I could, using all diligence in making the sail. My exertions seemed to please him, and he frequently addressed me in a cheerful manner. Our attention was now excited by a cry of "a sail, a sail" from the mast-head, and I was driven up aloft with the usual threat, to reconnoitre, while the vessel got under weigh. I informed them that she was a merchant brig, and orders were given to go in chase immediately; the pilot undertaking to take her through the channels, while I was called down and consulted as to the best mode of fighting in case she should resist. The corsair having gained on the brig, fired a gun, and hoisted Spanish colours, which the other an-swered by heaving to and displaying the English ensign. From the painted ports and figure-head of the brig, the pirate began to suspect that she was a man of war, and was fearful of approaching any nearer; he therefore ordered the fore-top-sail to be laid aback, and said that he should send the boat to board her under my directions.

This intimation greatly alarmed me, and I pointed out to him the perils I should run in obeying his orders, and that, should I be captured hereafter, I should assuredly suffer an ignominious death. "And what are you, sir," cried he ferociously, "that you should not suffer as well as myself? The schooner shall never be captured; for when I can no longer defend her, I shall blow her up: if you do not instantly go, I will shoot you." I told him that he might shoot me if he pleased; but that I would not commit an act that might subject me and my family to disgrace. Seeing me resolute, and inclined to dispute his authority, he ordered his crew to blindfold me and carry me forward, and told me to prepare myself for death. I was carried as he had directed, and he then came to me, and asked me if I was prepared; I answered firmly, "yes." He then left me, and immediately a volley of musquetry was fired, but, evidently, only with a view to frighten me. The captain immediately came up to me, and asked if I was not desperately wounded? I answered, I was not; but begged if it was his intention to destroy me, to do it at once, and not trifle with me, as I preferred death to disgrace and ignominy. He then gave directions that I should be taken and lashed to the main-mast, and the bandage removed from my eyes. This order was quickly obeyed by his myrmidons. As soon as I was fastened to the mast, the captain cut up a number of cartridges, and placed the powder round me on the deck, with a train to it, and gave orders for the cook to light a match and send it aft. He then repeated his order, and asked if I would obey him; I persisted in my refusal, and, without any further hesitation, he communicated the fire to the powder. The explosion deprived me of my senses, and stunned me for the moment; but I soon recovered, to undergo the most horrid torture: the flames had caught my clothes, which were blazing round me, and my hands were so pinioned, that I could not relieve myself. I begged them, for God's sake, to despatch me at once; but they only laughed at me, and the captain tauntingly asked me if I would obey him now? The excruciating agony in which I was, extorted my acquiescence, and I was ordered to be released; but I fainted before that could be done.

When I recovered my senses, I found myself stretched on a mattress in the cabin, and in the most dreadful pain. In the frenzy and delirium of the moment, I meditated self-destruction; but no weapons were near me, and the shattered state of my legs did not allow me to seek any. The steward was below, and I begged him to lend me his knife; but he suspected my intention, and informed the captain, who descended in a fury. "You want to kill yourself, young man, I understand," cried he, "but I do not mean that you should die yet; I shall blow you up again, for I see it is the only way to make you obey me." He then ordered them to keep watch over me, and help me to sit up and dress my wounds. I found my legs dreadfully injured, the flesh lacerated, and the bone in some parts laid bare; and by this time, large blisters had risen on various parts of my body. I asked for a sheet to cover me, and a pillow for my head; and the captain, who now seemed to relent, ordered the steward to give me all that I required. I begged that the medicine chest might be placed near me, which they did, & I seized that opportunity of swallowing the contents of a small vial of laudanum, about a hundred and thirty drops, hoping that I should wake no more in this world.

The cook, who seemed to pity and feel for my sufferings, now brought me a little arrow-root and wine, and made up my bed for me. I asked him where the corsair was, and he told me in the harbour at anchor. I expressed my surprise at the circumstance; when he informed me the captain was so convinced that the brig was a man of war, and that I had meant to decoy them to be taken, that he was afraid to attack, and had returned into harbour shortly after I was brought down below.

From this poor fellow I received a great deal of kindness, and he seemed possessed of much humanity. "The captain," said he, bending over me with a look of compassion, "is a very bad man, and has killed more than twenty people with his own hand, in cool blood; and he would kill you too, were he not in want of your services." He then cautioned me to appear cheerful and satisfied at all times, and that then they would treat me well: he also told me that he would prepare any little thing for me that I might want, and attend me by day and by night; and, with this kind assurance, left me to my repose.

I now began to feel the soporiferous effects of the laudanum, and, laying myself down upon my mattress, commended my soul into the hands of the God who gave it, beseeching him to forgive me for the act I had committed, and resigned myself, as I thought into the arms of death. I soon fell into a profound sleep, which lasted the whole night, and in the morning they found such difficulty to arouse me, that they imagined I had poisoned myself and was dead. The captain accused me of having done so, and threatened me with a second torturing if I ever made another attempt.

Smith eventually escaped the pirates – but only to arrested for piracy and forwarded to England in chains. A trial at the Old Bailey found him not guilty.

THE PIRATE'S SONG

To the mast nail our flag it is dark as the grave,
Or the death which it bears while it sweeps o'er the wave;
Let our deck clear for action, our guns be prepared;
Be the boarding-axe sharpened, the scimetar bared:
Set the canisters ready, and then bring to me,
For the last of my duties, the powder-room key.
It shall never be lowered, the black flag we bear;
If the sea be denied us, we sweep through the air.
Unshared have we left our last victory's prey;
It is mine to divide it, and yours to obey:
There are shawls that might suit a sultana's white neck,
And pearls that are fair as the arms they will deck;
There are flasks which, unseal them, the air will disclose
Diametta's fair summers, the home of the rose.
I claim not a portion: I ask but as mine –
'Tis to drink to our victory – one cup of red wine.
Some fight, 'tis for riches – some fight, 'tis for fame:
The first I despise, and the last is a name.
I fight, 'tis for vengeance! I love to see flow,
At the stroke of my sabre, the life of my foe.
I strike for the memory of long-vanished years;
I only shed blood where another shed tears.
I come, as the lightning comes red from above,
O'er the race that I loathe, to the battle I love.

Reprinted from *The Pirates Own Book*, 1924

APPENDIX I: THE CORSAIR

Lord Byron

Published in 1814, Lord Byron's tale in verse couplets enjoyed phenomenal success: 10,000 copies were sold on the first day of publication alone. Byron's protagonist, the pirate chief Conrad, captured the hearts of readers and the imagination of artists. Ballets, operas and plays based on The Corsair *all followed.*

Byron himself based Conrad on the exploits of the real-life Caribbean pirate, Lafitte, but took the licence of setting the exploits of Conrad – the original romantic swashbuckler – in the Aegean.

The First Canto

"———— nessun maggior dolore,
Che ricordarsi del tempo felice
Nelle miseria,"   DANTE

I

"O'er the glad waters of the dark blue sea,
Our thoughts as boundless, and our souls as free
Far as the breeze can bear, the billows foam,
Survey our empire, and behold our home!
These are our realms, no limits to their sway –
Our flag the sceptre all who meet obey.
Ours the wild life in tumult still to range
From toil to rest, and joy in every change.
Oh, who can tell? not thou, luxurious slave!
Whose soul would sicken o'er the heaving wave;

Not thou, vain lord of wantonness and ease!
Whom slumber soothes not – pleasure cannot please –
Oh, who can tell, save he whose heart hath tried,
And danced in triumph o'er the waters wide,
The exulting sense – the pulse's maddening play,
That thrills the wanderer of that trackless way?
That for itself can woo the approaching fight,
And turn what some deem danger to delight;
That seeks what cravens shun with more than zeal,
And where the feebler faint can only feel –
Feel – to the rising bosom's inmost core,
Its hope awaken and its spirit soar?
No dread of death if with us die our foes –
Save that it seems even duller than repose:
Come when it will – we snatch the life of life –
When lost – what recks it but disease or strife?
Let him who crawls enamour'd of decay,
Cling to his couch, and sicken years away:
Heave his thick breath, and shake his palsied head;
Ours – the fresh turf; and not the feverish bed.
While gasp by gasp he falters forth his soul,
Ours with one pang – one bound – escapes control.
His corse may boast its urn and narrow cave,
And they who loath'd his life may gild his grave:
Ours are the tears, though few, sincerely shed,
When Ocean shrouds and sepulchres our dead.
For us, even banquets fond regret supply
In the red cup that crowns our memory;
And the brief epitaph in danger's day,
When those who win at length divide the prey,
And cry, Remembrance saddening o'er each brow,
How had the brave who fell exulted now!"

II

Such were the notes that from the Pirate's isle
Around the kindling watch-fire rang the while:
Such were the sounds that thrill'd the rocks along,
And unto ears as rugged seem'd a song!

In scatter'd groups upon the golden sand,
They game – carouse – converse – or whet the brand:
Select the arms – to each his blade assign,
And careless eye the blood that dims its shine.
Repair the boat, replace the helm or oar,
While others straggling muse along the shore:
For the wild bird the busy springes set,
Or spread beneath the sun the dripping net:
Gaze where some distant sail a speck supplies
With all the thirsting eve of Enterprise:
Tell o'er the tales of many a night of toil,
And marvel where they next shall seize a spoil:
No matter where – their chief's allotment this;
Theirs, to believe no prey nor plan amiss.
But who that CHIEF? his name on every shore
Is famed and fear'd – they ask and know no more.
With these he mingles not but to command;
Few are his words, but keen his eye and hand.
Ne'er seasons he with mirth their jovial mess
But they forgive his silence for success.
Ne'er for his lip the purpling cup they fill,
That goblet passes him untasted still –
And for his fare – the rudest of his crew
Would that, in turn, have pass'd untasted too;
Earth's coarsest bread, the garden's homeliest roots,
And scarce the summer luxury of fruits,
His short repast in humbleness supply
With all a hermit's board would scarce deny.
But while he shuns the grosser joys of sense,
His mind seems nourish'd by that abstinence.
"Steer to that shore!" – they sail. "Do this!" – 'tis done:
"Now form and follow me!" – the spoil is won.
Thus prompt his accents and his actions still,
And all obey and few inquire his will;
So to such, brief answer and contemptuous eye
Convey reproof, nor further deign reply.

III

"A sail! – sail!" – a promised prize to Hope!
Her nation – flag – how speaks the telescope?
No prize, alas! but yet a welcome sail:
The blood-red signal glitters in the gale.
Yes – she is ours – a home-returning bark –
Blow fair thou breeze! – she anchors ere the dark.
Already doubled is the cape – our bay
Receives that prow which proudly spurns the spray.
How gloriously her gallant course she goes!
Her white wings flying – never from her foes –
She walks the waters like a thing of life,
And seems to dare the elements to strife.
Who would not brave the battle-fire, the wreck,
To move the monarch of her peopled deck?

IV

Hoarse o'er her side the rustling cable rings;
The sails are furl'd; and anchoring round she swings;
And gathering loiterers on the land discern
Her boat descending from the latticed stem.
'Tis mann'd – the oars keep concert to the strand,
Till grates her keel upon the shallow sand.
Hail to the welcome shout! – the friendly speech!
When hand grasps hand uniting on the beach;
The smile, the question, and the quick reply,
And the heart's promise of festivity!

V

The tidings spread, and gathering grows the crowd;
The hum of voices, and the laughter loud,
And woman's gentler anxious tone is heard –
Friends', husbands', lovers' names in each dear word:
"Oh! are they safe? we ask not of success –
But shall we see them? Will their accents bless?

From where the battle roars, the billows chafe
They doubtless boldly did – but who are safe?
Here let them haste to gladden and surprise,
And kiss the doubt from these delighted eyes!"

VI

"Where is our chief? for him we bear report –
And doubt that joy – which hails our coming short;
Yet thus sincere, 'tis cheering, though so brief;
But, Juan! instant guide us to our chief:
Our greeting paid, we'll feast on our return,
And all shall hear what each may wish to learn."
Ascending slowly by the rock-hewn way,
To where his watch-tower beetles o'er the bay,
By bushy brake, and wild flowers blossoming,
And freshness breathing from each silver spring,
Whose scatter'd streams from granite basins burst,
Leap into life, and sparkling woo your thirst;
From crag to cliff they mount – near yonder cave,
What lonely straggler looks along the wave?
In pensive posture leaning on the brand,
Not oft a resting-staff to that red hand?
" 'Tis he 'tis Conrad – here, as wont, alone;
On – Juan! – on – and make our purpose known.
The bark he views – and tell him we would greet
His ear with tidings he must quickly meet:
We dare not yet approach – thou know'st his mood
When strange or uninvited steps intrude."

VII

Him Juan sought, and told of their intent; –
He spake not, but a sign express'd assent.
These Juan calls – they come – to their salute
He bends him slightly, but his lips are mute.
"These letters, Chief, are from the Greek – the spy,
Who still proclaims our spoil or peril nigh:

Whate'er his tidings, we can well report,
Much that" – "Peace, peace!" – he cuts their prating short.
Wondering they turn, abash'd, while each to each
Conjecture whispers in his muttering speech:
They watch his glance with many a stealing look
To gather how that eye the tidings took;
But, this as if he guess'd, with head aside,
Perchance from some emotion, doubt, or pride,
He read the scroll – "My tablets, Juan, hark –
Where is Gonsalvo?"
"In the anchor'd bark"
"There let him stay – to him this order bear –
Back to your duty – for my course prepare:
Myself this enterprise to-night will share."
"To-night, Lord Conrad!"
"Ay! at set of sun:
The breeze will freshen when the day is done.
My corslet, cloak – one hour and we are gone.
Sling on thy bugle – see that free from rust
My carbine-lock springs worthy of my trust.
Be the edge sharpen'd of my boarding-brand,
And give its guard more room to fit my hand.
This let the armourer with speed dispose
Last time, it more fatigued my arm than foes:
Mark that the signal-gun be duly fired,
To tell us when the hour of stay's expired."

VIII

They make obeisance, and retire in haste,
Too soon to seek again the watery waste:
Yet they repine not – so that Conrad guides;
And who dare question aught that he decides?
That man of loneliness and mystery
Scarce seen to smile, and seldom heard to sigh;
Whose name appals the fiercest of his crew,
And tints each swarthy cheek with sallower hue;
Still sways their souls with that commanding art
That dazzles, leads, yet chills the vulgar heart.

What is that spell, that thus his lawless train
Confess and envy, yet oppose in vain?
What should it be, that thus their faith can bind?
The power of Thought – the magic of the Mind!
Link'd with success, assumed and kept with skill,
That moulds another's weakness to its will;
Wields with their hands, but, still to these unknown,
Makes even their mightiest deeds appear his own
Such hath it been shall be – beneath the sun
The many still must labour for the one!
'Tis Nature's doom – but let the wretch who toils
Accuse not, hate not him who wears the spoils.
Oh! if he knew the weight of splendid chains,
How light the balance of his humbler pains!

IX

Unlike the heroes of each ancient race,
Demons in act, but Gods at least in face,
In Conrad's form seems little to admire,
Though his dark eyebrow shades a glance of fire:
Robust but not Herculean – to the sight
No giant frame sets forth his common height;
Yet, in the whole, who paused to look again,
Saw more than marks the crowd of vulgar men;
They gaze and marvel how – and still confess
That thus it is, but why they cannot guess.
Sun-burnt his cheek, his forehead high and pale
The sable curls in wild profusion veil;
And oft perforce his rising lip reveals
The haughtier thought it curbs, but scarce conceals
Though smooth his voice, and calm his general mien
Still seems there something he would not have seen
His features' deepening lines and varying hue
At times attracted, yet perplex'd the view,
As if within that murkiness of mind
Work'd feelings fearful, and yet undefined
Such might it be – that none could truly tell –
Too close inquiry his stern glance would quell.

There breathe but few whose aspect might defy
The full encounter of his searching eye;
He had the skill, when Cunning's gaze would seek
To probe his heart and watch his changing cheek
At once the observer's purpose to espy,
And on himself roll back his scrutiny,
Lest he to Conrad rather should betray
Some secret thought, than drag that chief's to day.
There was a laughing Devil in his sneer,
That raised emotions both of rage and fear;
And where his frown of hatred darkly fell,
Hope withering fled, and Mercy sigh'd farewell!

X

Slight are the outward signs of evil thought,
Within—within – 'twas there the spirit wrought!
Love shows all changes – Hate, Ambition, Guile,
Betray no further than the bitter smile;
The lip's least curl, the lightest paleness thrown
Along the govern'd aspect, speak alone
Of deeper passions; and to judge their mien,
He, who would see, must be himself unseen.
Then – with the hurried tread, the upward eye,
The clenched hand, the pause of agony,
That listens, starting, lest the step too near
Approach intrusive on that mood of fear;
Then – with each feature working from the heart,
With feelings, loosed to strengthen – not depart,
That rise, convulse, contend – that freeze, or glow
Flush in the cheek, or damp upon the brow;
Then, Stranger! if thou canst, and tremblest not
Behold his soul – the rest that soothes his lot!
Mark how that lone and blighted bosom sears
The scathing thought of execrated years!
Behold – but who hath seen, or e'er shall see,
Man as himself – the secret spirit free?

XI

Yet was not Conrad thus by Nature sent
To lead the guilty – guilt's worse instrument –
His soul was changed, before his deeds had driven
Him forth to war with man and forfeit heaven
Warp'd by the world in Disappointment's school,
In words too wise, in conduct there a fool;
Too firm to yield, and far too proud to stoop,
Doom'd by his very virtues for a dupe,
He cursed those virtues as the cause of ill,
And not the traitors who betray'd him still;
Nor deem'd that gifts bestow'd on better men
Had left him joy, and means to give again
Fear'd, shunn'd, belied, ere youth had lost her force,
He hated man too much to feel remorse,
And thought the voice of wrath a sacred call,
To pay the injuries of some on all.
He knew himself a villain – but he deem'd
The rest no better than the thing he seem'd
And scorn'd the best as hypocrites who hid
Those deeds the bolder spirit plainly did.
He knew himself detested, but he knew
The hearts that loath'd him, crouch'd and dreaded too.
Lone, wild, and strange, he stood alike exempt
From all affection and from all contempt;
His name could sadden, and his acts surprise;
But they that fear'd him dared not to despise;
Man spurns the worm, but pauses ere he wake
The slumbering venom of the folded snake:
The first may turn, but not avenge the blow;
The last expires, but leaves no living foe;
Fast to the doom'd offender's form it clings,
And he may crush – not conquer – still it stings!

XII

None are all evil – quickening round his heart
One softer feeling would not yet depart

Oft could he sneer at others as beguiled
By passions worthy of a fool or child;
Yet 'gainst that passion vainly still he strove,
And even in him it asks the name of Love!
Yes, it was love – unchangeable – unchanged,
Felt but for one from whom he never ranged;
Though fairest captives daily met his eye,
He shunn'd, nor sought, but coldly pass'd them by;
Though many a beauty droop'd in prison'd bower,
None ever sooth'd his most unguarded hour.
Yes – it was Love – if thoughts of tenderness
Tried in temptation, strengthen'd by distress
Unmoved by absence, firm in every clime,
And yet – oh more than all! untired by time;
Which nor defeated hope, nor baffled wile,
Could render sullen were she near to smile,
Nor rage could fire, nor sickness fret to vent
On her one murmur of his discontent;
Which still would meet with joy, with calmness part,
Lest that his look of grief should reach her heart;
Which nought removed, nor menaced to remove –
If there be love in mortals – this was love!
He was a villain – ay, reproaches shower
On him – but not the passion, nor its power,
Which only proved, all other virtues gone,
Not guilt itself could quench this loveliest one!

XIII

He paused a moment – till his hastening men
Pass'd the first winding downward to the glen.
"Strange tidings! – many a peril have I pass'd
Nor know I why this next appears the last!
Yet so my heart forebodes, but must not fear
Nor shall my followers find me falter here.
'Tis rash to meet, but surer death to wait
Till here they hunt us to undoubted fate;
And, if my plan but hold, and Fortune smile,
We'll furnish mourners for our funeral pile.

Ay, let them slumber – peaceful be their dreams!
Morn ne'er awoke them with such brilliant beams
As kindle high to – flight (but blow, thou breeze!)
To warm these slow avengers of the sea
Now to Medora – oh! my sinking heart,
Long may her own be lighter than thou art!
Yet was I brave – mean boast where all are brave!
Ev'n insects sting for aught they seek to save.
This common courage which with brutes we share
That owes its deadliest efforts to despair,
Small merit claims – but 'twas my nobler hope
To teach my few with numbers still to cope;
Long have I led them – not to vainly bleed:
No medium now – we perish or succeed;
So let it be – it irks not me to die;
But thus to urge them whence they cannot fly.
My lot hath long had little of my care,
But chafes my pride thus baffled in the snare:
Is this my skill? my craft? to set at last
Hope, power, and life upon a single cast?
Oh, Fate! – accuse thy folly, not thy fate!
She may redeem thee still, not yet too late."

XIV

Thus with himself communion held he, till
He reach'd the summit of his towercrown'd hill:
There at the portal paused – or wild and soft
He heard those accents never heard too oft
Through the high lattice far yet sweet they rung,
And these the notes his bird of beauty sung:

1
"Deep in my soul that tender secret dwells,
    Lonely and lost to light for evermore,
Save when to thine my heart responsive swells,
    Then trembles into silence as before.

2

"There, in its centre a sepulchral lamp
   Burns the slow flame, eternal, but unseen;
Which not the darkness of despair can damp,
   Though vain its ray as it had never been.

3

"Remember me – oh! pass not thou my grave
   Without one thought whose relics there recline
The only pang my bosom dare not brave
   Must be to find forgetfulness in thine.

4

"My fondest, faintest, latest accents hear–
   Grief for the dead not virtue can reprove;
Then give me all I ever ask'd – a tear,
   The first – last – sole reward of so much love! –
He pass'd the portal, cross'd the corridor,

And reach'd the chamber as the strain gave o'er:
"My own Medora! sure thy song is sad–"
"In Conrad's absence wouldst thou have it glad?
Without thine ear to listen to my lay,
Still must my song my thoughts, my soul betray:
Still must each action to my bosom suit,
My heart unhush'd, although my lips were mute!
Oh! many a night on this lone couch reclined,
My dreaming fear with storms hath wing'd the wind,
And deem'd the breath that faintly fann'd thy sail
The murmuring prelude of the ruder gale;
Though soft, it seem'd the low prophetic dirge,
That mourn'd thee floating on the savage surge;
Still would I rise to rouse the beacon fire,
Lest spies less true should let the blaze expire;
And many a restless hour outwatch'd each star,
And morning came – and still thou wert afar.
Oh! how the chill blast on my bosom blew,
And day broke dreary on my troubled view,
And still I gazed and gazed – and not a prow
Was granted to my tears, my truth, my vow!

At length 'twas noon – I hail'd and blest the mast
That met my sight – it near'd – Alas! it pass'd!
Another came – oh God! 'twas thine at last!
Would that those days were over! wilt thou ne'er,
My Conrad! learn the joys of peace to share?
Sure thou hast more than wealth, and many a home
As bright as this invites us not to roam:
Thou know'st it is not peril that I fear,
I only tremble when thou art not here;
Then not for mine, but that far dearer life,
Which flies from love and languishes for strife –
How strange that heart, to me so tender still,
Should war with nature and its better will!"
"Yea, strange indeed – that heart hath long been changed;
Worm-like 'twas trampled, adder-like avenged,
Without one hope on earth beyond thy love,
And scarce a glimpse of mercy from above.
Yet the same feeling which thou dost condemn,
My very love to thee is hate to them,
So closely mingling here, that disentwined,
I cease to love thee when I love mankind:
Yet dread not this – the proof of all the past
Assures the future that my love will last;
But – oh, Medora! nerve thy gentler heart;
This hour again – but not for long – we part."
"This hour we part – my heart foreboded this:
Thus ever fade my fairy dreams of bliss.
This hour – it cannot be – this hour away!
Yon bark hath hardly anchor'd in the bay:
Her consort still is absent, and her crew
Have need of rest before they toil anew:
My love! thou mock'st my weakness; and wouldst steel
My breast before the time when it must feel;
But trifle now no more with my distress,
Such mirth hath less of play than bitterness.
Be silent, Conrad! – dearest! come and share
The feast these hands delighted to prepare;
Light toil! to cull and dress thy frugal fare!
See, I have pluck'd the fruit that promised best,
And where not sure, perplex'd, but pleased, I guess'd

At such as seem'd the fairest; thrice the hill
My steps have wound to try the coolest rill;
Yes! thy sherbet tonight will sweetly flow,
See how it sparkles in its vase of snow!
The grapes' gay juice thy bosom never cheers;
Thou more than Moslem when the cup appears:
Think not I mean to chide – for I rejoice
What others deem a penance is thy choice.
But come, the board is spread; our silver lamp
Is trimm'd, and heeds not the sirocco's damp:
Then shall my handmaids while the time along,
And join with me the dance, or wake the song;
Or my guitar, which still thou lov'st to hear,
Shall soothe or lull – or, should it vex thine ear
We'll turn the tale by Ariosto told,
Of fair Olympia loved and left of old.
Why, thou wert worse than he who broke his vow
To that lost damsel, shouldst thou leave me now;
Or even that traitor chief – I've seen thee smile,
When the dear sky show'd Ariadne's Isle,
Which I have pointed from these cliffs the while:
And thus half sportive, half in fear, I said,
Lest time should rake that doubt to more than dread,
Thus Conrad, too, win quit me for the main;
And he deceived me – for he came again!"
"Again, again – and oft again – my love!
If there be life below, and hope above,
He will return – but now, the moments bring
The time of parting with redoubled wing:
The why, the where – what boots it now to tell?
Since all must end in that wild word – farewell!
Yet would I fain – did time allow disclose –
Fear not – these are no formidable foes
And here shall watch a more than wonted guard,
For sudden siege and long defence prepared:
Nor be thou lonely, though thy lord's away,
Our matrons and thy handmaids with thee stay;
And this thy comfort – that, when next we meet,
Security shall make repose more sweet.
List! – 'tis the bugle!" – Juan shrilly blew –

"One kiss – one more – another – oh! Adieu!"
She rose – she sprung – she clung to his embrace,
Till his heart heaved beneath her hidden face:
He dared not raise to his that deep-blue eye,
Which downcast droop'd in tearless agony.
Her long fair hair lay floating o'er his arms,
In all the wildness of dishevell'd charms;
Scarce beat that bosom where his image dwelt
So full – that feeling seem'd almost Unfelt!
Hark – peals the thunder of the signal-gun
It told 'twas sunset, and he cursed that sun.
Again – again – that form he madly press'd,
Which mutely clasp'd, imploringly caress'd!
And tottering to the couch his bride he bore,
One moment gazed, as if to gaze no more;
Felt that for him earth held but her alone,
Kiss'd her cold forehead – turn'd – is Conrad gone?

XV

"And is he gone?" on sudden solitude
How oft that fearful question will intrude
"'Twas but an instant past, and here he stood!
And now" – without the portal's porch she rush'd,
And then at length her tears in freedom gush'd;
Big, bright, and fast, unknown to her they fell;
But still her lips refused to send – "Farewell!"
For in that word – that fatal word – how e'er
We promise, hope, believe, there breathes despair.
O'er every feature of that still, pale face,
Had sorrow fix'd what time can ne'er erase:
The tender blue of that large loving eye
Grew frozen with its gaze on vacancy,
Till – oh? how far! – it caught a glimpse of him,
And then it flow'd, and phrensied seem'd to swim
Through those long, dark, and glistening lashes dew'd
With drops of sadness oft to be renew'd.
"He's gone!" – against her heart that hand is driven,
Convulsed and quick – then gently raised to heaven:

She look'd and saw the heaving of the main;
The white sail set she dared not look again;
But turn'd with sickening soul within the gate
"It is no dream – and I am desolate!"

XVI

From crag to crag descending, swiftly sped
Stern Conrad down, nor once he turn'd his head;
But shrunk whene'er the windings of his way
Forced on his eye what he would not survey,
His lone but lovely dwelling on the steep,
That hail'd him first when homeward from the deep
And she – the dim and melancholy star,
Whose ray of beauty reach'd him from afar
On her he must not gaze, he must not think,
There he might rest – but on Destruction's brink:
Yet once almost he stopp'd, and nearly gave
His fate to chance, his projects to the wave:
But no – it must not be – a worthy chief
May melt, but not betray to woman's grief.
He sees his bark, he notes how fair the wind,
And sternly gathers all his might of mind:
Again he hurries on – and as he hears
The clang of tumult vibrate on his ears,
The busy sounds, the bustle of the shore,
The shout, the signal, and the dashing oar;
As marks his eye the seaboy on the mast,
The anchors rise, the sails unfurling fast,
The waving kerchiefs of the crowd that urge
That mute adieu to those who stem the surge;
And more than all, his blood-red flag aloft,
He marvell'd how his heart could seem so soft.
Fire in his glance, and wildness in his breast
He feels of all his former self possest;
He bounds – he flies – until his footsteps reach
The verge where ends the cliff, begins the beach,
There checks his speed; but pauses less to breathe
The breezy freshness of the deep beneath,

Than there his wonted statelier step renew;
Nor rush, disturb'd by haste, to vulgar view:
For well had Conrad learn'd to curb the crowd,
By arts that veil and oft preserve the proud;
His was the lofty port, the distant mien,
That seems to shun the sight – and awes if seen:
The solemn aspect, and the high-born eye,
That checks low mirth, but lacks not courtesy;
All these he wielded to command assent:
But where he wish'd to win, so well unbent
That kindness cancell'd fear in those who heard,
And others' gifts show'd mean beside his word,
When echo'd to the heart as from his own
His deep yet tender melody of tone:
But such was foreign to his wonted mood,
He cared not what he soften'd, but subdued:
The evil passions of his youth had made
Him value less who loved – than what obey'd.

XVII

Around him mustering ranged his ready guard,
Before him Juan stands – "Are all prepared?'"
"They are – nay more – embark'd: the boats
Waits but my Chief –"
"My sword, and my capote."
Soon firmly girded on, and lightly slung,
His belt and cloak were o'er his shoulders flung:
"Call Pedro here!" He comes – and Conrad bends,
With all the courtesy he deign'd his friends;
"Receive these tablets, and peruse with care,
Words of high trust and truth are graven there;
Double the guard, and when Anselmo's bark
Arrives, let him alike these orders mark:
In three days (serve the breeze) the sun shall shine
On our return – till then all peace be thine!"
This said, his brother Pirate's hand he wrung,
Then to his boat with haughty gesture sprung.
Flash'd the dipt oars, and sparkling with the stroke,

Around the waves' phosphoric brightness broke;
They gain the vessel – on the deck he stands, –
Shrieks the shrill whistle, ply the busy hands –
He marks how well the ship her helm obeys,
How gallant all her crew, and deigns to praise.
His eyes of pride to young Gonsalvo turn –
Why doth he start, and inly seem to mourn?
Alas! those eyes beheld his rocky tower
And live a moment o'er the parting hour;
She – his Medora – did she mark the prow?
Ah! never loved he half so much as now!
But much must yet be done ere dawn of day –
Again he mans himself and turns away;
Down to the cabin with Gonsalvo bends,
And there unfolds his plan, his means, and ends;
Before them burns the lamp, and spreads the chart,
And all that speaks and aids the naval art;
They to the midnight watch protract debate;
To anxious eyes what hour is ever late?
Meantime, the steady breeze serenely blew,
And fast and falcon-like the vessel flew;
Pass'd the high headlands of each clustering isle,
To gain their port – long – long ere morning smile:
And soon the night-glass through the narrow bay
Discovers where the Pacha's galleys lay.
Count they each sail, and mark how there supine
The lights in vain o'er heedless Moslem shine.
Secure, unnoted, Conrad's prow pass'd by,
And anchor'd where his ambush meant to lie;
Screen'd from espial by the jutting cape,
That rears on high its rude fantastic shape.
Then rose his band to duty – not from sleep –
Equipp'd for deeds alike on land or deep;
While lean'd their leader o'er the fretting flood,
And calmly talk'd –and yet he talk'd of blood!

The Second Canto

"Conoscestci dubiosi desiri?" – Dante

I

In Coron's bay floats many a galley light,
Through Coron's lattices the lamps are bright
For Seyd, the Pacha, makes a feast to-night:
A feast for promised triumph yet to come,
When he shall drag the fetter'd Rovers home;
This hath he sworn by Allah and his sword,
And faithful to his firman and his word,
His summon'd prows collect along the coast,
And great the gathering crews, and loud the boast;
Already shared the captives and the prize,
Though far the distant foe they thus despise
'Tis but to sail – no doubt to-morrow's Sun
Will see the Pirates bound, their haven won!
Meantime the watch may slumber, if they will,
Nor only wake to war, but dreaming kill.
Though all, who can, disperse on shore and seek
To flesh their glowing valour on the Greek;
How well such deed becomes the turban'd brave –
To bare the sabre's edge before a slave!
Infest his dwelling – but forbear to slay,
Their arms are strong, yet merciful to-day,
And do not deign to smite because they may!
Unless some gay caprice suggests the blow,
To keep in practice for the coming foe.
Revel and rout the evening hours beguile,
And they who wish to wear a head must smile
For Moslem mouths produce their choicest cheer,
And hoard their curses, till the coast is clear.

II

High in his hall reclines the turban'd Seyd;
Around – the bearded chiefs he came to lead,
Removed the banquet, and the last pilaff –
Forbidden draughts, 'tis said, he dared to quaff,
Though to the rest the sober berry's juice
The slaves bear round for rigid Moslems' use;

The long chibouque's dissolving cloud supply,
While dance the Almas to wild minstrelsy.
The rising morn will view the chiefs embark;
But waves are somewhat treacherous in the dark:
And revellers may more securely sleep
On silken couch than o'er the rugged deep:
Feast there who can – nor combat till they must,
And less to conquest than to Korans trust:
And yet the numbers crowded in his host
Might warrant more than even the Pacha's boast.

III

With cautious reverence from the outer gate
Slow stalks the slave, whose office there to wait,
Bows his bent head, his hand salutes the floor,
Ere yet his tongue the trusted tidings bore:
"A captive Dervise, from the Pirate's nest
Escaped, is here – himself would tell the rest."
He took the sign from Seyd's assenting eye,
And led the holy man in silence nigh.
His arms were folded on his dark-green vest,
His step was feeble, and his look deprest;
Yet worn he seem'd of hardship more than years,
And pale his cheek with penance, not from fears.
Vow'd to his God – his sable locks he wore,
And these his lofty cap rose proudly o'er:
Around his form his loose long robe was thrown
And wrapt a breast bestow'd on heaven alone;
Submissive, yet with self-possession mann'd,
He calmly, met the curious eyes that scann'd;
And question of his coming fain would seek,
Before the Pacha's will allow'd to speak.

IV

"Whence com'st thou, Dervise?'
"From the outlaw's den,

A fugitive –"
"Thy capture where and when?"
"From Scalanova's port to Scio's isle,
The Saick was bound; but Allah did not smile
Upon our course – the Moslem merchant's gains
The Rovers won; our limbs have worn their chains.
I had no death to fear, nor wealth to boast
Beyond the wandering freedom which I lost;
At length a fisher's humble boat by night
Afforded hope, and offer'd chance of flight;
I seized the hour, and find my safety here –
With thee – most mighty Pacha! who can fear?"
"How speed the outlaws? stand they well prepared,
Their plunder'd wealth, and robber's rock, to guard?
Dream they of this our preparation, doom'd
To view with fire their scorpion nest consumed?"
"Pacha! the fetter'd captive's mourning eye,
That weeps for flight, but ill can play the spy;
I only heard the reckless waters roar
Those waves that would not bear me from the shore;
I only mark'd the glorious sun and sky,
Too bright, too blue, or my captivity;
And felt that all which Freedom's bosom cheers
Must break my chain before it dried my tears.
This may'st thou judge, at least, from my escape,
They little deem of aught in peril's shape;
Else vainly had I pray'd or sought the chance
That leads me here – if eyed with vigilance
The careless guard that did not see me fly
May watch as idly when thy power is nigh.
Pacha! my limbs are faint – and nature craves
Food for my hunger, rest from tossing waves:
Permit my absence – peace be with thee! Peace
With all around! – now grant repose – release."
"Stay, Dervise! I have more to question – stay,
I do command thee – sit – dost hear? – obey!
More I must ask, and food the slaves shall bring
Thou shalt not pine where all are banqueting:
The supper done – prepare thee to reply,
Clearly and full – I love not mystery."

'Twere vain to guess what shook the pious man,
Who look'd not lovingly on that Divan;
Nor show'd high relish for the banquet prest,
And less respect for every fellow guest.
'Twas but a moment's peevish hectic pass'd
Along his cheek, and tranquillised as fast:
He sate him down in silence, and his look
Resumed the calmness which before forsook:
This feast was usher'd in, but sumptuous fare
He shunn'd as if some poison mingled there.
For one so long condemn'd to toil and fast,
Methinks he strangely spares the rich re-past.
"What ails thee, Dervise? eat – dost thou suppose
This feast a Christian's? or my friends thy foes?
Why dost thou shun the salt? that sacred pledge,
Which once partaken, blunts the sabre's edge,
Makes ev'n contending tribes in peace unite,
And hated hosts seem brethren to the sight!"
"Salt seasons dainties – and my food is still
The humblest root, my drink the simplest rill;
And my stern vow and order's laws oppose
To break or mingle bread with friends or foes;
It may seem strange – if there be aught to dread,
That peril rests upon my single head;
But for thy sway – nay more – thy Sultan's throne,
I taste nor bread nor banquet – save alone;
Infringed our order's rule, the Prophet's rage
To Mecca's dome might bar my pilgrimage."
"Well – as thou wilt – ascetic as thou art –
One question answer; then in peace depart.
How many? – Ha! it cannot sure be day?
What star – what sun is bursting on the bay?
It shines a lake of fire! – away – away!
Ho! treachery! my guards! my scimitar!
The galleys feed the flames – and I afar!
Accursed Dervise! – these thy tidings – thou
Some villain spy – seize cleave him – slay him now!"
Up rose the Dervise with that burst of light,
Nor less his change of form appall'd the sight:
Up rose that Dervise – not in saintly garb,

But like a warrior bounding on his barb,
Dash'd his high cap, and tore his robe away –
Shone his mail'd breast, and flash'd his sabre's ray!
His close but glittering casque, and sable plume,
More glittering eye, and black brow's sabler gloom,
Glared on the Moslems' eyes some Afrit sprite,
Whose demon death-blow left no hope for fight.
The wild confusion, and the swarthy glow
Of flames on high, and torches from below;
The shriek of terror, and the mingling yell –
For swords began to dash and shouts to swell –
Flung o'er that spot of earth the air of hell!
Distracted, to and fro, the flying slaves
Behold but bloody shore and fiery waves;
Nought heeded they the Pacha's angry cry,
They seize that Dervise! – seize on Zatanai!
He saw their terror – check'd the first dispair
That urged him but to stand and perish there,
Since far too early and too well obey'd,
The flame was kindled ere the signal made;
He saw their terror – from his baldric drew
His bugle – brief the blast – but shrilly blew;
'Tis answered – "Well ye speed, my gallant crew!
Why did I doubt their quickness of career?
And deem design had left me single here?"
Sweeps his long arm – that sabre's whirling sway
Sheds fast atonement for its first delay;
Completes his fury what their fear begun,
And makes the many basely quail to one.
The cloven turbans o'er the chamber spread,
And scarce an arm dare rise to guard its head:
Even Seyd, convulsed, o'erwhelm'd, with rage surprise,
Retreats before him, though he still defies.
No craven he – and yet he dreads the blow,
So much Confusion magnifies his foe!
His blazing galleys still distract his sight,
He tore his beard, and foaming fled the fight;
For now the pirates pass'd the Haram gate,
And burst within – and it were death to wait
Where wild Amazement shrieking – kneeling throws

The sword aside – in vain the blood o'erflows!
The Corsairs pouring, haste to where within
Invited Conrad's bugle, and the din
Of groaning victims, and wild cries for life,
Proclaim'd how well he did the work of strife.
They shout to find him grim and lonely there,
A glutted tiger mangling in his lair!
But short their greeting, shorter his reply
"'Tis well but Seyd escapes, and he must die –
Much hath been done, but more remains to do –
Their galleys blaze – why not their city too?"

V

Quick at the word they seized him each a torch
And fire the dome from minaret to porch.
A stern delight was fix'd in Conrad's eye,
But sudden sunk – for on his ear the cry
Of women struck, and like a deadly knell
Knock'd at that heart unmoved by battle's yell.
"Oh! burst the Haram – wrong not on your lives
One female form remember – we have wives.
On them such outrage Vengeance will repay;
Man is our foe, and such 'tis ours to slay:
But still we spared – must spare the weaker prey.
Oh! I forgot – but Heaven will not forgive
If at my word the helpless cease to live;
Follow who will – I go – we yet have time
Our souls to lighten of at least a crime."
He climbs the crackling stair, he bursts the door,
Nor feels his feet glow scorching with the floor;
His breath choked gasping with the volumed smoke,
But still from room to room his way he broke.
They search – they find – they save: with lusty arms
Each bears a prize of unregarded charms;
Calm their loud fears; sustain their sinking frames
With all the care defenceless beauty claims
So well could Conrad tame their fiercest mood,
And check the very hands with gore imbrued.

But who is she? whom Conrad's arms convey
From reeking pile and combat's wreck away –
Who but the love of him he dooms to bleed?
The Haram queen – but still the slave of Seyd!

VI

Brief time had Conrad now to greet Gulnare,
Few words to re-assure the trembling fair
For in that pause compassion snatch'd from war,
The foe before retiring, fast and far,
With wonder saw their footsteps unpursued,
First slowlier fled – then rallied – then withstood.
This Seyd perceives, then first perceives how few?
Compared with his, the Corsair's roving crew,
And blushes o'er his error, as he eyes
The ruin wrought by panic and surprise.
Alla il Alla! Vengeance swells the cry –
Shame mounts to rage that must atone or die!
And flame for flame and blood for blood must tell,
The tide of triumph ebbs that flow'd too well –
When wrath returns to renovated strife,
And those who fought for conquest strike for life
Conrad beheld the danger – he beheld
His followers faint by freshening foes repell'd:
"One effort – one – to break the circling host!"
They form – unite – charge – waver – all is lost!
Within a narrower ring compress'd, beset,
Hopeless, not heartless, strive and struggle yet –
Ah! now they fight in firmest file no more,
Hemm'd in, cut off, cleft down, and trampled o'er,
But each strikes singly, silently, and home,
And sinks outwearied rather than o'ercome,
His last faint quittance rendering with his breath,
Till the blade glimmers in the grasp of death!

VII

But first, ere came the rallying host to blows,
And rank to rank, and hand to hand oppose,
Gulnare and all her Haram handmaids freed,
Safe in the dome of one who held their creed,
By Conrad's mandate safely were bestow'd
And dried those tears for life and fame that flow'd:
And when that dark-eyed lady, young Gulnare
Recall'd those thoughts late wandering in despair
Much did she marvel o'er the courtesy
That smooth'd his accents, soften'd in his eye:
'Twas strange – that robber thus with gore bedew'd
Seem'd gentler then than Seyd in fondest mood.
The Pacha woo'd as if he deem'd the slave
Must seem delighted with the heart he gave
The Corsair vow'd protection, soothed affright
As if his homage were a woman's right.
"The wish is wrong – nay, worse for female – vain:
Yet much I long to view that chief again;
If but to thank for, what my fear forget,
The life my loving lord remember'd not!"

VIII

And him she saw, where thickest carnage spread,
But gather'd breathing from the happier dead;
Far from his band, and battling with a host
That deem right dearly won the field he lost,
Fell'd – bleeding – baffled of the death he sought,
And snatch'd to expiate all the ills he wrought;
Preserved to linger and to live in vain,
While Vengeance ponder'd o'er new plans of pain,
And stanch'd the blood she saves to shed again –
But drop for drop, for Seyd's unglutted eye
Would doom him ever dying – ne'er to die!
Can this be he? triumphant late she saw
When his red hand's wild gesture waved a law!
'Tis he indeed – disarm'd but undeprest,

His sole regret the life he still possest;
His wounds too slight, though taken with that will,
Which would have kiss'd the hand that then could kill.
Oh were there none, of all the many given,
To send his soul – he scarcely ask'd to heaven?
Must he alone of all retain his breath,
Who more than all had striven and struck for death?
He deeply felt – what mortal hearts must feel,
When thus reversed on faithless fortune's wheel,
For crimes committed, and the victor's threat
Of lingering tortures to repay the debt –
He deeply, darkly felt; but evil pride
That led to perpetrate, now serves to hide.
Still in his stern and self-collected mien
A conqueror's more than captive's air is seen
Though faint with wasting toil and stiffening wound,
But few that saw – so calmly gazed around:
Though the far shouting of the distant crowd,
Their tremors o'er, rose insolently loud,
The better warriors who beheld him near,
Insulted not the foe who taught them fear;
And the grim guards that to his durance led,
In silence eyed him with a secret dread.

IX

The Leech was sent – but not in mercy – there,
To note how much the life yet left could bear;
He found enough to load with heaviest chain,
And promise feeling for the wrench of pain;
To-morrow – yea – tomorrow's evening gun
Will sinking see impalement's pangs begun
And rising with the wonted blush of morn
Behold how well or ill those pangs are borne.
Of torments this the longest and the worst,
Which adds all other agony to thirst,
That day by day death still forbears to slake,
While famish'd vultures flit around the stake.
"Oh! Water – water!" smiling Hate denies

The victim's prayer, for if he drinks he dies.
This was his doom; – the Leech, the guard were gone,
And left proud Conrad fetter'd and alone.

X

'Twere vain to paint to what his feelings grew –
It even were doubtful if their victim knew.
There is a war, a chaos of the mind,
When all its elements convulsed, combined,
Lie dark and jarring with perturbed force,
And gnashing with impenitent Remorse –
That juggling fiend, who never spake before
But cries "I warn'd thee!" When the deed is o'er.
Vain voice! the spirit burning but unbent
May writhe, rebel – the weak alone repent!
Even in that lonely hour when most it feels,
And, to itself; all, all that self reveals, –
No single passion, and no ruling thought
That leaves the rest, as once, unseen, unsought,
But the wild prospect when the soul reviews,
All rushing through their thousand avenues –
Ambition's dreams expiring, love's regret,
Endanger'd glory, life itself beset:
The joy untasted, the contempt or hate
'Gainst those who fain would triumph in our fate
The hopeless past, the hasting future driven
Too quickly on to guess of hell or heaven;
Deeds, thoughts, and words, perhaps remember'd not
So keenly till that hour, but ne'er forgot;
Things light or lovely in their acted time,
But now to stern reflection each a crime;
The withering sense of evil unreveal'd,
Not cankering less because the more conceal'd –
All, in a word, from which all eyes must start,
That opening sepulchre – the naked heart
Bares with its buried woes, till Pride awake,
To snatch the mirror from the soul – and break
Ay, Pride can veil, and courage brave it all –

All – all – before – beyond – the deadliest fall.
Each hath some fear, and he who least betrays,
The only hypocrite deserving praise:
Not the loud recreant wretch who boasts and flies;
But he who looks on death – and silent dies.
So steel'd by pondering o'er his far career,
He half-way meets him should he menace near!

XI

In the high chamber of his highest tower
Sate Conrad, fetter'd in the Pacha's power.
His palace perish'd in the flame – this fort
Contain'd at once his captive and his court.
Not much could Conrad of his sentence blame,
His foe, if vanquish'd, had but shared the same: –
Alone he sate – in solitude had scann'd
His guilty bosom, but that breast he mann'd:
One thought alone he could not – dared not meet –
"Oh, how these tidings will Medora greet?"
Then – only then – his clanking hands he raised,
And strain'd with rage the chain on which he gazed
But soon he found, or feign'd, or dream'd relief,
And smiled in self-derision of his grief,
"And now come torture when it will – or may,
More need of rest to nerve me for the day!"
This said, with languor to his mat he crept,
And, whatsoe' er his visions, quickly slept
'Twas hardly midnight when that fray begun,
For Conrad's plans matured, at once were done:
And Havoc loathes so much the waste of time,
She scarce had left an uncommitted crime.
One hour beheld him since the tide he stemm'd –
Disguised, discover'd, conquering, ta'en, condemn'd –
A chief on land, an outlaw on the deep
Destroying, saving, prison'd, and asleep!

XII

He slept in calmest seeming, for his breath
Was hush'd so deep – Ah! happy if in death!
He slept – Who o'er his placid slumber bends?
His foes are gone, and here he hath no friends;
Is it some seraph sent to grant him grace?
No, 'tis an earthly form with heavenly face!
Its white arm raised a lamp – yet gently hid,
Lest the ray flash abruptly on the lid
Of that closed eye, which opens but to pain,
And once unclosed – but once may close again
That form, with eye so dark, and cheek so fair,
And auburn waves of gemm'd and braided hair;
With shape of fairy lightness – naked foot,
That shines like snow, and falls on earth as mute –
Through guards and dunnest night how came it there?
Ah! rather ask what will not woman dare?
Whom youth and pity lead like thee, Gulnare!
She could not sleep – and while the Pacha's rest
In muttering dreams yet saw his pirate-guest
She left his side – his signet-ring she bore
Which oft in sport adorn'd her hand before –
And with it, scarcely question'd, won her way
Through drowsy guards that must that sign obey.
Worn out with toil, and tired with changing blows
Their eyes had envied Conrad his repose;
And chill and nodding at the turret door,
They stretch their listless limbs, and watch no more;
Just raised their heads to hail the signet-ring,
Nor ask or what or who the sign may bring.

XIII

She gazed in wonder, "Can he calmly sleep,
While other eyes his fall or ravage weep?
And mine in restlessness are wandering here –
What sudden spell hath made this man so dear?
True – 'tis to him my life, and more, I owe,

And me and mine he spared from worse than woe:
'Tis late to think – but soft, his slumber breaks –
How heavily he sighs! – he starts – awakes!"
He raised his head, and dazzled with the light,
His eye seem'd dubious if it saw aright:
He moved his hand – the grating of his chain
Too harshly told him that he lived again.
"What is that form? if not a shape of air,
Methinks, my jailor's face shows wondrous fair!"
"Pirate! thou know'st me not – but I am one,
Grateful for deeds thou hast too rarely done;
Look on me – and remember her, thy hand
Snatch'd from the flames, and thy more fearful band.
I come through darkness and I scarce know why –
Yet not to hurt – I would not see thee die."
"If so, kind lady! thine the only eye
That would not here in that gay hope delight:
Theirs is the chance – and let them use their right.
But still I thank their courtesy or thine,
That would confess me at so fair a shrine!"
Strange though it seem – yet with extremest grief
Is link'd a mirth – it doth not bring relief –
That playfulness of Sorrow ne'er beguiles,
And smiles in bitterness – but still it smiles;
And sometimes with the wisest and the best,
Till even the scaffold echoes with their jest!
Yet not the joy to which it seems akin –
It may deceive all hearts, save that within.
Whate'er it was that flash'd on Conrad, now
A laughing wildness half unbent his brow
And these his accents had a sound of mirth,
As if the last he could enjoy on earth;
Yet 'gainst his nature – for through that short life,
Few thoughts had he to spare from gloom and strife.

XIV

"Corsair! thy doom is named – but I have power
To soothe the Pacha in his weaker hour.

Thee would I spare – nay more – would save thee now,
But this – time – hope – nor even thy strength allow;
But all I can, I will: at least, delay
The sentence that remits thee scarce a day.
More now were ruin – even thyself were loth
The vain attempt should bring but doom to both."
"Yes! loth indeed: – my soul is nerved to all,
Or fall'n too low to fear a further fall:
Tempt not thyself with peril – me with hope
Of flight from foes with whom I could not cope:
Unfit to vanquish, shall I meanly fly,
The one of all my band that would not die?
Yet there is one to whom my memory clings,
Till to these eyes her own wild softness springs.
My sole resources in the path I trod
Were these – my bark, my sword, my love, my God!
The last I left in youth! – he leaves me now –
And Man but works his will to lay me low.
I have no thought to mock his throne with prayer
Wrung from the coward crouching of despair;
It is enough – I breathe, and I can bear.
My sword is shaken from the worthless hand
That might have better kept so true a brand;
My bark is sunk or captive – but my love –
For her in sooth my voice would mount above:
Oh! she is all that still to earth can bind –
And this will break a heart so more than kind,
And blight a form – till thine appear'd, Gulnare!
Mine eye ne'er ask'd if others were as fair."
"Thou lov'st another then? – but what to me
Is this – 'tis nothing – nothing e'er can be:
But yet – thou lov'st – and – oh! I envy those
Whose hearts on hearts as faithful can repose,
Who never feel the void – the wandering thought
That sighs o'er vision – such as mine hath wrought."
"Lady – methought thy love was his, for whom
This arm redeem'd thee from a fiery tomb."
"My love stern Seyd's! Oh – No – No – not my love –
Yet much this heart, that strives no more, once strove
To meet his passion but it would not be.

I felt – I feel – love dwells with – with the free.
I am a slave, a favour'd slave at best,
To share his splendour, and seem very blest!
Oft must my soul the question undergo,
Of – 'Dost thou love?' and burn to answer, 'No!'
Oh! hard it is that fondness to sustain,
And struggle not to feel averse in vain;
But harder still the heart's recoil to bear,
And hide from one – perhaps another there.
He takes the hand I give not, nor withhold –
Its pulse nor check'd, nor quicken'd – calmly cold:
And when resign'd, it drops a lifeless weight
From one I never loved enough to hate.
No warmth these lips return by his imprest,
And chill'd remembrance shudders o'er the rest.
Yes – had lever proved that passion's zeal,
The change to hatred were at least to feel:
But still he goes unmourn'd, returns unsought,
And oft when present – absent from my thought.
Or when reflection comes – and come it must –
I fear that henceforth 'twill but bring disgust;
I am his slave – but, in despite of pride,
'Twere worse than bondage to become his bride.
Oh! that this dotage of his breast would cease:
Or seek another and give mine release,
But yesterday – I could have said, to peace!
Yes, if unwonted fondness now I feign,
Remember captive! 'tis to break thy chain;
Repay the life that to thy hand I owe
To give thee back to all endear'd below,
Who share such love as I can never know.
Farewell, morn breaks, and I must now away:
'Twill cost me dear – but dread no death to-day!"

XV

She press'd his fetter'd fingers to her heart,
And bow'd her head, and turn'd her to depart,
And noiseless as a lovely dream is gone.

And was she here? and is he now alone?
What gem hath dropp'd and sparkles o'er his chain?
The tear most sacred, shed for others' pain,
That starts at once – bright – pure – from Pity's mine
Already polish'd by the hand divine!
Oh! too convincing – dangerously dear –
In woman's eye the unanswerable tear
That weapon of her weakness she can wield,
To save, subdue at once her spear and shield:
Avoid it – Virtue ebbs and Wisdom errs,
Too fondly gazing on that grief of hers!
What lost a world, and bade a hero fly?
The timid tear in Cleopatra's eye.
Yet be the soft triumvir's fault forgiven;
By this – how many lose not earth – but heaven!
Consign their souls to man's eternal foe,
And seal their own to spare some wanton's woe!

XVI

'Tis morn, and o'er his alter'd features play
The beams – without the hope of yester-day.
What shall he be ere night? perchance a thing
O'er which the raven flaps her funeral wing
By his closed eye unheeded and unfelt;
While sets that sun, and dews of evening melt,
Chin wet, and misty round each stiffen'd limb,
Refreshing earth – reviving all but him!

The Third Canto

"Come vedi – ancor non m'abbandona" – Dante

I

Slow sinks, more lovely ere his race be run,
Along Morea's hills the setting sun;

Not, as in Northern climes, obscurely bright,
But one unclouded blaze of living light!
O'er the hush'd deep the yellow beam he throws,
Gilds the green wave, that trembles as it glows.
On old Agina's rock and Idra's isle,
The god of gladness sheds his parting smile;
O'er his own regions lingering, loves to shine,
Though there his altars are no more divine.
Descending fast the mountain shadows kiss
Thy glorious gulf; unconquer'd Salamis!
Their azure arches through the long expanse
More deeply purpled meet his mellowing glance,
And tenderest tints, along their summits driven,
Mark his gay course, and own the hues of heaven;
Till, darkly shaded from the land and deep,
Behind his Delphian cliff he sinks to sleep.
On such an eve, his palest beam he cast,
When – Athens! here thy Wisest look'd his last.
How watch'd thy better sons his farewell ray,
That closed their murder'd sage's latest day!
Not yet – not yet – Sol pauses on the hill –
The precious hour of parting lingers still;
But sad his light to agonising eyes,
And dark the mountain's once delightful dyes:
Gloom o'er the lovely land he seem'd to pour,
The land, where Phoebus never frown'd before;
But ere he sank below Cithæron's head,
The cup of woe was quaff'd – the spirit fled
The soul of him who scorn'd to fear or fly –
Who lived and died, as none can live or die!
But lo! from high Hymettus to the plain,
The queen of night asserts her silent reign.
No murky vapour, herald of the storm,
Hides her fair face, nor girds her glowing form:
With cornice glimmering as the moon-beams play,
There the white column greets her grateful ray,
And, bright around with quivering beams beset,
Her emblem sparkles o'er the minaret:
The groves of olive scatter'd dark and wide
Where meek Cephisus pours his scanty tide,

The cypress saddening by the sacred mosque,
The gleaming turret of the gay kiosk,
And, dun and sombre 'mid the holy calm,
Near Theseus' fane yon solitary palm,
All tinged with varied hues arrest the eye –
And dull were his that pass'd them heedless by.
Again the Agean, heard no more afar,
Lulls his chafed breast from elemental war;
Again his waves in milder tints unfold
Their long array of sapphire and of gold,
Mix'd with the shades of many a distant isle,
That frown – where gentler ocean seems to smile.

II

Not now my theme – why turn my thoughts to thee?
Oh! who can look along thy native sea.
Nor dwell upon thy name, whate'er the tale
So much its magic must o'er all prevail?
Who that beheld that Sun upon thee set,
Fair Athens! could thine evening face for get?
Not he – whose heart nor time nor distance frees,
Spell-bound within the clustering Cyclades!
Nor seems this homage foreign to its strain,
His Corsair's isle was once thine own domain –
Would that with freedom it were thine again!

III

The Sun hath sunk – and, darker than the night,
Sinks with its beam upon the beacon height
Medora's heart – the third day's come and gone –
With it he comes not – sends not – faithless one!
The wind was fair though light; and storms were none.
Last eve Anselmo's bark return'd, and yet
His only tidings that they had not met!
Though wild, as now, far different were the tale
Had Conrad waited for that single sail.

The night-breeze freshens – she that day had pass'd
In watching all that Hope proclaim'd a mast;
Sadly she sate on high – Impatience bore
At last her footsteps to the midnight shore,
And there she wander'd, heedless of the spray
That dash'd her garments oft, and warn'd away:
She saw not, felt not this – nor dared depart,
Nor deem'd it cold – her chill was at her heart;
Till grew such certainty from that suspense
His very sight had shock'd from life or sense!
It came at last – a sad and shatter'd boat,
Whose inmates first beheld whom first they sought;
Some bleeding – all most wretched – these the few –
Scarce knew they how escaped – this all they knew.
In silence, darkling, each appear'd to wait
His fellow's mournful guess at Conrad's fate:
Something they would have said; but seem'd to fear
To trust their accents to Medora's ear.
She saw at once, yet sunk not – trembled not –
Beneath that grief, that loneliness of lot;
Within that meek fair form were feelings high,
That deem'd not, till they found, their energy
While yet was Hope they soften'd, flutter'd wept –
All lost – that softness died not – but it slept;
And o'er its slumber rose that Strength which said,
"With nothing left to love, there's nought to dread."
'Tis more than nature's; like the burning night
Delirium gathers from the fever's height.
"Silent you stand – nor would I hear you tell
What – speak not – breathe not – for I know it well –
Yet would I ask – almost my lip denies
The – quick your answer – tell me where he lies."
"Lady! we know not – scarce with life we fled
But here is one denies that he is dead:
He saw him bound: and bleeding – but alive."
She heard no further – 'twas in vain to strive –
So throbb'd each vein – each thought – till then withstood;
Her own dark soul – these words at once subdued:
She totters – falls – and senseless had the wave
Perchance but snatched her from another grave,

But that with hands though rude, yet weeping eyes,
They yield such aid as Pity's haste supplies:
Dash o'er her deathlike cheek the ocean dew,
Raise, fan, sustain – till life returns anew;
Awake her handmaids, with the matrons leave
That fainting form o'er which they gaze and grieve;
Then seek Anselmo's cavern, to report
The tale too tedious – when the triumph short.

IV

In that wild council words wax'd warm and strange
With thoughts of ransom, rescue, and revenge;
All, save repose or flight: still lingering there
Breathed Conrad's spirit, and forbade despair
Whate'er his fate – the breasts he form'd and led
Will save him living, or appease him dead
Woe to his foes! there yet survive a few
Whose deeds are daring, as their hearts are true.

V

Within the Haram's Secret chamber sate
Stern Seyd, still pondering o'er his Captive's fate;
His thoughts on love and hate alternate dwell,
Now with Gulnare, and now in Conrad's cell;
Here at his feet the lovely slave reclined
Surveys his brow – would soothe his gloom of mind;
While many an anxious glance her large dark eye
Sends in its idle search for sympathy,
His only bends in seeming o'er his beads,
But inly views his victim as he bleeds,
"Pacha! the day is time; and on the crest
Sits Triumph – Conrad taken – fall'n the rest!
His doom is fix'd – he dies; and well his fate
Was earn'd – yet much too worthless for thy hate:
Methinks, a short release, for ransom told
With all his treasure, not unwisely sold;

Report speaks largely of his pirate-hoard –
Would that of this my Pacha were the lord!
While baffled, weaken'd by this fatal fray –
Watch'd – follow'd – he were then an easier prey;
But once cut off – the remnant of his band
Embark their wealth, and seek a safer strand."
"Gulnare! – if for each drop of blood a gem
Were offer'd rich as Stamboul's diadem;
If for each hair of his a massy mine
Of virgin ore should supplicating shine;
If all our Arab tales divulge or dream
Of wealth were here – that gold should not redeem!
It had not now redeem'd a single hour,
But that I know him fetter'd, in my power;
And, thirsting for revenge, I ponder still
On pangs that longest rack, and latest kill."
"Nay, Seyd! I seek not to restrain thy rage,
Too justly moved for mercy to assuage;
My thoughts were only to secure for thee
His riches – thus released, he were not free:
Disabled, shorn of half his might and band,
His capture could but wait thy first command."
"His capture could! shall I then resign
One day to him – the wretch already mine?
Release my foe! – at whose remonstrance? – thine!
Fair suitor! – to thy virtuous gratitude,
That thus repays this Giaour's relenting mood,
Which thee and thine alone of all could spare,
No doubt – regardless if the prize were fair,
My thanks and praise alike are due – now hear!
I have a counsel for thy gentler ear:
I do mistrust thee, woman! and each word
Of thine stamps truth on all Suspicion heard.
Borne in his arms through fire from yon Serai –
Say, wert thou lingering there with him to fly?
Thou need'st not answer – thy confession speaks
Already reddening on thy guilty cheeks;
Then, lovely dame, bethink thee! and beware:
'Tis not his: life alone may claim such care!
Another word and – nay – I need no more.

Accursed was the moment when he bore
Thee from the flames, which better far – but no –
I then had mourn'd thee with a lover's woe –
Now 'tis thy lord that warns – deceitful thing!
Know'st thou that I can clip thy wanton wing?
In words alone I am not wont to chafe:
Look to thyself – nor deem thy falsehood safe!"
He rose – and slowly, sternly thence withdrew,
Rage in his eye and threats in his adieu:
Ah! little reck'd that chief of womanhood –
Which frowns ne'er quell'd, nor menaces subdued
And little deem'd he what thy heart, Gulnare!
When soft could feel, and when incensed could dare.
His doubts appear'd to wrong – nor yet she knew
How deep the root from whence compassion grew –
She was a slave – from such may captives claim
A fellow-feeling, differing but in name;
Still half unconscious – heedless of his wrath,
Again she ventured on the dangerous path,
Again his rage repell'd – until arose
That strife of thought, the source of woman's woes!

VI

Meanwhile, long, anxious, weary, still the same
Roll'd day and night: his soul could terror tame –
This fearful interval of doubt and dread,
When every hour might doom him worse than dead,
When every step that echo'd by the gate,
Might entering lead where axe and stake await;
When every voice that grated on his ear
Might be the last that he could ever hear;
Could terror tame – that spirit stern and high
Had proved unwilling as unfit to die;
'Twas worn – perhaps decay'd – yet silent bore
That conflict, deadlier far than all before:
The heat of fight, the hurry of the gale,
Leave scarce one thought inert enough to quail;
But bound and fix'd in fetter'd solitude,

To pine, the prey of every changing mood;
To gaze on thine own heart; and meditate
Irrevocable faults, and coming fate –
Too late the last to shun – the first to mend –
To count the hours that struggle to thine end,
With not a friend to animate, and tell
To other ears that death became thee well;
Around thee foes to forge the ready lie,
And blot life's latest scene with calumny;
Before thee tortures, which the soul can dare,
Yet doubts how well the shrinking flesh may bear
But deeply feels a single cry would shame –
To valour's praise thy last and dearest claim;
The life thou leav'st below, denied above
By kind monopolists of heavenly love;
And more than doubtful paradise – thy heaven
Of earthly hope – thy loved one from thee riven.
Such were the thoughts that outlaw must sustain,
And govern pangs surpassing mortal pain:
And those sustain'd he – boots it well or ill?
Since not to sink beneath, is something still!

VII

The first day pass'd – he saw not her – Gulnare –
The second, third – and still she came not there;
But what her words avouch'd, her charms had done,
Or else he had not seen another sun.
The fourth day roll'd along, and with the night
Came storm and darkness in their mingling might.
Oh! how he listen'd to the rushing deep,
That ne'er till now so broke upon his sleep;
And his wild spirit wilder wishes sent,
Roused by the roar of his own element!
Oft had he ridden on that winged wave,
And loved its roughness for the speed it gave;
And now its dashing echo'd on his ear,
Along known voice – alas! too vainly near!
Loud sung the wind above; and, doubly

Shook o'er his turret cell the thunder-cloud;
And flash'd the lightning by the latticed bar,
To him more genial than the midnight star:
Close to the glimmering grate he dragg'd his chain
And hoped that peril might not prove in vain.
He raised his iron hand to Heaven, and pray'd
One pitying flash to mar the form it made:
His steel and impious prayer attract alike –
The storm roll'd onward, and disdain'd to strike;
Its peal wax'd fainter – eased – he felt alone,
As if some faithless friend had spurn'd his groan!

VIII

The midnight pass'd, and to the massy door
A light step came – it paused – it moved once more;
Slow turns the grating bolt and sullen key:
'Tis as his heart foreboded – that fair she!
Whate'er her sins, to him a guardian saint,
And beauteous still as hermit's hope can paint;
Yet changed since last within that cell she came,
More pale her cheek, more tremulous her frame:
On him she cast her dark and hurried eye,
Which spoke before her accents – "Thou must die!
Yes, thou must die – there is but one resource
The last – the worst – if torture were not worse."
"Lady! I look to none; my lips proclaim
What last proclaim'd they – Conrad still the same:
Why shouldst thou seek an outlaw's life to spare,
And change the sentence I deserve to bear?
Well have I earn'd – nor here alone – the meed
Of Seyd's revenge, by many a lawless deed."
"Why should I seek? Because – Oh! didst thou not
Redeem my life from worse than slavery's lot?
Why should I seek? – hath misery made thee blind
To the fond workings of a woman's mind?
And must I say? – albeit my heart rebel
With all that woman feels, but should not tell –
Because, despite thy crimes, that heart is moved:

It fear'd thee, thank'd thee, pitied, madden'd, loved.
Reply not, tell not now thy tale again,
Thou lov'st another, and I love in vain:
Though fond as mine her bosom, form more fair,
I rush through peril which she would not dare.
If that thy heart to hers were truly dear,
Were I thine own thou wert not lonely here:
An outlaw's spouse and leave her lord to roam!
What hath such gentle dame to do with home?
But speak not now – o'er thine and o'er my head
Hangs the keen sabre by a single thread;
If thou hast courage still, and wouldst be free,
Receive this poniard – rise and follow me!"
"Ay – in my chains! my steps will gently tread,
With these adornments, o'er each slumbering head!
Thou hast forgot – is this a garb for flight?
Or is that instrument more fit for fight?"
"Misdoubting Corsair! I have gain'd the guard,
Ripe for revolt, and greedy for reward.
A single word of mine removes that chain:
Without some aid how here could I remain?
Well, since we met, hath sped my busy time,
If in aught evil, for thy sake the crime:
The crime – 'tis none to punish those of Seyd.
That hated tyrant, Conrad – he must bleed!
I see thee shudder, but my soul is changed –
Wrong'd, spurn'd, reviled, and it shall be avenged –
Accused of what till now my heart disdain'd –
Too faithful, though to bitter bondage chain'd.
Yes, smile! – but he had little cause to sneer,
I was not treacherous then, nor thou too dear:
But he has said it – and the jealous well –
Those tyrants, teasing, tempting to rebel –
Deserve the fate their fretting lips foretell
I never loved – he bought me – somewhat high –
Since with me came a heart he could not buy.
I was a slave unmurmuring; he hath said,
But for his rescue I with thee had fled.
'Twas false thou know'st – but let such augurs rue,
Their words are omens insult renders true.

Nor was thy respite granted to my prayer;
This fleeting grace was only to prepare
New torments for thy life, and my despair.
Mine too he threatens; but his dotage still
Would fain reserve me for his lordly will:
When wearier of these fleeting charms and me,
There yawns the sack, and yonder rolls the sea!
What, am I then a toy for dotard's play,
To wear but till the gilding frets away?
I saw thee – loved thee – owe thee all – would save,
If but to show how grateful is a slave.
But had he not thus menaced fame and life –
(And well he keeps his oaths pronounced in strife) –
I still had saved thee, but the Pacha spared.
Now I am all thine own, for all prepared:
Thou lov'st me not, nor know'st – or but the worst.
Alas! this love – that hatred – are the first –
Oh! couldst thou prove my truth, thou wouldst not start,
Nor fear the fire that lights an Eastern heart;
'Tis now the beacon of thy safety – now
It points within the port a Mainote prow:
But in one chamber, where our path must lead,
There sleeps – he must not wake – the oppressor Seyd!"
"Gulnar – Gulnare – I never felt till now
My abject fortune, wither'd fame so low:
Seyd is mine enemy; had swept my band
From earth with ruthless but with open hand,
And therefore came I, in my bark of war,
To smite the smiter with the scimitar;
Such is my weapon – not the secret knife;
Who spares a woman's seeks not slumber's life.
Thine saved I gladly, Lady – not for this;
Let me not deem that mercy shown amiss.
Now fare thee well – more peace be with thy breast!
Night wears apace, my last of earthly rest!"
"Rest! rest! by sunrise must thy sinews shake,
And thy limbs writhe around the ready stake.
I heard the order – saw – I will not see –
If thou wilt perish, I will fall with thee.
My life, my love, my hatred – all below

Are on this cast – Corsair! 'tis but a blow!
Without it flight were idle – how evade
His sure pursuit? – my wrongs too unrepaid,
My youth disgraced, the long, long wasted years,
One blow shall cancel with our future fears;
But since the dagger suits thee less than brand,
I'll try the firmness of a female hand.
The guards, are gain'd – one moment all were o'er –
Corsair! we meet in safety or no more;
If errs my feeble hand, the morning cloud
Will hover o'er thy scaffold, and my shroud."

IX

She turn'd, and vanish'd ere he could reply,
But his glance follow'd far with eager eye;
And gathering, as he could, the links that bound
His form, to curl their length, and curb their sound,
Since bar and bolt no more his steps preclude,
He, fast as fetter'd limbs allow, pursued.
'Twas dark and winding, and he knew not where
That passage led; nor lamp nor guard was there:
He sees a dusky glimmering – shall he seek
Or shun that ray so indistinct and weak?
Chance guides his steps – a freshness seems to bear
Full on his brow, as if from morning air;
He reach'd an open gallery – on his eye
Gleam'd the last star of night, the clearing sky:
Yet scarcely heeded these – another light
From a lone chamber struck upon his sight.
Towards it he moved; a scarcely closing door
Reveal'd the ray within, but nothing more.
With hasty step a figure outward pass'd,
Then paused, and turn'd – and paused – 'tis she at last!
No poniard in that hand, nor sign of ill –
"Thanks to that softening heart – she could not kill!"
Again he look'd, the wildness of her eye
Starts from the day abrupt and fearfully.
She stopp'd – threw back her dark far-floating hair,

That nearly veil'd her face and bosom fair,
As if she late had bent her leaning head
Above some object of her doubt or dread.
They meet – upon her brow – unknown, forgot –
Her hurrying hand had left – 'twas but a spot
Its hue was all he saw, and scarce withstood –
Oh! slight but certain pledge of crime – 'tis blood!

X

He had seen battle – he had brooded lone
O'er promised pangs to sentenced guilt foreshown;
He had been tempted, chasten'd, and the chain
Yet on his arms might ever there remain:
But ne'er from strife, captivity, remorse –
From all his feelings in their inmost force –
So thrill'd, so shudder'd every creeping vein
As now they froze before that purple stain.
That spot of blood, that light but guilty streak,
Had banish'd all the beauty from her cheek!
Blood he had view'd, could view unmoved – but then
It flow'd in combat, or was shed by men!

XI

"'Tis done – he nearly waked – but it is done.
Corsair! he perish'd – thou art dearly won.
All words would now be vain – away – away!
Our bark is tossing – 'tis already day.
The few gain'd over, now are wholly mine
And these thy yet surviving band shall join:
Anon my voice shall vindicate my hand,
When once our sail forsakes this hated strand."

XII

She clapp'd her hands, and through the gallery pour,
Equipp'd for flight, her vassals – Greek and Moor;
Silent but quick they stoop, his chains unbind;
Once more his limbs are free as mountain wind!
But on his heavy heart such sadness sate,
As if they there transfer'd that iron weight.
No words are utter'd – at her sign, a door
Reveals the secret passage to the shore:
The city lies behind – they speed, they reach
The glad waves dancing on the yellow beach;
And Conrad following, at her beck, obey'd,
Nor cared he now if rescued or betray'd;
Resistance were as useless as if Seyd
Yet lived to view the doom his ire decreed.

XIII

Embark'd, the sail unfurl'd, the light breeze blew –
How much had Conrad's memory to re-view!
Sunk be in contemplation, till the cape
Where last he anchor'd rear'd its giant shape.
Ah! since that fatal night, though brief the time,
Had swept an age of terror, grief, and crime.
As its far shadow frown'd above the mast,
He veil'd his face, and sorrow'd as he pass'd;
He thought of all – Gonsalvo and his band,
His fleeting triumph and his failing hand;
He thought on her afar, his lonely bride:
He turn'd and saw – Gulnare, the homicide!

XIV

Sbe watch'd his features till she could not bear
Their freezing aspect and averted air;
And that strange fierceness, foreign to her eye,
Fell quench'd in tears, too late to shed or dry.

She knelt beside him and his hand she press'd,
"Thou may'st forgive, though Allah's self detest;
But for that deed of darkness what wert thou?
Reproach me – but not yet – Oh! spare me now!
I am not what I seem – this fearful night
My brain bewilder'd – do not madden quite
If I had never loved though less my guilt,
Thou hadst not lived to – hate me – if thou wilt."

XV

She wrongs his thoughts, they more himself upbraid
Than her, though undesign'd' the wretch be made;
But speechless all, deep, dark, and unexprest,
They bleed within that silent cell – his breast
Still onward, fair the breeze, nor rough the surge,
The blue waves sport around the stern they urge;
Far on the horizon's verge appears a speck
A spot – a mast – a sail – an armed deck!
Their little bark her men of watch descry,
And ampler canvas woos the wind from high;
She bears her down majestically near,
Speed on her prow, and terror in her tier;
A flash is seen – the ball beyond their bow
Booms harmless, hissing to the deep below.
Uprose keen Conrad from his silent trance,
A long, long absent gladness in his glance;
" 'Tis mine – my blood-red flag! Again – again –
I am not all deserted on the main!"
They own the signal, answer to the ball,
Hoist out the boat at once, and slacken sail.
" 'Tis Conrad! Conrad!" shouting from the deck,
Command nor duty could their transport check!
With light alacrity and gaze of pride,
They view him mount once more his vessel's side;
A smile relaxing in each rugged face,
Their arms can scarce forbear a rough embrace.
He, half forgetting danger and defeat,
Returns their greeting as a chief may greet,

Wrings with a cordial grasp Anselmo's hand,
And feels he yet can conquer and command!

XVI

These greetings o'er, the feelings that o'erflow,
Yet grieve to win him back without a blow;
They sail'd prepared for vengeance – had they known
A woman's hand secured that deed her own,
She were their queen – less scrupulous are they
Than haughty Conrad how they win their way.
With many an asking smile, and wondering stare,
They whisper round, and gaze upon Gulnare;
And her – at once above – beneath her sex
Whom blood appall'd not, their regards perplex.
To Conrad turns her faint imploring eye,
She drops her veil, and stands in silence by;
Her arms are meekly folded on that breast,
Which – Conrad safe – to fate resign'd the rest.
Though worse than frenzy could that bosom fill,
Extreme in love or hate, in good or ill,
The worst of crimes had left her woman still!

XVII

This Conrad mark'd, and felt – ah! could he less? –
Hate of that deed, but grief for her distress;
What she has done no tears can wash away,
And Heaven must punish on its angry day:
But – it was done: he knew, whate'er her guilt,
For him that poniard smote, that blood was spilt;
And he was free! and she for him had given
Her all on earth, and more than all in heaven!
And now he turn'd him to that dark-eyed slave
Whose brow was bow'd beneath the glance he gave,
Who now seem'd changed and humbled, faint and meek,
But varying oft the colour of her cheek
To deeper shades of paleness – all its red

That fearful spot which stain'd it from the dead!
He took that hand – it trembled – now too late –
So soft in love, so wildly nerved in hate;
He clasp'd that hand – it trembled – and his own
Had lost its firmness, and his voice its tone.
"Gulnare!" – but she replied not – "dear Gulnare!"
She raised her eye – her only answer there –
At once she sought and sunk in his embrace:
If he had driven her from that resting-place,
His had been more or less than mortal heart,
But – good or ill – it bade her not depart.
Perchance, but for the bodings of his breast,
His latest virtue then had join'd the rest.
Yet even Medora might forgive the kiss
That ask'd from form so fair no more than this,
The first, the last that Frailty stole from Faith –
To lips where Love had lavish'd all his breath
To lips – whose broken sighs such fragrance fling,
As he had fann'd them freshly with his wing!

XVIII

They gain by twilight's hour their lonely isle
To them the very rocks appear to smile;
The haven hums with many a cheering sound,
The beacons him their wonted stations round,
The boats are darting o'er the curly bay,
And sportive dolphins bend them through the spray;
Even the hoarse sea-bird's shrill, discordant shriek
Greets like the welcome of his tuneless beak!
Beneath each lamp that through its lattice gleams,
Their fancy paints the friends that trim the beams
Oh! what can sanctify the joys of home,
Like Hope's gay glance from Ocean's troubled foam?

XIX

The lights are high on beacon and from bower,
And 'midst them Conrad seeks Medora's tower:
He looks in vain – 'tis strange – and all remark,
Amid so many, hers alone is dark
'Tis strange of yore its welcome never fall'd,
Nor now, perchance, extinguish'd, only veil'd.
With the first boat descends he for the shore,
And looks impatient on the lingering oar.
Oh! for a wing beyond the falcon's flight,
To bear him like an arrow to that height!
With the first pause the resting rowers gave,
He waits not, looks not – leaps into the wave,
Strives through the surge, bestrides the beach, and high
Ascends the path familiar to his eye.
He reach'd his turret door – he paused – no sound
Broke from within; and all was night around
He knock'd, and loudly – footstep nor reply
Announced that any heard or deem'd him nigh;
He knock'd, but faintly – for his trembling hand
Refused to aid his heavy heart's demand.
The portal opens – 'tis a well-known face,
But not the form he panted to embrace.
Its lips are silent – twice his own essay'd,
And fail'd to frame the question they delay'd;
It quits his grasp expiring in the fall.
He would not wait for that reviving ray –
As soon could he have linger'd there for day;
But, glimmering through the dusky corridor,
Another chequers o'er the shadow'd floor.
His steps the chamber gain – his eyes behold
All that his heart believed not – yet fortold!

XX

He turn'd not – spoke not – sunk not – fix'd his look,
And set the anxious frame that lately shook:
He gazed – how long we gaze despite of pain,

And know, but dare not own, we gaze in vain!
In life itself she was so still and fair,
That death with gender aspect wither'd there;
And the cold flowers her colder hand contain'd,
In that last grasp as tenderly were strain'd
As if she scarcely felt, but feign'd asleep,
And made it almost mockery yet to weep:
The long dark lashes fringed her lids of snow
And veil'd – thought shrinks from all that lurk'd below –
Oh! o'er the eye Death most exerts his might,
And hurls the spirit from her throne of light;
Sinks those blue orbs in that long last eclipse,
But spares, as yet, the charm around her lips –
Yet, yet they seem as they forbore to smile,
And wish'd repose, – but only for awhile;
But the white shroud, and each extended tress?
Long, fair – but spread in utter lifelessness,
Which, late the sport of every summer wind,
Escaped the baffled wreath that strove to bind;
These – and the pale pure cheek, became the bier –
But she is nothing – wherefore is he here?

XXI

He ask'd no question – all were answer'd now
By the first glance on that still, marble brow.
It was enough – she died – what reck'd it how?
The love of youth, the hope of better years,
The source of softest wishes, tenderest fears,
The only living thing he could not hate,
Was reft at once – and he deserved his fate,
But did not feel it less, – the good explore,
For peace, those realms where guilt can never soar:
The proud, the wayward – who have fix'd below
Their joy, and find this earth enough for woe,
Lose in that one their all – perchance a mite –
But who in patience parts with all delight?
Full many a stoic eye and aspect stern
Mask hearts where grief hath little left to learn;

And many a withering thought lies hid, not lost
In smiles that least befit who wear them most.

XXII

By those, that deepest feel, is ill exprest
The indistinctness of the suffering breast;
Where thousand thoughts begin to end in one,
Which seeks from all the refuge found in none;
No words suffice the secret soul to show,
For Truth denies all eloquence to Woe.
On Conrad's stricken soul exhaustion prest,
And stupor almost lull'd it into rest;
So feeble now – his mother's softness crept
To those wild eyes, which like an infant's wept:
It was the very weakness of his brain,
Which thus confess'd without relieving pain.
None saw his trickling tears – perchance if seen,
That useless flood of grief had never been:
Nor long they flow'd – he dried them to
In helpless – hopeless – brokenness of heart:
The sun goes forth, but Conrad's day is dim;
And the night cometh – ne'er to pass from him.
There is no darkness like the cloud of mind,
On Grief's vain eye – the blindest of the blind!
Which may not – dare not see but turns aside
To blackest shade – nor will endure a guide!

XXIII

His heart was form'd for softness – warp'd to wrong;
Betray'd too early, and beguiled too long;
Each feeling pure – as falls the dropping dew
Within the grot – like that had harden'd too;
Less clear perchance, its earthly trials pass'd,
But sunk, and chill'd, and petrified at last.
Yet tempests wear, and lightning cleaves the rock,
If such his heart, so shatter'd it the shock.

There grew one flower beneath its rugged brow,
Though dark the shade – it shelter'd – saved till now.
The thunder came – that bolt hath blasted both,
The Granite's firmness, and the Lily's growth:
The gentle plant hath left no leaf to tell
Its tale, but shrunk and wither'd where it fell
And of its cold protector, blacken round
But shiver'd fragments on the barren ground!

XXIV

'Tis morn – to venture on his lonely hour
Few dare; though now Anselmo sought his tower.
He was not there, nor seen along the shore;
Ere night, alarm'd, their isle is traversed o'er:
Another morn – another bids them seek,
And shout his name till echo waxeth weak;
Mount: grotto, cavern, valley search'd in vain,
They find on shore a sea-boat's broken chain:
Their hope revives – they follow o'er the main.
'Tis idle all – moons roll on moons away,
And Conrad comes not, came not since that day:
Nor trace, nor tidings of his doom declare
Where lives his grief, or perish'd his despair!
Long mourn'd his band whom none could mourn beside;
And fair the monument they gave his bride:
For him they raise not the recording stone –
His death yet dubious, deeds too widely known;
He left a Corsair's name to other times,
Link'd with one virtue, and a thousand crimes.

APPENDIX II: AN ABSTRACT OF THE CIVIL LAW AND STATUTE LAW NOW IN FORCE IN RELATION TO PIRACY, 1724.

A Pyrate is Hostis humanis generis, a common Enemy, with whom neither Faith nor Oath is to be kept, according to Tully. And by the Laws of Nature, Princes and States are responsible for their Neglect, if they do not provide Remedies for restraining these sort of Robberies. Though Pyrates are called common Enemies, yet they are properly not to be term'd so. He is only to be honour'd with that Name, says Cicero, who hath a Commonwealth, a Court, a Treasury, Consent & Concord of Citizens, and some Way, if Occasion be, of Peace and League: but when they have reduced themselves into a Government or State, as those of Algier, Sally, Tripoly, Tunis, and the like, they then are allowed the Solemnities of War, and the Rights of Legation.

If Letters of Marque be granted to a Merchant, and he furnishes a Ship, with a Captain & Mariners, and they, instead of taking the Goods, or Ships of that Nation against whom their Commission is awarded, take the Ship & Goods of a Friend, this is Pyracy; and if the Ship arrive in any Part of his Majesty's Dominions, it will be seized, and for ever lost to the Owners; but they are no way liable to make Satisfaction.

If a Ship is assaulted & taken by the Pyrates, for Redemption of which, the Master becomes a Slave to the Captors, by the Law Marine, the Ship and Lading are tacitly obliged for his Redemption, by a general Contribution; but if it happen through his own Folly, then no Contribution is to be made.

If Subjects in Enmity with the Crown of England, are abord an English Pyrate, in Company with English, and a Robbery is committed, and they are taken; it is Felony in the English, but not in the Stranger; for it was no Pyracy in them, but the Depredation of an Enemy, and they will be tried by a Martial Law.

If Pyracy is committed by Subjects in Enmity with England upon the British Seas, it is properly only punishable by the Crown of England, who have istud regimen & Dominum exclusive of all other Power.

If Pyracy be committed on the Ocean, and the Pyrates in the attempt be overcome, the Captors may, without any Solemnity of Condemnation, hang them up at the Main-Yard; if they are brought to the next Port, & the Judge rejects the Tryal, or the Captors cannot wait for the Judge, without Peril or Loss, Justice may be done upon them by the Captors.

If Merchandize be delivered to a Master, to carry to one Port and he carries it to another, & sells and disposes of it, this is not Felony; but if, after unlading it at the first Port, he retakes it, it is Pyracy.

If a Pyrate attack a Ship, & the Master for Redemption, gives his Oath to pay a Sum of Money, tho' there be nothing taken, yet is it Pyracy by the Law Marine.

If a Ship is riding at Anchor, & the Mariners all ashore, and a Pyrate attack her, and rob her, this is Pyracy.

If a Man commit Pyracy upon the Subjects of any Prince, or Republick, (though in Amity with us,) and brings the Goods into England, & sells them in a Market Overt, the same shall bind, and the Owners are for ever excluded.

If a Pyrate enters a Port of this Kingdom, and robs a Ship at Anchor there, it is not Pyracy, because not done Super Altum Mare; but is Robbery at common Law, because infra Corpus Comitatus. A Pardon of all Felonies does not extend to Pyracy, but the same ought to be especially named.

By 28 H. 8. Murthers and Robberies committed upon the Sea, or in other Places, where the Admiral pretends Jurisdiction, shall be enquired into, try'd, heard, & determined, in such Places and Counties within the Realm, as shall be limited by the King's Commission, in like Manner as if such Offences were done at Land. And such Commissions (being under the Great Seal) shall be directed to the Lord Admiral, his Lieutenant or

Deputy, and to three or four such others as the Lord Chancellor shall name.

The said Commissioners, or three of them, have Power to enquire of such Offences by twelve lawful Men of the County, so limited in their Commission, as if such Offences were done at Land, within the same County; and every Indictment so found & presented, shall be good in Law; & such Order, Progress, Judgment, & Execution shall be used, had, done, and made thereupon, as against Offenders for Murder & Felony done at Land. Also the Tryal of such Offences (if they be denied) shall be had by twelve Men of the County, limited in the said Commission (as aforesaid,) and no Challenge shall be had for the Hundred: And such as shall be convict of such Offences, shall suffer Death without Benefit of Clergy, and forfeit Land & Goods, as in Case of Felonies & Murders done at Land.

This Act shall not prejudice any Person, or Persons, (urged by Necessity) for taking Victuals, Cables, Ropes, Anchors or Sails, out of another Ship, that may spare them, so as they either pay ready Money or Money worth for them, or give a Bill for the Payment thereof; if on this Side the Straits of Gibraltar, within four Months; if beyond, within twelve Months.

When any such Commission shall be sent to any Place within the Jurisdiction of the Cinque-Ports, it shall be directed to the Warden of the said Ports, or his Deputy with three or four other Persons, as the Lord Chancellor shall Name; and the Inquisition or Tryal of such Offences, there, shall be, made and had by the Inhabitants of the said Ports, and Members of the same.

By 11 & 12 W.3. c. 7. If any natural born Subjects or Denizons of England, commit Pyracy or any Act of Hostility, against his Majesty's Subjects at Sea, under Colour of a Commission or Authority, from any foreign Prince or State, or Person whatsoever, such Offenders shall be adjudged Pyrates.

If any Commander or Master of a Ship, or Seaman or Mariner, give up his Ship etc. to Pyrates, or combine to yield up, or run away with any Ship, or lay violent Hand on his Commander, or endeavour to make a Revolt in the Ship, he shall be adjudged a Pyrate.

All Persons who after the 29th of September 1720, shall set forth any Pyrate (or be aiding and assisting to any such Pyrate,) committing Pyracy on Land or Sea, or shall conceal such Pyrates, or receive any Vessel or Goods pyratically taken, shall be adjudged accessory to such Pyracy, & suffer as Principals.

By 4 G. c. 11. Sect. 7. All Persons who have committed, or shall commit, any Offences, for which they ought to be adjudged Pyrates, by the Act 11 and 12 W. 3. c. 7. may be tried for every such Offence, in such Manner as by the Act 28 H. 8. c. 15. is directed for the Tryal of Pyrates; and shall not have the Benefit of Clergy.

Sect. 8. This Act shall not extend to Persons convicted or attainted in Scotland. Sect. 9. This Act shall extend to his Maiesty's Dominions in America, & be taken as a publick Act.

GLOSSARY

ARTICLES – rules of conduct for a ship's crew.

BAGNIO – Italian-derived name for slave market and prison as operated by the rulers of the **BARBARY COAST**.

BARBARY COAST – European name for the North African Muslim states of Algiers, Tunis and Tripoli which sponsored anti-Christian piracy. This was regulated by the Taife Reisi guild. The piracy of the Barbary states was brought to an end by the Anglo-Dutch bombardment of Algiers in 1816. See **CORSAIR**.

BARQUE – a small three-master, the sternmost rigged fore-and-aft.

BUCCANEER – From the French *boucan*, to barbecue. The original *bucanier* were hunters of wild cattle and pigs in western Hispaniola (now Dominica and Haiti) who were driven out by the Spanish to join deserters and slaves in preying on Spanish shipping. By the end of the seventeenth century the term "buccaneer" applied to all pirates and privateers working the West Indies.

CAREEN – To heel over a ship and clean its hull.

CORSAIR – Synonym for **PRIVATEER** operating in the Mediterranean, especially an Islamic raider authorized by the **BARBARY COAST** states to attack Christian shipping.

FLOGGING – standard nautical punishment for misbehaviour, often carried out with the cat-o'-nine-tails comprising nine length of rope tied to a main rope or wooden handle.

GALLEON – English term for the heavy two- or three-deck ships of the Spanish.

GUNDELOE – Ship's landing boat

JOLLY ROGER – black pirate flag, invented by British and

American pirates circa 1700 and used in the Atlantic and
Indian oceans until around 1752. Among the first to fly a
black banner was John Quelch in 1703; his depicted a man
holding an hour glass and a bleeding heart pierced by an arrow.
Edward England flew the classic, bare skull and crossed bones;
Jack Rackham hoisted a skull and crossed swords, Christopher
Condent three skull and crossed bones in a row. Probably the
term "Jolly Roger" is derived from the French *joli rouge*, the
"beautiful red", the scarlet flag flown to mean "no quarter";
another plausible origin is the English world "roger", meaning
vagabond or devil.

JUNK – Malayan or Chinese flat-bottomed, high-sterned ship.
From the Portuguese *unco*, itself a corruption of the Japanese
for ship, *djong*.

LETTER OF MARQUE – A licence permitting a vessel to
capture enemy merchant shipping.

MAROONING – piratical punishment in which the errant
person is abandoned in a remote place. Derived from the
Spanish for untamed, *cimarron*. Alexander Selkirk, abandoned
on Juan Fernandez Island in 1704, was the model for *Robinson
Crusoe*.

MATELOT – French term for sailor, corrupted by English
buccaneers to mean a close comrade or buddy with whom
possessions and responsibilities were shared. It has been suggested by at least one social historian, Hans Turley, that the
permanent relationships formed by matelots indicated high
levels of homosexuality amongst pirates giving "a whole new
meaning to the phrase 'Jolly Roger'". Indisputably a number
of pirate captains, either from necessity or inclination, were
homosexual (e.g. Captain Edward Cook and Chang Pao).
Christian slaves complained that sodomy was rife amongst
the Barbary corsairs.

PICAROON – English synonym for privateer or buccaneer.

PIECES OF EIGHT – colloquial term for silver coins properly
known as "eight reales", the common currency in the **SPAN-
ISH MAIN**.

PINNACE – ship's boat.

PIRATE – One who robs or plunders on the high seas or (in
Britain) within the jurisdiction of the Admiralty, that is up to
the low-water mark.

PRIVATEER – Vessel (or commander or crewman of said vessel) authorized by a state commission or **LETTER OF MARQUE** to capture the merchant vessels of an enemy nation.

SPANISH MAIN – Spain's empire in the New World.

TACK – to make headway against wind by setting sails at an angle to it.

WEAR – to reach opposite **TACK** by turning against the wind and coming about in a three-quarter circle.

SOURCES

Cochrane, Thomas, *Adventures Afloat*, Thomas Nelson & Sons, 1907.

Dampier, William, *A New Voyage Around the World*, Hummingbird Press, 1988. Revisions copyright © Mark Beken 1988.

Defoe, Daniel, *The Pirate Gow*, Gordon Wright Publishing, n.d.

Ellms, Charles, *The Pirates Own Book*, Marine Research Society, 1924/Project Gutenberg eBook 12216.

Exquemelin, A. O., *The Buccaneers of America*, Editoria Corripio, 1981.

Grant, Neil, *Buccaneers*, Angus & Robertson, 1976.

Hampden, John and Janet, *Sir Francis Drake's Raid on the Treasure Trains*, Folio Society, 1954.

Johnson, Captain Charles, *A General History of the Robberies & Murders of the Most Notorious Pirates*, Conway Maritime Press, 1998. Copyright © 1998 Conway Maritime Press (Major Bonnet, Calico Jack Rackam)/*A General History of the Robberies & Murders of the Most Notorious Pirates*, Manuel Schonhorn (ed.), 1972 (Blackbeard).

Le Golif, Louis, *The Memoirs of a Buccaneer*, G. Alaux and A. t'Serstevens (eds), trans M. Barnes, George Allen & Unwin, 1954.

Leslie, Edward, *Desperate Journeys, Abandoned Souls*, Macmillan, 1988. Copyright © 1988 Edward E. Leslie.

Little, George, *Life on the Ocean: or, Twenty Years at Sea: Being the Personal Adventures of the Author*, Waite, Pierce, 1845.

Lloyd, Christopher, *English Corsairs on the Barbary Coast*, Collins, 1981. Copyright © 1981 Christopher Lloyd.

Mitchell, David, *Pirates*, Thames & Hudson, 1976. Copyright © 1976 David Mitchell/Thames & Hudson.

Pyle, Howard, *Buccaneers & Marooners of America*, T. Fisher Unwin, 1891.

Senior, Clive, *A Nation of Pirates*, David & Charles 1976. Copyright © 1976 C.M. Senior.

Smith, Aaron, *The Atrocities of the Pirates*, Prion 1997. Copyright © 1997 Prion Books Ltd.

Winton, Alexander, *No Purchase, No Pay*, Eyre & Spottiswoode, 1970. Copyright © 1969 A. Winton.